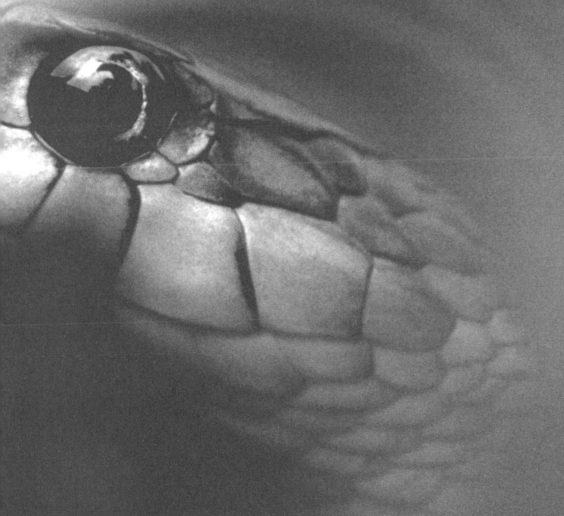

SNAKE

SNAKE

CHRIS MATTISON

DK PUBLISHING, INC.
www.dk.com

A DK PUBLISHING BOOK

www.dk.com

Senior Editor Adèle Hayward
Senior Art Editor Tracy Hambleton-Miles
Production Controller Silvia La Greca

Managing Editor Stephanie Jackson
Managing Art Editor Nigel Duffield
US Editor Iris Rosoff

Produced by Schermuly Design Co.
The Church Hall, York Rise, Dartmouth Park,
London NW5 1SB
Designers Hugh Schermuly, Nick Buzzard, Masumi Higo
Editors Sally MacEachern, Josie Bryan, Claire Calman

First American Edition, 1999
2 4 6 8 10 9 7 5 3 1

Published in the United States by
DK Publishing, Inc.
95 Madison Avenue
New York, New York 10016

Copyright © 1999
Dorling Kindersley Limited, London
Text copyright © 1999 Chris Mattison

Library of Congress Cataloging-in-Publication Data
Mattison, Christopher.
Snake / by Chris Mattison. - - 1st American ed.
p. cm.
ISBN 0-7894-4660-X (alk. paper)
1. Snakes. I. Title
QL666. O6M3385 1999
597. 96 - - dc21   99-19957
                                    CIP

Reproduction by Colorlito Rigogliosi s.r.l., Milan
Printed and bound in Slovakia by Neografia

CONTENTS

Introduction 6

— THE ESSENTIAL SNAKE —

Introduction 7
Evolution 8
Environment 10
Size and Shape 12
Scales 14
Anatomy and Movement 16
Skull and Teeth 18
Sense Organs 20
Hunting and Feeding 22
Venomous Snakes 24
Passive Defense 26
Active Defense 28
Reproduction 30
Conservation 32
Classification of Snakes 34

— SNAKE GALLERY —

Introduction 35
Mexican Burrowing Snake 36
Sunbeam Snake 37
Emerald Tree Boa 38
Common Boa 40
Rainbow Boa 42
Green Anaconda 44

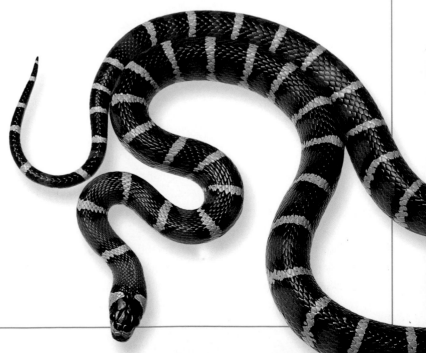

Rosy Boa	46
Dumeril's Ground Boa	48
Calabar Ground Boa	50
Carpet Python	52
Burmese Python	54
Reticulated Python	56
Blood Python	58
Children's Python	60
Spotted Python	61
Green Tree Python	62
Royal Python	64
Haitian Wood Snake	66
Cuban Wood Snake	67
Grass Snake	68
Common Egg-eater	70
Corn Snake	72
Baird's Rat Snake	74
Trans-Pecos Rat Snake	76
Mandarin Rat Snake	78
Rough Green Snake	80
Common Kingsnake	82
Gray-banded Kingsnake	84
Mexican Kingsnake	85
Sonoran Mountain Kingsnake	86
Milk Snake	88
Banded Water Snake	90
Pine Snake	92
Western Hognose Snake	94
Leopard Snake	96
Indigo Snake	98
Checkered Garter Snake	100
San Francisco Garter Snake	102
Brown House Snake	104
Red-tailed Rat Snake	106
Mangrove Snake	108
Green Cat-eyed Snake	109
Boomslang	110
Red Spitting Cobra	112
Chinese Cobra	114
Monocled Cobra	115
Collett's Snake	116
Northern Death Adder	118
West African Green Mamba	120
Puff Adder	122
Long-nosed Viper	124
Adder	126
Gaboon Viper	128
Desert Horned Viper	130
White-lipped Tree Viper	132
Saw-scaled Viper	134
Jararaca	136
Copperhead	138
Western Diamondback Rattlesnake	140
Tropical Rattlesnake	142
Sidewinder	144

— SNAKE DIRECTORY —

Introduction	145
Snake Directory	146
Glossary	188
Index	189
Acknowledgments	192

INTRODUCTION

There has always been something of a mystery about snakes. How can they move so quickly without legs? How can they kill prey with only a single bite, delivered at the speed of an eye-blink? And how do they swallow prey whole when it may be several times bigger than their jaws? It is little wonder that so many myths and legends have grown up around these amazing creatures.

Snakes can be frightening as well as fascinating. They are predators, like eagles, sharks, and tigers, and although we may have a sneaking admiration for their stealth and cunning, we know that some can be dangerous. For the snakes themselves, this has unfortunate consequences because, due to fear and ignorance, they are often killed on sight. In reality, however, only a small number of species can harm humans and, of these, the number that can actually kill us is even smaller.

There are many other interesting aspects to snakes' lives – their different forms, behaviors, defenses, habitats, and their feeding and breeding habits. These are the subjects that have been emphasized in this book. Wherever possible, rather than merely describing snakes, the evolutionary reasons behind snakes' development have also been given.

Much of this information is quite new, since snakes, being secretive, are among the most difficult animals to study in their own habitat. In recent years, professional biologists have pioneered new techniques for tracking and monitoring snakes in the wild, showing that snakes have an important role to play in the natural order. At the same time, amateur naturalists, perhaps alarmed by the rate at which flora and fauna are disappearing from our lives, are beginning to notice and appreciate their beauty.

Snake is written in the hope that the information provided by the text, combined with the stunning photographs, will give you a greater appreciation of snakes and will stimulate your interest in their lives. I hope it will answer some of your questions. Most important, I hope you will be convinced that "the only good snake is a live snake."

RHINOCEROS VIPER
One of the most flamboyant snakes, the rhinoceros viper becomes almost invisible when lying among the leaf-litter of its African rain forest home, hidden from predators and waiting for prey.

Chris Mattison

THE
ESSENTIAL
SNAKE

O ver the course of the millennia, thousands of species of snake have evolved and dispersed throughout the world. The 3,000 or more species of existing snakes are all different, yet all have several physical characteristics in common, such as a scaly covering, lack of functional limbs, a long, forked tongue, and lidless eyes. Perhaps more important, all snakes have to interact with their environment, they all have to find enough food to eat, while avoiding being eaten themselves, and, if they are to pass on their successful qualities and features, they all have to reproduce. The following introductory section concentrates on these themes, cutting across the boundaries that distinguish one family or species from another, and looking at aspects of their lifestyles that are common to all snakes. It also gives a comprehensive explanation of how snakes are classified.

— FORM

Through the ages, snakes have been shaped by natural selection. This has resulted in some species that are very large and others that are very small. Large snakes are in the minority, although they attract the most

attention. The vast majority of snakes are less than 3 ft 3 in (1 m) long. Other variations in shape have also evolved to allow snakes to succeed in a range of different environments – snakes may be fat or thin, rounded or flattened, and so on.

The same selective pressures that have caused snakes to evolve into elongated, tubelike animals have also molded their internal organs to fit the shape of their bodies. It might be surprising to learn that snakes have fundamentally the same set of organs as humans. However, these are arranged differently to fit into the available space. Many organs are elongated, and the paired organs are often staggered rather than positioned side by side.

— BEHAVIOR

The need to survive has as strong an influence on snakes' behavior patterns as on their shape and appearance. Indeed, the way in which each species behaves is often linked to the way it looks. It is no surprise, therefore, that snakes have diverse methods of hunting, subduing prey, defending themselves, and reproducing. These strategies are also influenced by natural

selection, although the reason why one species lays eggs while another gives birth to live young, for example, is not always obvious. Finding the answers to questions such as this provides a continually absorbing challenge for zoologists.

The links between snakes' appearance and their activities are not always clear, nor do we fully understand why they behave as they do. Some of the questions often asked about snakes can be answered quite simply, but other answers are speculative. For, no matter how much we continue to learn, we will never know all the answers.

— THE FUTURE

Sadly, snakes are disappearing from many parts of the globe where they used to be common, just when we are starting to understand their place in our world. Most snakes cannot respond quickly enough to the habitat destruction caused by encroaching urban development, intensive agricultural policies, and pollution, so they need human help if they are to survive. This section includes an exploration of the threats snakes face as well as examples of successful conservation actions.

EVOLUTION

T o the best of our knowledge, snakes first appeared 100–150 million years ago, during the early Cretaceous period. Today there are nearly 3,000 distinct species that have evolved over millennia, perhaps from just one group of lizards. The evolution and spread of snakes has been highly successful – different species survive in a remarkable range of habitats and climatic conditions, and snakes have established themselves in almost every country in the world.

ORIGINS

Within the diverse assemblage of animals known as reptiles, snakes are most closely related to lizards and amphisbaenians (burrowing reptiles that superficially resemble worms), all of which are subdivisions of the order Squamata.

The first snakes are thought to have arisen from a group of lizards that gradually lost their legs in response to a burrowing lifestyle A subterranean habitat makes legs redundant; in fact, they get in the way. Lizards belonging to several surviving families still have a tendency to lose their legs for the same reason, but it is unlikely that snakes evolved from any of the legless lizards that exist today.

The earliest known snake is a terrestrial species called *Lapparentophis defrennei,* which lived in the region that is now North Africa between 100–150 million years ago. The next fossil record is that of a marine snake, *Simoliophis,* whose remains are about 100 million years old and occur in parts of Europe and North Africa that were once the seabed. The fossil records are intermittent after this, but fossils that have been found all over the world and that date from about 65 million years ago show that, by this time, many more species of snakes were present. Some fossils belong to species that later became extinct, but a number are evidently closely related to living species belonging to a couple of the older families, the pipe snakes and the boas. There are no existing fossil records representing the most primitive living snakes, the thread and blind snakes, since the skeletons of their predecessors were too small and fragile to survive.

LEGLESS LIZARD

With no front legs and only vestigial hind legs, this legless glass lizard is believed to resemble the earliest ancestors of today's snakes. Living a largely subterranean existence, the burrowing forms of snakes that evolved with no legs may have been better equipped to survive than limbed forms.

DISPERSAL

At the same time that snakes were evolving, the Earth was undergoing dramatic changes (see "Land drift," above right), with the continental land masses separating and joining together. Because the vast majority of snakes are land creatures, with little chance of dispersing across the oceans, these land movements had important implications for their distribution. The earliest, most primitive snake families were able to disperse across continents that were still joined to one another, while the spread of more recent snake families was limited by the barriers of surrounding seas.

By looking at the present-day distribution of snakes, therefore, it is possible to tell, to a large extent, when they evolved and how they spread. It is clear, for example, that snakes in North America have more in common with those in Europe and Asia than with those in South America, and that South American snakes have affinities with

LAND DRIFT

The shape and position of the Earth's land masses have altered radically during the evolution of snakes. After the formation of the supercontinent Pangaea, the land mass split into two vast continents and continued to drift to form the map of Earth known today.

200 MILLION YEARS AGO

100 MILLION YEARS AGO

TODAY

species in Africa and Madagascar. In both cases, it is possible to reach the conclusion that these snakes were actively dispersing when the ancient southern continent, Gondwanaland, was separate from the northern continent, Laurasia.

Similarly, vipers, generally considered to be the most recently evolved family of snakes, are found throughout the warmer regions of the world except Australia, suggesting that they evolved after Australia separated from the large landmasses.

Some species have made remarkable journeys. The boas on New Guinea and neighboring South Pacific islands arrived from the west coast of South America. They may have been transported on an uprooted vegetable raft, their ability to go for long periods without food being essential to their survival. Perhaps a single pregnant female was washed ashore, and from this small beginning a new colony arose.

RADIATION

The evolution of snakes into creatures with a wide variety of behaviors and anatomies has been largely influenced by changes in their environment, due either to their spread into new territories or to changes in the environment itself. Snakes finding themselves in new or changing habitats need to adapt, either to avoid direct competition with another species, or to exploit a resource, such as a food source or living space. They may change physically, for instance, growing longer, shorter, stouter, or more slender, or their coloration may be modified to blend in with the new habitat.

In this way, snakes "radiate," reinventing themselves in new forms over thousands of generations. Although the majority of species do not adapt in time and die out, those that are successful may eventually oust other species. This situation remains dynamic today - populations expand into and withdraw from their geographical ranges, so that the existing set of species is in flux, with some increasing and others dwindling in number.

EVOLUTIONARY CONVERGENCE

The environment in which any species lives presents it with a series of challenges to its survival – how to find enough food, avoid being eaten by predators, find a mate, and produce offspring. Through the evolutionary process, each species arrives at distinct solutions to these problems. Sometimes different species in distant yet similar habitats face almost identical problems and have developed parallel solutions.

These pairs, or sets, of species typically have a similar appearance and behavior pattern – known as evolutionary convergence – even though they may live thousands of miles apart.

There are numerous examples of this fascinating aspect of evolution. For example, the green tree python of New Guinea and Australia and the emerald tree boa of South America look so similar that they are hard to tell apart. Both are arboreal snakes living in forest habitats and, in response to similar conditions, they have both evolved with bright green coloring and white markings. They even drape themselves over branches in exactly the same way.

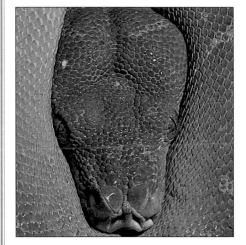

GREEN TREE PYTHON

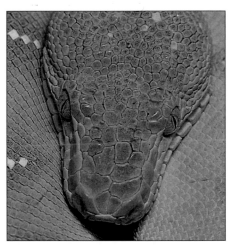

EMERALD TREE BOA

FILLING A NICHE
Some species have only evolved because of a vacant ecological niche. There are no vipers in Australia, but the death adder, a member of the cobra family, has come to look and behave like one, using its thick, heavy body to ambush prey.

ENVIRONMENT

I n contrast to birds and mammals, snakes are unable to migrate or move over long distances and are, therefore, very much at the mercy of conditions in their immediate surroundings. Because every environment is different, each snake species has, over time, evolved various ways of adapting in order to survive. The most important environmental components that affect snakes are temperature, light, and water.

LIVING IN WARM CLIMATES
Many snake species, including Dumeril's boa, inhabit warm parts of the world where there is little climatic variation.

— REGULATING BODY TEMPERATURE —

Unlike mammals and birds, which generate body heat internally, snakes are ectotherms. This means that their body temperatures are determined by outside sources, such as the heat of the sun, and can be regulated only by basking or seeking shade. For most species, the ideal temperature is around 85°F (30°C) At low body temperatures, snakes become sluggish, and body functions slow down. To digest meals, they need high body temperatures.

How snakes regulate body heat depends on where they live. In the tropics, temperatures are usually stable, so snakes rarely need to bask. In very cold or cool places, they may need to frequently change position. This is partly why snakes are more numerous in warm regions, and why species diversity falls off toward the poles.

Only highly specialized snakes can survive in extreme conditions, so there are few species living in regions far from the equator or at high altitudes. In these places, temperatures do not rise much above

freezing for most of the year. Snakes here are invariably small so that they can warm up quickly, and they are often dark for the same reason. They hibernate in winter, and most give birth to live young because, by basking, they can use their bodies to provide a better

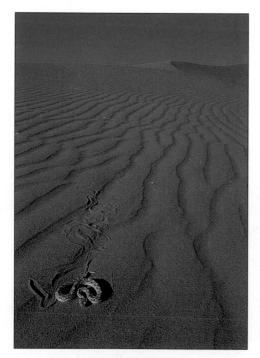

ADAPTING TO THE DESERT
Many desert snakes shuffle down below the surface of the sand during the day to escape the lethally hot temperatures. Where traction is a problem, they may move across the surface by sidewinding (see p. 17).

(see p. 17)

KEEPING COOL IN ARID REGIONS
Snakes from arid regions are often pale in color to reflect heat and to blend with the sand, soil, or rock on which they live. These snakes shelter in burrows to avoid temperature.extremes

HIBERNATING IN COLD CONDITIONS
The few species of snake that occupy mountainous regions with harsh environments often hibernate for up to eight months. For the rest of the year they are active only during the middle of the day.

environment for the developing embryos than if they were to lay eggs (see p. 30). Snakes from deserts have also adapted their behavior patterns to cope with extreme conditions. They may be active for only part of the year, hiding in burrows during the hottest season or becoming active for a few short hours in the middle of the night. During the winter, these same species may become active only during the day to avoid cold night temperatures. Desert snakes tend to live near rocky outcrops or in canyons and gullies, where they can find water and gain protection from temperature extremes.

Many burrowing and highly aquatic snakes have little opportunity to regulate their body temperatures, so most live in places such as tropical forests and swamps, where temperatures are warm and even.

— SURVIVING COLD —

Snakes in high latitudes hibernate in burrows and underground chambers to escape the worst of winter. But in late autumn and early spring they may be caught out above ground by a sudden drop in the air temperature. At these times, some species, including some North American garter snakes, produce substances to prevent damage if ice crystals form inside their cells. For a short period, as much as 40 percent of the fluid in their cells may turn to ice.

— SAVING ENERGY —

Ectotherms have the ability to exploit scarce or seasonal food sources because they do not need to use their metabolic energy for heat production, as mammals do. It is estimated that snakes can survive on less than 10 percent of the food needed by birds or mammals of equivalent size. Furthermore, when food is scarce, they can shut down their systems, for months if necessary, until food sources improve.

— BALANCING MOISTURE —

A scaly skin is only one of the methods snakes use to resist dehydration. The skin's degree of impermeability depends on the snake's origins. Those from dry, desert regions are often very efficient at conserving moisture, while those from humid or wet habitats quickly dehydrate without access to water. Snakes also minimize water loss by excreting their nitrogenous waste as uric acid, a white, crystalline substance needing very little water to carry it out of the body.

Some snakes conserve water by coiling to reduce the surface area from which water can evaporate. Certain desert species avoid hissing so that valuable water vapor is not exhaled. Instead, these species have specialized scales that they rub together (stridulation) or tails that rattle to sound a warning to other creatures (see p. 29).

Sea and wart snakes live in saltwater and feed on marine animals that contain a high proportion of salt. This creates an imbalance in the ratio of salt to water in their bodies, which they correct by using a special gland on the floor of the mouth. Concentrated salty water collects here and is transferred to the sheath surrounding the tongue. When a snake flicks out its tongue underwater, it pushes out a small quantity of this solution, keeping the balance within acceptable limits.

WARMING UP IN TEMPERATE REGIONS
In temperate regions, where the weather is often cool, snakes, to raise their body temperatures, exploit periods of sunshine by basking on open ground or rocks, which retain the heat of the sun.

THRIVING IN THE TROPICS
Tropical regions are host to a rich diversity of snake species because they provide ideal conditions — warm temperatures with little fluctuation and a humid atmosphere that prevents dehydration.

MAINTAINING BODY HEAT IN WATER
In an aquatic habitat, it is hard for snakes to adjust their body temperatures by changing position, so these snakes are rare outside tropical regions, which are usually consistently warm all year.

SIZE AND SHAPE

All snakes have fundamentally the same form, long and thin with no limbs. Yet different species can vary considerably in size, and there is even some difference in shape. The smallest snakes may be barely longer than a human finger, while the largest can extend to five or six times the height of a person. These variations are a result of natural selection as evolving species have adapted to different environments and ways of life.

RUBBER BOA

LARGE AND SMALL
Even within a single group snakes may range in size from gigantic to tiny. Among boas, anacondas can grow to over 33 ft (10 m) long, while the rubber boa, Charina bottae, rarely exceeds 2½ ft (75 cm). Here, a young rubber boa is shown in true proportion to a green anaconda.

GREEN ANACONDA

— LARGE SNAKES —

The six largest snakes belong to just two families, the boas and the pythons. The two largest species are the green anaconda and the reticulated python. The python is usually regarded as the longest, growing to about 33 ft (10 m), but the green anaconda is far heavier. Not surprising, wild stories about the sizes of both species abound. In 1907 explorer Sir Percy Fawcett claimed to have killed an anaconda in Brazil measuring 62 ft (18.9 m).

Somewhat smaller are the giant pythons from India and Burma, *Python molurus*, and from Africa, *Python sebae*. Both species reportedly grow to 20 ft (6 m), although large specimens are becoming rarer as their habitats dwindle. The equivalent snake in Australia is the amethystine python, *Morelia amethistina*, which has been reliably recorded at over 26 ft (8 m), although it is more usually 10–13 ft (3–4 m).

The smallest of the "Big Six" is the common boa. This has only once been reliably recorded at over 13 ft (4 m) and usually grows to about 10 ft (3 m) .

There are few species of large snakes for two main reasons. First, such snakes need to eat a lot, but their size restricts them to hunting by ambush, which can limit the food available to them. Second, snakes rely on outside sources to raise their body temperatures, and large snakes take a long time to warm up. All activity, whether hunting, breeding, or self-defense, is curtailed until they can do so.

TYPES OF BODY SHAPE

A snake's shape gives clues to its lifestyle. Burrowing snakes are mostly cylindrical (A), while ground-dwellers have a flattened underside (B) to allow the body to grasp irregular surfaces. The flat underside is also seen in species that climb, such as rat snakes, which are loaf-shaped in cross section (C) with a corner at the bottom of each flank to grip bark. Some arboreal snakes are flattened from side to side (D) for rigidity as they cantilever their bodies out, supporting their own weight, to cross from branch to branch. Steel girders are shaped like this for the same reason. Aquatic snakes may also have flattened sides (E) to enable them to propel their bodies through water. A few snakes, such as the kraits, are triangular (F), but the reason for this is not clear.

A   B   C   D   E   F

SHEDDING SKIN
Even small snakes never stop growing. Throughout their lives, all snakes regularly shed the outer layer of skin to allow for growth. A snake will rub its snout on a rough surface to free the skin, then crawl forward to pull the skin off, leaving it intact. Young snakes grow more quickly than adults, so shed most often.

It is significant that the six largest snakes as well as several other large species, including the king cobra, *Ophiophagus hannah*, the Taipan, *Oxyuranus scutellatus*, and the Gaboon viper, all live in or near the tropics. Toward the poles, the average size of snakes decreases, as does the number of species.

SMALL SNAKES

In contrast, there are many species so small that they are often overlooked. Snakes in the three most primitive families - leptotyphlopids, anomalepids, and typhlopids - rarely grow to more than 12 in (30 cm). These families total about 300 species – over 10 percent of all snakes. The smallest may be the Martinique thread snake, *Leptotyphlops bilineatus*, the longest of which was recorded at just 4¼ in (10.8 cm). Small snakes require little food – most eat ants or termites and their larvae – and their bodies warm up quickly. However, their size makes them easy prey.

GREEN-EYED CAT SNAKE

FAT AND THIN
A snake's shape and weight often reveal how it hunts. Thin snakes can stalk prey, while thick, heavy species may rely on camouflage to ambush prey.

SHAPE

Snakes vary in shape, depending on how each species has evolved in relation to its environment. Snakes that are long and thin tend to be tree-dwellers or to rely on speed to hunt down prey. Arboreal snakes must be light in weight so that branches will support them. Most have long, prehensile tails to enable them to hang down and pluck lizards and birds from the tree. Snakes that live in open country, such as whipsnakes, racers, and sand snakes, are also long and thin. They use their large eyes to spot prey at a distance and then chase it. The long tail is used as a counterbalance when the snake is flashing through grasses or low vegetation.

Short, thick snakes, such as many vipers and a number of pythons, do not chase prey or climb trees. Instead, they ambush their food. The heavy body is used to anchor the snake firmly as it lunges its head forward to strike its prey.

GABOON VIPER

SCALES

L ike chain mail worn by medieval crusaders, the scaly skin of the snake combines protection with flexibility. It consists of platelike scales connected by an elastic skin. Snakes have different types of scales on different parts of the body. Each type serves a specific purpose, and each one varies according to the snake's habitat and lifestyle. The pigment in the scales gives the snake its color and markings and provides another key element in its armory, whether for camouflage in its habitat or as a warning to potential predators.

— FUNCTIONS OF SCALES —

A snake's skin is made up of two distinct parts: thickened areas, which are the scales, and the thinner, flexible areas between the scales, the interstitial skin. Unlike fish scales, the scales of snakes cannot be scraped off, but the outer layer of skin is shed regularly to allow for growth (see p. 13).

Scales protect the snake from injury as it moves over rough ground. They also provide some defense against attack from parasites, biting insects, small predators, and from the snakes' own prey, which often fights back.

Scales may help locomotion. Irregularities in the scales, especially along the trailing edges of those on the underside, help the snake grip the surface and pull itself forward horizontally or vertically.

Scales also help minimize water loss through evaporation. This feature is most important in desert species. Experiments

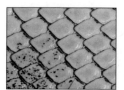

RELAXED SKIN.   **STRETCHED SKIN.**

INTERSTITIAL SKIN
Unlike the thickened areas, or scales, the thinner interstitial, or interscalar, skin is able to stretch. This gives the whole skin elasticity and flexibility of movement, while, at the same time, the snake benefits from the shieldlike rigidity of the scales.

Head scales vary in shape according to their position.

SCALE LOCATION
Snakes have different types of scale covering the back and sides, underside, head, and underside of the tail. They protect the snake from the elements and predators and help it to move.

have shown that the scales on these snakes give more protection against dehydration than those of other species, such as snakes from humid tropical rain forests.

— TYPES OF SCALE —

A snake may have three or more types of scales on different parts of its body, each with a particular form and function (see "Scale characteristics," opposite).

Dorsal scales Found on the back and sides, these are usually arranged in rows, the number of which can identify a species. Dorsal scales may be keeled, as in most vipers, or smooth, as in burrowing snakes.

Ventral scales Located on the underside, these are smooth to aid locomotion. The last one, the pre-anal scale, may be single or paired. Entirely aquatic snakes have greatly reduced ventral scales, sometimes visible only as a narrow ridge along the belly. This may be because these snakes do not haul their full body weight over rough surfaces.

— MODIFIED SCALES —

The Madagascan vine snake, *Langaha madagascariensis*, demonstrates a unique and remarkable example of modification of the head scales. Its snout ends in a long protuberance, but while the male's is straight, the female's is broad and ornamented with numerous small spines. The purpose of this is unclear.

FEMALE MADAGASCAN VINE SNAKE

MALE MADAGASCAN VINE SNAKE

Ventral scales occur on the underside, from the chin to the cloaca.

Dorsal scales cover the back and sides.

Head scales These are large and platelike in many species. They include the rostral scale, at the tip of the snout, the subocular scales, immediately below the eyes, and the labial scales, bordering the mouth. Some snakes, notably most boas and many vipers, have large labial scales, with small scales

SCALE CHARACTERISTICS

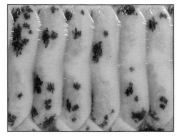

VENTRAL SCALES
The ventral scales of Dumeril's boa are typical of most snakes, forming a single row of short, wide, overlapping scales. They are always smooth to facilitate movement over the ground.

SMOOTH DORSAL SCALES
Triangular, overlapping dorsal scales, such as those seen on Baird's rat snake, create a smooth, polished surface. Snakes with smooth scales include the majority of boas and pythons.

KEELED DORSAL SCALES
The Pacific boa is one of a number of species that have keeled dorsal scales. This type of scale has a ridge, or a pair of ridges, along its center, giving the snake a rough appearance.

GRANULAR DORSAL SCALES
Small and conical in shape and rough in texture, granular dorsal scales occur in only a few species of snake, including the aquatic wart, or file, snakes, which use them to grip fish.

LARGE HEAD SCALES
Seen here on the American rat snake, large head scales are arranged in distinctive patterns that help identify the snake. They occur in most colubrids, cobras, and some vipers.

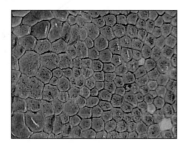

SMALL HEAD SCALES
The emerald tree boa is one of many species of boa to have a large number of small, fairly uniform scales covering the top of the head. Such scales are also found in vipers.

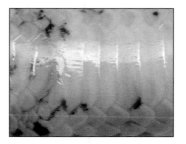

SINGLE SUBCAUDAL SCALES
Subcaudal scales are similar to ventral scales. Here, the underside of a rosy boa's tail shows typical single subcaudal scales. In some species of snake these scales are paired.

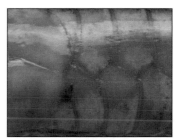

PAIRED SUBCAUDAL SCALES
Certain species, including Baird's rat snake, have paired subcaudal scales. Occasionally, however, single subcaudal scales may be found scattered among the double scales.

covering the upper surfaces of the head. These probably evolved from larger scales that became fragmented over time.

Subcaudal scales Found beneath the snake's tail, these scales are similar to the ventral scales, but may be either single or paired. In some snakes, single scales appear in places among the paired scales.

Subcaudal scales are located underneath the snake's tail.

SCALE COLORATION

The cells containing pigments are located in the scales and give each species its characteristic pattern and coloration. Snakes may be a single, uniform color or, more frequently, patterned with spots, blotches, saddles, bands, or stripes, which often help them merge with their surroundings (see pp. 26–27). In some species, such as the rainbow boa, the surface structure of the cells reflects and refracts the light, creating a shifting, iridescent effect.

Some species change color during their lifetime. Newborn emerald tree boas, for example, are yellow or red but turn green after about a year. A few species can change shade within minutes (usually becoming paler at night), although this ability is less well developed than in many lizards.

SPECIALIZED SCALES

Some snakes have evolved specialized scales, such as the thornlike projections on the horned adder, *Bitis Caudalis*, or the short, fleshy horns or tentacles on the snout of the aquatic Asian tentacled snake, *Erpeton tentaculatum*.

In a few species, the tail ends in a sharp, pointed tip that can be pressed into the flesh of a predator. By contrast, shield-tailed snakes have obliquely truncated tails covered with small spines at the ends. These burrowing snakes are thought to use their tails to plug their burrows and so protect themselves from pursuing predatory snakes.

Some species, such as rattlesnakes, have modified scales on the tail that stay in place when the snake sheds its skin, forming a chain that can be vibrated to produce a warning sound (see p. 29).

ANATOMY AND MOVEMENT

D espite its elongated shape, the anatomy of the snake has much in common with other vertebrates, including humans. It relies on the same systems to support life and shares many of the same organs, such as a heart, lungs, liver, and kidneys. The main differences lie in the shape and arrangement of these, determined by the snake's narrow body. A snake's skeleton looks complex, with hundreds of ribs, but is very simple in comparison with that of lizards and other reptiles.

— INTERNAL SYSTEMS —

Most of a snake's organs are contained in its long rib cage. Together they make up the various systems for breathing, circulation, digestion, excretion, and reproduction.

Respiratory system Snakes inhale and exhale via their mouths and trachea. All snakes, except boas and pythons, lack a functional left lung. In every species, the right lung is greatly enlarged in order to compensate. The right lung is especially large in aquatic snakes, and the lower end is modified so that it is able to control the snake's buoyancy in water.

In some species, the lack of a left lung is also compensated for by a tracheal lung, which is an extension of the right lung. It provides extra capacity and may help the snake breathe while swallowing large prey. To prevent choking, snakes also have a muscular windpipe that they can push forward, forcing it under the prey so that they can continue breathing.

Circulatory system The snake's circulatory system is similar to that of most other animals (without the branches that extend into limbs, of course), except that the heart has only three chambers instead of four. It has just a single ventricle, which is partly divided, and the bloodstreams that pass through it do not mix.

Digestive system The digestive process begins in the snake's mouth, where oral glands secrete digestive juices while the snake is feeding. In venomous species, these substances incapacitate the prey as

THE SKELETON
Made up of a skull, spine, and ribs, the skeleton's most notable features are the strength and flexibility of the spine and the unusually large number of vertebrae – up to 400 in some species, although even small snakes may have 180.

THE INTERNAL ORGANS
The male snake's anatomy shows the elongated shape of many of the organs, including the stomach. Organs in pairs, such as the kidneys, are staggered.

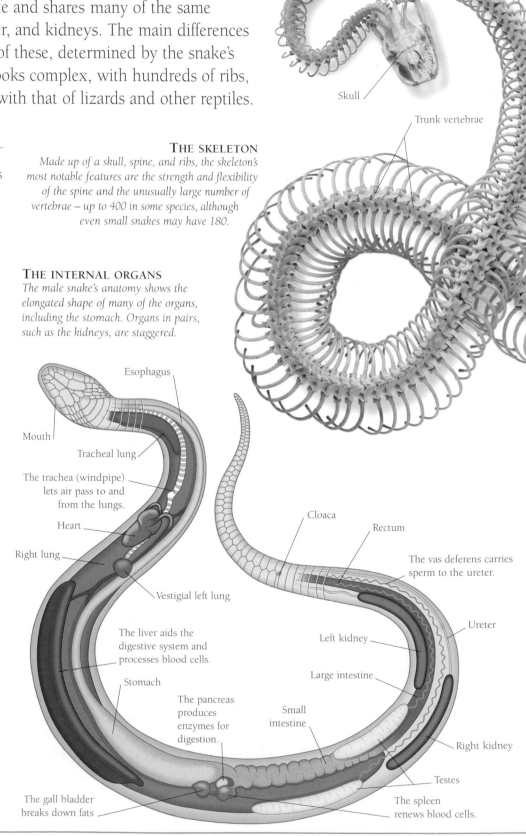

Neck vertebrae

Skull

Trunk vertebrae

Esophagus

Mouth

Tracheal lung

The trachea (windpipe) lets air pass to and from the lungs.

Heart

Right lung

Vestigial left lung

The liver aids the digestive system and processes blood cells.

Stomach

The pancreas produces enzymes for digestion.

The gall bladder breaks down fats

Cloaca

Rectum

The vas deferens carries sperm to the ureter.

Ureter

Left kidney

Large intestine

Small intestine

Right kidney

Testes

The spleen renews blood cells.

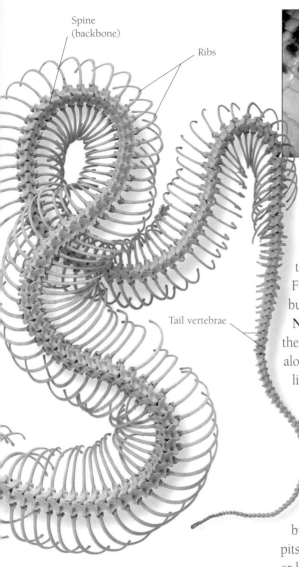

Spine
(backbone)

Ribs

Tail vertebrae

VESTIGIAL LIMBS
Members of the most primitive snake families have pelvic girdles, and, in some cases, vestigial hind limbs, retaining the link between snakes and their ancestral lizards.

the testes to the hemipenes via the ureter. Females usually have staggered ovaries, but some species have no left ovary.

Nervous system This is made up of the brain and spinal cord, which extends along the entire backbone. The lack of limbs means that the nerve network is simplified, although snakes have additional nerves that serve the Jacobson's organ (see p. 20), and, in some species, the heat-sensitive pits (see p. 21). The function of nerve endings sited below the pits and tubercles in the scales is unclear, but their presence indicates that the pits are sensitive, perhaps to touch, heat, or light, or that they are used in some form of chemical communication.

— INTERNAL STRUCTURE —

Skeleton Since a snake has no limbs, its skeleton consists only of a skull (see pp. 18–19), spine (backbone), ribs, and sometimes a vestigial pelvic girdle. The numerous vertebrae that make up the highly flexible spine are especially strong to cope with the strain imposed by the muscles. There is one pair of ribs attached to each of the neck and trunk vertebrae, but not to the tail vertebrae. The ribs are not joined along the snake's belly and are easily able to expand when the snake swallows large prey.

Muscles Animating the skeleton are many muscles attached to each vertebra and rib. It is the coordination of these muscles, coupled with the spine's flexibility, that gives a snake its characteristic weaving action.

well as aid digestion (see pp. 22–25). The throat and esophagus are muscular and help the snake push food into its stomach, which is merely a wide section of the gut. Due to the snake's narrow shape, the large and small intestines are less coiled, and so shorter overall, than in other creatures. Food that is undigested is expelled by snakes through the rectum and the cloaca.

Excretory system Snakes do not have a bladder. Waste filtered through the kidneys is excreted as uric acid, a white, crystalline material that contains very little water, enabling the snake to conserve moisture.

Reproductive system Like mammals and other reptiles, snakes use internal fertilization (see pp. 30–31). Males have elongated testes and a pair of copulatory organs, the hemipenes, although only one is used during mating. Sperm is carried from

— LOCOMOTION —

Snakes owe their efficient locomotion to their complex system of muscles. They use four principal types of motion, which they vary primarily according to the kind of terrain they have to traverse. Most marine snakes have a flattened, paddlelike tail to assist them in swimming.

LINEAR PROGRESSION
Waves of muscle contractions along the length of its body move the snake directly forward. The trailing edges of its large ventral scales provide grip.

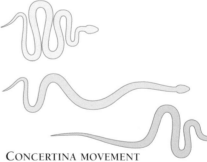

LATERAL UNDULATION
This is the most common type of motion. The snake moves forward by pushing the sides of its body against rocks or other ground irregularities.

CONCERTINA MOVEMENT
In a tight space, the snake proceeds by bunching its muscles in turn, first at the rear as it extends its front, then at the front as it draws up the rear.

SIDEWINDING
On loose sand or a smooth surface, the snake lifts loops of its body clear as it moves sideways, creating downward pressure as it lifts to prevent sliding.

SKULL AND TEETH

Vital clues to understanding the relationships between snake families, genera, and species can be found in their skulls. As different species have evolved, their changing feeding habits have brought about changes to the shape and relative positions of the bones in the skull. The construction of the jaw and the arrangement of the teeth have been most affected. More advanced snakes, which swallow large prey whole, have jaws that expand, and even temporarily dislocate.

EATING LARGE PREY
Many snakes have jaws that are highly mobile, with some bones that can move away from each other. This allows a snake to eat prey that is considerably broader than its own head.

THE SKULL

Unlike most carnivores, which can chew their prey, tear it apart, or hold it while they feed, snakes have no limbs and so have to swallow their food whole.

In the most primitive snakes, the jaws have only limited movement, if any. These species feed mainly on ants and termites, so a large gape is unnecessary. The more advanced snakes eat larger prey, so the capacity to open the jaws wide is essential. To do this, they have evolved skulls that are only loosely articulated. Bones that, in other animals, would normally be heavily built and solidly fused together are delicate and able to move apart from each other when the jaws are stretched. The skulls in these species are constructed so that the upper and lower jawbones can move backward, forward, and outward independently of each other or the rest of the skull. Further flexibility is provided by the lower jawbones, which are not joined at the chin, but can stretch apart or be thrust forward one side at a time. This enables the snake to hook its teeth into the prey and drag it into its gullet.

THE TEETH

Snakes have either hardly any teeth or a large number, depending on their feeding habits. Teeth are arranged along the lower jaws, the outer set of upper jaws (the maxilla), and an inner set of upper jawbones (the palatine bones). The palatine bones in back are fused to the pterygoid bones, which also usually have teeth.

THE EVOLVING SKULL

The evolution of flexible jaws resulted in changes to other parts of the skull. Some bones became smaller, while others grew larger or longer. The skulls of five different families of snake, from the earliest to the most recently evolved, show how the shapes of different bones have changed.

The most notable changes are to the jawbones. A small maxilla in primitive thread snakes becomes elongated in pythons and colubrids, then shortens again in cobras and vipers. The compound bone lengthens, while the tooth-bearing lower jawbone (the dentary) becomes shorter.

RIGID SKULL
The skulls of primitive snakes such as thread snakes are rigid and heavy, and the jawbones are very short.

LIGHTWEIGHT SKULL
The skull and lower jaw of colubrids are reduced in size but highly mobile. Some species have large fangs below the eyes.

HINGED FRONT FANGS
The fangs are very long and, by rotating the maxilla to which they are attached, the snake can fold them away until needed.

ELONGATED JAWS
Pythons have elongated jaws. The upper jawbones can spread apart, although the lower jaw is still relatively rigid.

FIXED FRONT FANGS
Mambas and other cobras have short, hollow, fixed front fangs with no teeth immediately behind them.

KEY TO EVOLVING BONES

- MAXILLA
- DENTARY BONE
- COMPOUND BONE
- QUADRATE BONE
- STAPES

Groove carries venom
to an aperture at the tip.

Movable maxilla allows
the fang to be folded away
until it is needed.

Eye socket

Hinged front fang
is erected and
ready to strike.

Venom duct delivers
venom to the fang.

Palatine bone is greatly
reduced in vipers.

Venom gland
produces venom.

Pterygoid bone is
the main tooth-
bearing upper jaw.

VIPER SKULL

*The viper skull represents the pinnacle of snake
evolution. All the bones are greatly reduced in size
and are highly mobile, unlike the human skull, for
example, in which the bones are heavy and fused
together. Vipers are also equipped with long,
hollow fangs attached to short maxillae.*

Compound bone is
long and has no teeth.

Dentary bone
carries the teeth,
which hold the
prey secure.

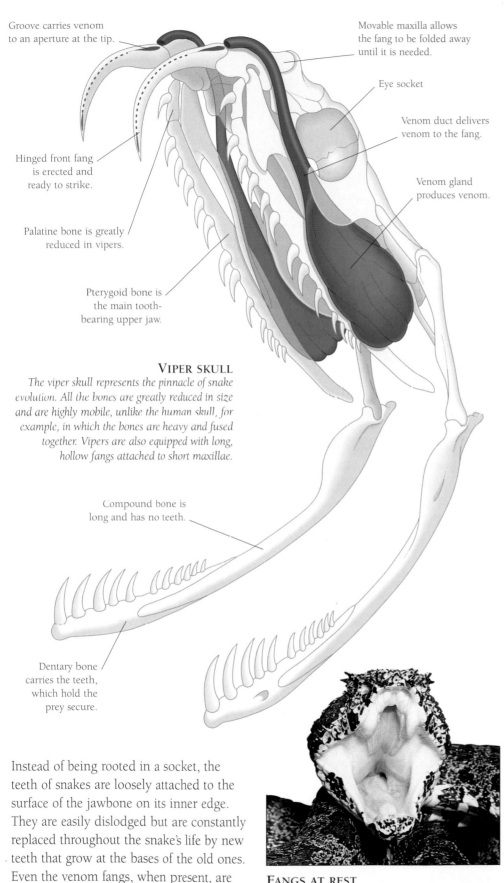

Instead of being rooted in a socket, the
teeth of snakes are loosely attached to the
surface of the jawbone on its inner edge.
They are easily dislodged but are constantly
replaced throughout the snake's life by new
teeth that grow at the bases of the old ones.
Even the venom fangs, when present, are
lost in this way, but replacements grow
quickly. The shed teeth often become
embedded in prey as it is dragged into the
snake's mouth and are then swallowed.

FANGS AT REST

*Vipers inject venom deep into prey with their long
fangs to kill it before it has had time to stagger far.
The fangs are attached to short bones, the maxillae,
which can rotate through an angle of about 90 degrees
so that they can be folded away when not in use.*

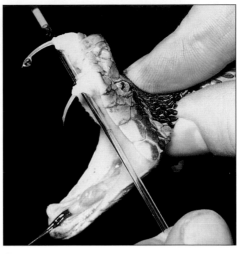

FLEXIBLE SKULL

*The extent to which the whole skull can flex in the
more advanced families of snakes is shown here.
The fleshy sheath that normally covers the fangs
has been pushed back and a drop of venom can
be seen at the tip of one of the fangs. The snake's
tongue and windpipe are on the floor of its mouth.*

FANGS

Some snakes have teeth of several different
types, notably enlarged fangs for injecting
venom. These snakes are divided into two
groups, opistoglyphous, or rear-fanged,
snakes, and proteroglyphous, or front-
fanged, snakes. Within these categories, there
are many variations (see pp. 24–25).

Rear-fanged snakes These comprise
about one-third of species in the colubrid
family. They may have a single pair of fangs
towards the backs of their mouths, or there
may be two on each side. In some snakes,
the enlarged fangs are grooved to facilitate
the delivery of the venom to their tips. In
a few species, the rear fangs are relatively
close to the front of the snake's jaws, so
they are capable of injecting venom even
with a single bite. Only a few rear-fanged
snakes are harmful to humans.

Front-fanged snakes Snakes with front
fangs belong to the burrowing asps, cobra,
and viper families. Cobra and viper fangs
are hollow so that the venom can flow
along their lengths, exiting near their tips,
and penetrating deep into prey. An important
difference between the cobra and viper
families is the ability of vipers to fold their
fangs against the roof of the mouth when
not in use (see "Viper skull", above left).

SENSE ORGANS

Because the evolutionary history of snakes includes a long period when they lived underground, their sense organs have evolved in ways different from those of most other animals. Most important, many species have poor eyesight, and many, especially the burrowing species, are almost blind. To compensate, some of their other senses are highly developed, and some species have evolved systems for exploring their surroundings that are not found in other animals.

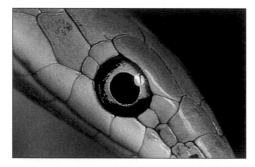

ROUND PUPIL (ROUGH GREEN SNAKE)

VERTICAL PUPIL (COMMON BOA)

HORIZONTAL PUPIL (LONG-NOSED TREE SNAKE)

PUPIL SHAPES
The shape of a snake's pupil indicates the probable period of its hunting activity. Generally, snakes with round pupils hunt by day, and snakes with vertical pupils hunt at night. Horizontal pupils occur only in some species of tree and twig snakes. These snakes have good binocular vision and are able to judge distances between branches accurately.

— SEEING —

Many burrowing snakes have eyes that have degenerated to the point where they are only able to distinguish light from dark. This is true for almost all the species in the most primitive families – leptotyphlopids, anomalepids, and typhlopids – as well as burrowing snakes in other families.

The eyes of the remaining species have one of three pupil shapes: round, vertical, or horizontal. Most species of snakes have round pupils. Snakes with small, round pupils tend to be secretive and are nocturnal hunters. Snakes with large, round pupils are usually diurnal (day) hunters and have good eyesight, although they find it difficult to see stationary objects clearly. To give them a better view when they are hunting, they may raise their heads and necks off the ground. All the water snakes, garter snakes, whip-snakes, and racers of North America, Europe, and Asia have eyes with large, round pupils.

Vertical pupils are typical of nocturnal species, such as vipers and tropical colubrids.

These species have adapted to poor light conditions. In bright light, their pupils contract to slits to protect their retinas.

Horizontal pupils occur in only a few species: the eight Asian tree snakes in the genus *Ahaetulla* and the two African species of twig snake, *Thelotornis*. Because of the shape of the pupils and the size and position of the eyes, these snakes have good binocular vision – something that is not possible for snakes with eyes situated on the sides of the head. Binocular vision allows snakes to judge distances very accurately. This is important for species that use their bodies to bridge gaps between branches or need to reach out to pluck their prey from leaves and twigs.

— SMELLING —

Like other vertebrates, snakes have nostrils that are connected to the olfactory parts of the brain. They also have an extra organ called the Jacobson's organ, consisting of a pair of depressions, or sacs, in the roof of the snake's mouth into which it inserts the tips of its forked tongue. The snake extends and flickers its tongue briefly, searching for scent molecules in the atmosphere. It brings its tongue back inside its mouth to the Jacobson's organ, where the molecules are analyzed and the information passed to the brain. This is why a snake will flicker its tongue repeatedly when disturbed or exploring new surroundings.

ANALYZING SCENTS
Scent molecules that are picked up by the tongue are transferred to the Jacobson's organ. This connects with the same part of the brain as the nostrils, adding to the information from them, and so enhancing the snake's sense of smell.

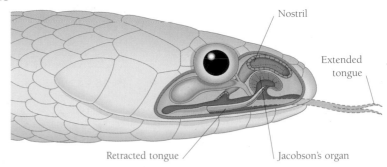

Nostril

Extended tongue

Retracted tongue

Jacobson's organ

HEARING

Although snakes have no external ears, vestiges of the internal structure of the ear are still present in the form of a small bone, the stapes, which transmits vibrations to the inner ear. To detect these, the lower jaw must be in contact with the ground. The vibrations are then transmitted via the jawbones, the stapes, and the quadrate bone to the inner ear. In addition to the footsteps of enemies and the scurryings of potential meals, snakes can almost certainly pick up low-frequency airborne sounds.

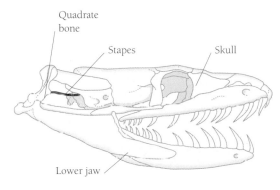

THE HEARING SYSTEM
A system of small bones in the skull allows the snake to "hear" vibrations that are picked up by the lower jawbone. This articulates with the stapes, which transmits the vibrations to the quadrate bone.

SENSING HEAT

Certain snakes have unique sense organs called heat pits. These are found in the members of three families: the boas, pythons, and pit vipers. Where present, boas have rows of pits between the scales that border the jaws, while those of pythons are within the scales. Pit vipers have a pair of pits between their eyes and nostrils – some of them are called *cuatro natrices* (four nostrils) in parts of Latin America for this reason.

In all species, the heat pits are lined with a layer of cells that contains many thermoreceptors, each of which is linked to the brain. Using these cells, snakes can detect minute rises in temperature, such as those radiated by the small, warm-blooded creatures that are their prey. (Even lizards, despite being cold-blooded, radiate some heat, because basking in the warm sun raises their body temperature above that of their surroundings.) The heat pits allow snakes to detect changes in temperature as small as 0.002°F (0.001°C).

The heat pits are directed forward, and by analyzing the heat messages received on either side of its head, the snake can work out its prey's position and range. This means it can strike out accurately, even in total darkness. In experiments, a blind rattlesnake scored a direct hit on its prey 98 percent of the time, but when its pits were covered, its success rate dropped to 27 per cent.

PIT VIPER HEAT PITS
The red diamond rattlesnake, Crotalus ruber, *like all pit vipers, has a pair of heat pits situated just below the level of its eyes. They act in stereo to pinpoint the direction and range of their target.*

OTHER SENSES

Many snakes have small tubercles or pits in their scales, just visible to the naked eye. Tubercles are the most common and seem to be present in every species, even though they are sparse and localized in some. Although their exact function is not clear, it seems most likely that tubercles have some sensory purpose because there is always a concentration of nerve endings in the region immediately below them. They may, for instance, be associated with touch, since they tend to be more numerous on parts of the body that come into contact with the substrate when the snake moves around.

Not all species of snake have pits. When present, the pits are most numerous on the snake's head, but they are also found in pairs at the tip of each dorsal (back) scale. The pits may possibly be light-sensitive, letting the snake know if any part of its body is still exposed when it shelters under a rock or enters a burrow.

Alternatively, the pits may play a role in chemical communication. Little is known about this form of communication in snakes, but individual snakes can sense the presence of other members of the same species (and perhaps other species) by scent. This helps them find mates or follow trails to mass hibernation sites.

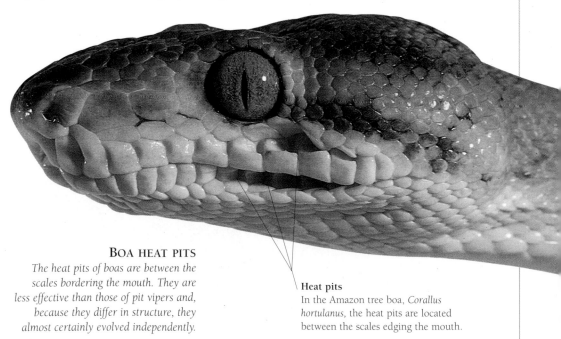

BOA HEAT PITS
The heat pits of boas are between the scales bordering the mouth. They are less effective than those of pit vipers and, because they differ in structure, they almost certainly evolved independently.

Heat pits
In the Amazon tree boa, *Corallus hortulanus,* the heat pits are located between the scales edging the mouth.

HUNTING AND FEEDING

A ll snakes are carnivores, but different species eat a huge variety of prey, from ants to antelopes and almost anything in between, as long as it is alive or has only recently died. Despite their lack of limbs, snakes are impressive hunters, whether they hunt by stealth, scent, or speed. All must swallow their prey whole, eating small or helpless creatures alive, and killing larger prey first by constriction or venom.

— TYPES OF PREY

Some snakes are specialists, feeding only on one group of animals, such as slugs or snails, or even on just a single species. Others are generalists and eat more or less anything they can swallow – a kingsnake, for instance, may eat frogs and toads, lizards, small birds, mammals, and other snakes.

Freshwater fish are eaten by many aquatic and semiaquatic snakes, including a few vipers, such as the cottonmouth, whose Latin name, *Agkistrodon piscivorus*, means "fish-eater." Three species of sea snakes feed only on fish eggs along coral reefs. As a result, they have effectively lost their venom apparatus through evolution.

Many species eat frogs, toads, and salamanders. Hognose snakes, for example, use their plow-shaped snouts to root out toads that have burrowed down into the soil to escape summer drought. Other species hunt frogs at night when they are feeding or calling for mates. A Central American snake, *Leptodeira septentrionalis*, eats frogs' eggs that have been stuck to leaves. Ironically, the frogs place them there to keep them safe from predatory fish.

— PASSIVE HUNTERS

Some snakes do not actively look for food, but wait for it to come to them. These snakes are found in several families, especially among the vipers and some of the larger boas and pythons. Sit-and-wait predators typically have thickset, heavy bodies that anchor them firmly when they

FEEDING ON SNAKES
Most snakes will tackle and eat other reptiles, including snakes, which are an easy shape to swallow. Some species specialize in eating lizards and snakes, while others, such as the common king-snake, eat them only as part of a varied diet, which may also include frogs, birds, and mammals.

EATING LIVE PREY
Snakes such as the grass snake, that eat frogs, toads, and fish, all of which are defenseless, have few problems in overpowering their prey. They do not need to kill it first and can swallow it alive, although they may turn it around in their mouths so that it goes down headfirst.

strike. They are well camouflaged so that prey may come close without detecting them. Certain species sense the presence of prey with their heat-sensitive facial pits (see p. 21), and they can strike accurately, even on dark nights. Despite this, many snakes have to wait for long periods of time, often returning to the same spot on several successive nights, before they successfully ambush a meal.

Snakes increase their chances of a kill

by waiting in a spot where prey, often small mammals, is likely to pass by. They can probably identify these places by scent. Others use the tip of the tail to lure prey close. Often, the tip is colored differently from the rest of the snake so that it resembles a worm or a caterpillar. Typically, the snake lies with its body partially hidden in sand or among vegetation and curls its tail around so that the lure is close to the snake's head. If a likely target appears, the snake wriggles its tail enticingly. When the prey moves closer to investigate, it strikes.

FEEDING ON LARGE PREY
A Thompson's gazelle makes a large meal for an African python, Python sebae, and may last for several weeks, or even months. Prey as large as this may be too much to handle, and pythons sometimes have to release a prospective meal. Animals with horns or antlers are especially hazardous to swallow.

ACTIVE HUNTERS

Other snakes go looking for their food. Nocturnal species may search rock crevices or among vegetation for sleeping lizards. Some species investigate rodent burrows, tree holes, and other refuges. Snail- and slug-eating snakes track their victims by following their distinctive slime trails. Many other snakes also hunt by scent.

Snakes with large eyes tend to hunt by day, using their vision to detect prey. They are often long and slender in shape, and many raise their heads off the ground to survey their surroundings. If they see or sense a potential victim, they usually approach stealthily at first, then make a short, fast dash. These snakes are often known as whipsnakes or racers in their countries of origin, even though they may not belong to these genera.

KILLING BY CONSTRICTION
Constrictors such as the African python throw one or two loops of their bodies around the prey and tighten their coils each time it breathes out. The prey dies from asphyxiation rather than being crushed. The coils may also speed up the process by restricting the blood flow to parts of the body.

CONSTRICTORS

Although small prey, such as frogs, may be picked up and swallowed alive, larger prey may put up more of a struggle or fight back, so they must be killed before being eaten. Some snakes kill using venom (see pp. 24–25), while others use constriction.

Constrictors are found in several families, but are most often associated with boas, pythons, and several groups of colubrids, notably rat snakes and their relatives.

A constrictor asphyxiates its prey by looping its body around the victim, then squeezing until it stops breathing.

SWALLOWING CONSTRICTED PREY
Like all constrictors, the common boa does not begin to swallow until it is sure its prey is dead. Once struggling has ceased, the snake slackens its coils and begins to search for the head. It starts to loosen its hold so that it can swallow the prey more easily. As it swallows, it pulls the body from its coils, which are now relatively loose.

EATING EGGS

A number of snakes eat soft-shelled eggs, such as those laid by lizards or other snakes. A few also eat birds' eggs as part of a varied diet. The African egg-eating snakes, however, feed exclusively on birds' eggs and have evolved unique characteristics to deal with them.

These snakes, of which there are six species, lack functional teeth but have toothlike spines in their throats, on the underside of the neck vertebrae. They use these to pierce through the top of the eggshell. This allows the snake to swallow the contents of the egg without the shell, which would otherwise take up valuable space in its stomach.

ENGULFING THE EGG
The egg-eater opens its jaws widely and pushes slightly downward as it begins to engulf an egg at least twice the diameter of its head and body.

CRACKING THE SHELL
In the snake's throat the egg is forced against the bony spines that project downward through the esophagus.

SWALLOWING THE CONTENTS
As soon as the shell begins to collapse, the snake's throat muscles work in waves to squeeze out the contents, which run down into the snake's stomach.

DISPOSING OF THE REMAINS
Once the shell is empty the snake forces it back into its mouth and regurgitates it in the form of a boat-shaped pellet, held together by sticky membrane.

VENOMOUS SNAKES

Although venomous snakes are notorious, they make up only a small minority of all snakes. About 250 species are regarded as dangerous to humans – less than one-tenth of all species – and only 50 or so are potentially lethal. Venomous snakes occur in four families. The burrowing asps, the elapids (cobras and their relatives), and the vipers are all venomous, while about one third of snakes in the colubrid family have modified salivary glands that produce a type of venom.

PRODUCING VENOM

Snakes' ability to produce venom evolved primarily as a means of subduing prey, although they also use it as a defense. Venom is formed from modified saliva, a mixture of proteins and enzymes that originally served to aid digestion of the prey. The stronger these digestive juices, the more powerful the venom, so the distinction between venomous and nonvenomous snakes is blurred. Generally, snakes classified as venomous are those with specialized teeth that deliver venom deep into the body of their prey, although there are some species without modified teeth that also produce venom.

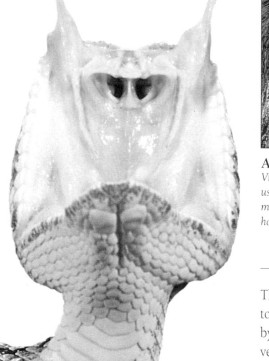

ATTACKING WITH FRONT FANGS
Vipers have long, hinged front fangs, which they use to inject venom and to pull their prey into the mouth. The snake uses them alternately, like mobile hooks, working first on one side and then the other.

PREPARING TO STRIKE
A viper erects its long front fangs as soon as its mouth is open, ready to strike at enemies or prey and deliver its venom deep into its victim.

TOXICITY

The potency of venom varies from species to species, the most potent being produced by those that feed on fast-moving prey. The venom of some marine elapids, for example, is among the most toxic in the world, since they eat reef fish, which would elude them if the venom did not act rapidly. Certain snakes have specialized venom, adapted to a particular prey – it will affect a lizard, for example, but not a similar-sized bird.

Among land snakes, the Australian inland taipan, *Oxyuranus microlepidotus*, the black mamba, *Dendroaspis polylepis*, and the king cobra, *Ophiophagus hannah*,

SIDE STRIKE

Some members of the burrowing asp family, Atractaspididae, hunt their prey in narrow tunnels where there is insufficient space for a normal strike. These species have specialized front fangs that they can pivot to the side and expose without opening their mouths. The snake slides its head alongside its victim, then stabs it with a rapid sideways or backwards motion.

BURROWING ASP

are considered to be the most venomous. They kill only a handful of people each year, however, since they are rare and not very aggressive unless cornered. Asiatic cobras, Russell's vipers, and saw-scaled vipers have less toxic venom, but account for up to 100,000 human deaths a year.

Not all venom has the same effect. Cobra venom typically acts on the nervous system (neurotoxic venom), and that of vipers on the blood cells (hemotoxic venom). Neurotoxic venom acts fastest, paralyzing the victim. Hemotoxic venom acts more slowly, causing death by hemorrhaging or blood clotting. Sea snakes and a few Australian land elapids have myotoxic venom, which affects muscles.

A single species may have more than one type of venom – some populations of the Mojave rattlesnake, *Crotalus scutulatus*, have a largely neurotoxic type, for example, while in others it is mainly hemotoxic.

PREYING ON LIZARDS
Although there are plenty of exceptions, lizards are often the preferred prey of rear-fanged snakes, which hold on to them while their venom takes effect. Lizards can be worked into the back of the mouth easily and are unlikely to do much damage to the snake in the struggle to escape.

STRIKING AT PREY

The way venomous snakes strike their prey varies from species to species. Members of the viper family usually draw back the front part of the body into an S-shaped loop, then straighten out suddenly to strike. At the same time, they open their jaws wide and swing their fangs down so that they point forward. Snakes in the cobra family make short, fast strikes, while some snakes strike sideways (see "Side strike," left).

INJECTING VENOM

Most venomous snakes are equipped with enlarged fangs, which may be hollow or grooved, for delivering venom into their prey quickly and effectively. The fangs may be situated at the rear or at the front of the snake's mouth (see p. 19).

SWALLOWING DEAD PREY
The adder kills its prey with its venom before eating it. Like most snakes, whether venomous or non-venomous, it swallows its victim headfirst, using its tongue to locate the head. The limbs of prey such as lizards fold backward, allowing the body to slide easily down the snake's gullet.

Snakes with rear fangs need to have a good grip on their victims to inject their venom. They work the prey into the back of the mouth, then bite down on it to produce a deep wound into which the venom runs. If the prey struggles, the snake may bite repeatedly, as though chewing, until it is dead. Because of this method of killing prey, these snakes are not often a threat to humans. However, a few species, including twig snakes and the boomslang, have been known to cause deaths. Rear-fanged colubrids produce venom in modified salivary glands known as the Duvernoy's glands.

Front-fanged snakes are well adapted to their method of hunting. They may strike the prey, then release it at once to avoid the risk of injury as it struggles. The prey succumbs quickly and cannot travel far, so the snake is able to track it by following the scent trail it leaves behind.

FAST-ACTING VENOM
The world's longest venomous snake, the king cobra, produces a particularly potent venom and feeds exclusively on other snakes (its Latin name, Ophiophagus hannah, means "snake-eater"). By the time the meal reaches its stomach, the venom will already have started the digestive process.

PASSIVE DEFENSE

S nakes are undoubtedly fearsome predators, but they are also regarded as a potential meal by numerous creatures. These range from birds of prey to carnivorous mammals, and even include some types of snake. All snakes prefer to avoid direct conflict and rely on passive strategies as a first line of defense, although some species actively defend themselves against predators (see pp. 28–29). Passive defenses include concealment, camouflage – helping the snake merge with its surroundings – and mimicry, in which a harmless snake looks like a venomous species, deterring potential predators.

— PREDATORS OF SNAKES —

Snakes, especially small ones, have many enemies. Birds of prey such as hawks, eagles, hornbills, storks, roadrunners, and secretary birds feed on them extensively, while smaller birds, such as members of the crow family, are opportunist predators and will prey on snakes if they have the chance. Other predators include small mammals, for example, mongooses, raccoons, skunks, and foxes. Large lizards, frogs, toads, insects, and even spiders also feed on snakes.

In many areas, however, snakes are often the most efficient hunters of other snakes. A long, thin body shape means that they are easy to swallow and fit neatly inside each other. Snakes are also able to follow one another into small spaces.

Some snakes are able to defend themselves actively against predators. Others rely entirely on a range of subtle defenses.

— CAMOUFLAGE —

The body shape of snakes is important in helping them stay camouflaged. Snakes can easily change from being stretched out to coiling up tightly, and forming any shape in between, making it difficult for predators to build up a mental image of what the prey looks like. This allows many snakes to go undetected unless they move.

Most snakes are colored to match the rock, vegetation, or other substrate on which they live. Where a species occurs over a wide geographic range and the substrate varies,

its coloration is also likely to vary. This often accounts for differences in color between populations of the same species.

However, few species use color alone to produce their camouflaged effect. A plain brown snake, for example, would not be well camouflaged on dead leaves. Nearly all snakes have dark or light markings, in the form of spots or blotches, that help disguise their outlines. Some species are marked with a spectacular arrangement of geometrical shapes in different colors, which, while conspicuous on a plain background, make the snake disappear in its preferred habitat. Many camouflaged species have lines passing through their eyes to help disguise a feature that can often give away their location to a predator.

DISAPPEARING ACT
Lying still in the leaf litter of the forest floor in tropical Africa, the Gaboon viper is almost invisible, especially in dappled light and shade.

— WARNING COLORATION -

Some species use the very opposite strategy to that of camouflage: bold coloration helps protect them. These snakes are brightly colored to warn predators that they are venomous, therefore avoiding confrontation and conserving venom. The most common color scheme is red, black, and white (or yellow), usually arranged in rings. Snakes of this type are generally called coral snakes. All belong to the Elapidae, or cobra, family.

Some nonvenomous species, the harmless "false" coral snakes, protect themselves with

MILK SNAKE

MIMICKING VENOMOUS SNAKES
With its bands of red, black, and white, this harmless Milk Snake is strikingly similar in appearance to the unrelated, and highly venomous, coral snakes, providing it with a measure of protection against predators. Mimicry of this kind is also seen in other snakes. As their name suggests, Viper Boas, Candoia aspera, *resemble vipers.*

CORAL SNAKE

— CONCEALMENT —

Snakes are expert at squeezing into tight spaces, such as cavities under rocks and logs, burrows made by themselves or other animals, rocky crevices, and, in areas inhabited by humans, holes in walls. Desert species, such as the desert horned viper, often bury themselves in the sand to avoid detection by potential predators or prey, as well as to escape from the scorching heat of the midday sun. The snake wriggles and rocks its body downward, shoveling sand upward and over its back.

THE VIPER RETREATS INTO THE SAND.

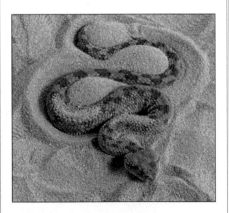

IT FLICKS SAND OVER ITS BACK.

SOON ONLY THE TOP OF ITS HEAD IS VISIBLE.

the same defensive coloration. These snakes include mountain kingsnakes and others of the genus *Lampropeltis*.

Warning colors are not restricted to coral snakes and their mimics. A number of snakes from around the world have brightly colored undersides, for instance, which they display when they are alarmed.

DIFFERING FORMS
In polymorphic species such as the Amazon tree boa, two or more colors or patterns occur within the same population. Several distinct color forms can even be present in a single litter, as here. This phenomenon is a means of defense, helping to confuse predators, which tend to recognize only one form.

— POLYMORPHISM —

Snake species in which two or more distinct colors or patterns occur in the same population, irrespective of the substrate on which the snakes live, are known as polymorphic. This is another defense strategy based on the way predators build up search images of their prey. Since only one of the polymorphic forms will fit this image, the other is likely to be overlooked by predators, and thus improve its survival rate. When the most common form has been preyed on so heavily that it becomes the less common of the two, predators' attention switches to the other form.

Polymorphic species may occur in striped or blotched forms, as in the European leopard snake, or banded and striped forms, as in some populations of the California kingsnake. Other species exhibit a bewildering variety of color forms. The Amazon tree boa, *Corallus enhydris*, for example, occurs in a great variety of colors from mottled gray to orange.

ACTIVE DEFENSE

I f passive defenses such as concealment or camouflage fail to deter a predator, a snake must defend itself actively. Different species employ a variety of strategies, ranging from playing dead to drawing attention away from the snake's vulnerable head by feigning a counterattack with the tail. Many snakes make a ferocious display to intimidate predators, inflating their bodies, hissing, or lunging in mock strikes. Some snakes have specialized defenses. They include the rattlesnakes, which vibrate their tails to create an alarming buzz, and the spitting cobras of Africa and Asia, which can spray venom over a long distance.

FEIGNING DEATH
If intimidation fails to ward off a predator, the grass snake plays dead, rolling onto its back and writhing to imitate death throes. It then lies completely still with its tongue hanging out.

— BALLING AND TAIL LOSS

A number of snakes, such as the royal python and some West Indian wood snakes, react to danger by balling, or hiding their heads in their coils. Other snakes conceal the head but raise the tail above their coils, diverting the predator's attention and reducing the risk of life-threatening damage to the head. Species that do this have blunt tails, which may be marked to mimic their heads. For example, some calabar ground boas have imitation eye markings.

Some snakes are even able to discard part of the tail, as lizards do, to escape from their predators. The South American snakes

HEAD OR TAIL?
Certain snakes, such as the Asian pipe snake, Cylindrophis ruffus, *protect themselves by concealing their heads, the most vulnerable part of the body. They also draw attention toward their blunt tails, which they move in a headlike manner, sometimes even using them to make false strikes.*

Pliocercus elapoides and *Scaphiodontophis venustissimus* have fracture planes across the tail vertebrae to help them break easily. Certain African snakes, such as *Psammophis* and *Natriciteres* species, spin their bodies rapidly if grasped, so the tail may break off even though it has no fracture planes.

— PLAYING DEAD

A few species of snake feign death as part of their defensive repertoire. These include the grass snake, hognose snakes, and the African spitting cobra, or Ringhals, *Haemachatus hemachatus*. The snake flips over onoto its back with its mouth gaping open and its tongue lolling out. A foul-smelling secretion is often produced at the same time, which may contribute to the effect by suggesting decomposition. This is still a risky strategy, however, for, although many predators avoid prey that is already dead, some are not averse to eating carrion. For this reason, it is possible that snakes play dead only as a last resort.

— INTIMIDATION

Many snakes, including those that are actually harmless, try to intimidate attackers. Some inflate the body to make themselves look less like easy prey. This is often accompanied by hissing as the snake expels air forcibly through its windpipe.

BALLING
The royal python, here emerging to check if danger is past, frequently uses the strategy of balling, protecting its head in the center of its coils. For this reason, it is also called the ball python.

THREATENING POSTURE
One of a number of snakes that enlarge their bodies to deter attackers, the king cobra, Ophiophagus hannah, rears its head and flattens its neck to form the characteristic hood. Some cobras have a large, eyelike marking, seen when the hood is spread, that also intimidates the aggressor.

INTIMIDATION STRATEGIES
Snakes such as the reticulated python have a whole repertoire of intimidating behavior, including hissing, inflating the body in order to look threatening, and opening the mouth wide as if about to strike.

WARNING RATTLE
Rather than waste venom in a strike, the western diamondback rattlesnake often uses its rattle as a deterrent if threatened. It raises its tail and vibrates the tip rapidly, making a buzzing noise.

snake vibrates its tail. The segments are formed from the hardened remains (epidermis) of the scale at the tip of the tail. Like an hourglass, this scale is constricted around the middle, so the epidermis is trapped loosely at the tip each time the snake sloughs, and another segment is added. Adult snakes may accumulate ten segments or more, but six or seven is more usual because the oldest part is brittle and periodically breaks off.

Desert vipers in Africa and the Middle East also use audible warnings. The desert horned viper and the carpet vipers have serrated scales on their flanks that may be rubbed together like pieces of sandpaper to make a warning rasp. These snakes coil in a characteristic horseshoe shape and move different parts of their bodies in opposite directions to create the sound.

— SPITTING —

The spitting cobras of Africa and Asia can defend themselves by spraying venom. In these species, the venom canals in the fangs have a sharp kink near the end. The opening at the front of the fang is so tiny that venom is forced through it under pressure and may land over 3 ft (1 m) away. To improve the trajectory, the snake raises its front half as it spits. When hunting, spitting cobras inject their venom by biting in the same way as other front-fanged snakes (see p. 25).

African twig snakes and boomslangs puff up their throats, revealing bold markings or colors between their scales, while parrot snakes gape their jaws, displaying bright mouths quite unlike their camouflaged scales.

Defensive displays are sometimes followed by mock strikes in which the snake lunges, but does not make contact. Only if this fails does it launch into a real attack. Even non-venomous snakes may inflict a painful bite, since many have long, curved fangs that penetrate deeply. This is often enough to deter all but the most persistent predator.

— WARNING SIGNALS —

Many snakes hiss when disturbed, but some make more unusual warning sounds, such as the rattling or buzzing produced by rattlesnakes. The rattle consists of segments of old scales that clatter together when the

SPRAYING VENOM
The venom from a spitting cobra is aimed at the eyes and other mucous membranes of any creature regarded as a potential threat. It causes instant pain, but is not fatal to humans.

REPRODUCTION

M ost snakes lead a solitary lifestyle and may not come into contact with a suitable mate very often. To increase their chances of breeding successfully, snakes have the highly unusual capability of delaying fertilization after mating. Females can store sperm until conditions are favorable for the young to develop, giving the offspring a good chance of survival. While most species are egg-layers, some are live-bearers, with the young being incubated inside the mother's body.

HEMIPENES
The male has a pair of sex organs, the hemipenes. Only one of these is used at each mating, but they may be alternated in subsequent matings.

— COURTSHIP —

Although some species of snake mate several times with the same partner, in most cases the male departs immediately after mating to look for other females. The female may then also mate with other males and eventually produce offspring from several different fathers.

Snakes find their mates during the breeding season in a number of ways. Some species hibernate communally in a den that may contain several hundred snakes. These species tend to mate in early spring, almost as soon as they emerge from hibernation and before they disperse. In certain species, including mambas, most vipers, and the most northerly-occurring rattlesnakes, males wrestle for the privilege of mating with females. In male-to-male combat, two rivals rear up and entwine the front parts of their bodies, trying to push each other to the ground.

These movements are so graceful that early observers thought they were witnessing a courtship dance. Eventually, one snake, usually the largest, succeeds in driving away the other. It can then mate with the female, who has usually remained coiled quietly nearby.

It is thought that tropical species, which do not hibernate in a group, may find each other by chance, probably using chemical clues such as scent to track each other down.

— FERTILIZATION —

Fertilization may take place shortly after mating, or the sperm may be stored in the female's oviduct. Certain species that, because of climatic conditions, have a very brief period of activity, will mate one year and produce young the next. The ridge-nosed rattlesnake, *Crotalus willardi*, for example, mates in summer, but the eggs do not begin to develop until the next spring. These species, therefore, breed only every other year, or even less often. The aquatic and slow-moving file snakes, *Acrochordus* species, probably the slowest breeders, have ten years or more between litters.

MATING BALL
Some northern populations of garter snake, notably those of the red-sided garter snake, Thamnophis sirtalis parietalis, *form huge mating balls, with numerous males all trying to mate with a receptive female.*

ENTWINED MATES
When mating, snakes start by lying side by side, then the male crawls along the female's back, flicking his tongue over her and twitching as he goes. If receptive, she may also twitch before raising her tail so that they can mate. They often remain joined for several minutes or even hours.

Species from regions with markedly distinct seasons, such as summer and winter, wet and dry, ensure that the young emerge at a favorable time, usually when food is in abundance, while many tropical species may breed almost continually through the year.

— EGG-LAYING SNAKES —

Most species lay eggs. The eggs are left to the mercy of the weather, developing best in a warm environment, so egg-laying species are usually found in tropical and subtropical locations.

Snakes lay their eggs in sites that are likely to provide stable conditions for their development, which can take up to three months. Some species burrow in sand or sandy soil, or make an egg chamber beneath a rock. Dead vegetation or rotting wood is favored because it is easy to dig into, has good insulating properties, often generating its own heat, and retains moisture. The eggs need a moist place because the shells are soft and permeable and can absorb water and oxygen as the embryo develops.

Clutches vary in size, depending on the species and size of the mother. They range from one or two to up to 100 eggs in the case of the large pythons, including the Indian python, *Python molurus,* African rock python, *Python sebae,* and reticulated python.

— LIVE-BEARING SNAKES —

Live-bearers carry their developing young inside them. They do not nourish them via a placenta as mammals do, but retain the eggs in their oviducts rather than laying them. The young develop inside a thin membrane, instead of a shell, from which they break out around the time of birth.

BROODING EGGS
Once snakes have laid their eggs, they usually take no further interest in them, although pythons coil around their eggs throughout the incubation period to regulate their temperature, and cobras and a few other species stay nearby to guard their clutches.

— SINGLE-SEX SNAKE —

Not all snakes need to mate in order to reproduce their species successfully. The Brahminy blind snake, a native of India and Southeast Asia but now found in many other warm countries, including South Africa and Australia, is the only parthenogen (female-only) species. As soon as each snake is mature, it begins to lay fertile eggs, without having mated. All of these eggs subsequently hatch into females that are clones of their mother. In general, parthenogen species tend to be very successful for a while, but, in the long term, they lack the variability that would allow them to adapt to changing conditions.

BRAHMINY BLIND SNAKE

BEARING LIVE YOUNG
In the majority of cases, live-bearing snakes give birth in a secluded place – a space underneath a rock, for example – usually during warm weather. Even though a birth occasionally takes place in the open, this has rarely been observed.

By basking to raise its body temperature, the female can hasten the development of the unborn young, making successful breeding less dependent on the external temperature. It is no coincidence that vipers, many of which are live-bearers, thrive in mountain habitats or at extreme latitudes too cold for other snakes. Aquatic snakes, including most of the sea snakes, are live-bearers because they rarely come ashore. Similarly, many arboreal snakes bear live young, avoiding the need to descend to ground level, where many of them are defenseless.

The most prolific live-bearers include two vipers, the puff adder and the fer-de-lance, and three colubrids, the common garter snake, the green water snake, *Nerodia cyclopion,* and the African mole snake, *Pseudaspis cana.* Each of these has been known to produce litters of over 100 young, the puff adder holding the record at 157.

HATCHING OUT
Like all snakes that hatch from an egg, when the young rat snake is fully developed, it slashes its way out of the shell by using a temporary "egg-tooth" on its snout. Although it may remain near the egg site for a few days, the young snake is fully independent, and venomous species can even produce venom.

BREAKING THE SHELL   TASTING THE AIR   STARTING TO EMERGE   LEAVING THE EGG

CONSERVATION

S nakes spend much of their lives hidden from view, so their increasing rarity may easily pass unnoticed. Yet unless conservation is made an urgent priority, hundreds of species are likely to become extinct in the near future. The most serious threat comes from humans and is mainly due to habitat destruction. Snakes are also killed out of misplaced fear, and many fall prey to traffic and the skin trade.

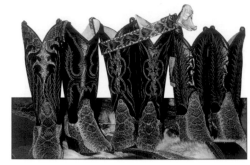

PRODUCTS OF THE SNAKE TRADE
Snakes have long been prized for their skins, used in the manufacturing of boots, shoes, belts, handbags, wallets, and other goods. Over a million snakes are killed each year for their skin, especially pythons and other species from the Far East.

— THREATS TO SNAKES —

The natural habitats of snakes, like those of many other creatures, have been ravaged by the activities of man. The effects have been devastating in the rain forests of Central and South America and Southeast Asia, where land clearance for agriculture involves logging and burning. The situation is made worse by erosion and climatic changes that arise from these and other human activities.

Many snake species in these areas have already been exterminated, often partly because they cannot escape from threatened habitats as easily as mammals and birds. In some cases, species have become extinct even before we knew they existed.

Some species are killed by introduced predators, including cats, dogs, mongooses, and rats, that have been released either deliberately or accidentally by man. Island species are especially vulnerable. On Round Island, in the Indian Ocean, for example, both members of the family Bolyeriidae are threatened by nonindigenous predators. Rats and cats prey on snakes, while goats eroded their habitat. The Round Island Boa

has not been seen since 1975 and is probably extinct. The other species, *Casarea dussumieri*, has only been brought back from the brink of extinction by drastic conservation measures.

Other human activities have contributed to the decline of snakes. Industrial and commercial development often drives out their prey, depriving them of food. Snakes are killed on sight in many countries, whether venomous or not, and thousands die on the roads. Snakes are also deliberately exploited, principally for the skin trade. Smaller numbers are captured for the pet trade, zoos, and research. In parts of North America, rattlesnakes are even killed as a recreational activity, in "rattlesnake roundups."

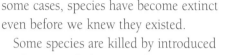

DEFORESTATION
Vast tracts of tropical forest have been cleared for the timber trade and for mining, agriculture, and cattle ranching. Irreplaceable trees have been felled, destroying the habitats of snakes and numerous other species.

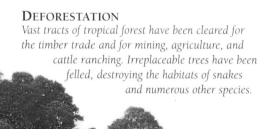

CONSERVATION MEASURES

There is no doubt that snakes need immediate help if they are to survive. For many species, it is already too late, but the growing interest in saving and protecting endangered species is now filtering through to include snake conservation.

Research A vital priority is more funding for research to fill in the many gaps in our knowledge of snakes. Some snake species are known from only a handful of preserved specimens, making it difficult for conservationists to provide appropriate help.

Nature reserves The development of reserves dedicated to snakes is still a long way off, but snakes do gain some incidental protection where they share habitats with other endangered species. For this reason, national parks and nature preserves are of great value in helping to conserve species.

Captive breeding For some species, captive breeding programs may be the only answer as conservationists, including enthusiastic amateurs, race against time to save them from extinction. For example, many American and European zoos have co-operated in breeding three threatened boa species of Madagascar, while colonies of a further three critically endangered snake species are maintained at Jersey Zoo in the Channel Islands. The aim of captive breeding should be to release snakes back into the wild, but if a species is rare due to habitat destruction, effective conservation measures need to be put in place first.

SAVING THE MILOS VIPER

A MILOS VIPER KILLED BY TRAFFIC.

FITTING A RADIO TRANSMITTER FOR RESEARCH.

The Milos Viper, *Macrovipera schweizeri*, lives on three small Greek islands, where it is threatened by gypsum mining. There are moves to preserve parts of its habitat, but numbers are rapidly dwindling and captive breeding programs have been set up. Miniaturized radio transmitters are used by conservationists to study this and other snake species in the wild. The transmitter is implanted in the snake and used to track its movements and to gather data such as body temperature.

On Round Island, the goats and rabbits introduced by man, which were eating the vegetation, were eradicated in the 1970s and 1980s. This allowed trees and undergrowth to recover, benefiting the lizards that are the boas' main prey. As a result, the island is now better able to support snakes than at any time in the past 100 years.

Education The greatest conservation tool is education, and people in many countries are starting to appreciate the value of their wildlife. While snakes are not the main focus of attention, they benefit from a more tolerant approach to wildlife, a move against the use of animal products in the fashion industry, and the growth of eco-tourism in places that once attracted few visitors.

Legislation Many species of snake around the world now have some legal protection with laws that restrict and regulate the collection, trade, and export of rare snakes (or snake products), and, in a few cases, even protect native snake species from interference by humans.

FACING EXTINCTION
The Antiguan Racer, Alsophis antigua, is among the world's rarest snakes, found only on the island of Antigua. By 1985, as few as 60–80 adults remained. The decline of the species was caused by rats, introduced by man, eating the eggs and young.

CAPTURED FOR CONSERVATION
Antiguan Racers were collected by conservationists and sent to the Jersey Wildlife Preservation Trust in the Channel Islands. These snakes were used to establish a captive breeding colony while the rat population on Antigua was eradicated.

BREEDING IN CAPTIVITY
After their arrival at Jersey Zoo, the snakes were kept in breeding cages in a part of the zoo not open to the public. Their offspring will one day be released back into the wild. Captive breeding is a valuable safety net in the fight to save endangered species.

CLASSIFICATION OF SNAKES

T he science of establishing relationships between different organisms and arranging them in a way that reflects these relationships is called classification. Snakes belong to the class Reptilia, or reptiles. The reptiles are divided into four orders: the Testudines (turtles and tortoises), the Crocodylia (crocodiles and alligators), the Rhynchocephalia (tuataras), and the Squamata. The Squamata are divided into three sub-orders: the Serpentes (snakes), Sauria (lizards), and Amphisbaenia (amphisbaenians, or worm-lizards).

WHITE-LIPPED TREE VIPER
The arrangement of the fangs and the numerous small head scales identify this species as a member of the Viperidae, or viper, family. Heat pits place it in the subfamily Crotalinae, or pit vipers. It is not always this easy to classify snakes on the basis of external characteristics.

— FAMILIES

Within the suborder Serpentes, snakes are divided into two major groups, or superfamilies, the Scolecophidia and the Alethinophidia. Each superfamily is further divided into families, the total number of which varies according to the classification scheme. The following classification reflects a conservative view in which 18 families are recognized. Families are further divided into related groups of snakes (genera), which are made up of the different species.

Snake classification is in a constant state of flux, however, as new discoveries come to light and new technologies give fresh insights into the relationships between families or species. There are four key differences of opinion among herpetologists at the current time.

First, are boas and pythons branches of the same family, or separate families? Here they have been placed in separate families.

Second, should sea snakes be placed in the same family as the cobras, or do they deserve a family of their own? They have been kept in the same family here.

Third, where do the burrowing asps belong? Over the years, they have been included in the cobra family, the viper family, and the colubrid family. At present, they are usually placed in a separate family; this policy has been followed here. Even

FAMILY TREE
This diagram shows how the suborder Serpentes divides into two superfamilies, then into the 18 snake families, shown in the order in which they evolved (top to bottom). The subdivision Caenophidia contains the most advanced families.

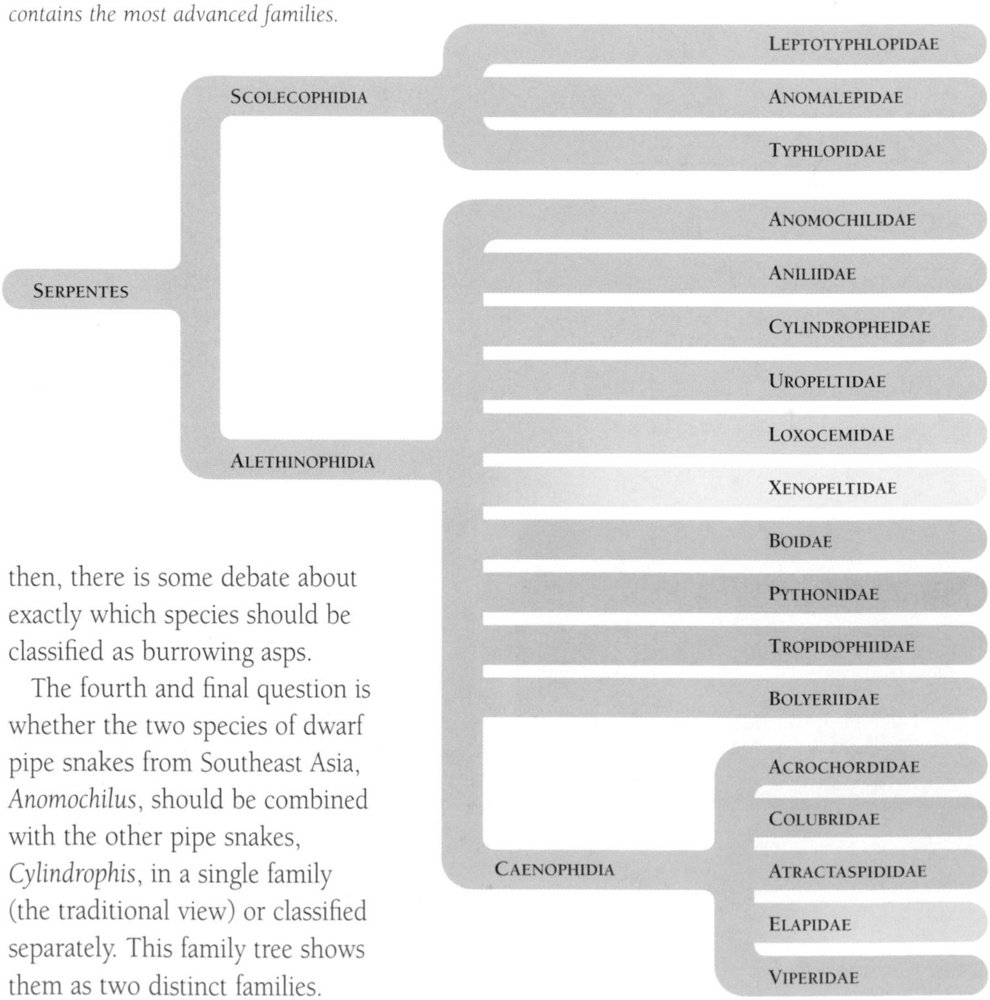

then, there is some debate about exactly which species should be classified as burrowing asps.

The fourth and final question is whether the two species of dwarf pipe snakes from Southeast Asia, *Anomochilus*, should be combined with the other pipe snakes, *Cylindrophis*, in a single family (the traditional view) or classified separately. This family tree shows them as two distinct families.

SCOLECOPHIDIA
- LEPTOTYPHLOPIDAE
- ANOMALEPIDAE
- TYPHLOPIDAE

SERPENTES

ALETHINOPHIDIA
- ANOMOCHILIDAE
- ANILIIDAE
- CYLINDROPHEIDAE
- UROPELTIDAE
- LOXOCEMIDAE
- XENOPELTIDAE
- BOIDAE
- PYTHONIDAE
- TROPIDOPHIIDAE
- BOLYERIIDAE

CAENOPHIDIA
- ACROCHORDIDAE
- COLUBRIDAE
- ATRACTASPIDIDAE
- ELAPIDAE
- VIPERIDAE

SNAKE GALLERY

The Snake Gallery illustrates 61 species of snake, chosen to reflect the fantastic diversity of size, shape, color, and markings found among these remarkable creatures. Some species have also been included for their fascinating behavior. Together they represent all major regions of the world.

The species have been arranged according to the traditional classification, which starts with the most primitive family and ends with the most recently evolved. Snakes in some families are either extremely rare or seldom seen and are not often photographed, so not all the snake families are represented.

Each snake is introduced with a description of its most interesting features. Captions, annotations, and boxes explain important aspects of behavior, physical characteristics, camouflage, and unusual methods of locomotion, providing fascinating and, in some cases, little-known facts.

GALLERY DETAILS
Each spread features one or two species of snake. This annotated example shows how the information on each spread is organized.

Species name
This gives the common name of the species that is being described.

Main characteristics
The most useful pointers in helping to identify the featured species are given here.

Footprint
The footprint shows the relative size of the snake. It represents a size 12 shoe – equal to 12 in (30 cm) .

Additional pictures
These show particular features or behavioral practices that help identify the featured snake.

Fact File
This gives key information about the species: its Latin name, family, natural habitat, breeding details, preferred food, and distribution.

World map
The approximate geographic range of the species is shown in red.

Average adult length
The dark gray snake indicates the typical length reached by an adult of the species.

Record length
Four of the six snake species that reach a noteworthy length are featured. The pale gray snake gives the largest recorded size.

Box
This covers a topic relevant to the featured snake – from conservation issues to other species with similar characteristics.

MEXICAN BURROWING SNAKE

The Mexican burrowing snake is something of a mystery. It is the sole member of its family, and it is not fully understood how its characteristics relate to those of other snakes. It shares some features with pythons, for instance, although pythons are not found in the Americas. Its burrowing habits and secretive lifestyle make it difficult to study. However, it has been observed eating iguana eggs.

FACT FILE

SPECIES: *Loxocemus bicolor.*
FAMILY: Loxocemidae.
HABITAT: Tropical, moist, dry, and arid forests.
BREEDING: Egg-layers, producing small clutches of eggs.
FEEDING: Rodents, lizards, and lizard eggs.
DISTRIBUTION: Southern Mexico to Costa Rica.

— MAIN CHARACTERISTICS

This species is stout with a very muscular body. Its small, shiny body scales are mostly dark gray, with white patches. The narrow head, spade-shaped snout, and small eyes are all adaptations to its burrowing lifestyle, helping it to tunnel through loose soil.

HEAD SCALES
Large scales cover the top of the head, unlike most other primitive snakes. Its shallow shape is an adaptation to a burrowing lifestyle.

Small eyes
The eyes are small, and the snake is thought to rely on its sense of smell when hunting.

AVERAGE ADULT LENGTH

0 cm	50 cm	1 m	1.5 m
0 in	1 ft 8 in	3 ft 3 in	4 ft 11 in

MEXICAN BURROWING SNAKE
The adult Loxocemus has irregular patches of white scales on the body. These appear as the snake ages, and the pale neck collar typical of the hatchling snakes disappears.

COLOR CHANGE
This unusual specimen lost all its gray pigment after shedding its skin except for a small patch on the head.

SUNBEAM SNAKE

Although they are only distantly related, the sunbeam snake is the Asian counterpart of the Mexican burrowing snake (see opposite). It too comes from a very small family that contains just one other similar species from China. Like the Mexican burrowing snake, the sunbeam snake spends most of its life below the ground, feeding on rodents and other burrowing vertebrates, including other snakes.

FACT FILE

SPECIES: *Xenopeltis unicolor.*
FAMILY: Xenopeltidae (sunbeam snakes).
HABITAT: Forest clearings, plantations, gardens, and parks.
BREEDING: Egg-layers, producing up to 10 eggs.
FEEDING: Almost anything, but especially frogs, reptiles, and small mammals.
DISTRIBUTION: Southern China and Southeast Asia.

MAIN CHARACTERISTICS

The most obvious distinguishing feature of the sunbeam snake is its highly polished, iridescent scales; no other species of snake shines so brightly. It has a thickset, powerful body with a narrow head, which is scarcely distinct from its neck.

SUNBEAM SNAKE
Shimmering scales give this snake its common name. It is also known occasionally as the iridescent earth snake. Its Latin name, Xenopeltis, means "strange covering."

Iridescence
A layer of dark pigmentation just below the surface of each scale enhances the iridescence.

Narrow neck
The narrow head blends almost imperceptibly into the slender neck.

WEDGE-SHAPED HEAD
The shape of the head enables the snake to push through loose soil. The eyes are small.

Head scales
Large, iridescent scales completely cover the top of the head.

AVERAGE ADULT LENGTH

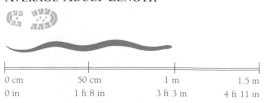

0 cm	50 cm	1 m	1.5 m
0 in	1 ft 8 in	3 ft 3 in	4 ft 11 in

EMERALD TREE BOA

T his bright green snake lives in the dense rain forests of South America, where it spends its days coiled inconspicuously over a horizontal branch. At night, it hangs downward in the hopes of ambushing prey – usually a bird, bat, or small arboreal mammal. It never descends to the ground, and even gives birth to live young in the canopy. Totally undisturbed forest habitats are essential for its survival.

— MAIN CHARACTERISTICS —

Bright green coloration and white markings along the back make the emerald tree boa unmistakable among South American snakes, although the green tree python (see p. 62), from Southeast Asia and the northern tip of Australia is almost identical. Differences include the larger scales on the top of the emerald tree boa's head and the position of the heat pits between scales bordering the mouth; those of the python are within the scales.

Stable anchor
The tail curls around a branch, providing an anchor for the hanging snake.

Heat pits
These are deep and very conspicuous. They are most useful for a nocturnal hunter, enabling the snake to strike accurately at prey.

BROAD HEAD
Like most boas, the broad head is covered with small scales. The muscles around the jaws are large, enabling the snake to clamp down firmly on its prey as it plunges long, curved teeth deeply into the victim's body.

EMERALD TREE BOA
Bright green coloration and slender body proportions reflect the emerald tree boa's arboreal habits. White crossbars help break up the snake's outline and camouflage it when it is coiled at rest.

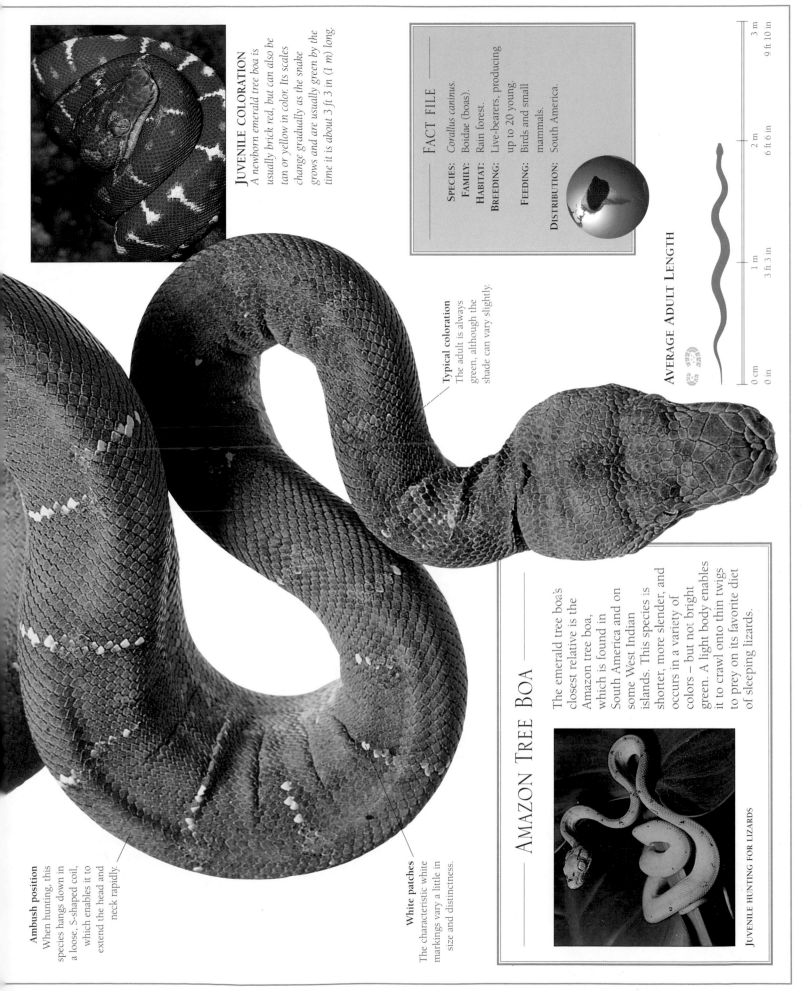

JUVENILE COLORATION
A newborn emerald tree boa is usually brick red, but can also be tan or yellow in color. Its scales change gradually as the snake grows and are usually green by the time it is about 3 ft 3 in (1 m) long.

FACT FILE

SPECIES: *Corallus caninus.*
FAMILY: Boidae (boas).
HABITAT: Rain forest.
BREEDING: Live-bearers, producing up to 20 young.
FEEDING: Birds and small mammals.
DISTRIBUTION: South America.

AVERAGE ADULT LENGTH

3 m
9 ft 10 in

2 m
6 ft 6 in

1 m
3 ft 3 in

0 cm
0 in

Typical coloration
The adult is always green, although the shade can vary slightly.

Ambush position
When hunting, this species hangs down in a loose, S-shaped coil, which enables it to extend the head and neck rapidly.

White patches
The characteristic white markings vary a little in size and distinctness.

AMAZON TREE BOA

The emerald tree boa's closest relative is the Amazon tree boa, which is found in South America and on some West Indian islands. This species is shorter, more slender, and occurs in a variety of colors – but not bright green. A light body enables it to crawl onto thin twigs to prey on its favorite diet of sleeping lizards.

JUVENILE HUNTING FOR LIZARDS

COMMON BOA

P robably among the most widely known of snake species, the boa constrictor, as it is popularly known, is a magnificent predator from the jungles of Central and South America that has adapted itself to a wide range of different habitats and lifestyles. It has few enemies once it reaches its adult length of 9 ft 10 in (3 m) or more.

MAIN CHARACTERISTICS

The common boa has a relatively small head in comparison to its stout, powerful body. Owing to its wide geographic range, the color and markings vary greatly, being silver, gray, or tan, with large blotches, or saddle-shaped markings, which may be dark red or brown. Some forms are suffused with black, while others are a pale, grayish pink.

VARIED HABITATS
Although the common boa is usually found in rain forests, it also occurs in drier environments in Mexico and on the grasslands of northern Argentina. It lives in trees or on the ground, but becomes increasingly terrestrial as it gets larger.

Narrow head
The head is thin, with a squared-off snout, and is covered with many small scales. The markings emphasize the shape and break up the outline.

AT RISK

Although the common boa is widespread, some local populations are endangered. Among these is a small form living on groups of islands off the north coast of Honduras, whose numbers have been greatly reduced due to their being collected for the pet trade and habitat destruction. They may already have been eliminated from some of the islands.

COMMON BOA FROM HOG ISLAND

Thick body
The common boa has a thick, muscular body, used for gripping branches while it is climbing and for constricting its prey.

FACT FILE

SPECIES:	*Boa constrictor.*
FAMILY:	Boidae (boas).
HABITAT:	Varied, from semiarid scrub to rain forests.
BREEDING:	Live-bearers, producing up to 50 young.
FEEDING:	Birds and small mammals.
DISTRIBUTION:	Central and South America.

COMMON BOA
The formidable size and powerful body of the common boa allow it to feed easily on a variety of warm-blooded prey. It may be active by day or at night, depending on the climate and time of year.

SWALLOWING PREY
The common boa begins to swallow its meal once the prey is dead. The snake gradually spreads its jaws as it slowly pulls the prey through the coils and down the throat.

Tail color
The saddles on the tail are often dark red, although they vary in intensity from one local population to another.

Expanding scales
The skin on the neck and throat is very elastic, allowing the snake to swallow prey that is relatively large.

AVERAGE ADULT LENGTH

RECORD LENGTH

0 cm	1 m	2 m	3 m	4 m	5 m
0 in	3 ft 3 in	6 ft 6 in	9 ft 10 in	13 ft 1 in	16 ft 5 in

RAINBOW BOA

T he rainbow boa occurs in several distinct forms, or subspecies, each varying slightly in size and coloration. All, however, have a dazzling, iridescent skin. Rainbow boas are equally at home on the ground or in trees, and in a variety of habitats.

— MAIN CHARACTERISTICS

The rainbow boa is usually slender, although the body shapes of the various forms vary. It has a narrow head, often with a dark line down the center and another over each eye. There is a row of shallow heat pits along the upper jaw. Juvenile rainbow boas are more brightly colored than the adults, regardless of the subspecies they belong to.

Large eyes
Rainbow boas have moderately large eyes; they hunt by sight on occasion.

BRAZILIAN RAINBOW BOA
The Brazilian rainbow boa is the most colorful of the forms. Its orange or rich red background is decorated with black circles and a row of eyespot markings along the flanks.

Shimmering scales
The smooth, iridescent scales shimmer and appear to change color as the snake moves.

PARAGUAYAN RAINBOW BOA
The Paraguayan rainbow boa,
Epicrates cenchria crassus, is
heavy-bodied. It has bold circles
down the back and very dark lines
running down the narrow head.

LIVE YOUNG
Rainbow boas give birth to live
young, which develop inside a thin
membrane. They break out just
before or just after they are born.

ARGENTINE RAINBOW BOA
The appearance of the Argentine rainbow
boa, Epicrates cenchria alvarezi, *makes it*
a very distinct subspecies. The scales are less
shiny than other forms, with a complex
pattern of light circles and semicircles on
a dark background.

Dark eyespots
Lateral rings, or eyespots,
are more pronounced in
juveniles, but are always
dark in color.

AVERAGE ADULT LENGTH

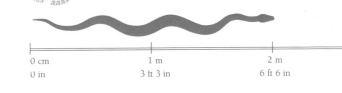

0 cm	1 m	2 m	3 m
0 in	3 ft 3 in	6 ft 6 in	9 ft 10 in

FACT FILE

SPECIES: *Epicrates cenchria.*
FAMILY: Boidae (boas).
HABITAT: Rain forest and grassland.
BREEDING: Live-bearers, producing up to 25 young.
FEEDING: Birds and small mammals.
DISTRIBUTION: Northern and central South America.

GREEN ANACONDA

N ative to South America, this gigantic snake is thought to grow to a greater size than any other species, once its weight and girth are taken into account. Because it becomes so heavy, it has to live partially in water to support its weight, and must catch its prey by ambush. Early accounts by Victorian explorers of anacondas measuring up to 60 ft (18 m) long were certainly exaggerations, but even so, adult anacondas are impressive. They have few enemies other than humans, and their life span can exceed 20 years.

— MAIN CHARACTERISTICS

The green anaconda is a massive olive-green or brown snake that has a number of circular, or oval, black blotches scattered at random over the entire body. There are very few similar snakes anywhere in the world, so its size, coloration, and habitat make this species easy to identify.

Aquatic camouflage
Dappled markings provide camouflage when the snake lies among vegetation in shallow water.

High-set eyes
The green anaconda's eyes are set toward the top of the head, which allows the snake to submerge its body, leaving little more than the eyes above the surface.

GREEN ANACONDA
A supple, sinuous body helps propel the green anaconda through swamps and shallow water, and also to constrict its prey. On land, however, its heavy body makes the snake sluggish, especially as it ages and its length and girth increase.

LARGE HEAD
The thick, powerful neck merges with the large head. A dark stripe passes from each eye to the angle of the jaw, although this can be obscured in old snakes since they darken over the entire body.

AVERAGE ADULT LENGTH

RECORD LENGTH

0 cm	1 m	2 m	3 m	4 m	5 m	6 m	7 m	8 m	9 m
0 in	3 ft 3 in	6 ft 6 in	9 ft 10 in	13 ft 1 in	16 ft 5 in	19 ft 8 in	23 ft	26 ft 3 in	29 ft 6 in

FORMIDABLE PREDATOR
Apart from mammals and birds, this snake also eats freshwater turtles and even caiman and crocodiles. Tussles with such formidable adversaries can take several hours, but the snake rarely loses. There have been a few authenticated reports of anacondas eating humans.

Mighty body
The powerful coils rarely allow the snake's prey to escape once captured.

FACT FILE

SPECIES: *Eunectes murinus.*
FAMILY: Boidae (boas).
HABITAT: Swamps and flooded forests.
BREEDING: Live-bearers, producing up to 40 young.
FEEDING: Almost anything, including fish, reptiles, birds, and mammals.
DISTRIBUTION: South America, primarily the Amazon basin and Trinidad.

YELLOW ANACONDA

The yellow anaconda, *Eunectes notaeus*, is a much smaller species than the green anaconda, growing to "only" 6 ft 6 in–9 ft 10 in (2–3 m). It is more colorful, being yellow or ocher with bold, black blotches on the body. The behavior and habits of the yellow anaconda are similar to those of the green anaconda. Both species, for instance, are aquatic and bear live young. Juvenile yellow anacondas frequently feed on fish.

A JUVENILE LYING IN SHALLOW WATER

ROSY BOA

T he rosy boa is an attractive but secretive inhabitant of the deserts of southwestern North America. It frequents rocky places, hiding by day in crevices and burrows, and emerging at night to hunt for rodents and other small mammals. The movements of the rosy boa are slow and deliberate, although it can strike quickly. Like all boas, it is a powerful constrictor. It is completely inoffensive toward humans, and is frequently kept as a pet.

— MAIN CHARACTERISTICS

A thick-bodied snake, the rosy boa has a small head and a short tail. The small scales are smooth and glossy. The body is cylindrical in shape, with a pattern consisting of three broad, longitudinal stripes on a light background. The color of the stripes varies from one form to another.

MEXICAN ROSY BOA
The Mexican rosy boa, C. trivirgata trivirgata, has dark brown or black stripes on cream, giving it the boldest pattern of all the subspecies. It is found in southern Baja California and Sonora, extending into a small part of southern Arizona.

COASTAL ROSY BOA
The stripes of the coastal rosy boa, C. trivirgata roseofusca, have ragged edges, especially in old adults. This species lives along the coastal region of southern California and adjacent parts of Baja California.

LONG HEAD
The head is elongated and covered with many small scales. The eye is small with a vertical pupil, which is typical of nocturnal foragers. The rosy boa does not have heat-sensitive pits.

CENTRAL BAJA ROSY BOA
This form of rosy boa, C. trivirgata saslowi, has orange stripes, which are usually well-defined with straight edges, and its eyes have orange irises. It occurs in central Baja California.

Thick neck
The thick, powerful neck is only barely distinct from the snake's head.

FACT FILE

SPECIES: *Charina trivirgata*.
FAMILY: Boidae (boas).
HABITAT: Deserts and rocky outcrops.
BREEDING: Live-bearers, producing up to 8 young.
FEEDING: Small mammals.
DISTRIBUTION: North America.

DESERT ROSY BOA

The desert form, C. trivirgata myriolepis, is cream with orange-brown stripes. These have ragged edges and are not as distinctive as those of the central Baja form. The desert rosy boa is found in northern Arizona and adjacent parts of neighboring desert states.

Variable coloration
This form, like most of the others, does not live up to its common name, since it is rarely "rosy" in color. Only a few individuals have an orange or pinkish hue.

AVERAGE ADULT LENGTH

0 cm	50 cm	1 m	1.5 m
0 in	1 ft 8 in	3 ft 3 in	4 ft 11 in

47

DUMERIL'S GROUND BOA

H abitat destruction and collection for the skin trade have much reduced the numbers of Dumeril's ground boa, a species that lives among the leaf-litter on the forest floor of southern and southwestern Madagascar. It is being widely bred by zoos, which are cooperating in a captive breeding program.

— MAIN CHARACTERISTICS

A stocky snake, Dumeril's ground boa starts life with a pinkish flush to its markings, but this soon fades. Adults display an intricate brown and tan pattern in different shades. The inky black blotches on the scales bordering the mouth are characteristic.

FACT FILE

SPECIES: *Acrantophis dumerili.*
FAMILY: Boidae (boas).
HABITAT: Dry forests.
BREEDING: Live-bearers, producing up to 20 young.
FEEDING: Birds and mammals.
DISTRIBUTION: Madagascar.

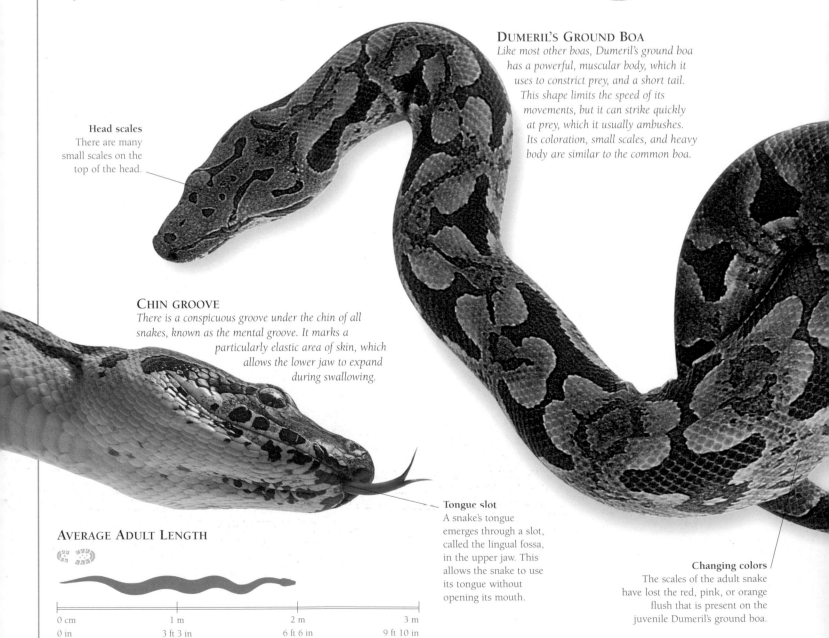

Head scales
There are many small scales on the top of the head.

DUMERIL'S GROUND BOA
Like most other boas, Dumeril's ground boa has a powerful, muscular body, which it uses to constrict prey, and a short tail. This shape limits the speed of its movements, but it can strike quickly at prey, which it usually ambushes. Its coloration, small scales, and heavy body are similar to the common boa.

CHIN GROOVE
There is a conspicuous groove under the chin of all snakes, known as the mental groove. It marks a particularly elastic area of skin, which allows the lower jaw to expand during swallowing.

Tongue slot
A snake's tongue emerges through a slot, called the lingual fossa, in the upper jaw. This allows the snake to use its tongue without opening its mouth.

Changing colors
The scales of the adult snake have lost the red, pink, or orange flush that is present on the juvenile Dumeril's ground boa.

AVERAGE ADULT LENGTH

0 cm	1 m	2 m	3 m
0 in	3 ft 3 in	6 ft 6 in	9 ft 10 in

DEFORESTATION

Dumeril's ground boa is only one of many unique reptiles, amphibians, mammals, and plants on Madagascar that is threatened by the destruction of its habitat. Many are in grave danger of extinction if deforestation continues at its current rate. Only a small proportion of Madagascar's forests remains. Lumbering to provide agricultural land not only removes the forest cover but also results in soil erosion and the subsequent silting up of rivers.

LAND CLEARED FOR CATTLE GRAZING, MADAGASCAR

Unique markings
The markings are highly variable, and no two snakes are exactly alike. The saddles along the midline form perfect ovals in places, while in others, the halves of the saddles do not match.

Cylindrical body
The thick, stocky body is roughly cylindrical in shape.

CAMOUFLAGE
Dumeril's ground boa's markings in shades of brown, tan, orange, and olive-green are a good match for the mosaic of leaves and other debris covering the forest floor.

CALABAR GROUND BOA

V ery little is known about the natural history of the Calabar ground boa, which leads a hidden existence in tunnels beneath the soil. It lives in tropical forests and probably feeds mainly on nestling rodents, which it tracks down in their burrows. Inoffensive to humans, it never attempts to bite. Calabar was the former name for the part of West Africa in which this snake lives.

— MAIN CHARACTERISTICS —

The Calabar ground boa appears to have two heads. Both head and tail are blunt, and the tail is short. Its body is almost perfectly cylindrical and has smooth scales. All these characteristics are found in several other species of burrowing snake, but the Calabar ground boa is probably the most perfect example, making it easily identifiable.

DECEPTIVE TAIL
The tail is clearly intended to imitate the head of the snake. It is the same shape and color, and even has similar white scales under the "chin." Many individuals have scars on their tails, where they have been attacked by predators who mistook the snake's tail for its head.

CALABAR GROUND BOA
The blunt snout, thick neck, cylindrical body, and short tail of the Calabar ground boa are all the result of its burrowing lifestyle, helping it to force its way through soil.

Heavy body
Unlike many other heavy-bodied snakes, this species does not crawl on its belly, but braces part of its body against the burrow walls while it pushes or pulls another part forward.

Blunt head
Used as a ram, the blunt head moves from side to side as the snake progresses, compacting displaced soil against the walls of its burrow.

Varied coloration
This individual has many red or orange patches, while the coloration of others is uniform. The reddish scales are scattered randomly over the entire body.

DEFENSIVE POSTURE
When threatened, the Calabar ground boa hides its head in its coils and raises its tail. It may even make mock strikes with the tail, deflecting the attack away from the vulnerable head.

FACT FILE

SPECIES: *Charina reinhardtii.*
FAMILY: Boidae (boas).
HABITAT: Forests.
BREEDING: Egg-layers, producing 1–4 moderately large eggs.
FEEDING: Small mammals.
DISTRIBUTION: West Africa.

AVERAGE ADULT LENGTH

0 cm	50 cm	1 m	1.5 m
0 in	1 ft 8 in	3 ft 3 in	4 ft 11 in

CARPET PYTHON

T his slender, graceful python occurs in many color forms throughout its wide geographic range in Australia and New Guinea. It occupies a number of different types of habitat and is usually nocturnal, but, depending on the climate, it can also be diurnal. The carpet python is often found around human habitations, where it does a useful job eating rats and other vermin.

— MAIN CHARACTERISTICS

Most forms have intricate markings consisting of light and dark bands, or reticulations, on a background of gray, brown, or reddish brown. All forms have triangular heads, which are distinct from the neck and covered with many small scales. There is a conspicuous row of heat pits in the scales bordering the mouth, and the eyes are moderately large with vertical pupils.

Effective camouflage
The irregular pattern serves to conceal the snake's outline from predators.

Triangular head
The distinctive shape of the head is characteristic of this species.

— FACT FILE —

SPECIES: *Morelia spilota*.
FAMILY: Pythonidae (pythons).
HABITAT: Dry forests,rocky scrublands, along river courses, rain forests
BREEDING: Egg-layers, producing 10-50 eggs.
FEEDING: Reptiles, birds, and small mammals.
DISTRIBUTION: Australia and New Guinea.

AVERAGE ADULT LENGTH

0 cm	1 m	2 m	3 m
0 in	3 ft 3 in	6 ft 6 in	9 ft 10 in

JUNGLE CARPET PYTHON

The black and yellow coloration of the jungle carpet python is spectacular. In its natural habitat, however, these markings make it difficult to see when it is coiled in the branches of a tree or resting in the mottled light of the Queensland rain forest, where it lives. One of several subspecies of carpet python, the jungle carpet python is partially arboreal.

Strong body
Powerful body muscles prevent the heart and lungs of the snake's prey from functioning, thus causing rapid unconsciousness and a quick death.

Exotic markings
Light and dark bands on a pale background give the effect of an Oriental carpet, hence the common name.

ADULT ON CLIFF LEDGE, CAMOUFLAGED AGAINST THE ROCK

CENTRAL AUSTRALIAN CARPET PYTHON

The Central Australian carpet python, *Morelia bredli*, is a close relative of the carpet python, although it is slightly smaller. Also known as the desert carpet python, it was not considered to be a distinct species until 1981. It differs mainly in having smaller (and therefore more numerous) scales on the top of the head. *Morelia bredli* occurs in the central Australian deserts, where it lives among rocky outcrops or near trees and shrubs. Its reddish-brown coloration is a perfect match with the red earth and rock of its habitat. In most other respects, this species is similar to the carpet python.

HUNTING METHODS

The carpet python uses its heat-sensitive pits to locate warm-blooded prey such as rodents. Once it has pinpointed the prey's whereabouts, it strikes rapidly, throwing a number of coils around the creature and then tightening them until the victim is unable to draw breath. The snake begins to swallow its meal only when the prey has been squeezed to death.

BURMESE PYTHON

C ommonly found near villages and even cities, the Burmese python performs a useful function by eating rats and other vermin. Unfortunately, it is not always welcome because it also attacks chickens and other domestic animals. All pythons coil around their eggs, but the Burmese python is able to raise its body temperature by a process that is not yet fully understood.

— MAIN CHARACTERISTICS

Apart from its large size – commonly up to 9 ft 10 in (3 m), and occasionally longer – the Burmese python can be distinguished by its rich chestnut and tan coloration, smooth scales, large scales on the top of the head, and the presence of heat pits. Out of its habitat, it could be confused with the African rock python, which is similar in size and coloration, but has a different pattern.

ALBINO FORM
Through a genetic anomaly, some Burmese pythons lack the dark pigments that give them their rich coloration. These albinos are selectively bred in captivity to produce pure strains, called golden pythons.

BURMESE PYTHON
This richly colored form has a geographic range centered around Myanmar (Burma), as its name suggests. The large, interlocking blotches along the back are always present, even in paler forms. Its markings blend perfectly with the flecked light of its natural habitat.

AVERAGE ADULT LENGTH

RECORD LENGTH

0 cm	1 m	2 m	3 m	4 m	5 m	6 m	7 m	8 m	9 m
0 in	3 ft 3 in	6 ft 6 in	9 ft 10 in	13 ft 1 in	16 ft 5 in	19 ft 8 in	23 ft	26 ft 3 in	29 ft 6 in

Desirable skin
Rich colors and smooth scales have resulted in the Burmese python being widely hunted for the skin trade. Exterminated in several regions, it is now rare in many of the places where it was formerly common.

HEAD MARKINGS
Dark arrowhead markings help identify this species. A wedge-shaped mark runs from each eye to the angle of the jaw, with another immediately below each eye.

Prominent heat pits
Heat pits help the snake pinpoint its prey, even in total darkness.

FACT FILE

SPECIES:	*Python molurus.*
FAMILY:	Pythonidae (pythons).
HABITAT:	Rain forests, plantations, and fields.
BREEDING:	Egg-layers, producing up to 50 eggs.
FEEDING:	Birds and mammals.
DISTRIBUTION:	South and Southeast Asia.

RETICULATED PYTHON

T hought to be the world's longest snake, the reticulated python is an inhabitant of the steamy tropical rain forests of Southeast Asia. It leads a secretive life, well camouflaged among forest vegetation. Occasionally, it strays into villages and the outskirts of large towns, probably attracted by potential prey in the form of rats and domestic animals. It is one of only a handful of snakes that are known to have eaten humans, although cases are exceptionally rare.

— MAIN CHARACTERISTICS

The reticulated python has a complex, geometric pattern, which incorporates a number of different colors. A series of irregular diamond shapes along the back is flanked with smaller markings, which often have light centers. Its size and unmarked head are usually enough to identify this species, even though there is some variation in pattern. Despite its wide distribution and the variation in size, color, and markings, no subspecies has been described so far. This is partly due to the difficulties involved in capturing, preserving, and transporting a snake of this size.

FACT FILE

SPECIES: *Python reticulatus*.
FAMILY: Pythonidae (pythons).
HABITAT: Rain forest.
BREEDING: Egg-layers, producing around 60 eggs, occasionally up to 100.
FEEDING: Birds and mammals, including, on rare occasions, people.
DISTRIBUTION: Southeast Asia.

RETICULATED PYTHON
A reticulated, or netlike, pattern gives this snake its common and Latin names. A broad head and a huge gape enable it to swallow large prey and make it an efficient hunter. Long, curved teeth ensure that once the snake has caught its prey, it rarely loses its grip on its victim.

Geometric markings
There are irregular diamond shapes along the back.

Large body
A powerful constrictor, the adult snake's size allows it to easily overpower and kill animals as large as deer, pigs, and dogs.

NIGHT VISION
The reticulated python has vertical pupils with bright orange irises. It is a nocturnal hunter that relies heavily on ambush tactics to catch prey.

Plain head
A conspicuous line running from each eye to the angle of the jaw is the only marking on an otherwise plain head.

Smooth scales
This species has smooth scales. Most are of a single color, so that the markings appear ragged at the edges.

FOREST CAMOUFLAGE
Despite its massive size, the reticulated python is surprisingly hard to spot, even in places where it is common. This is partly due to excellent camouflage and partly because it is not very active during the day, when it rests in thick vegetation, in a hollow tree, or lies partially buried in forest debris.

AVERAGE ADULT LENGTH

RECORD LENGTH

0 cm	1 m	2 m	3 m	4 m	5 m	6 m	7 m	8 m	9 m
0 in	3 ft 3 in	6 ft 6 in	9 ft 10 in	13 ft 1 in	16 ft 5 in	19 ft 8 in	23 ft	26 ft 3 in	29 ft 6 in

BLOOD PYTHON

A stocky snake, the blood python is at home in the soggy jungles of Southeast Asia. It leads a sedentary lifestyle, hiding among the leaf-litter and forest debris and waiting for its next meal to come within range. Its great bulk provides a firm anchor from which it can launch a sudden strike, taking its victim completely by surprise.

BLOOD PYTHON
The blood python derives its name from its orange or red coloration. Not all forms have this coloration, however, and the name can be misleading. It has a stubby tail, which provides it with an alternative name, the short-tailed python.

— MAIN CHARACTERISTICS

The blood python is the most thickset of the pythons, and it is quite easy to identify by its proportions alone. The head is light on top and dark at the sides, and the eyes are small. The scales are smooth and shiny, and the body is invariably marked with large, dark blotches on a lighter background. The colors of the different forms can be highly variable.

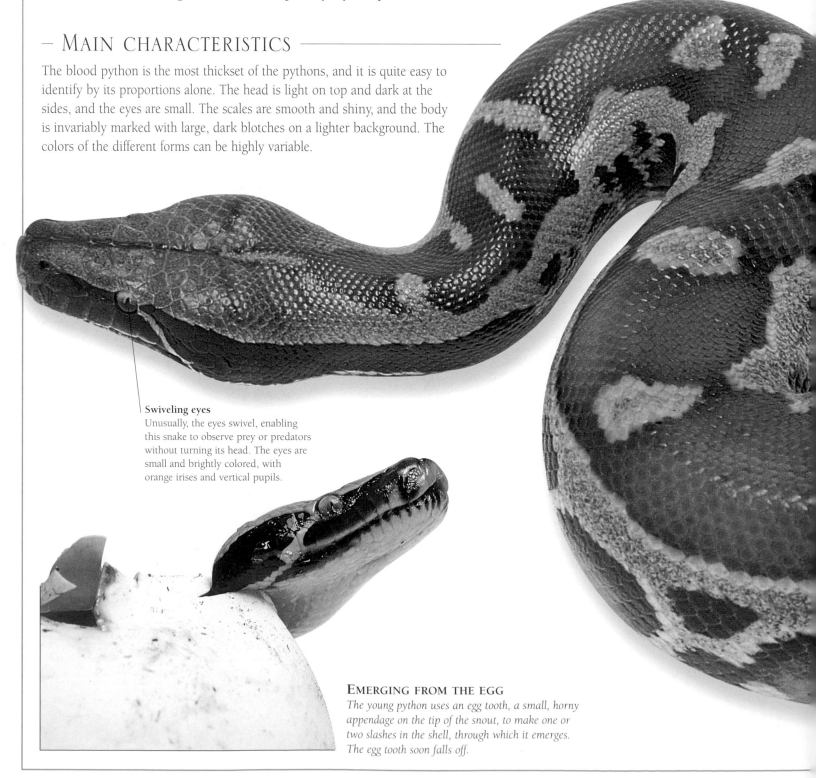

Swiveling eyes
Unusually, the eyes swivel, enabling this snake to observe prey or predators without turning its head. The eyes are small and brightly colored, with orange irises and vertical pupils.

EMERGING FROM THE EGG
The young python uses an egg tooth, a small, horny appendage on the tip of the snout, to make one or two slashes in the shell, through which it emerges. The egg tooth soon falls off.

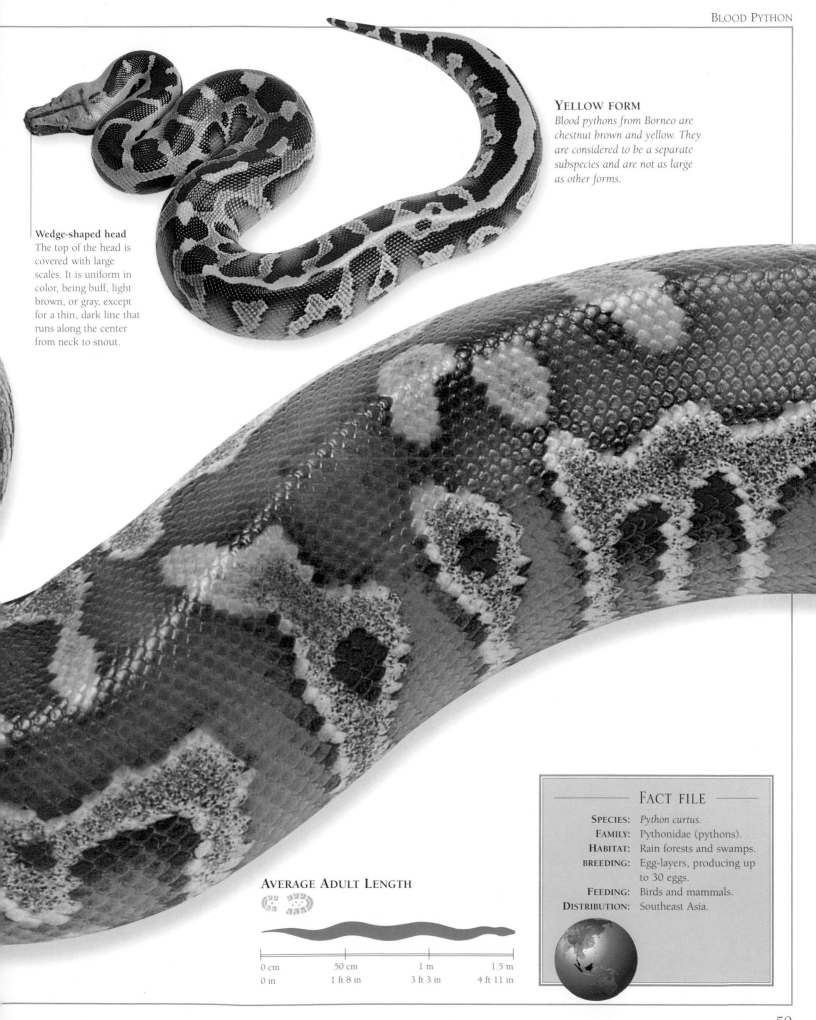

YELLOW FORM
Blood pythons from Borneo are chestnut brown and yellow. They are considered to be a separate subspecies and are not as large as other forms.

Wedge-shaped head
The top of the head is covered with large scales. It is uniform in color, being buff, light brown, or gray, except for a thin, dark line that runs along the center from neck to snout.

AVERAGE ADULT LENGTH

| 0 cm | 50 cm | 1 m | 1.5 m |
| 0 in | 1 ft 8 in | 3 ft 3 in | 4 ft 11 in |

FACT FILE

SPECIES: *Python curtus.*
FAMILY: Pythonidae (pythons).
HABITAT: Rain forests and swamps.
BREEDING: Egg-layers, producing up to 30 eggs.
FEEDING: Birds and mammals.
DISTRIBUTION: Southeast Asia.

CHILDREN'S PYTHON

Named in honor of J.G. Children, who was in charge of the zoological collection at the British Museum, London, in the first half of the nineteenth century, Children's python lives in a variety of habitats, usually on the ground but sometimes in trees too. This species is active at night, hunting lizards, small birds, and mammals.

MAIN CHARACTERISTICS

The young Children's python is heavily blotched, then becomes brown or reddish brown as it grows. Large scales on the top of the head contrast with small, smooth ones on the body. This characteristic is typical of the species and its close relatives; most pythons have small head scales. There are heat pits in some of the scales bordering the mouth.

FACT FILE

SPECIES:	*Antaresia childreni.*
FAMILY:	Pythonidae (pythons).
HABITAT:	Woodlands, monsoon forests, and dry scrub, usually among rocks.
BREEDING:	Egg-layers, producing up to 20 eggs.
FEEDING:	Reptiles, birds, and small mammals.
DISTRIBUTION:	Northern Australia.

CHILDREN'S PYTHON
The Children's python is among the smallest species of python, rarely exceeding 3 ft 3 in (1 m) in length. Despite its small size, it is a powerful constrictor. This snake is half-grown, but will become less marked as it ages.

Prominent eyes
The eyes are prominent and have the vertical pupils of a nocturnal hunter.

EGG INCUBATION
Like all pythons, the female Children's python broods her eggs by coiling herself around them throughout the incubation period, which lasts for about seven weeks. This behavior helps hide and protect the eggs from the snake's predators. It also maintains constant temperature and humidity levels around the eggs.

AVERAGE ADULT LENGTH

0 cm	50 cm	1 m	1.5 m
0 in	1 ft 8 in	3 ft 3 in	4 ft 11 in

SPOTTED PYTHON

This small python occurs in most types of habitat, but is especially fond of rocky hillsides and outcrops with crevices and caves. It is active at night, when it goes in search of prey. Insect-eating bats, which it catches at cave entrances, are a favorite food.

— MAIN CHARACTERISTICS

The spotted python has a slender, cylindrical body covered with smooth, iridescent scales. It keeps this irregularly blotched pattern throughout its life, but the size of the blotches and their contrast with the background color can vary. In some members the spots join together in places to produce a ragged zigzag pattern along the back.

FACT FILE

SPECIES: *Antaresia maculosa.*
FAMILY: Pythonidae (pythons).
HABITAT: Moist and dry forests, grasslands, rocky outcrops, and tree hollows.
BREEDING: Egg-layers, producing up to 15 eggs.
FEEDING: Frogs, lizards, birds, and small mammals, including bats.
DISTRIBUTION: Northeastern Australia.

Large scales
There are large scales on top of the head and shallow heat pits in some of the scales bordering the mouth.

Irregular pattern
The characteristic blotches have ragged edges, like a rug or tapestry. This is because the dark pigmentation is restricted to complete scales.

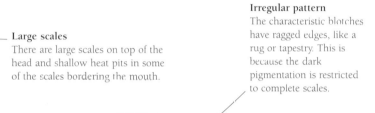

KILLING PREY
A powerful constrictor, the spotted python wraps several coils of its body around the prey and squeezes, swallowing only when it is sure that the prey is dead. Even then, the snake does not release its quarry, but pulls the body through its coils as it swallows.

SPOTTED PYTHON
This species and the Children's python (see opposite) have until recently been considered variations of the same species. Distinguishing the two can be difficult, especially in juveniles, although the more heavily spotted pattern, larger size, and darker overall coloration of the spotted python are usually good identification characteristics.

AVERAGE ADULT LENGTH

0 cm	50 cm	1 m	1.5 m
0 in	1 ft 8 in	3 ft 3 in	4 ft 11 in

GREEN TREE PYTHON

A beautiful snake that conforms to the popular vision of a jungle serpent, the green tree python is found only in the rain forests of New Guinea and extreme northern Queensland. It spends its entire life in the canopy, draped spectacularly over branches during the day and hunting for its prey of arboreal mammals and roosting birds at night.

GREEN TREE PYTHON
This is the only python that is predominantly green in color. It is also more slender than most other pythons. Both characteristics are adaptations to living in the forest canopy.

MAIN CHARACTERISTICS

The green tree python is similar in appearance to the emerald tree boa (see pp. 38–39), which comes from South America. The adult snake is bright green and usually has a broken line of white markings along the midline of the back. Juveniles are bright yellow or, rarely, red; the young become green when they are about a year old. Other important distinguishing characteristics of the green tree python are the small scales on the head and the heat pits situated in the scales bordering the mouth.

Strong muscles
The greater part of the snake's weight is supported by powerful muscles. The ability to stretch out unsupported helps this snake move efficiently from branch to branch.

Head bulges
The bulges conceal powerful jaw muscles. A firm grip is important for an arboreal species because it would be unlikely to recover dropped animals.

Large eyes
Vertical pupils and large eyes identify this snake as a nocturnal hunter. Adults have cream eyes, while those of juveniles are white with a dark line passing through their centers.

SCALY HEAD
The head is covered with numerous small, granular scales. The nasal scales are large. Adults have uniform green heads with pale green, yellowish, or white lips. Occasional specimens have scattered blue scales on their heads.

AVERAGE ADULT LENGTH

0 cm	50 cm	1 m	1.5 m
0 in	1 ft 8 in	3 ft 3 in	4 ft 11 in

Heat pits
These are located in the scales, while those of the emerald tree boa are found between the scales.

FACT FILE

SPECIES: *Morelia viridis.*
FAMILY: Pythonidae (pythons).
HABITAT: Rain forests.
BREEDING: Egg-layers, producing up to 25 eggs.
FEEDING: Reptiles, birds, and small mammals.
DISTRIBUTION: New Guinea and surrounding islands, extreme northern Queensland, Australia.

YELLOW YOUNG
Like all female pythons, the green tree python coils around her eggs throughout the incubation period to protect them from predators and temperature extremes. The young hatch after about two months and are usually brilliant yellow. This coloration is paralleled in the emerald tree boa, but the reason for it is still unknown to zoologists.

ROYAL PYTHON

I noffensive to humans, the royal python is the smallest of the three African pythons. Its home is the grasslands and sparse woodlands of the West African savanna, where it spends much of its life in underground burrows. It is active mainly at night, although during the long dry season it may remain permanently in hiding.

— MAIN CHARACTERISTICS

A short, stocky snake, the royal python is boldly marked in black and tan, which makes it hard to see when it is nestled among short vegetation. It has a short tail and a powerful, muscular body, which it uses to constrict prey. Its scales are small and shiny and do not overlap. It grows to a maximum length of about 6 ft 6 in (2 m).

Visible heat pits
The heat pits, used for detecting prey, are well developed and clearly visible.

BROAD HEAD
This species has a rounded snout and small scales covering the top of the broad head. The eyes are large and the pupils are vertical, as in most snakes that are active at night.

Sturdy body
The body is short and stout. It is slightly triangular when seen in cross section.

TIGHT DEFENSE
The royal python rolls itself into a ball whenever it feels threatened, hiding its head in the center of the coils and exposing only its scaly armor to enemies.

AVERAGE ADULT LENGTH

0 cm	50 cm	1 m	1.5 m
0 in	1 ft 8 in	3 ft 3 in	4 ft 11 in

FACT FILE

SPECIES: *Python regius.*
FAMILY: Pythonidae (pythons).
HABITAT: Grassland and dry forests.
BREEDING: Egg-layers, producing about 4–8 eggs.
FEEDING: Birds and small mammals.
DISTRIBUTION: West Africa.

Saddle variation
Slight variations in the shape and number of the saddles make each one individual.

Powerful coils
Like other pythons, this species uses powerful muscles to constrict warm-blooded prey such as rodents.

Eye stripe
The stripe on each side of the royal python's eye helps disguise the outline of the head, making it difficult for a predator to spot the snake.

ROYAL PYTHON
Dark brown and tan markings make this one of the most attractive pythons. Small scales and a handsome pattern make it a favorite in the skin trade, leading to large-scale slaughter.

Dark colors
The brown background, seen here in its darkest phase, may become paler at night.

HIDING PLACES
Wood snakes coil up in small spaces when they rest during the day. The rolled-up stems of palm fronds and the "vases" of air plants are favorite hiding places, but they may also crawl under logs, boards, or garbage. When exposed, they tend to remain still at first and can easily be overlooked.

HAITIAN WOOD SNAKE
A small head, supple body, and mottled coloration all help this little snake avoid detection. Moderately large eyes enable the Haitian wood snake to see at night, when it is out hunting for food.

AVERAGE ADULT LENGTH

0 cm	50 cm	1 m	1.5 m
0 in	1 ft 8 in	3 ft 3 in	4 ft 11 in

HAITIAN WOOD SNAKE

P reviously considered to be members of the boa family, the wood snakes now comprise a family in their own right. The Haitian wood snake feeds almost exclusively on lizards, which it stalks at night while they are asleep, and which it constricts. When disturbed, it may roll itself into a ball and produce a foul-smelling fluid from its cloaca.

— MAIN CHARACTERISTICS

The Haitian wood snake is slender and has smooth scales, a small head with large scales covering the top, and an unusual coloration of dark green blotches on a brown background. No other snake has the same color pattern, but in some cases dark members can be mistaken for other species. Unusual among snakes, it sometimes undergoes a color change, during which its dark background turns yellow.

FACT FILE

SPECIES: *Tropidophis haetianus.*
FAMILY: Tropidophiidae (wood snakes).
HABITAT: Woods.
BREEDING: Live-bearers, producing 5–10 young.
FEEDING: Lizards and small mammals.
DISTRIBUTION: Cuba, Hispaniola, and Jamaica.

CUBAN WOOD SNAKE

The most common species of wood snake, the Cuban wood snake is found in a wide variety of habitats, including rain forests, rocky hillsides, and plantations. It lives mostly on the ground, but also climbs into shrubs and up rocks in search of prey. Its diet includes tree frogs, lizards, small mammals, and, occasionally, birds. It never bites, but will release a foul-smelling slime from its cloaca when threatened.

Bright tail
The vivid tip may lure potential prey closer or deflect an attack from the head.

– MAIN CHARACTERISTICS –

The Cuban wood snake is the largest of the wood snakes. It has a stocky body, small head, small eyes with vertical pupils, and a short tail. The tail tip may be black or yellow, contrasting with the rest of the body. Its scales are smooth with a satin-like sheen.

FACT FILE

SPECIES	*Tropidophis melanurus.*
FAMILY:	Tropidophiidae (wood snakes).
HABITAT:	Deciduous forests.
BREEDING:	Live-bearers, producing about 8 young.
FEEDING:	Frogs, reptiles, and small mammals.
DISTRIBUTION:	Cuba.

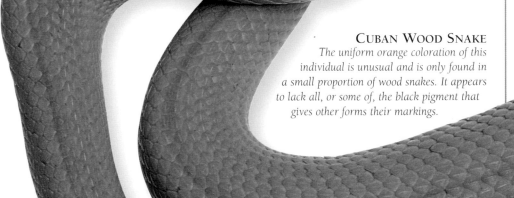

CUBAN WOOD SNAKE
The uniform orange coloration of this individual is unusual and is only found in a small proportion of wood snakes. It appears to lack all, or some of, the black pigment that gives other forms their markings.

COLOR DIFFERENCES
This species is highly variable in color. The most common form is tan, gray, or buff with irregular dark blotches along the back. This combination means that the snake is well camouflaged when it is resting among dead leaves or other forest debris.

AVERAGE ADULT LENGTH

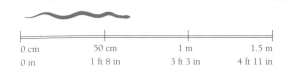

0 cm	50 cm	1 m	1.5 m
0 in	1 ft 8 in	3 ft 3 in	4 ft 11 in

Small eyes
The snake hunts more by smell than by sight, hence the small eyes.

GRASS SNAKE

Semiaquatic, this species is found in a variety of damp habitats. When it swims, it usually stays on the surface with the head well above water. It feeds largely on frogs, but also eats toads, newts, tadpoles, and fish. It is inoffensive and never attempts to bite. Within its huge geographic range, it is one of the most common and adaptable of species. Females are always larger than males, and all members from the south tend to be larger than those of northerly populations.

— MAIN CHARACTERISTICS —

The grass snake is generally easily identifiable by the distinctive collar behind the head, which is usually yellow, but may be orange, cream, or white, and has a pair of black crescents immediately behind it. The snake's coloration varies from brown or greenish gray to olive-green and, sometimes, black. The members of some populations from southeastern Europe and northern Italy have two pale lines running down their bodies. Spanish specimens are often more uniform in coloration and lack the light-colored collar and the bars on the flanks. The grass snake's distinctive collar can be obscure in very dark specimens.

GRASS SNAKE
Narrow, heavily keeled scales may help propel this snake through the water, and its sinuous body enables it to work its way through reeds, rushes, and other dense aquatic vegetation.

AVERAGE ADULT LENGTH

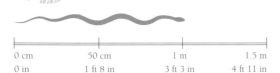

0 cm	50 cm	1 m	1.5 m
0 in	1 ft 8 in	3 ft 3 in	4 ft 11 in

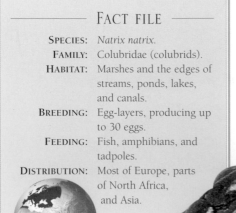

— FACT FILE —

SPECIES: *Natrix natrix.*
FAMILY: Colubridae (colubrids).
HABITAT: Marshes and the edges of streams, ponds, lakes, and canals.
BREEDING: Egg-layers, producing up to 30 eggs.
FEEDING: Fish, amphibians, and tadpoles.
DISTRIBUTION: Most of Europe, parts of North Africa, and Asia.

Plain head
The top of the head is covered with large scales, and is usually plain in color.

Distinctive marking
The bright collar, together with the two black patches behind it, is a good distinguishing characteristic.

Orange irises
This species has average-sized eyes with round pupils and orange irises.

Flank markings
The dark crossbars down the flanks are nearly always present, except in black specimens.

EGG INCUBATION
Because they tend to live in cold places, female grass snakes search out decaying vegetation in which to lay eggs. The heat generated by the process of decomposition speeds up the development of the eggs. Several females may lay eggs together in a particularly favorable site.

Defense mechanism
This snake has puffed up its body to make itself look bigger and intimidate enemies.

DEFENSE
If cornered, the grass snake may play dead by lying upside down with its mouth open and tongue hanging out. At the same time, it secretes a foul-smelling fluid from the cloaca. After a while it rights itself and makes off. Otherwise, it tries to escape by taking cover in water or in dense vegetation.

COMMON EGG-EATER

An anatomically modified head and thirty specialized vertebrae enable the common egg-eater to feed on birds' eggs. It lays its own eggs and devours most of its food in the spring when birds are nesting. For the rest of the year it fasts and is rarely seen, despite being a common species. Hatchlings, which are only about 8 in (20 cm) long, must find small eggs such as those of weaverbirds, tits, and finches.

MAIN CHARACTERISTICS

The common egg-eater can grow to about 3 ft 3 in (1 m), but is usually smaller. The combination of a narrow head, rounded snout, and very rough scales makes it easily identifiable. It may be gray, light brown, or olive, but there is always a series of irregular dark blotches along the back. The top of the head is marked with two dark chevrons pointing forward. There is a similar marking on the back of the neck.

Expanding jaw
The snake's jaw can easily accommodate an egg four to five times the size of its head.

THE SNAKE STRETCHES ITS JAW AND NECK

THE EGG IS ALMOST ENTIRELY ENGULFED

CONSUMING AN EGG
An egg-eater engulfs whole eggs by wedging them against a firm object before forcing them into its throat. The 22nd and 28th vertebrae then penetrate the shell, while vertebrae 29 and 30 prevent the egg from moving, and vertebrae 1 to 21 prevent it from slipping out of the snake's mouth. The egg is crushed by vertebrae 23 to 27. The contents of the egg are swallowed, but the shell, folded into a characteristic pellet, is regurgitated.

AVERAGE ADULT LENGTH

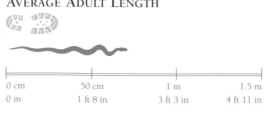

0 cm	50 cm	1 m	1.5 m
0 in	1 ft 8 in	3 ft 3 in	4 ft 11 in

DEFENSE

The common egg-eater, which has no functional teeth, is harmless to humans. To protect itself from its potential predators, such as birds of prey and mammals, it mimics the venomous vipers that live in the same part of the world. A gray individual, for instance, looks like a night adder or a carpet viper. The common egg-eater may even imitate the defensive behavior of the viper by forming semicircular coils, rasping the rough scales on its flanks together, and spreading its jaws to make its head look as broad as possible.

COMMON EGG-EATER

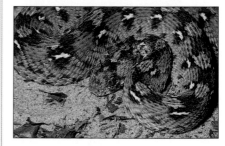

CARPET VIPER

Distinctive marking
There are two dark chevrons on the top of the head and a similar marking on the neck.

COMMON EGG-EATER
Heavily keeled scales give the common egg-eater a superficial similarity to the carpet and saw-scaled vipers. This deception is even extended to the obliquely arranged keels on its flanks, enabling it to imitate the rasping sound these vipers make.

Varying coloration
The background color is usually gray, but this may vary in other specimens to match the soil on which they live.

Keeled scales
The scales along the center of the snake's back are elongated and heavily keeled.

FACT FILE

SPECIES: *Dasypeltis scabra.*
FAMILY: Colubridae (colubrids).
HABITAT: Savannas, scrub, and open woodlands.
BREEDING: Egg-layers, producing up to 18 eggs.
FEEDING: Birds' eggs.
DISTRIBUTION: Africa, south of the Sahara.

Back markings
A series of irregular dark blotches run along the snake's back.

CORN SNAKE

Also known as the red rat snake, the corn snake is a common and beautiful species native to the southeastern region of the US. It is found around houses and gardens as well as in natural habitats. The corn snake has become a very popular domestic pet, and selective breeding has produced forms that bear little resemblance to their wild ancestors. All, however, belong to the same species.

— MAIN CHARACTERISTICS

Corn snakes are slender with narrow heads and well-defined neck regions. The number and size of the saddles, or blotches, down the back can vary, as can the color, although the differences are less extreme in snakes from the wild. In some forms the blotches merge to form a broad stripe or an irregular zigzag.

WILD FORM
The coloration and pattern of this form are the same as those of the wild form of the corn snake.

CORN SNAKES
These captive-bred corn snakes display some of the many variations in color and pattern that are the result of many years of selective breeding from occasional, naturally occurring mutations.

TREE CLIMBER
A wild corn snake climbs well, although it is not classified as an arboreal species. It climbs in order to search for prey. Here, it is searching for birds' nests containing unguarded eggs and nestlings.

FACT FILE

SPECIES:	*Elaphe guttata.*
FAMILY:	Colubridae (colubrids).
HABITAT:	Old fields, open woodlands, and pine barrens.
BREEDING:	Egg-layers, producing up to 30 eggs.
FEEDING:	Lizards, birds, and small mammals.
DISTRIBUTION:	Southeastern US.

Platelike scales
Like nearly all colubrids, the corn snake has large, platelike scales on the top of the head.

Large eyes
The corn snake has large eyes and round pupils. It has moderately good daytime vision, even though it is mainly active at night.

AVERAGE ADULT LENGTH

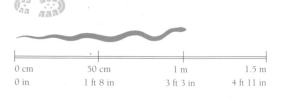

0 cm	50 cm	1 m	1.5 m
0 in	1 ft 8 in	3 ft 3 in	4 ft 11 in

Amelanistic form
When a form lacks black pigment, it is known as amelanistic. Only shades of red and orange remain, and the eyes are pink.

Snow Corn Snake
Specimens lacking black and red pigmentation are known as snow corns. They are almost pure white, with just a faint tinge of pink.

Dorsal markings
These are usually square and well separated but become elongated and may touch each other toward the snake's neck.

BAIRD'S RAT SNAKE

A long, slender, elegant snake, Baird's rat snake was named in honor of Spencer Fullerton Baird, a nineteenth-century zoologist. It is found in the rocky deserts of Texas and adjacent parts of northeastern Mexico. It is seldom seen, hiding by day and emerging at night, especially after rain, to hunt for small rodents and birds.

— MAIN CHARACTERISTICS —

Baird's rat snake changes color as it grows. Juveniles are gray with dark crossbars. These fade with age, and the snake turns first plain gray, then orange and gray, as each scale develops an orange crescent at its base. There is often, though not always, a pair of dusky lines along the back.

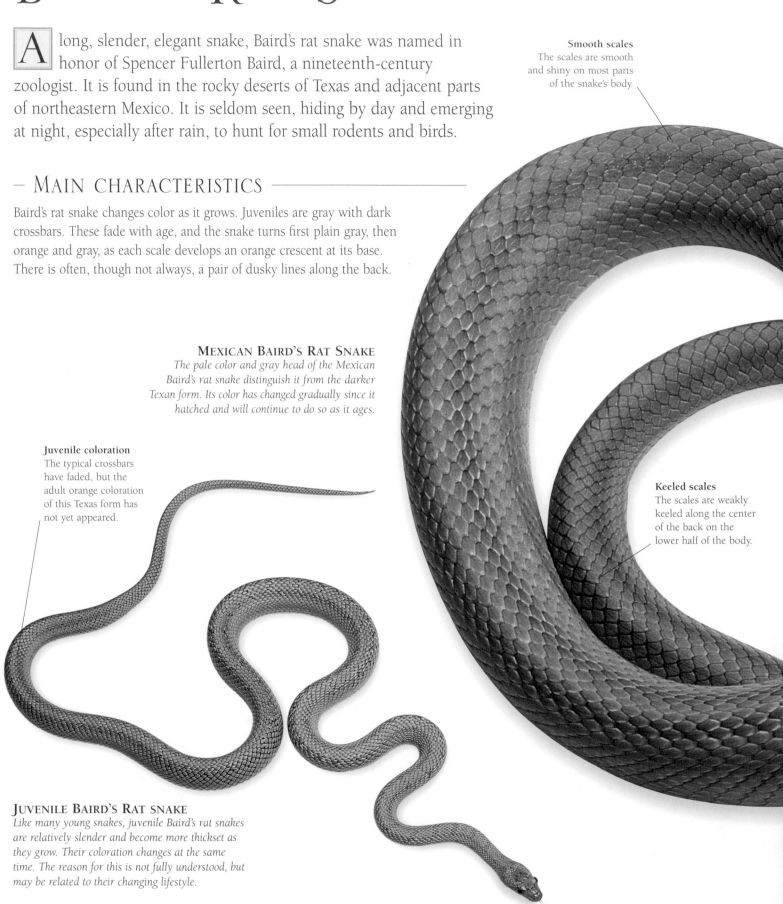

Smooth scales
The scales are smooth and shiny on most parts of the snake's body.

MEXICAN BAIRD'S RAT SNAKE
The pale color and gray head of the Mexican Baird's rat snake distinguish it from the darker Texan form. Its color has changed gradually since it hatched and will continue to do so as it ages.

Juvenile coloration
The typical crossbars have faded, but the adult orange coloration of this Texas form has not yet appeared.

Keeled scales
The scales are weakly keeled along the center of the back on the lower half of the body.

JUVENILE BAIRD'S RAT SNAKE
Like many young snakes, juvenile Baird's rat snakes are relatively slender and become more thickset as they grow. Their coloration changes at the same time. The reason for this is not fully understood, but may be related to their changing lifestyle.

Gray head
The color of the Mexican form's head remains gray – the head of the Texan form changes color.

UNMARKED HEAD
The adult snake has no markings on the head, so the large scales are very distinct. The large eyes have round pupils.

Body shape
The underside of the body is flattened to create a pair of edges along the bottom of each flank. The snake uses these to grip rough surfaces such as bark and rock.

FACT FILE

SPECIES: *Elaphe bairdi.*
FAMILY: Colubridae (colubrids).
HABITAT: Limestone canyons, desert, montane forest.
BREEDING: Egg-layers, usually fewer than 10 eggs.
FEEDING: Small mammals, including bats and birds, and lizards.
DISTRIBUTION: Central and west Texas and adjacent Mexico.

AVERAGE ADULT LENGTH

0 cm	50 cm	1 m	1.5 m
0 in	1 ft 8 in	3 ft 3 in	4 ft 11 in

TRANS-PECOS RAT SNAKE

I nhabiting the dry mountains and valleys of the Chihuahuan Desert in southern Texas and northeastern Mexico, the Trans-Pecos rat snake hunts at night for the small rodents on which it feeds. During the day, it hides among rocks or in rodent burrows, avoiding the lethally high temperatures. Because of its secretive habits, it is rarely seen, even though it can be present in large numbers in favorable habitats.

— MAIN CHARACTERISTICS

Two types of pattern occur on this snake: the typical form and the "blonde" form, but both are essentially yellow or tan with darker blotches. The head is unmarked, and the margins of the large scales covering it are easily seen. The prominent eyes with their round pupils are very distinctive and are unlike those of any other American rat snake.

"BLONDE" FORM
This coloration is less common than that of the typical form. The markings are smaller and have a washed-out appearance, and the background color is lighter.

FACT FILE

SPECIES: *Bogertophis subocularis.*
FAMILY: Colubridae (colubrids).
HABITAT: Barren desert flats, cactus dominated hillsides with rocky outcrops.
BREEDING: Egg-layers, producing up to 12 eggs.
FEEDING: Small mammals, lizards, and birds.
DISTRIBUTION: West Texas and adjacent. Mexico.

TYPICAL FORM
The most common form of this species has dorsal blotches arranged as a series of H-shaped markings down the back, often touching, or nearly touching, each other. The markings tend to be most concentrated and darkest toward the snake's tail.

Large eyes
Large eyes help this species hunt at night.

Dorsal blotches
Distinctive blotches form a series of H-shaped markings down the back.

Juvenile body shape
Young adults and juveniles have elongated bodies, but well-fed, older individuals often become thick-bodied.

AVERAGE ADULT LENGTH

0 cm	50 cm	1 m	1.5 m
0 in	1 ft 8 in	3 ft 3 in	4 ft 11 in

TRANS-PECOS RAT SNAKE
*Among the longest and most slender species
of rat snake, the Trans-Pecos rat snake
occasionally grows to a length of nearly
6 ft 6 in (2 m)*

Ridged body
The Trans-Pecos rat snake has
flattened flanks, which form a
pair of ridges where they join
the underside and help the snake
climb over rock faces.

Back scales
The back scales are slightly keeled,
but those on the flanks are smooth.
They all have a velvety sheen. The
belly scales are silvery white and
perfectly smooth.

MANDARIN RAT SNAKE

U nusual colors and markings distinguish this Far Eastern rat snake from other members of the genus. It usually lives in cool montane habitats up to 9,800 ft (3,000 m), such as forests and rocky scrub, but it also occurs at lower elevations, where it may be found in agricultural settings such as rice fields, probably attracted by the large populations of small rodents that frequent such areas.

MAIN CHARACTERISTICS

The yellow bull's-eye body markings, surrounded by black circles or triangles, and the boldly marked head, are unique among snakes. The background color may be gray, brown, or reddish brown. The size and shape of the dorsal blotches vary slightly.

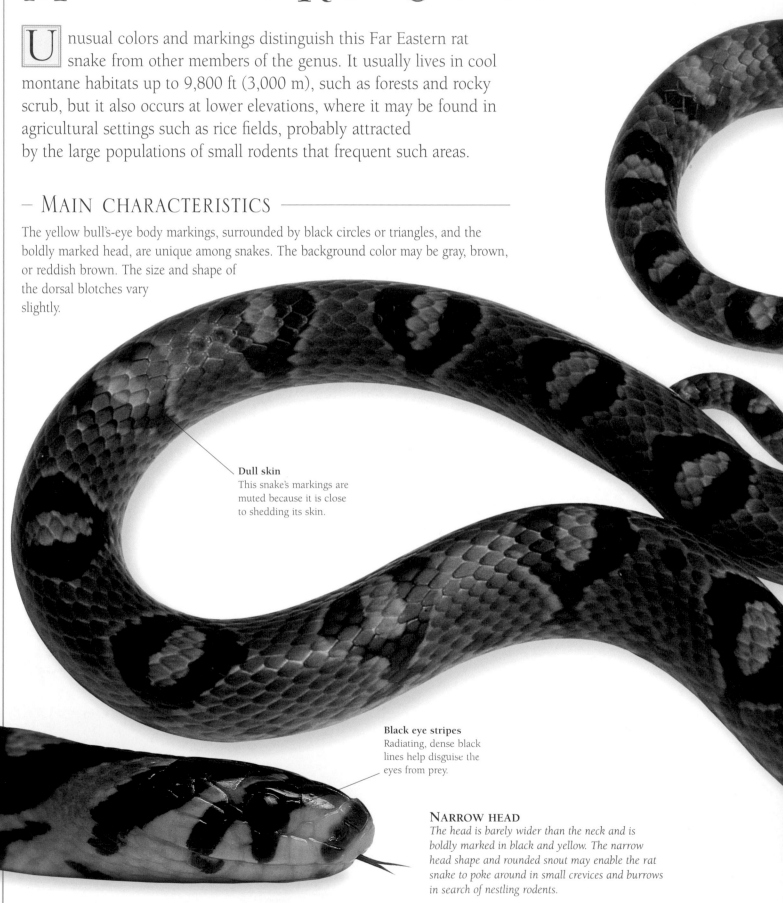

Dull skin
This snake's markings are muted because it is close to shedding its skin.

Black eye stripes
Radiating, dense black lines help disguise the eyes from prey.

NARROW HEAD
The head is barely wider than the neck and is boldly marked in black and yellow. The narrow head shape and rounded snout may enable the rat snake to poke around in small crevices and burrows in search of nestling rodents.

Scale variation
Individual scales can be smooth or slightly keeled.

MANDARIN RAT SNAKE
Contrasting black and yellow markings, especially on the face, seem to suggest this snake's Asian origins and make its common name particularly apt. It is more slender than most rat snakes, perhaps as a result of its semi-burrowing habits.

Slender shape
This species is longer and more slender than most rat snakes.

Background coloration
This specimen has a gray background color, but this may vary.

Unique markings
The bull's-eye markings may help break up the snake's outline when it is lying among leaf-litter in patches of light and shade.

AVERAGE ADULT LENGTH

0 cm	50 cm	1 m	1.5 m
0 in	1 ft 8 in	3 ft 3 in	4 ft 11 in

FACT FILE

SPECIES: *Elaphe mandarina.*
FAMILY: Colubridae (colubrids).
HABITAT: Lightly wooded and scrub-covered mountain slopes.
BREEDING: Egg-layers, producing 3–8 eggs.
FEEDING: Rodents, especially nestlings.
DISTRIBUTION: China.

ROUGH GREEN SNAKE

A dainty, slender species, the rough green snake lives in shrubs and thickets close to water, particularly favoring the lush growth around the margins of streams and lakes. It frequents branches that overhang the water's edge and may even enter the water on occasion. It is largely insectivorous, living off crickets, grasshoppers, grubs, caterpillars, and spiders.

— MAIN CHARACTERISTICS —

The rough green snake is long and very thin with a bright green upper surface and a white or pale green underside. Its scales are keeled, giving it a rough appearance. This characteristic separates it from the only other similar species in North America, the smooth green snake.

Head scales
Large scales cover the head. The dark color of the top scales gives good camouflage.

Large eyes
This species has relatively large eyes with round pupils. It hunts by sight during the day.

NARROW HEAD
The head is only just wider than the neck. The snout is pointed. This species eats small items of food and does not need a large gape.

Rough scales
Each scale has a distinct keel, giving the snake's skin a rough texture.

ROUGH GREEN SNAKE
The bright green coloration and slender shape of this species camouflage it well. As long as it remains still, it is hard to find, and it is probably more common than rare sightings suggest.

EXPERT CAMOUFLAGE
The rough green snake occasionally climbs into shrubs and bushes, but spends most of its time among grass and other understory (lower-level) vegetation, where its excellent camouflage makes it very hard to see among the greenery.

Light body
The long, thin body is typical of climbing species. The snake is able to span gaps between branches and, because it weighs very little, can move along small twigs with minimum disturbance.

Long tail
The long tail acts as a counter-balance to the body weight and may also grip branches and twigs.

AVERAGE ADULT LENGTH

0 cm	50 cm	1 m	1.5 m
0 in	1 ft 8 in	3 ft 3 in	4 ft 11 in

FACT FILE

SPECIES: *Opheodrys aestivus.*

FAMILY: Colubridae (colubrids).

HABITAT: Thick vegetation, often near lakes, rivers, and streams.

BREEDING: Egg-layers, producing 3–12 eggs.

FEEDING: Insects, such as crickets, grasshoppers, butterfly and moth caterpillars, and spiders.

DISTRIBUTION: Eastern North America.

SHOVEL-NOSED SNAKE

CENTRAL AMERICAN CENTIPEDE SNAKE

ASIAN SLUG-EATING SNAKE

INVERTEBRATE EATERS

The rough green snake is one of a large number of snakes that prey entirely on invertebrates. They include specialized feeders such as the Asian slug-eating snake, *Aplopeltura boa*, and the Central American centipede snake, *Scolecophis atrocinctus*, as well as generalized feeders such as the shovel-nosed snake, *Chionactis occipitalis*, which eats scorpions, spiders, cockroaches, and larvae.

COMMON KINGSNAKE

Familiar throughout most of North America, the common kingsnake can be found in habitats as diverse as the swamps of
Florida and the deserts of Arizona and northern Mexico. The snake's
adaptability is reflected in its feeding habits, and it will eat almost any
animal, including fish, frogs, lizards, rodents, and venomous snakes.

– MAIN CHARACTERISTICS

The common kingsnake has a cylindrical body, smooth, shiny scales, and a narrow
head. The head is approximately the same diameter as the rest of the body.
Coloration varies from one locality to another, but it is usually black or dark
brown with white or cream markings in a variety of patterns. One of the
Mexican forms is totally black.

NARROW HEAD
*The head ends in a blunt snout. The common
kingsnake usually has white spots on the front
of the head. White bars on the scales
bordering the mouth are
common to many of
the subspecies.*

Round pupils
The eyes have round pupils and are set
further forward than those of many
other species of snake.

Shiny scales
The scales are smooth
and shiny. The Latin
name, *Lampropeltis*,
means "shiny-shields."

FACT FILE ---

SPECIES:	*Lampropeltis getula.*
FAMILY:	Colubridae (colubrids).
HABITAT:	Marshlands to dry forests and deserts.
BREEDING:	Egg-layers, producing 3-24 eggs.
FEEDING:	Reptiles, birds, and mammals.
DISTRIBUTION:	North America.

SNAKE EATS SNAKE
*Common kingsnakes eat a large variety of prey, including other snakes.
Some prey species, such as rattlesnakes, are venomous, but the common
kingsnake has some immunity to the venom. When a rattlesnake is
approached, it arches its body off the ground so as to look bigger. This
strategy has only a limited success, however, and most are quickly
overpowered by the common kingsnake's powerful coils.*

Distinctive markings
This snake, from southern California, is boldly marked with wide, contrasting bands, or rings. In some members, a number of the bands are broken, or divided, usually near the dorsal midline.

CALIFORNIA KINGSNAKE
The California subspecies, Lampropeltis getula californiae, is among the most distinctive of the kingsnakes, with wide, pale bands on a darker background. The black and white coloration is typical of inland specimens, but on the coast they are brown and cream. Very occasionally, the markings may consist of stripes rather than bands.

AVERAGE ADULT LENGTH

0 cm	50 cm	1 m	1.5 m
0 in	1 ft 8 in	3 ft 3 in	4 ft 11 in

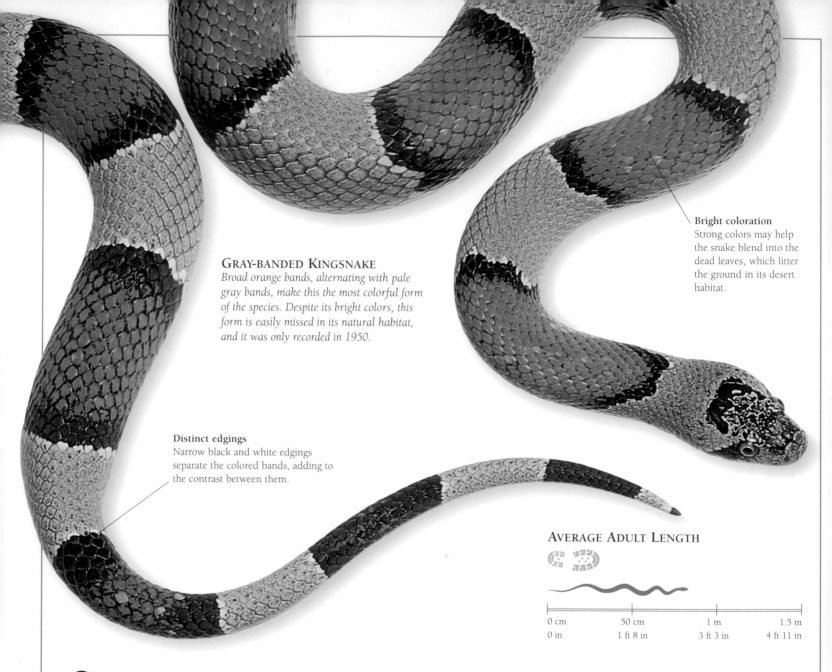

GRAY-BANDED KINGSNAKE
Broad orange bands, alternating with pale gray bands, make this the most colorful form of the species. Despite its bright colors, this form is easily missed in its natural habitat, and it was only recorded in 1950.

Bright coloration
Strong colors may help the snake blend into the dead leaves, which litter the ground in its desert habitat.

Distinct edgings
Narrow black and white edgings separate the colored bands, adding to the contrast between them.

AVERAGE ADULT LENGTH

0 cm	50 cm	1 m	1.5 m
0 in	1 ft 8 in	3 ft 3 in	4 ft 11 in

GRAY-BANDED KINGSNAKE

A colorful snake that is native to west Texas and adjacent parts of Mexico, this species lives in the Chihuahuan Desert, where the underlying limestone provides the crevices and subterranean cavities in which it hides. It seldom ventures out, except in the spring, when males search for mates. Even then, it only comes out at night.

— MAIN CHARACTERISTICS

The gray-banded kingsnake is highly variable in color – even offspring from the same clutch of eggs can differ markedly. The dorsal bands may be orange, red, or brownish red, or they may be absent altogether, leaving only narrow black bars. It has a small head with small eyes. The smooth scales have a texture that is satinlike rather than glossy.

FACT FILE

SPECIES: *Lampropeltis alterna.*
FAMILY: Colubridae (colubrids).
HABITAT: Rocky deserts with underlying limestone.
BREEDING: Egg-layers, producing 3–18 eggs.
FEEDING: Lizards, reptile eggs, and frogs.
DISTRIBUTION: West Texas, and adjacent parts of Mexico.

MEXICAN KINGSNAKE

Other kingsnakes are found in Mexico, but this species lives only there. It inhabits the mountainous northeast, where it hunts for lizards and small rodents among the rocks in valleys and on hillsides. At least three subspecies are recognized; all forms are very colorful, but both color and markings vary considerably.

FACT FILE

SPECIES:	*Lampropeltis mexicana.*
FAMILY:	Colubridae (colubrids).
HABITAT:	Rocky deserts and valleys.
BREEDING:	Egg-layers, producing up to 12 eggs.
FEEDING:	Reptiles, small birds, and mammals.
DISTRIBUTION:	Northeastern Mexico.

— MAIN CHARACTERISTICS

The Mexican kingsnake has a cylindrical body, a small head, and smooth scales. The red or orange markings are shaped like large saddles or narrow crossbars. All markings are invariably edged in black. The background color may be gray, cream, or pinkish. Of the three forms, one, the San Luis Potosí kingsnake, has a distinctive red marking on the head, which is lacking in the other two forms.

COLOR VARIATION
The Mexican kingsnake from Nuevo Leon belongs to the subspecies Lampropeltis mexicana thayeri. It is often cream with narrow slashes of red edged in black, but specimens from the same region may have varied patterns.

MEXICAN KINGSNAKE
The large red saddles and intricate head marking immediately identify Lampropeltis mexicana mexicana as belonging to the population from San Luis Potosí.

AVERAGE ADULT LENGTH

0 cm	50 cm	1 m	1.5 m
0 in	1 ft 8 in	3 ft 3 in	4 ft 11 in

Saddle markings
These cover the top of the body only and are, therefore, known as saddles, despite looking like bands from above.

SONORAN MOUNTAIN KINGSNAKE

F ormerly known as the Arizona mountain kingsnake, this species' name has been changed so that it more accurately describes its natural geographic range, which extends to the north, east, and south of Arizona. However, it is restricted exclusively to mountainous areas within this region. It is thought to undergo long periods of hibernation. When active, it feeds on lizards, small snakes, and mammals.

— MAIN CHARACTERISTICS

Striking markings make this snake easy to identify. The white rings, which are always complete, alternate with the red rings, which may sometimes be reduced to wedges along the flanks where the black bands widen as they reach the dorsal midline. The red rings lack the black tips that are typical of most forms of the milk snake (see pp. 88–89), which have similar markings. The snout is always white, in contrast to the California mountain kingsnake (see opposite), which has a black snout.

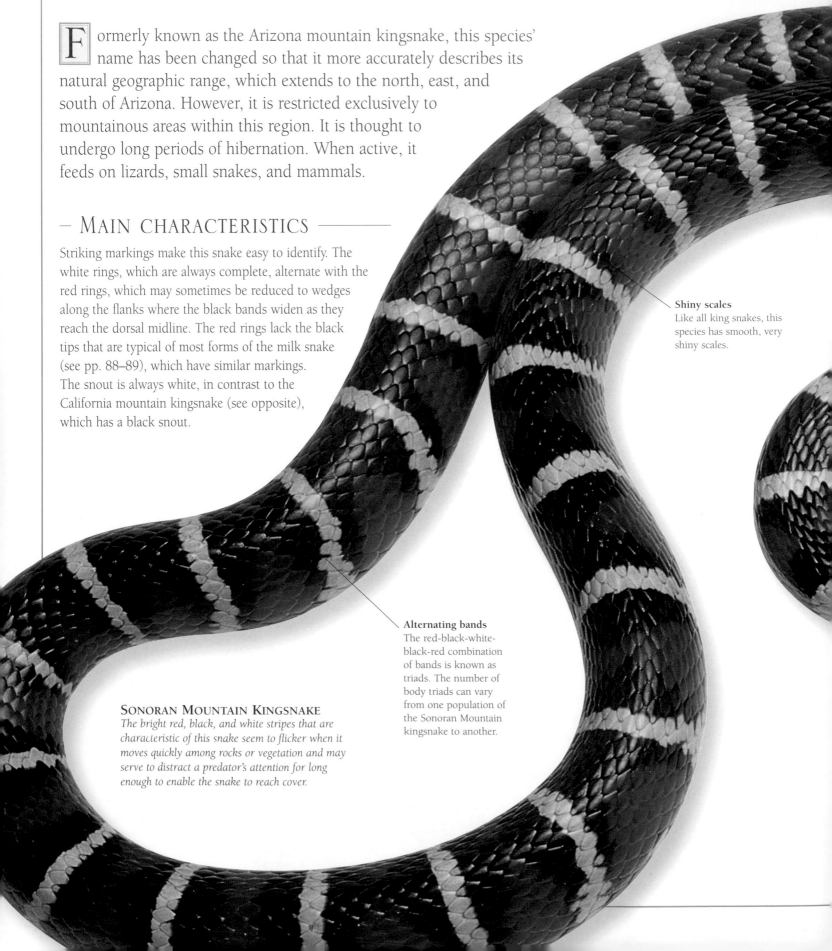

Shiny scales
Like all king snakes, this species has smooth, very shiny scales.

Alternating bands
The red-black-white-black-red combination of bands is known as triads. The number of body triads can vary from one population of the Sonoran Mountain kingsnake to another.

SONORAN MOUNTAIN KINGSNAKE
The bright red, black, and white stripes that are characteristic of this snake seem to flicker when it moves quickly among rocks or vegetation and may serve to distract a predator's attention for long enough to enable the snake to reach cover.

AVERAGE ADULT LENGTH

0 cm	50 cm	1 m	1.5 m
0 in	1 ft 8 in	3 ft 3 in	4 ft 11 in

FACT FILE

SPECIES: *Lampropeltis pyromelana.*
FAMILY: Colubridae (colubrids).
HABITAT: Scrub and conifer woods on scree and rocky mountainsides, often near water.
BREEDING: Egg-layers, producing 2–8 elongated eggs.
FEEDING: Lizards, small snakes, and rodents.
DISTRIBUTION: Southwestern US and northwestern Mexico.

Slim body
The long slender body helps this snake slide among the rocks and boulders among which it lives and hunts.

MOUNTAIN HABITAT
Rarely seen in the open, although active mainly during the day, the Sonoran Mountain kingsnake lives among rock piles and scree in undisturbed places on rocky mountainsides, which are often covered with snow for several months in the winter.

White snout
A white snout distinguishes this species from the other mountain kingsnakes.

CALIFORNIA MOUNTAIN KINGSNAKE

The California mountain kingsnake, *Lampropeltis zonata*, occupies a similar habitat to that of the Sonoran Mountain kingsnake, but is found further west. There is also an isolated population on a small rocky island off the Atlantic coast of Mexico that is unusual in lacking red rings. The main population is often a bright cherry red, and snakes have a black snout. Mating takes place in the spring, following hibernation, during which the snake's mountain habitat may be buried under several feet of snow.

MALE AND FEMALE MATING

MILK SNAKE

The milk snake is a variable species that is currently divided into 28 subspecies. Throughout its wide geographic range, from Canada in the north to Ecuador in the south, it occupies a number of different types of habitat, from forests to mountains and from rain forests to deserts, although it avoids the most arid regions. When frightened, its movements are quick and jerky, so that its colorful bands startle predators. In some places the snake can easily be confused with the venomous coral snakes (see opposite).

Wide neck band
A black snout and wide, white band distinguish the Pueblan milk snake.

— MAIN CHARACTERISTICS

The milk snake has a slender, cylindrical body, smooth, shiny scales, and a narrow head, which is barely wider than its neck. Most forms have red, white, and black bands around the body. These may be approximately equal in width or the red bands may be widest. A few forms have saddles rather than complete bands. Hatchlings are especially brightly colored, but their markings dull slightly as they become older, and small dusky areas develop on the scales.

Flickering colors
The red, white, and black colored bands flicker when the snake moves quickly, making it difficult to follow and confusing predators.

SINALOAN MILK SNAKE
The Sinaloan form, from parts of north-western Mexico, is distinct from most other forms of the milk snake because it has extremely wide, red bands and narrow, black-white-black bands. It is more slender and slightly shorter than the Pueblan subspecies.

LAYING EGGS
The milk snake lays between 3 and 24 eggs in the spring or early summer. The young hatch about ten weeks later and measure 8–12 in (20–30 cm).

MIMICRY

The milk snake shares parts of its geographic range with several species of the venomous coral snake, which belongs to the cobra family. It is thought that by imitating the markings and behavior of coral snakes, the milk snake gains a degree of immunity from attack by predators. Other experts, however, consider that their similarity in markings stems from the innate fear that animals have for all brightly colored animals, which they associate with danger.

CORAL SNAKE.

PUEBLAN MILK SNAKE

This is one of the largest and most boldly marked subspecies, with wide white bands, especially on the neck. Its stocky shape probably helps it to store enough food to last it through the long winters it experiences in the mountains of south-central Mexico, where it lives.

FACT FILE

SPECIES:	*Lampropeltis triangulum.*
FAMILY:	Colubridae (colubrids).
HABITAT:	Varied: wetlands to deserts.
BREEDING:	Egg-layers, producing up to 24 eggs.
FEEDING:	Reptiles and small mammals.
DISTRIBUTION:	North, Central, and parts of South America.

AVERAGE ADULT LENGTH

0 cm	50 cm	1 m	1.5 m
0 in	1 ft 8 in	3 ft 3 in	4 ft 11 in

BANDED WATER SNAKE

I nhabiting the swamps, lake edges, rivers, and wetlands of the American southeast, the banded water snake feeds on fish and amphibians, and basks on branches and riverbanks. It is often bad-tempered, striking and biting vigorously in self-defense. Although it is harmless, it is sometimes killed in the belief that it is a venomous cottonmouth – a pit viper with which it shares its habitat. There are a number of forms, or subspecies.

— MAIN CHARACTERISTICS

A narrow head distinguishes this species from the venomous cottonmouth with which it is sometimes confused; the cottonmouth has a broad, triangular head. Unlike the viper, the banded water snake is slender, although females can become very bulky, especially when pregnant. A banded pattern is common to the species, although the width and coloration may vary.

BANDED WATER SNAKE
Broad bands distinguish this form, which occurs throughout the Mississippi basin. It can be difficult to see the banded pattern, especially if the snake has been swimming in muddy water.

MATING BALL
Water snakes sometimes form a mating ball as several males try to mate with the same female. In snakes with this breeding system, males are often significantly smaller than females because they do not need to fight to win a mate. Females give birth to young about three to four months after mating.

Keeled scales
The scales are keeled, perhaps as an aid to pushing the snake through water.

Camouflage markings
Irregular, blotchy markings disguise the snake's outline when it lies motionless in mud and vegetation at the water's edge.

AVERAGE ADULT LENGTH

0 cm	50 cm	1 m	1.5 m
0 in	1 ft 8 in	3 ft 3 in	4 ft 11 in

FACT FILE

SPECIES: *Nerodia fasciata.*
FAMILY: Colubridae (colubrids).
HABITAT: All types of freshwater habitats, including ponds, lakes, swamps, streams, and canals.
BREEDING: Live-bearers, producing 10–20 young (exceptionally over 50).
FEEDING: Fish and amphibians.
DISTRIBUTION: Southeastern United States.

Flattened body
The body is slightly flattened toward the tail, which helps propel the snake through water.

Cuts and grazes
Small areas of damaged skin will be repaired when the snake sheds its skin.

ENDANGERED HABITAT

In southern Florida, the banded water snake's preferred habitat is cypress swamps. However, the demands of a rapidly expanding human population are steadily reducing water levels in the swamps. As a result, the plants and wildlife of the swamps are now seriously threatened.

CYPRESS SWAMP IN SOUTHERN FLORIDA

PINE SNAKE

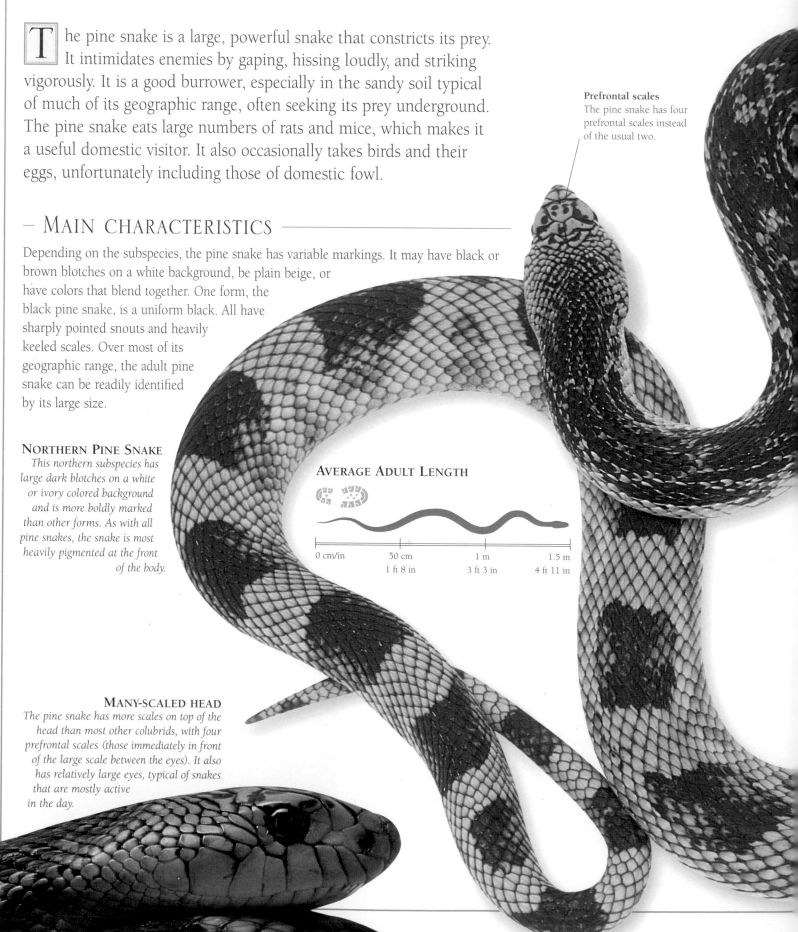

The pine snake is a large, powerful snake that constricts its prey. It intimidates enemies by gaping, hissing loudly, and striking vigorously. It is a good burrower, especially in the sandy soil typical of much of its geographic range, often seeking its prey underground. The pine snake eats large numbers of rats and mice, which makes it a useful domestic visitor. It also occasionally takes birds and their eggs, unfortunately including those of domestic fowl.

Prefrontal scales
The pine snake has four prefrontal scales instead of the usual two.

— MAIN CHARACTERISTICS

Depending on the subspecies, the pine snake has variable markings. It may have black or brown blotches on a white background, be plain beige, or have colors that blend together. One form, the black pine snake, is a uniform black. All have sharply pointed snouts and heavily keeled scales. Over most of its geographic range, the adult pine snake can be readily identified by its large size.

NORTHERN PINE SNAKE
This northern subspecies has large dark blotches on a white or ivory colored background and is more boldly marked than other forms. As with all pine snakes, the snake is most heavily pigmented at the front of the body.

AVERAGE ADULT LENGTH

0 cm/in	50 cm	1 m	1.5 m
	1 ft 8 in	3 ft 3 in	4 ft 11 in

MANY-SCALED HEAD
The pine snake has more scales on top of the head than most other colubrids, with four prefrontal scales (those immediately in front of the large scale between the eyes). It also has relatively large eyes, typical of snakes that are mostly active in the day.

Keeled scales
The scales on the back and flanks of the snake are heavily keeled.

Camouflage coloration
Pale coloration helps the snake avoid detection by potential predators when on pale, sandy soil.

PINEWOOD HABITAT
As its name suggests, the pine snake is most at home among pinewoods, although it also occurs in fields, around human dwellings, and along rocky ridges. Its main requirement is some loose, sandy soil in which to dig a burrow.

FACT FILE

SPECIES:	*Pituophis melanoleucus.*
FAMILY:	Colubridae (colubrids).
HABITAT:	Pinewoods, grasslands, and farms.
BREEDING:	Egg-layers, producing 16 or more eggs.
FEEDING:	Small mammals.
DISTRIBUTION:	Eastern and south-eastern United States.

– GOPHER AND BULL SNAKES –

Other members of the genus *Pituophis* are the gopher snakes and the bull snake. They are the counterpart of the pine snake in the western region of the US and were formerly classified as the same species. These snakes are found in many different habitats, including prairies, dry hillsides, semiarid places, and even true deserts. They are commonly found near cultivated and irrigated land, probably attracted by large numbers of rodents. Like the pine snake, they are expert ratters and are, therefore, beneficial to humans.

SAN DIEGO GOPHER SNAKE.

WESTERN HOGNOSE SNAKE

A skilled exponent of the art of bluffing, the western hognose snake puffs up its body and hisses loudly when confronted by an enemy. If this tactic fails, it rolls over and pretends to be dead. It is perfectly harmless and spends its time searching for frogs and toads on the prairies and in woodlands. It is one of the few species of snake that will eat dead prey that is beginning to decompose.

— MAIN CHARACTERISTICS

There are three species of hognose snake in North America, all with similar physical and behavioral characteristics. The western hognose snake is a short, stout species with rough scales, a blotched pattern down the back, and an unmistakable, upturned snout. It is usually brown in color, although it can also have a greenish or reddish tinge. In addition some forms have blotches on their backs that are not sharply defined.

CHUNKY HEAD
Hognose snakes have broad, chunky heads. There is a bar of color stretching across the snout from eye to eye. This helps break up the outline, protecting the snake from the attention of predators.

Rostral scale
The sharp-edged, shovel-shaped rostral scale at the tip of the snout is used to dig up toads and reptile eggs, which form the bulk of its diet.

FACT FILE

SPECIES: *Heterodon nasicus.*
FAMILY: Colubridae (colubrids).
HABITAT: Dry sandy prairies, sand bushlands, and farms.
BREEDING: Egg-layers, producing 4-23 eggs.
FEEDING: Amphibians, lizards, and small birds and mammals.
DISTRIBUTION: North America

AVERAGE ADULT LENGTH

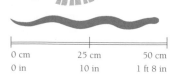

0 cm	25 cm	50 cm
0 in	10 in	1 ft 8 in

WESTERN HOGNOSE SNAKE
This form has a row of well-defined blotches down the back, which alternate with smaller ones on the flanks. The blotches are usually brown, but are sometimes olive or reddish in color. Other forms have less obvious markings.

Rough scales
Hognose snakes have heavily keeled scales, perhaps to provide a firm grip when they dig.

STAPLE FOOD

All hognose snakes prefer to eat toads rather than small mammals. They are efficient, diurnal burrowers, rooting out any buried prey they find. It is thought that the snakes are immune to the poisons that the toads produce in the warty glands on their heads and backs. Because toads puff themselves up, the hognose snake has to be capable of stretching its mouth to an enormous extent in order to swallow them.

EASTERN HOGNOSE SNAKE SWALLOWING A TOAD

Western coloration
The western hognose snake is lighter in color than its eastern relatives.

Short tail
This snake has a short tail, which is typical of species that burrow.

HATCHING OUT
The young hatch about two months after the eggs are laid. They immediately shed their skins and begin to search for food, in the shape of juvenile frogs and toads, and lizards.

95

LEOPARD SNAKE

This small rat snake is arguably the most attractive of all the European snakes. It lives among rocks and dry stone walls, often near fields and human dwellings, where it hunts for mice. Because it is active mainly at night, it is rarely seen, even in places where it is common. Although there is considerable variation in its markings, it is always brightly colored. It is sometimes mistaken for a viper and, therefore, killed needlessly, despite its beneficial feeding habits.

— MAIN CHARACTERISTICS

The leopard snake is slender and dainty in appearance. It is usually cream, yellowish, or light gray with dark-red or reddish-brown markings finely outlined in black. These markings may be arranged in a number of different ways, depending on the snake's geographic origins. The bold markings on its head are characteristic.

AVERAGE ADULT LENGTH

0 cm	50 cm	1 m	1.5 m
0 in	1 ft 8 in	3 ft 3 in	4 ft 11 in

LEOPARD SNAKE
The spotted form is the most common and is found throughout the species' geographic range. On parts of the body the spots narrow in the middle, resembling little dumbbells. Occasionally, the spots divide to form a double row.

Narrow head
The slim head restricts the size of prey the snake can consume.

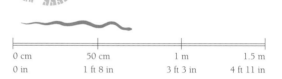

Large eyes
The large eyes have orange irises and round pupils. Their outlines are disguised by several dark markings, which radiate outward.

HEAD MARKINGS
The head is light in color with a bold, black marking between the eyes, and another running from the top of each eye to the angle of the jaw. The head is covered in large scales.

FACT FILE

SPECIES: *Elaphe situla.*
FAMILY: Colubridae (colubrids).
HABITAT: Rocky hillsides and walls, sparse woods, and farmland.
BREEDING: Egg-layers, producing up to 6 eggs.
FEEDING: Small mammals.
DISTRIBUTION: Southern Europe and western Asia.

STRIPED FORM

In some parts of the species' geographic range, individuals have reddish markings arranged as parallel lines instead of spots. The stripes may be very even or, more commonly, slightly ragged along the edges and joined at irregular intervals.

Cylindrical body
The body is roughly cylindrical, although the underside is slightly flattened.

Smooth scales
Unlike most rat snakes, the leopard snake has smooth scales.

INDIGO SNAKE

This large, handsome snake is one of a variety of forms of a species found on the American continent. The indigo snake lives in dry, sandy places in Florida and Texas. Despite its size, it is inoffensive and never attempts to bite, although it may hiss and flatten its neck when alarmed. In Central and South America, snakes belonging to the same species are brown rather than glossy black, live in a wider variety of habitats, and tend to be more aggressive. Active during the day, all forms are alert, fast-moving hunters of a wide variety of prey from fish to birds' eggs. They also consume snakes, including venomous species.

— MAIN CHARACTERISTICS

In southeastern US, the species is jet black with a deep red, pink, or cream chin. It lives in pine hummocks and other slightly raised, dry habitats. In Texas, the front part of the body is brown, and in Central and South America the entire body may be brown, tan, or yellowish brown, with darker markings in the form of irregular crossbars. Key identification features for all forms are the size, the large, glossy scales, and the slightly triangular cross section.

Dark coloration
The black scales of the Florida indigo snake help it absorb heat efficiently.

FOREST CAMOUFLAGE
Snakes belonging to the same species from Central America are known by the local name of cribo. *Their coloring gives them excellent camouflage on the floor of their tropical forest habitat.*

FACT FILE

SPECIES:	*Drymarchon corais.*
FAMILY:	Colubridae (colubrids).
HABITAT:	Clearings, pinewoods, and tropical dry forests.
BREEDING:	Egg-layers, producing up to 12 eggs.
FEEDING:	Wide-ranging, including fish, amphibians, reptiles, birds, eggs, and small mammals.
DISTRIBUTION:	North, Central, and South America.

INDIGO SNAKE
This is the longest species of snake in North America, often exceeding 6 ft 6 in (2 m) There are records of specimens measuring over 8 ft 2 in (2.5 m), but these are rare.

AVERAGE ADULT LENGTH

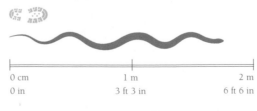

0 cm	1 m	2 m
0 in	3 ft 3 in	6 ft 6 in

Contrasting chin
In dramatic contrast to
the jet black body, the
chin may be deep red,
cream, or pink.

Glossy scales
The large scales are
very glossy and are a
distinctive feature of the
snake's appearance.

99

CHECKERED GARTER SNAKE

O ne of the most adaptable species of garter snake, the checkered garter snake never occurs far from water, and it has extended its geographic range into deserts and semiarid regions by living alongside seasonal streambeds and irrigation ditches. Usually diurnal, in such places it sometimes becomes nocturnal in order to avoid high daytime temperatures. It also reduces its dependency on fish and amphibians for food by adding nestling rodents to its diet.

— MAIN CHARACTERISTICS

This is the only garter snake with a pattern of bold, squarish blotches on either side of a cream mid-dorsal stripe. The dark collar marking just behind the head is also characteristic. The head is uniform in color with the exception of a small light-colored marking on the top. Like all garter snakes, this species has heavily keeled scales and a slender body shape, although it is more stocky than many of the other species.

— FACT FILE —

SPECIES: *Thamnophis marcianus.*
FAMILY: Colubridae (colubrids).
HABITAT: Ponds, streams, rivers, and ditches, often in otherwise arid places.
BREEDING: Live-bearers, producing 5–31 young.
FEEDING: Fish, frogs, toads, tadpoles, lizards, and small mammals.
DISTRIBUTION: Southwestern US to Central America.

CHECKERED GARTER SNAKE
The checkerboard pattern is distinctive enough to give this species its common name; other garter snakes are boldly striped.

Head scales
Large platelike scales cover the head. There is a small marking on the top of the head.

— PLAINS GARTER SNAKE —

The plains garter snake is found farther north than the checkered garter snake. It is one of several garter snakes with a striped pattern, but the bright, orange, mid-dorsal stripe is a reliable identification characteristic. More dependent on water than the checkered species, it is only common in river valleys and around the edges of ponds, lakes, and marshes.

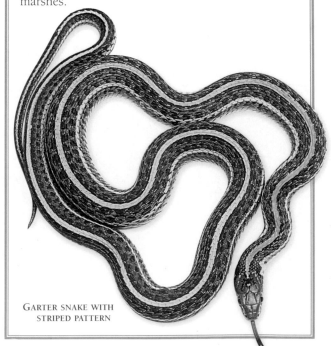

GARTER SNAKE WITH STRIPED PATTERN

Tapering snout
The snout is long and tapering, like that of all garter snakes.

Large eyes
The checkered garter snake has large eyes with round pupils and hunts by day.

HEAD COLOR
The head is invariably light on top. The light-colored lip scales often have short, dark bars along the edges that radiate out from the region of the eyes.

Slender tail
The tail is long and slender. The thickness of the tail toward the base shows that this is a male snake – in females it is thinner.

AVERAGE ADULT LENGTH

0 cm	50 cm	1 m	1.5 m
0 in	1 ft 8 in	3 ft 3 in	4 ft 11 in

NARROW HEAD
As in other garter snakes, this species has a narrow head, which is only just wider than the neck. The snout is pointed.

Large eyes
Large eyes give this snake good vision. It hunts mainly during the day.

SAN FRANCISCO GARTER SNAKE

T he San Francisco garter snake is a subspecies of the common, or eastern, garter snake. The species is widely distributed over North America, where it occurs in several color forms and 10 subspecies. Many of these forms are quite common, but this particular one is critically endangered because most of its habitat has already been destroyed. The remaining portions are threatened by encroaching development and channeling of water sources underground.

— MAIN CHARACTERISTICS —

Two broad red stripes on either side of a greenish-yellow stripe along the center of the back, all edged in black, make this one of the most distinctive garter snakes. The top of the head is also red. A slender body shape and heavily keeled scales distinguish the San Francisco garter snake from all other striped snakes found in the region.

Striking coloration
Bright stripes edged in
black cover the upper
part of the body.

Keeled scales
The scales are long and narrow,
and have a keel, or ridge,
down the center.

SAN FRANCISCO GARTER SNAKE

*The uninterrupted, bright carmine-red stripes along the
San Francisco garter snake's body contrast sharply with
the wide greenish-yellow mid-dorsal stripe. It is one of
North America's most beautiful snakes as well
as one of its rarest, despite being protected.*

BASKING IN SUNSHINE
*The San Francisco garter snake is most active in the
afternoon, after the typical San Francisco morning mist
has cleared and the sun has broken through.*

FACT FILE

SUBSPECIES: *Thamnophis sirtalis
tetrataenia.*

FAMILY: Colubridae (colubrids).

HABITAT: Ponds, marshes, roadside
ditches and streams.

BREEDING: Live-bearing, producing
12–24 young.

FEEDING: Frogs and toads, fish,
and small mammals.
Invertebrates on occasion.

DISTRIBUTION: Western parts of the San
Francisco Peninsula,
California.

AVERAGE ADULT LENGTH

```
0 cm        50 cm        1 m          1.5 m
0 in        1 ft 8 in    3 ft 3 in    4 ft 11 in
```

IDENTIFYING GARTER SNAKES

Garter snakes can be very
difficult to identify, especially
if several species occur in
the same area. One of the
most reliable guides to
identification is the position
of the stripes along the
center of the snake's back
and along the flanks. Species
tend to be highly consistent
in the arrangement of these
stripes and the scale rows
on which they occur. The
two species illustrated
demonstrate this point: note
the differences in the width
and coloration of the stripes.

SAN FRANCISCO GARTER SNAKE

PLAINS GARTER SNAKE

BROWN HOUSE SNAKE

An elegant and graceful species, the brown house snake is found in a wide range of habitats, including farm buildings and the outskirts of towns, where it is often tolerated for its beneficial effects on rodent populations. Its ability to enter narrow burrows and crevices makes it a formidable rodent hunter. It has an extensive geographic range, but in the driest deserts it is restricted to the vicinity of oases.

— MAIN CHARACTERISTICS —

The brown house snake is usually reddish brown in color, but is sometimes dark brown, dark olive, or even black. Very occasionally individuals are orange. The two cream stripes through the eyes, which sometimes extend onto the neck, help identify this species. Young snakes have indistinct blotches along the flanks, which are sometimes also visible in mature specimens.

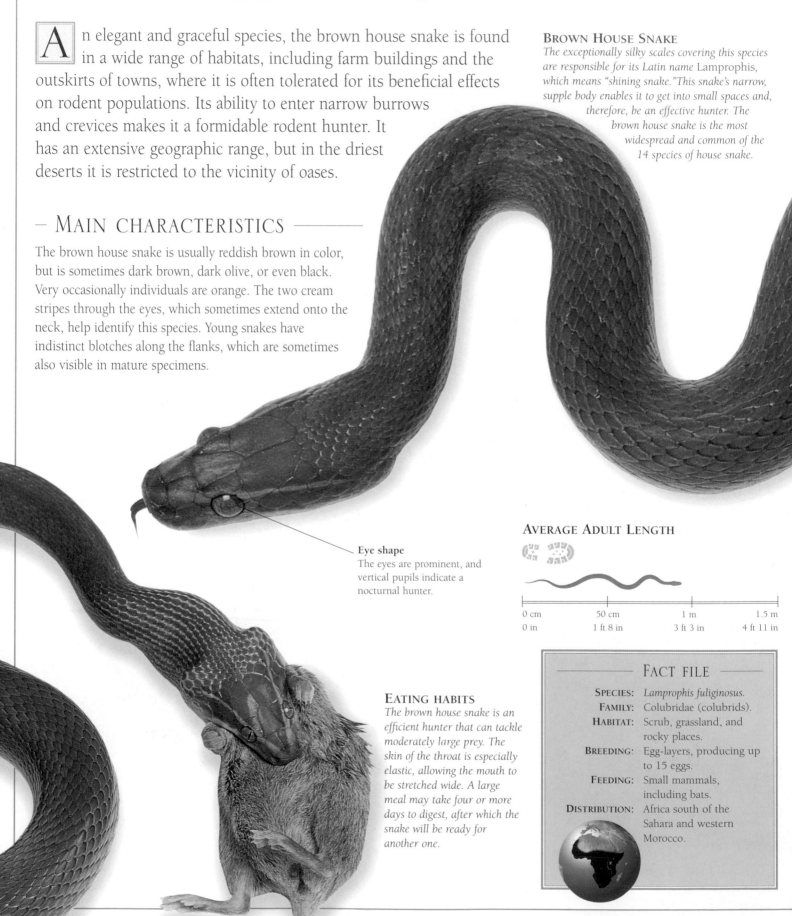

BROWN HOUSE SNAKE
The exceptionally silky scales covering this species are responsible for its Latin name Lamprophis, *which means "shining snake." This snake's narrow, supple body enables it to get into small spaces and, therefore, be an effective hunter. The brown house snake is the most widespread and common of the 14 species of house snake.*

Eye shape
The eyes are prominent, and vertical pupils indicate a nocturnal hunter.

AVERAGE ADULT LENGTH

0 cm	50 cm	1 m	1.5 m
0 in	1 ft 8 in	3 ft 3 in	4 ft 11 in

EATING HABITS
The brown house snake is an efficient hunter that can tackle moderately large prey. The skin of the throat is especially elastic, allowing the mouth to be stretched wide. A large meal may take four or more days to digest, after which the snake will be ready for another one.

— FACT FILE —

SPECIES: *Lamprophis fuliginosus.*
FAMILY: Colubridae (colubrids).
HABITAT: Scrub, grassland, and rocky places.
BREEDING: Egg-layers, producing up to 15 eggs.
FEEDING: Small mammals, including bats.
DISTRIBUTION: Africa south of the Sahara and western Morocco.

Pale coloration
The scales pale in color low down on the flanks and become creamy white underneath the snake.

Smooth scales
The body scales are smooth and, instead of being glossy, have a silky texture.

Strong muscles
Powerful muscles are used to constrict prey. The strength of the brown house snake is at least equal, size for size, to that of boas and pythons.

DESERT FORM

Brown house snakes from the deserts of Namaqualand, South Africa, tend to be pale and have large eyes. Bright streaks run from the snout through the eyes and along the side of the head above the jaw. These snakes are sometimes considered to be a separate subspecies, Lamprophis fuliginosus mentalis.

RED-TAILED RAT SNAKE

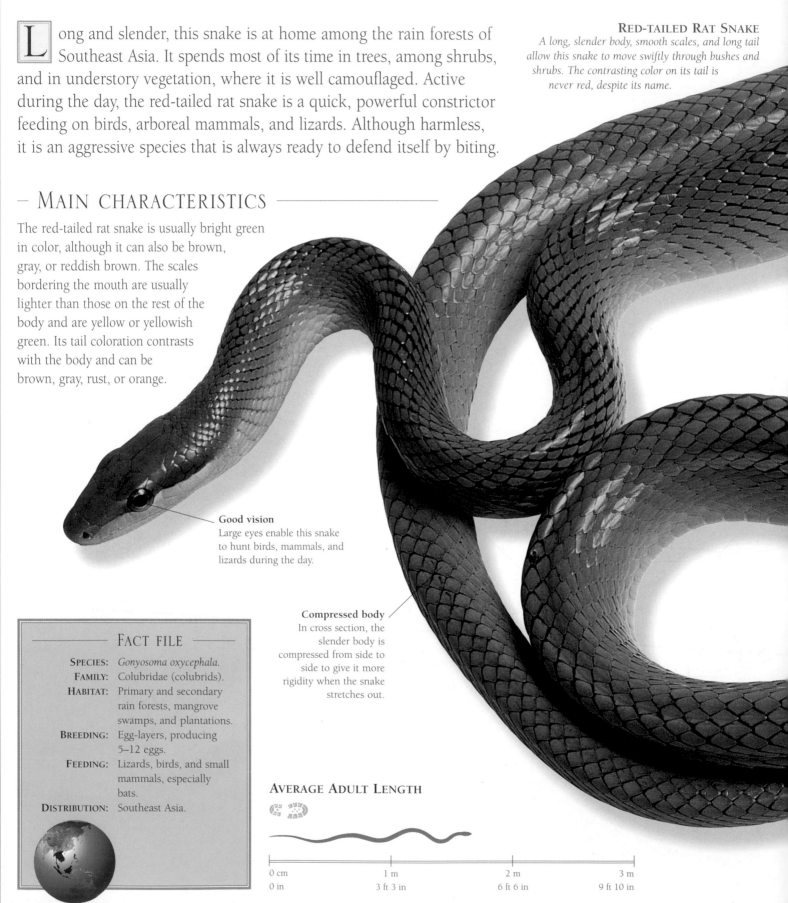

RED-TAILED RAT SNAKE
A long, slender body, smooth scales, and long tail allow this snake to move swiftly through bushes and shrubs. The contrasting color on its tail is never red, despite its name.

L ong and slender, this snake is at home among the rain forests of Southeast Asia. It spends most of its time in trees, among shrubs, and in understory vegetation, where it is well camouflaged. Active during the day, the red-tailed rat snake is a quick, powerful constrictor feeding on birds, arboreal mammals, and lizards. Although harmless, it is an aggressive species that is always ready to defend itself by biting.

— MAIN CHARACTERISTICS

The red-tailed rat snake is usually bright green in color, although it can also be brown, gray, or reddish brown. The scales bordering the mouth are usually lighter than those on the rest of the body and are yellow or yellowish green. Its tail coloration contrasts with the body and can be brown, gray, rust, or orange.

Good vision
Large eyes enable this snake to hunt birds, mammals, and lizards during the day.

Compressed body
In cross section, the slender body is compressed from side to side to give it more rigidity when the snake stretches out.

FACT FILE

SPECIES: *Gonyosoma oxycephala.*
FAMILY: Colubridae (colubrids).
HABITAT: Primary and secondary rain forests, mangrove swamps, and plantations.
BREEDING: Egg-layers, producing 5–12 eggs.
FEEDING: Lizards, birds, and small mammals, especially bats.
DISTRIBUTION: Southeast Asia.

AVERAGE ADULT LENGTH

0 cm	1 m	2 m	3 m
0 in	3 ft 3 in	6 ft 6 in	9 ft 10 in

— RED MOUNTAIN RACER —

Several other Asian snakes belonging to the genera *Gonyosoma* and *Elaphe* are known as racers. They include the red mountain racer, *Elaphe porphyracea*, which comes from montane habitats in the same region as the red-tailed rat snake. This species is completely terrestrial, however, so there is little or no competition between them. Members of the genus *Elaphe* are variously known as rat snakes or racers in different parts of the world.

ADULT CAMOUFLAGED AMONG DEAD LEAVES

Smooth scales
The smooth, shiny scales are easily differentiated since their edges are often picked out in black.

DEFENSE POSTURE
When threatened, the red-tailed rat snake flattens its throat from side to side and raises its head and neck and the front part of its body off the ground. This posture is intended to intimidate the snake's enemies, making it appear larger.

Striped marking
A dark eye-stripe divides the dark green area from the lighter color of the lip scales.

Blue tongue
This is one of several related Asian species that have blue tongues. The tongue often protrudes for several seconds at a time. The purpose of this display is not known.

MANGROVE SNAKE

L iving in trees, including mangroves, and shrubs near water, the brilliantly colored mangrove snake is a rear-fanged species, with long fangs below each eye, and it bites readily in self-defense. Although this can cause humans some pain and discomfort, the venom is mild, and the bites are unlikely to have serious consequences.

FACT FILE

SPECIES: *Boiga dendrophila.*
FAMILY: Colubridae (colubrids).
HABITAT: Lowland rain forests and mangrove swamps.
BREEDING: Egg-layers, producing 4–15 eggs.
FEEDING: Reptiles, birds, and small mammals.
DISTRIBUTION: Southeast Asia.

— MAIN CHARACTERISTICS

The mangrove snake is unlikely to be confused with any other snake because of its glossy scales and distinctive coloration. The only other similar species from Southeast Asia is the banded krait, which, in contrast, has wide yellow bands, a triangular cross section, and rarely climbs.

AVERAGE ADULT LENGTH

0 cm	1 m	2 m	3 m
0 in	3 ft 3 in	6 ft 6 in	9 ft 10 in

Spade-shaped head
The wide, spade-shaped head is very distinct from the slender neck. The top of the head has no markings.

Shiny scales
The scales are large, distinct, smooth, and very shiny.

MANGROVE SNAKE
The long, slender shape of this species enables it to coil among thin branches some distance from the ground. Its distinctive pattern may help the snake escape notice in the light and shade of its forest habitat, but equally may serve to warn of its venom.

THREATENING POSTURE
When annoyed, the mangrove snake flares its lips to display bright yellow and black scales. It may also open its mouth wide in an attempt to intimidate enemies.

GREEN CAT-EYED SNAKE

The green cat-eyed snake is at home in trees and bushes, where its green coloration and slow movements make it difficult to distinguish from vines and creepers. Its main defense is intimidation, opening its mouth wide so that the black lining shows. Although it is a rear-fanged species, its venom is mild and harmless to humans.

FACT FILE

SPECIES: *Boiga cyanea.*
FAMILY: Colubridae (colubrids).
HABITAT: Forests, especially near water.
BREEDING: Egg-layers, producing fewer than 10 eggs.
FEEDING: Frogs, reptiles, small birds and mammals.
DISTRIBUTION: Southeast Asia.

— MAIN CHARACTERISTICS

Bright green coloration and a slender body distinguish this species from most others. Its body is deeper than it is wide and is slightly triangular in cross section, with a ridge along the dorsal midline. The head is very wide in comparison with the neck. The green cat-eyed snake has an unusual row of very large scales along the center of the back. It is sometimes confused with the green tree viper from the same habitat and region, but this species is more heavily built and has a deeper head covered with small scales.

GREEN CAT-EYED SNAKE
The bright green color of this species is unique among cat-eyed snakes, although its build and habitat are similar. Distinctive, large eyes with vertical pupils give the snakes of this genus their common name. They are also known as cat snakes.

AVERAGE ADULT LENGTH

0 cm	50 cm	1 m	1.5 m
0 in	1 ft 8 in	3 ft 3 in	4 ft 11 in

Protruding eyes
Large eyes and a narrow snout give this species good forward vision.

Center scales
A row of very large scales covers a ridge running along the center of the back.

Slender body
The long, thin body is flattened from side to side. This high, narrow shape helps the snake span large gaps between branches.

WIDE HEAD
The pear-shaped head of the green cat-eyed snake is much wider than the slender neck. The large scales covering the top of the head are well defined.

Big eyes
Huge eyes and vertical pupils immediately identify this as a species that is active at night.

BOOMSLANG

T he boomslang hunts chameleons, birds, and other small animals during the day, using camouflage and a stealthy approach to get within striking distance, and then snatching its prey in a sudden rush. It kills with venom delivered through fangs that are situated below the eyes and is one of the few colubrids that can kill humans, although it only bites when cornered.

— MAIN CHARACTERISTICS —

An elongated shape and arboreal habits help identify this snake, but its variable color and markings can cause confusion. Juveniles are gray or grayish brown, and females are usually uniform olive-brown. Males, however, may be uniform brown or black, or they may be bright green, reddish, or even bluish green in color, often with dark edges to the scales. The eye is thought to be larger, relative to the size of its head, than that of any other species.

POINTED HEAD

The huge eye – which is green in juveniles – and sharply angled snout are the most conspicuous features of this head. The scales are very well defined and may be outlined with black in older individuals.

Ventral scales
Wide ventral scales with free trailing edges grip rough bark and tree branches, helping the snake move forward.

Large eyes
The pupils of the exceptionally large eyes are shaped like teardrops.

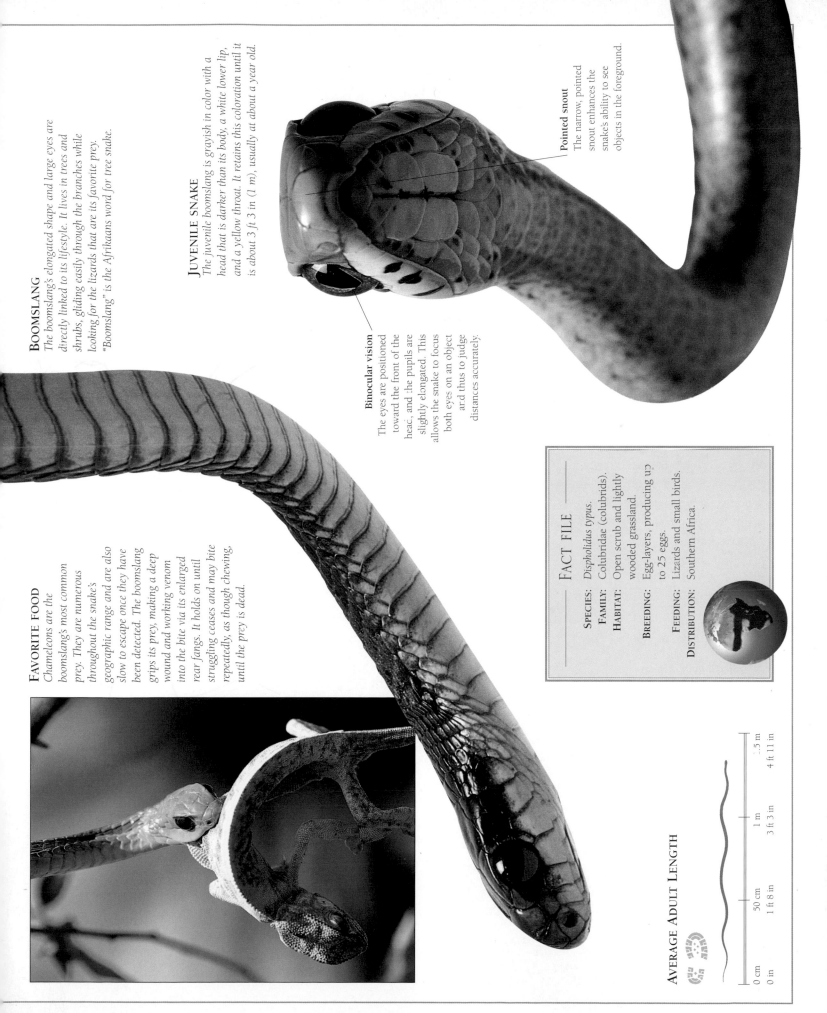

BOOMSLANG

The boomslang's elongated shape and large eyes are directly linked to its lifestyle. It lives in trees and shrubs, gliding easily through the branches while looking for the lizards that are its favorite prey. "Boomslang" is the Afrikaans word for tree snake.

JUVENILE SNAKE

The juvenile boomslang is grayish in color with a head that is darker than its body, a white lower lip, and a yellow throat. It retains this coloration until it is about 3 ft 3 in (1 m), usually at about a year old.

Pointed snout
The narrow, pointed snout enhances the snake's ability to see objects in the foreground.

Binocular vision
The eyes are positioned toward the front of the head, and the pupils are slightly elongated. This allows the snake to focus both eyes on an object and thus to judge distances accurately.

FAVORITE FOOD

Chameleons are the boomslang's most common prey. They are numerous throughout the snake's geographic range and are also slow to escape once they have been detected. The boomslang grips its prey, making a deep wound and working venom into the bite via its enlarged rear fangs. It holds on until struggling ceases and may bite repeatedly, as though chewing, until the prey is dead.

FACT FILE

SPECIES: Dispholidus typus.
FAMILY: Colubridae (colubrids).
HABITAT: Open scrub and lightly wooded grassland.
BREEDING: Egg-layers, producing up to 25 eggs.
FEEDING: Lizards and small birds.
DISTRIBUTION: Southern Africa.

AVERAGE ADULT LENGTH

0 cm	50 cm	1 m	1.5 m
0 in	1 ft 8 in	3 ft 3 in	4 ft 11 in

RED SPITTING COBRA

A small cobra from the dry grasslands and scrubby habitats of northeastern Africa, the red spitting cobra is set apart from other cobras by its spectacular color. This species defends itself from a distance by squirting jets of venom at high pressure through small apertures located in the front of each fang. If the venom enters the human eye, it is extremely painful. When hunting, the snake injects venom through biting. As a last resort, it will also defend itself in this way. However, bite victims usually recover quickly.

RED SPITTING COBRA
The deep red coloration of this individual is related to its maturity – juveniles are a brighter red and gradually become darker as they grow. The red spitting cobra's scales will also become dull when it is about to shed its skin.

— MAIN CHARACTERISTICS —

This cobra is moderately slender with smooth, shiny scales. It has a narrow hood, unlike the Asian cobras, which have wide, pear-shaped hoods. It is usually red or reddish brown, but can sometimes be olive or gray. It has a broad, dark band on the throat, which is plainly visible when the snake rears up. The hood is erected only when an individual feels threatened.

Venom glands
The venom glands are situated below and behind the eyes, and under the cheeks.

TAPERING HEAD
The broadest part of the head is well behind the eyes. It narrows sharply toward the snout, giving the snake good forward vision.

Narrow hood
The hood is not visible unless the snake senses danger.

Dark band
When disturbed, the snake lifts its head up, exposing the dark scales on the throat.

AVERAGE ADULT LENGTH

0 cm	50 cm	1 m	1.5 m
0 in	1 ft 8 in	3 ft 3 in	4 ft 11 in

ARID HABITAT
This snake lives among the sparse vegetation of oases, hillsides, and riverbanks. Adults hide among piles of vegetation or in burrows. They are predominantly nocturnal, but juveniles are sometimes active by day. If disturbed the red spitting cobra will move away rapidly.

Camouflage colors
The reddish-brown coloration blends into dry vegetation, but looks conspicuous when the snake is seen out of habitat.

FACT FILE

SPECIES:	*Naja pallida.*
FAMILY:	Elapidae (cobras and their relatives).
HABITAT:	Dry grassland and semidesert.
BREEDING:	Egg-layers, producing up to 15 eggs.
FEEDING:	Other snakes, birds, and small mammals
DISTRIBUTION:	Northeast Africa.

Shiny scales
This species has smooth, glossy scales.

CHINESE COBRA

T he most common species of cobra over much of southeastern China and adjoining countries, this snake lives mostly in open areas such as grasslands, fields, and lightly wooded places. It feeds on a variety of prey, including fish, amphibians, birds, and mammals. It is not an aggressive species, although its potentially lethal venom and habit of living in close proximity to humans make it a constant threat wherever it is found.

— MAIN CHARACTERISTICS —

Thickset for a cobra, this species is usually dark brown or black. Occasional specimens are lighter in color. It has a number of widely spaced, indistinct, light bands, one scale wide, around the body. There is an eyespot marking on the back of the hood, but this is also true of the monocled cobra (see opposite), and the two species may be confused: until recently, they were classified as a single species.

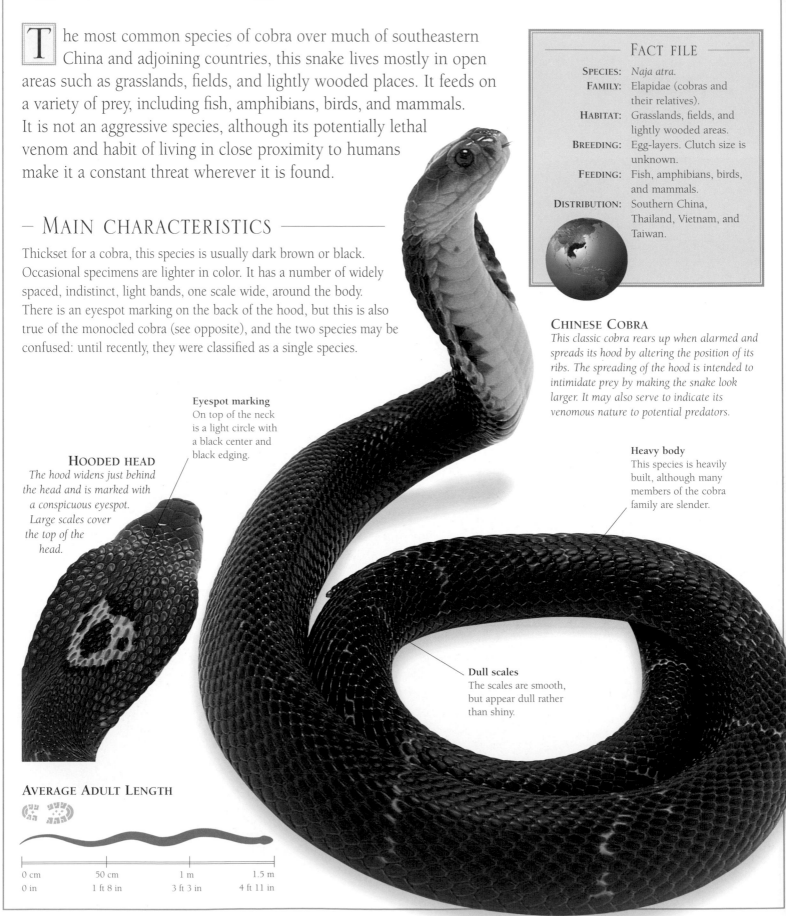

FACT FILE

SPECIES: *Naja atra.*
FAMILY: Elapidae (cobras and their relatives).
HABITAT: Grasslands, fields, and lightly wooded areas.
BREEDING: Egg-layers. Clutch size is unknown.
FEEDING: Fish, amphibians, birds, and mammals.
DISTRIBUTION: Southern China, Thailand, Vietnam, and Taiwan.

CHINESE COBRA
This classic cobra rears up when alarmed and spreads its hood by altering the position of its ribs. The spreading of the hood is intended to intimidate prey by making the snake look larger. It may also serve to indicate its venomous nature to potential predators.

Eyespot marking
On top of the neck is a light circle with a black center and black edging.

HOODED HEAD
The hood widens just behind the head and is marked with a conspicuous eyespot. Large scales cover the top of the head.

Heavy body
This species is heavily built, although many members of the cobra family are slender.

Dull scales
The scales are smooth, but appear dull rather than shiny.

AVERAGE ADULT LENGTH

0 cm	50 cm	1 m	1.5 m
0 in	1 ft 8 in	3 ft 3 in	4 ft 11 in

MONOCLED COBRA

S nake charmers often choose to work with the monocled cobra because, although it is instantly recognizable as a venomous snake, it normally has a placid disposition. Its name refers to the single eyespot marking on the hood, which looks like a monocle.

MAIN CHARACTERISTICS

Like the Chinese cobra (see opposite), this species is heavily built and has a single eyespot on the hood. However, on average, the monocled cobra is slightly smaller than the Chinese cobra. In addition, it is lighter in color, and the pale flecks on the back, if present, are more randomly scattered. The light-colored head is devoid of any markings.

FACT FILE

SPECIES: *Naja kaouthia.*
FAMILY: Elapidae (cobras and their relatives).
HABITAT: Fields and sparse forests.
BREEDING: Egg-layers. Clutch size is unknown.
FEEDING: Fish, amphibians, birds, and mammals.
DISTRIBUTION: Southeast Asia.

Large eyes
The eyes are moderately large and, being dark, contrast sharply with the scales around them.

Light coloration
This snake is light brown, with pale flecks

MONOCLED COBRA
The monocled cobra spreads its hood to look larger and thus intimidate enemies. It does not spread its hood when hunting, although it may raise its head to obtain a better view of its surroundings.

AVERAGE ADULT LENGTH

0 cm	50 cm	1 m	1.5 m
0 in	1 ft 8 in	3 ft 3 in	4 ft 11 in

HOOD MARKS
Eyespot markings such as this serve as a warning signal throughout the animal kingdom. The marking also gives the snake its name.

Smooth scales
This species has the typical smooth scales of the genus *Naja.*

Distinctive monocle
This is usually white or cream with a black border and two or three black spots.

COLLETT'S SNAKE

A handsome Australian cobra, living in an isolated region of semi-arid grasslands and lightly wooded places, collett's snake is thought to adapt its lifestyle to the seasons, being active by day during the winter and nocturnal during the hotter parts of summer. Little is known about its natural habits. As a venomous species, it is potentially dangerous, although it is unlikely to have caused human fatalities.

— MAIN CHARACTERISTICS

Collett's snake is a stocky species with a distinctive color pattern in which dark brown and reddish scales combine to create a coppery overall coloration. The scales on the lower flanks are often arranged in irregular patches, and sometimes suggest a cross-banded arrangement. The body may be speckled.

Copper pattern
The dark brown and red pattern is thought to camouflage this species when it is resting on the dark red soils of its desert habitat.

Smooth scales
The scales are smooth, but not very shiny. Each scale is a single color, resulting in a mosaic-like pattern with jagged edges.

COLLETT'S SNAKE
This snake is undoubtedly one of the more colorful Australian species. Although it only occurs with dark brown and reddish coloration, collett's snake belongs to a genus, Pseudechis, whose members are sometimes known collectively as black snakes.

AVERAGE ADULT LENGTH

0 cm	50 cm	1 m	1.5 m
0 in	1 ft 8 in	3 ft 3 in	4 ft 11 in

Large scales
Like most of the cobra family and the harmless colubrids, the scales on the snake's head are large and very well-defined.

Cylindrical body
The body is roughly cylindrical in cross section, indicating a burrowing or terrestrial lifestyle. Collett's snake is thought to hide in burrows or beneath dead vegetation and other debris, and hunts on the ground.

FACT FILE

SPECIES: *Pseudechis colletti.*
FAMILY: Elapidae (cobras and their relatives).
HABITAT: Grasslands and lightly wooded areas.
BREEDING: Live-bearers, producing 10 or more young.
FEEDING: Probably amphibians, lizards, snakes, and small mammals.
DISTRIBUTION: Central Queensland, Australia.

TIGER SNAKES

Tiger snakes, which belong to the genus *Notechis*, are close relatives of collett's snakes. There are two species, both very dangerous, which are responsible for most snake-bite deaths in Australia. The black tiger snake is found on the mainland, Tasmania, and many of the small islands in the Bass Straits. Some of these island populations, notably that of Chappel Island, are remarkable for their eating habits. The snakes gorge on mutton-bird chicks during the birds' nesting season, but for the rest of the year have little or no food, although juveniles eat small lizards. As an adaptation to this enforced feast and famine regime, the Chappel Island tiger snakes grow to roughly twice the size of tiger snakes on the mainland. This enables them to store fat efficiently, and thus to survive between nesting seasons.

BLACK TIGER SNAKE

CHAPPEL ISLAND TIGER SNAKE

NORTHERN DEATH ADDER

Although death adders look and behave like vipers, they are members of the cobra family. Because there are no vipers in Australasia, death adders have evolved to fill their ecological niche (see p. 8). Their potent, fast-acting venom and sluggish habits make them responsible for a high proportion of Australia's serious snakebites.

MAIN CHARACTERISTICS

A thickset body, superficially more like that of a viper than a member of the cobra family, and colors and markings that closely match those of its surroundings make the death adders unmistakable in Australia and New Guinea. The northern death adder can be identified by raised edges along the scales over the eyes (known as the supraocular scales).

ENTICING LURE
The snake rests with the body well hidden and its curled tail exposed near its head. The tail tip is a different color from the body and is twitched enticingly if potential prey appears.

FACT FILE
SPECIES: Acanthophis praelongus.
FAMILY: Elapidae (cobras and their relatives).
HABITAT: Wet and dry forests.
BREEDING: Live-bearers, producing up to 20 young.
FEEDING: Lizards and mammals.
DISTRIBUTION: Northern Australia and New Guinea.

AVERAGE ADULT LENGTH

0 cm   25 cm   50 cm
0 in   10 in   1 ft 8 in

NORTHERN DEATH ADDER
Its dark coloration, thick body, and chunky head give the northern death adder a rather sinister appearance. Although it is highly venomous, it never bites unless provoked and prefers to avoid confrontation.

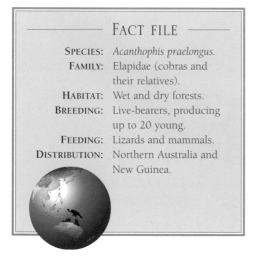

TRIANGULAR HEAD
The head is short and triangular with a sloping snout. The head scales are smaller than those of other members of the cobra family, but not fragmented like those of true vipers.

Thin tail
The tail tip is thin and roughened, and may look like a caterpillar or a worm to a foraging lizard or mouse. Jerky movements enhance the effect.

Raised edges
These hornlike structures directly above the eyes give the northern death adder its characteristic profile. Their function is still unknown.

DESERT DEATH ADDER

The desert death adder, *Acanthophis pyrrhus*, occurs in the remote desert regions of central Australia, where its striking reddish coloration matches the red soil and rock on which it lives. Its natural history is not as well known as that of the other species of death adder, but it is presumed to have a similar lifestyle.

RED COLORATION PROVIDES IDEAL DESERT CAMOUFLAGE

WEST AFRICAN GREEN MAMBA

The West African green mamba is one of three green species of mamba. All belong to the genus *Dendroaspis* (tree asp) and are similar in appearance. Mambas are among the most notorious of the venomous African snakes, even though bites are rare. If disturbed, they will try to escape and will only bite if cornered. The bite is highly dangerous, often proving fatal if not treated immediately.

— MAIN CHARACTERISTICS —

A brightly colored snake with large scales, the West African green mamba has an elegant, pointed head and conspicuous eyes. It is primarily green in color, but the scales on the long tail are yellow and edged in black, giving the impression of a braided rope. Its large dorsal scales are arranged in 13 rows, far fewer than are present on most snakes.

Gradated coloration
Each scale shades subtly from yellowish to bluish green.

WEST AFRICAN GREEN MAMBA
A long, thin snake, the West African green mamba uses its body to bridge gaps between the branches of the trees and shrubs where it lives. The long tail acts as a counterbalance. When the snake moves rapidly, it appears to flow through the foliage.

FACT FILE

SPECIES: *Dendroaspis viridis.*
FAMILY: Elapidae (cobras and their relatives).
HABITAT: Forests and woodlands.
BREEDING: Egg-layers. Number of eggs unknown.
FEEDING: Mainly small rodents, birds, and, possibly, bats.
DISTRIBUTION: West Africa, including Saõ Tome Island.

BLACK MAMBA

At a length of up to 11½ ft (3.5 m), the black mamba, *Dendroaspis polylepis*, is the longest, and probably the most feared, snake in Africa. It rears up when threatened, and a large one could easily look a human in the face! At breeding time, males entwine their bodies and attempt to force each other to the ground. The black mamba varies in color from brown to gray or olive, but is never black.

MALES IN COMBAT

Large eyes
Large eyes and excellent vision
mean that this snake is alert to
the slightest movement.

HEAD SCALES
*The platelike scales on the head are
black-edged and very clearly defined, making
it easy to pick out the various shapes.*

Large scales
The scales are huge,
especially down the
center of the back. They
are smooth, but not
particularly shiny.

AVERAGE ADULT LENGTH

0 cm	1 m	2 m	3 m
0 in	3 ft 3 in	6 ft 6 in	9 ft 10 in

Puff Adder

A large, slow-moving viper, the puff adder is responsible for a significant number of snakebite accidents in Africa. It is not aggressive, but relies heavily on its camouflage, so it is easily overlooked by humans and can inadvertently be stepped upon. It strikes quickly, and its long fangs penetrate deeply. Its potent venom is produced in huge quantities. Although this snake kills many people in rural areas, death is usually preventable if suitable medical treatment is available.

Puff Adder

The washed-out appearance of this puff adder is typical of forms from desert habitats. Its massive body becomes even larger when it is annoyed or cornered. It inflates itself with air, which it then releases, producing an intimidating, loud, low-pitched hiss or a drawn-out "sssssssh" sound.

— Main characteristics

It would be difficult to mistake the puff adder for any other species. Despite variations in color, the combination of wide body, broad head, and rounded snout, together with the pattern of clearly defined chevrons on the back, makes it instantly identifiable. Unless in a hurry, which is seldom, it moves slowly forward in a straight line.

Distinguishing pattern
A distinctive pattern of dark chevrons helps identify the puff adder.

Broad head
The head is broad in order to accommodate the huge venom glands.

Small eyes
The eyes are small with vertical pupils. They are positioned toward the top of the head.

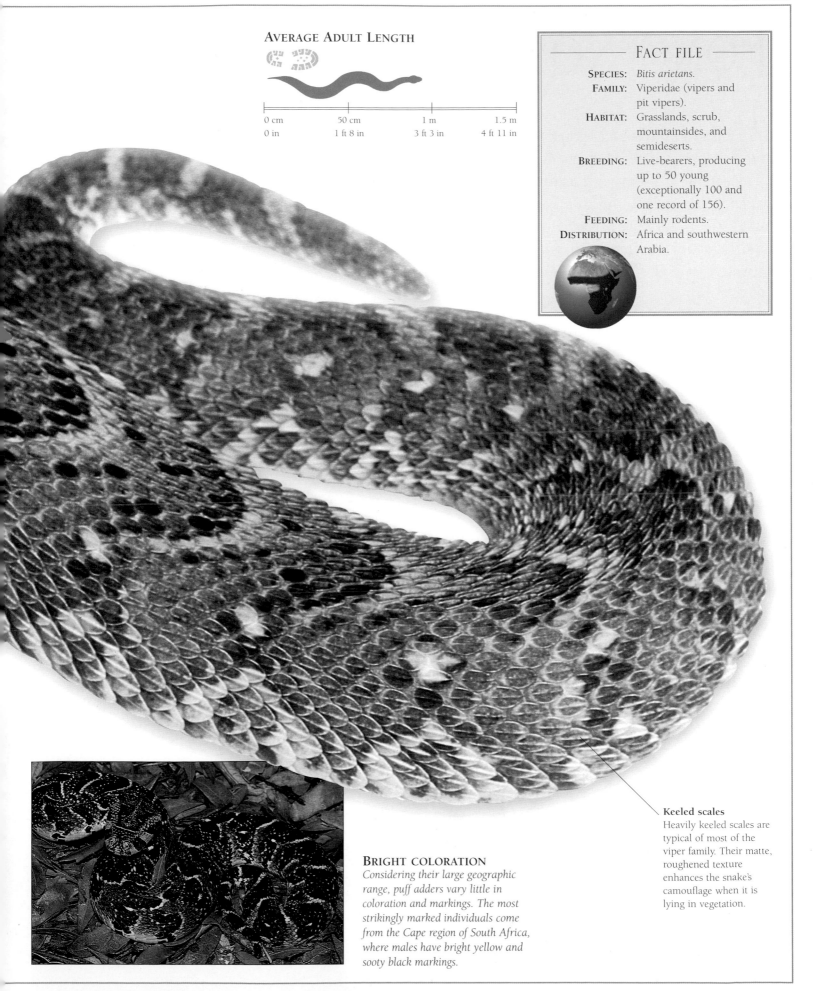

AVERAGE ADULT LENGTH

0 cm	50 cm	1 m	1.5 m
0 in	1 ft 8 in	3 ft 3 in	4 ft 11 in

FACT FILE

SPECIES: *Bitis arietans.*

FAMILY: Viperidae (vipers and pit vipers).

HABITAT: Grasslands, scrub, mountainsides, and semideserts.

BREEDING: Live-bearers, producing up to 50 young (exceptionally 100 and one record of 156).

FEEDING: Mainly rodents.

DISTRIBUTION: Africa and southwestern Arabia.

Keeled scales
Heavily keeled scales are typical of most of the viper family. Their matte, roughened texture enhances the snake's camouflage when it is lying in vegetation.

BRIGHT COLORATION
Considering their large geographic range, puff adders vary little in coloration and markings. The most strikingly marked individuals come from the Cape region of South Africa, where males have bright yellow and sooty black markings.

123

LONG-NOSED VIPER

The long-nosed viper inhabits the mountain slopes and hillsides of eastern Europe and Turkey. It may be active by day or at night and often lies, partially hidden, among a jumble of rocks, or at the base of a small bush. It forages for small rodents, lizards, and birds, and often climbs into low shrubs in search of the latter. Although it has fairly potent venom, it is generally inoffensive and reluctant to bite. The relict (isolated) populations of Switzerland and Austria have enjoyed full legal protection for many years.

— MAIN CHARACTERISTICS —

The horn on the snout and the bold zigzag dorsal marking are enough to distinguish the long-nosed viper from any other. Its color can vary greatly, however. Apart from geographical differences, the sexes are dimorphic (different in appearance). Males are bright and boldly marked in light gray with a black zigzag, while females tend to be brown or orange with dark markings. The zigzag stripe has a dark edging in both sexes. Occasional specimens have a yellowish or pinkish background color and, very rarely, completely black specimens appear. This is the most common species of viper in the area where it occurs.

Zigzag pattern
A zigzag marking with dark edges running down the back is common to the female and male.

LONG-NOSED VIPER

Brown or orange individuals of this species are invariably females; males are normally silver-gray with a dark zigzag. There is also some variation from one population to another, possibly as a result of differently colored rocks or soils.

— FACT FILE —

SPECIES: *Vipera ammodytes.*
FAMILY: Viperidae (vipers and pit vipers).
HABITAT: Dry, rocky, and sandy hillsides and valleys.
BREEDING: Live-bearers, producing 5–15 young.
FEEDING: Lizards, birds, and small mammals.
DISTRIBUTION: Southeastern Europe and southwestern Asia.

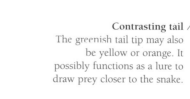

Contrasting tail
The greenish tail tip may also be yellow or orange. It possibly functions as a lure to draw prey closer to the snake.

AVERAGE ADULT LENGTH

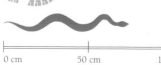

0 cm	50 cm	1 m
0 in	1 ft 8 in	3 ft 3 in

Keeled scales
All the European vipers, as well as most other species of viper, have strongly keeled scales.

LATASTE'S VIPER

ADULT ON A ROCKY SHELF

A smaller species of viper, which has only a slightly upturned snout, is found in Spain, Portugal, and parts of North Africa. Lataste's Viper, *Vipera latasti*, is found on lower mountain slopes, among rocks and scree, and sometimes in lightly wooded areas. In southern Spain it also lives among sand dunes. Its lifestyle, food preferences, and breeding habits are similar to those of the long-nosed viper.

Prominent horn
The horn is a fleshy projection on the snout covered with nine or ten small scales. Its function is not known.

GIVING BIRTH
All the members of the genus Vipera, *to which the long-nosed viper belongs, give birth to live young, although a few closely related vipers lay eggs. The long-nosed viper mates in April or May, and the young are born the following August or September. They measure 6–7 in (16–18 cm) at birth, and are born with fangs and a small amount of venom. Young snakes take two to four years to reach breeding size.*

WIDE HEAD
The head of the long-nosed viper is wide and flat. The scales on the head are small, and those over the eyes overhang slightly and slope down from back to front, giving the snake the appearance of having a permanent frown. It has moderately large eyes and vertical pupils.

ADDER

K nown also as the northern viper, the adder is a familiar species around which many folk tales and superstitions have been created. Nearly all of them are inaccurate: the adder does not swallow its young in times of danger, nor does it form itself into a hoop and roll away. It has the largest geographic range of any terrestrial snake, occurring from Western Europe, right across Central Asia to the Pacific Ocean. It is also found farther north than any other species of snake.

MALES IN COMBAT
Males fight in the spring in order to win the right to mate. A pair of males intertwine the front parts of their bodies and try to wrestle each other to the ground; they do not bite. The loser makes off, and the victor often mates immediately with the female.

— MAIN CHARACTERISTICS

The adder is a small snake with a narrow head and a distinctive zigzag pattern along the back. Unlike several other vipers, it does not have a darker edging to its dorsal marking, and additional blotches along the flanks alternate with the angles of the zigzag. There is nearly always a dark V- or X-shaped mark on the nape of the neck.

ADDER
The adder's markings help it hide in broken light, especially among fronds of bracken, which commonly grow in its habitat. The contrast between the zigzag and the background color can vary, but, otherwise, the adder's markings are remarkably consistent across its wide geographic range.

Dark marking
There is always a dark line from the eye to the angle of the jaw.

FOLDING FANGS
The adder's fangs, like those of all vipers, are hinged and can be folded against the roof of the mouth when not in use. They are erected just before the snake strikes and directed forward. Venom is forced out through small orifices located near the fang tips.

Dorsal pattern
The dorsal zigzag serves to camouflage the snake and to break up its outline. It is characteristic of most European vipers, although its appearance varies between species.

Color variation
Dark markings on a light background are typical of males, while females have brown or reddish markings that contrast less with the background color.

AVERAGE ADULT LENGTH

0 cm   25 cm   50 cm
0 in   10 in   1 ft 8 in

FACT FILE

SPECIES: *Vipera berus.*
FAMILY: Viperidae (vipers and pit vipers).
HABITAT: Varied, including lightly wooded areas, heaths, grasslands, and bogs.
BREEDING: Live-bearers, producing 3–20 young.
FEEDING: Lizards and small mammals.
DISTRIBUTION: Europe, Atlantic to Pacific.

SURVIVING COLD TEMPERATURES

The adder occurs as far north as 69 degrees latitude, which is well inside the Arctic Circle. The adder's small size and predominantly dark coloration help it heat up quickly in a cold environment, and its ability to hibernate for many months each winter enables it to survive conditions that would otherwise be fatal. Giving birth to live young is another adaptation to the cold environment.

BLACK ADDER

A small proportion of adders are completely black. They are more frequent in the colder, more northerly parts of the species' geographic range, as well as on small islands, especially in the Baltic Sea. The black coloration helps this adder warm up quickly, but it is not well camouflaged.

GABOON VIPER

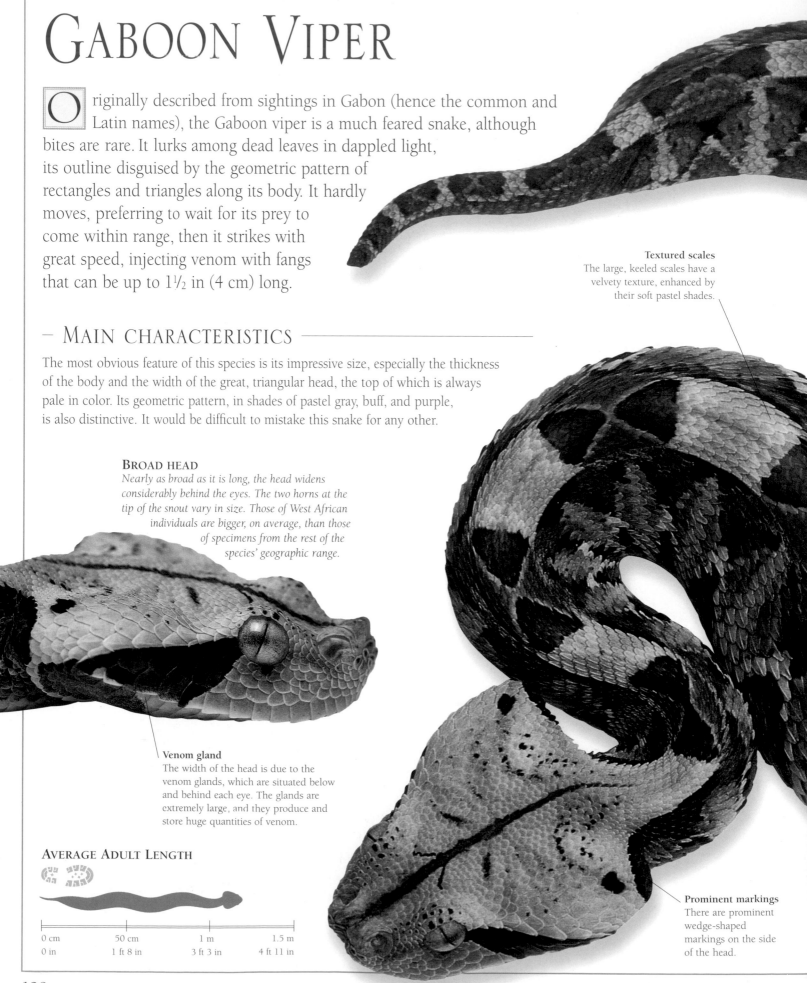

Originally described from sightings in Gabon (hence the common and Latin names), the Gaboon viper is a much feared snake, although bites are rare. It lurks among dead leaves in dappled light, its outline disguised by the geometric pattern of rectangles and triangles along its body. It hardly moves, preferring to wait for its prey to come within range, then it strikes with great speed, injecting venom with fangs that can be up to 1½ in (4 cm) long.

— MAIN CHARACTERISTICS

The most obvious feature of this species is its impressive size, especially the thickness of the body and the width of the great, triangular head, the top of which is always pale in color. Its geometric pattern, in shades of pastel gray, buff, and purple, is also distinctive. It would be difficult to mistake this snake for any other.

Textured scales
The large, keeled scales have a velvety texture, enhanced by their soft pastel shades.

BROAD HEAD
Nearly as broad as it is long, the head widens considerably behind the eyes. The two horns at the tip of the snout vary in size. Those of West African individuals are bigger, on average, than those of specimens from the rest of the species' geographic range.

Venom gland
The width of the head is due to the venom glands, which are situated below and behind each eye. The glands are extremely large, and they produce and store huge quantities of venom.

Prominent markings
There are prominent wedge-shaped markings on the side of the head.

AVERAGE ADULT LENGTH

0 cm	50 cm	1 m	1.5 m
0 in	1 ft 8 in	3 ft 3 in	4 ft 11 in

EXPERT CAMOUFLAGE
The ability of this species to blend into its forest surroundings is legendary. When lying on leaves, the Gaboon viper's kaleidoscopic patches of different colors serve to break up its outline, and the eyes are disguised by the head markings.

GABOON VIPER
A massive viper from the rain forests of West Africa, the coloration and markings seem garish when the snake is seen out of habitat. However, in its natural environment, the snake's camouflage is superb. Because of its markings, its sedentary lifestyle, and the sparse population of the area in which it lives, this snake is seldom seen.

Stout body
The stout body is typical of "sit-and-wait" predators, which do not need to chase after prey. When alarmed, the Gaboon viper can puff up its body to an even greater girth. It produces a loud, low-pitched hiss when it exhales.

Geometric markings
Gray, buff, and purple rectangles and triangles are arranged in a geometric pattern along the body.

FACT FILE

SPECIES:	*Bitis gabonica.*
FAMILY:	Viperidae (vipers and pit vipers).
HABITAT:	Edges of forests and forest clearings.
BREEDING:	Live-bearers, producing up to 60 young.
FEEDING:	Small and medium-sized mammals.
DISTRIBUTION:	West and Central Africa.

DESERT HORNED VIPER

An inhabitant of the Sahara Desert, the desert horned viper has made some interesting adaptations to its environment. To move across loose, windblown sand, it uses an unusual technique called sidewinding (see p. 17). To escape the notice of predators and to ambush its prey, it conceals itself beneath the sand. It adjusts its period of activity according to the season: in the hot summer it becomes nocturnal, but at cooler times of the year it is diurnal. It is unusual among vipers in that it lays eggs.

Ridged horns
Each horn has a ridge running along it, and the horns may bend forward slightly.

— MAIN CHARACTERISTICS

A short, stocky viper, this snake has rough scales and a distinctive "horn" over each eye. Its color varies slightly, but is usually dirty yellow, buff, cream, or light brown with scattered and irregular crossbars and blotches of a darker shade.

MYSTERIOUS HORNS
When the viper shuffles down into the sand, only the eyes and horns are visible. Each horn is a single scale, modified into a thornlike structure. The function of the horns is not certain. They may help reduce glare from the sun since they are found in other species of vipers from desert habitats.

BLUNT HEAD
The desert horned viper has the typical wide, blunt head found throughout the viper family. It has large eyes with vertical pupils. A covering of small, heavily keeled scales gives the head a rough texture.

AVERAGE ADULT LENGTH

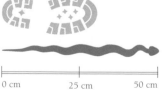

| 0 cm | 25 cm | 50 cm |
| 0 in | 10 in | 1 ft 8 in |

DESERT HORNED VIPER

When the desert horned viper rubs its keeled scales together, they produce a loud rasping or "zizzing" noise. The snake uses this device to warn potential predators of its presence.

Keeled scales
The scales are all heavily keeled. Those on its flanks have oblique keels with serrated ridges.

FACT FILE

SPECIES:	*Cerastes cerastes.*
FAMILY:	Viperidae (vipers and pit vipers).
HABITAT:	Deserts.
BREEDING:	Egg-layers, producing up to 23 eggs.
FEEDING:	Lizards, birds, and small mammals.
DISTRIBUTION:	North Africa.

DESERT CAMOUFLAGE

The desert horned viper is colored to match the sand on which it lives. This can vary from pale yellow to brown. The snake's hunting strategy is to shuffle down until its body is covered with a fine layer of sand, with just the top of its head showing. From this position, it can strike at small lizards, which make up the bulk of its prey.

Scale texture
The scales are lightly keeled. They are not shiny, but have a silky sheen, which intensifies the green color.

WHITE-LIPPED TREE VIPER

T he white-lipped tree viper has adapted to an arboreal life in the evergreen trees and lush undergrowth of rain forests and only occasionally descends to the ground. It is most active at night, and normally hunts by ambush, resting with its head and neck in an S-shaped loop, ready to strike when prey is within range. Although it is venomous and easily provoked, human fatalities are rare because the venom is mild.

— MAIN CHARACTERISTICS —

Although the white-lipped tree viper has a distinctive white or yellow band along the mouth, it is easily confused with several other green pit vipers from the same part of the world. The arboreal pit vipers are all more slender and agile than ground-dwelling related species, often have larger eyes, and are green, yellow, or bluish in color. They are easily distinguished from nonvenomous green snakes by the presence of prominent heat pits, a broad head, and lightly keeled scales.

AVERAGE ADULT LENGTH

0 cm	50 cm	1 m	1.5 m
0 in	1 ft 8 in	3 ft 3 in	4 ft 11 in

ISLAND PIT VIPERS

Pit vipers occur throughout the major archipelagos of the region, such as the Indonesian chain, the Philippines, and Celebes. Many island species, such as the Sumatran pit viper, have evolved in isolation from other mainland vipers. All of the island species are at home in rain forests, bamboo thickets, and plantations, where their predominantly green coloration provides excellent camouflage. Heat pits help them find prey in poor light.

SUMATRAN PIT VIPER REARING UP

Yellow eye
The size of the eye and the vertical pupil mark this species as a nocturnal hunter. The eyes are one of its most conspicuous features.

Large heat pits
The heat pits are set into the side of the head and are large. They point directly forwards and work as a pair.

WHITE-LIPPED TREE VIPER
The long, slim body of this snake and its green coloration are evidence of an arboreal lifestyle. It can remain motionless, head down and ready to strike, for many minutes – or even hours – waiting for suitable prey to stray within range.

FACT FILE

SPECIES: *Trimeresurus albolabris.*
FAMILY: Viperidae (vipers and pit vipers).
HABITAT: Forests and plantations, especially near streams.
BREEDING: Live-bearers, producing 10–11 young.
FEEDING: Frogs, birds, and small mammals.
DISTRIBUTION: Southern China to India and south to the Indonesian Archipelago, but absent from the Malay peninsula.

WIDE HEAD
The width of the white-lipped tree viper's head can be seen clearly from the front. The snake is poised to strike. Its head is drawn back, and the front of the body is tensed in readiness to straighten out suddenly.

Saw-scaled Viper

Although small, the saw-scaled or carpet viper is extremely dangerous because of its venom and its readiness to bite if stepped on or otherwise disturbed. It is responsible for most of the snakebite fatalities throughout its geographic range because of its abundance and habit of lying partially buried in the sand or soil. Its common name refers to the serrated keels on some of its scales, which are used to produce a hissing sound.

SAW-SCALED VIPER
Apart from producing a warning sound, the heavily keeled scales help this snake shuffle down into the sand or soil where it remains motionless, and almost invisible, lying in wait for its prey.

Main characteristics

This species is slender for a viper and has a very distinct, pear-shaped head. Its body pattern is intricate and varies according to the color of the soil on which it lives, occurring in different shades of brown, beige, or gray, with brown or reddish-brown blotches. However, all individuals have black and white spots along the back. There is usually a cross-shaped marking on the head.

Complex coloration
The intricate markings break up the viper's outline when it is resting on gravelly sand or among dry vegetation.

Defense posture

All saw-scaled vipers have the same distinctive defense posture. The snake coils its body into a horseshoe shape, so that the specialized serrated scales on one section of the flanks are next to those on another section, but facing the opposite way. When it moves its coils, the serrated keels rasp together, producing a harsh hissing, or zizzing, sound. At the same time, the snake defends itself by striking repeatedly and vigorously.

Distinctive spots
The indistinct black-edged white spots are a notable characteristic.

AFRICAN SAW-SCALED VIPER

Large eyes
The large eyes are positioned toward the top of the head.

PEAR-SHAPED HEAD
The saw-scaled viper has a pear-shaped head with a rounded snout that is covered with many small scales. The depth of the head and position of the eyes enable the snake to see when it is partially buried.

Keeled scales
The heavily keeled, rough scales are non-reflective, maintaining the snake's camouflage when it is lying on sand.

FACT FILE

SPECIES: *Echis carinatus.*
FAMILY: Viperidae (vipers and pit vipers).
HABITAT: Deserts, dry scrub forests, grasslands, and rocky places.
BREEDING: Live-bearers, producing up to 23 young.
FEEDING: Most small creatures, from invertebrates to amphibians, reptiles, birds, and mammals.
DISTRIBUTION: African and Asian desert belt.

Distinctive marking
A cross-shaped marking on the head is nearly always present. It gives the genus its Latin name, *Echis*, which means "x."

AVERAGE ADULT LENGTH

0 cm	50 cm	1 m	1.5 m
0 in	1 ft 8 in	3 ft 3 in	4 ft 11 in

JARARACA

The jararaca belongs to the group of snakes commonly known as lanceheads. The snake's common name is derived from Amerindian; alternative versions are *yararaca* and *yarar*. Due to the jararaca's excellent camouflage, abundance, and liking for cultivated areas and forest clearings, humans are frequently bitten. Although the venom is potent, medical intervention prevents most fatalities.

— MAIN CHARACTERISTICS

It can be difficult to distinguish this species of viper from several other lanceheads that are found in the same part of the world. The triangular head and pointed snout are common to all lanceheads, and the jararaca's coloration is too variable to be a good identification characteristic. Triangular blotches along the back are often obscured by dark pigmentation, especially in adults, and there is often more contrast in the markings of juveniles.

FACT FILE

SPECIES:	*Bothrops jararaca.*
FAMILY:	Viperidae (vipers and pit vipers).
HABITAT:	Open country.
BREEDING:	Live-bearers, thought to produce about 20 young.
FEEDING:	Birds and small mammals.
DISTRIBUTION:	Southern Brazil to Argentina.

AVERAGE ADULT LENGTH

0 cm	50 cm	1 m	1.5 m
0 in	1 ft 8 in	3 ft 3 in	4 ft 11 in

JARARACA
A long, dark body, obscure markings, and a preference for shady places make this snake hard to see and, therefore, dangerous to people working on the land. The triangular shape of its head is the result of large venom glands immediately behind its eyes.

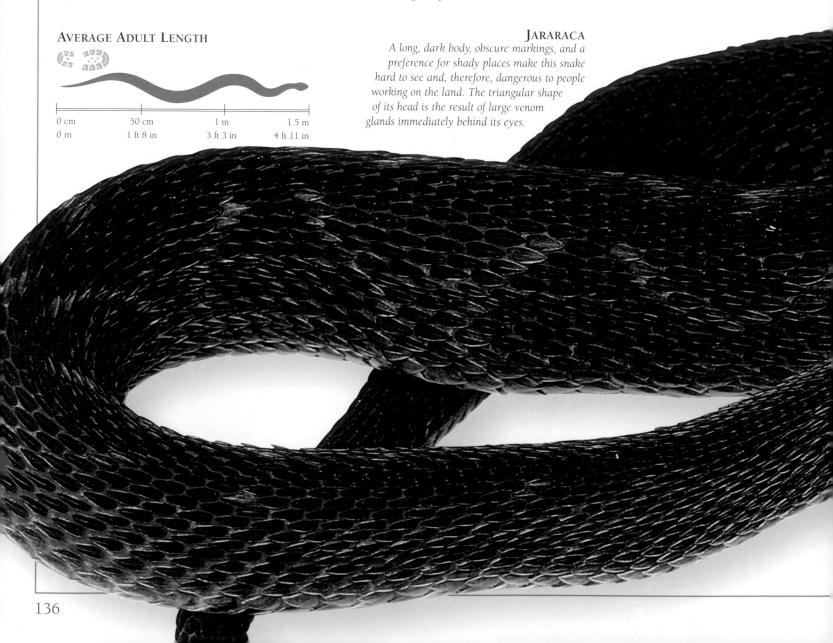

TRIANGULAR HEAD

The broad, triangular head and arrow-shaped marking are characteristic, and it is easy to see why this group of snakes has been given the common name of lancehead. The vertical pupils identify it as a nocturnal hunter.

Geometric coloration
The tips of triangular blotches meet along the center of the snake's back. However, these may be indistinct.

Conspicuous heat pits
Heat pits enable the jararaca to hunt effectively at night.

FER-DE-LANCE

Other lanceheads are found throughout Central and South America. The most common and, therefore, the most familiar, is *Bothrops asper*, from Central and northern South America. This is the species usually known as the Fer-de-lance. However, its Spanish name of *Terciopelo*, meaning "velvet," is a more appropriate description of its appearance. It is responsible for a large number of human fatalities.

JUVENILE EATING A TEIID LIZARD

Keeled scales
Dark coloration and heavily keeled scales give this snake a matte, almost sooty, appearance.

COPPERHEAD

Broad head
The venom glands behind the eyes give this viper a spade-shaped head.

D istinctively marked pit vipers, copperheads are closely related to rattlesnakes. They live in a variety of habitats and can be quite common in places. Excellent camouflage and their habit of remaining motionless, however, mean that they often go unnoticed. Although venomous, copperheads try to avoid confrontation. Its bite is only rarely serious.

— MAIN CHARACTERISTICS

A coppery colored head and broad bands of chestnut brown and orange, tan, or gray combine to give the copperhead its unmistakable appearance. The band colors vary among different populations, but always contrast sharply with the background color. A number of subspecies are recognized. Some water snakes have similar markings, but seen at close quarters, the facial pits distinguish the copperhead.

COPPERHEAD
The wide head, tapering quickly to a narrow neck, gives the copperhead its distinctive shape, and the coppery color gives the snake its name. It is also known as the moccasin, but this name is best avoided because it also applies to other snakes.

CHUNKY HEAD
The wide head ends in an upturned snout. Moderately large eyes and vertical pupils indicate that the snake is primarily nocturnal, although it can be active during the day in cool weather.

Faint markings
In contrast to the rest of the body, the head is uniform in color, with only faint traces of the facial markings found in many other pit vipers.

AVERAGE ADULT LENGTH

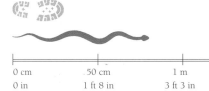

0 cm	50 cm	1 m	1.5 m
0 in	1 ft 8 in	3 ft 3 in	4 ft 11 in

TAIL TIP
The tip of a juvenile copperhead's tail is bright yellow and is used as a lure to entice small frogs and lizards to come within striking range. As the snake matures, its hunting methods and choice of prey alter. Consequently, the bright coloration gradually fades. The copperhead vibrates its tail when aroused to produce a warning rustling or rattling noise, especially when it makes contact with dead leaves.

FOREST CAMOUFLAGE
Although the copperhead's markings appear gaudy when seen in isolation, they provide exceptionally good camouflage when the snake is resting among dead leaves. The banded markings also serve to break up the snake's outline, making it hard for predators to identify its shape.

Varying band width
The dark bands widen on the flanks. Although the two halves of each band often correspond exactly, they are sometimes staggered or broken in places.

Matte scales
The matte texture of the scales, combined with pastel hues, enhances the snake's camouflage.

FACT FILE

SPECIES:	*Agkistrodon contortrix*.
FAMILY:	Viperidae (vipers and pit vipers).
HABITAT:	Rocky hillsides, semi-deserts, woodland, grassland, and swamps.
BREEDING:	Live-bearers, producing 3-21 young.
FEEDING:	Frogs, birds, and small mammals.
DISTRIBUTION:	North America.

WESTERN DIAMONDBACK RATTLESNAKE

A western diamondback rattlesnake in defensive posture is an awesome spectacle, and very few predators are prepared to tackle it. The snake raises its tail and draws up its body into an S-shape, like a coiled spring, flickering its tongue and vibrating its rattle every time it senses movement that might spell danger. It is active mainly at night, although it may emerge from its hiding place during late afternoon. Large, heavy-bodied individuals often crawl in a straight line rather than wriggle from side to side.

FACT FILE

SPECIES: *Crotalus atrox.*
FAMILY: Viperidae (vipers and pit vipers).
HABITAT: Deserts, scrub, and rocky hillsides.
BREEDING: Live-bearers, producing 4–21 young.
FEEDING: Birds and mammals.
DISTRIBUTION: Southwestern US and Mexico.

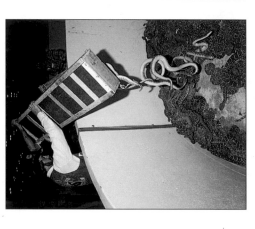

MAIN CHARACTERISTICS

The western diamondback rattlesnake is a large snake, which sometimes grows to over 4 ft 11 in.(1.5 m) It is heavy-bodied, often becoming even more bulky with age. The head is wide and triangular, and there is nearly always a dark streak, bordered by a pair of lighter ones, passing from the eye to the angle of the jaw. An obvious identification feature is the black and white banding on the tail just before the rattle.

RATTLESNAKE ROUNDUPS

A few states in the US still allow rattlesnake roundups, and the western diamondback is the species most affected. Large numbers are slaughtered for the amusement of spectators. As a result, some local populations of diamondback have been virtually eliminated.

Sheathed fangs

When not in use, the fangs are covered with a pair of fleshy sheaths. These slide back out of the way when the fangs are erected and ready for action.

Poison glands

Plump cheeks accommodate large poison glands, situated behind the eyes.

FANG ACTION

The snake swings the fangs forward as it strikes so that they stab, rather than bite, their victim. The bones to which the fangs are attached are short and mobile, allowing the whole apparatus to move through 90 degrees.

DIAMONDBACKS

Several large rattlesnakes have angular, blotched markings. Some common names reflect this, including those for the western and eastern diamondbacks, and the red diamond rattlesnake.

Banded tail

The stripes act as a visual warning to supplement the audible rattle.

AVERAGE ADULT LENGTH

0 cm	50 cm	1 m	1.5 m
0 in	1 ft 8 in	3 ft 3 in	4 ft 11 in

Heat pits
The heat pits point forward and work together to pinpoint the snake's prey.

Warning rattle
The rattle is raised, ready to sound a warning against any potential threat.

WESTERN DIAMONDBACK RATTLESNAKE

This species comes in many color variations to match the surface on which it lives. The rattle, which may have up to ten segments, is used as a warning signal. It prevents large mammals from trampling the snake by accident, for instance. A new segment is added to the rattle every time the rattlesnake sheds its skin.

Speckled scales
A pattern of small speckles is superimposed over the large dorsal blotches.

TROPICAL RATTLESNAKE

V ariable in appearance, the tropical rattlesnake has the largest geographic range of any rattlesnake. It is probably responsible for more cases of serious snakebite in South America than any other species, and mortality is high without treatment. The snake's Spanish name, *cascabel*, means little bell, which is a strangely inappropriate description of its rattle.

— MAIN CHARACTERISTICS

The pair of parallel stripes down the neck make this species easy to identify. In addition, it has a pronounced ridge along the back, caused by spines on top of each vertebra and high keels on the scales covering this part of the body. The body scales are rougher than those of any other species of rattlesnake. Markings are extremely variable, and at least 14 subspecies are recognized.

TROPICAL RATTLESNAKE
Pale markings in greenish gray are typical of the form of tropical rattlesnake from Brazil. Like all snakes belonging to the species, it is easily provoked into using its rattle as a warning signal when it senses danger.

Identifying stripes
A pair of parallel stripes runs down the neck into the upper part of the body. These tend to be dark in color.

FACT FILE

SPECIES: *Crotalus durissus.*
FAMILY: Viperidae (vipers and pit vipers).
HABITAT: Dry tropical forests and clearings.
BREEDING: Live-bearers.
FEEDING: Birds and mammals.
DISTRIBUTION: Central and South America.

AVERAGE ADULT LENGTH

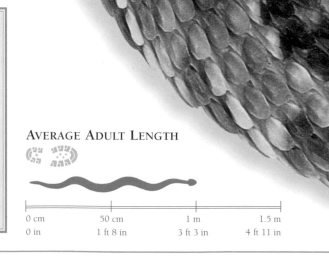

0 cm	50 cm	1 m	1.5 m
0 in	1 ft 8 in	3 ft 3 in	4 ft 11 in

VENEZUELAN SUBSPECIES

Of all the subspecies of the tropical rattlesnake, Crotalus durissus vegrandis, *from Venezuela, is the most distinctive. The dorsal markings and the stripes on the neck are mostly obscured by speckles of dark gray and white. This form is sometimes considered to be a full species in its own right.*

Loud rattle

The rattle produces a loud buzzing sound when the snake becomes alert to danger.

BREEDING HABITS

All rattlesnakes give birth to live young. They are born in a thin membrane, but soon break free and become fully independent. Tropical rattlesnakes probably breed every year, but other species from cooler climates may only breed every two or three years.

Keeled scales

This species has very heavily keeled scales, giving it the roughened texture and appearance of a pineapple.

SIDEWINDER

The sidewinder is a small rattlesnake that lives amidst dunes of loose, windblown sand. It moves rapidly over them, mostly at night, in a looping motion known as sidewinding (see p.17). Before morning, it digs itself into the sand, often at the base of a small bush, to escape from excessive heat. The sidewinder is not as dangerous as its reputation suggests, although its bites require medical attention.

MAIN CHARACTERISTICS

The sidewinder has raised scales over its eyes and a dark line through each eye. The head is much wider and flatter than that of other rattlesnakes. Its coloration varies to match the ground on which it lives, and can be yellow, gray, or orange, with indistinct spots of darker and lighter shades. Its method of locomotion is its most distinctive feature.

PARALLEL TRACKS
The sidewinder's tracks consist of a series of unconnected imprints at about 45 degrees to the direction of travel. Each track shows a small hook at either end where the snake curls its head and tail.

AVERAGE ADULT LENGTH

0 cm	25 cm	50 cm
0 in	10 in	1 ft 8 in

FACT FILE

SPECIES:	*Crotalus cerastes.*
FAMILY:	Viperidae (vipers and pit vipers).
HABITAT:	Deserts.
BREEDING:	Live-bearing, producing 7–18 young.
FEEDING:	Lizards and small mammals.
DISTRIBUTION:	Extreme southwestern US and adjacent Mexico.

SIDEWINDER
The sidewinder is the stoutest species of rattlesnake and has a flattened head. The body shape, also flattened, helps the snake move across the sand, putting the greatest possible area into contact with the ground.

Dark head marking
A dark line runs through each eye, disguising the shape of the head.

Small rattle
The rattle is small, relative to the body, but still acts as an effective warning to enemies.

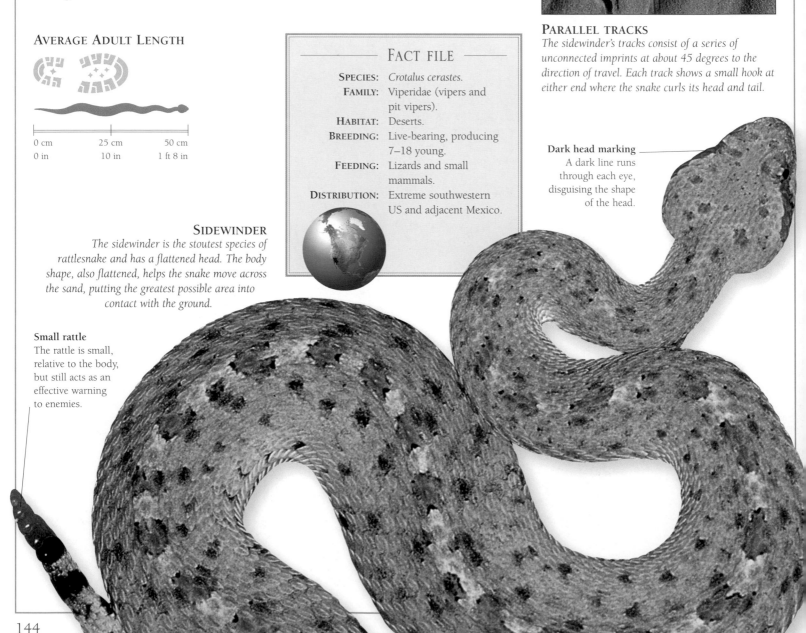

SNAKE DIRECTORY

— CONTENTS —

LEPTOTYPHLOPIDAE (*thread snakes*) .... p. 146

ANOMALEPIDAE .... p. 146

TYPHLOPIDAE (*blind snakes*) .... p. 146

ANOMOCHILIDAE (*dwarf pipe snakes*) .... p. 148

ANILIIDAE (*South American pipe snake*) .... p. 148

CYLINDROPHEIDAE (*Asian pipe snakes*) .... p. 148

UROPELTIDAE (*shield-tailed snakes*) .... p. 148

LOXOCEMIDAE (*Central American sunbeam snake*) .... p. 149

XENOPELTIDAE (*Asian sunbeam snakes*) .... p. 149

BOIDAE (*boas*) .... p. 149

PYTHONIDAE (*pythons*) .... p. 150

TROPIDOPHIIDAE (*wood snakes*) .... p. 151

BOLYERIIDAE (*Round Island boas*) .... p. 151

ACROCHORDIDAE (*wart or file snakes*) .... p. 152

COLUBRIDAE (*colubrids*) .... p. 152

ATRACTASPIDIDAE (*burrowing asps*) .... p. 177

ELAPIDAE (*cobras and their relatives*) .... p. 178

VIPERIDAE (*vipers*) .... p. 183

The Snake Directory is the most complete listing of snake species possible at present – undoubtedly many more species are yet to be described.

Several species of snake are poorly known. Indeed, some are known from only a single individual, and it is not always feasible to give precise information about some species.

— FAMILIES —

Snakes are currently grouped into 18 families. Each family is divided into genera, and these are further divided into species. Some families contain only one or a few species. In contrast, the largest family, the Colubridae, contains over 1,850 species.

The three most primitive families – Leptotyphlopidae, Anomalepidae, and Typhlopidae – differ from other snakes in that their skulls are very rigid and their eyes are either small and covered with scales or lacking altogether. They are sometimes grouped as a superfamily, known as the Scolecophidia, or blind snakes.

Of the other 15 families (sometimes known collectively as the Alethinophidia), ten contain relatively primitive snakes. They are scattered around the world and reflect the first wave of diversification among snakes. These families have few members and are thought to be in decline.

The remaining five families are the most advanced. Very diverse and including all the venomous snakes, they are grouped into one small family – the Acrochordidae – and four larger ones – the Colubridae, Atractaspididae, Elapidae, and Viperidae.

Some families are divided into subfamilies. The Boidae, for example, is divided into the Boinae and the Erycinae. The Colubridae has many subfamilies, but the placement of each species within them is often controversial.

In the Snake Directory, the families are arranged in order, from the most primitive to the most recently evolved. Within each family, subfamilies (where present), genera, and species are arranged alphabetically.

SNAKE LENGTHS
The following categories have been used to indicate snake lengths:

small	to about 2 ft 5$\frac{1}{2}$ in (75 cm)
medium	2 ft 5$\frac{1}{2}$ in–4 ft 11 in (75–150 cm)
large	4 ft 11 in–9 ft 10 in (1.5–3 m)
very large	over 9 ft 10 in (over 3 m)

LEPTOTYPHLOPIDAE
THREAD SNAKES

2 GENERA CONTAINING 86 SPECIES

The members of this family are small and slender with smooth, shiny scales. Most individuals are pink or silvery gray, but some are darker. All have teeth in the lower jaw only, and the upper jaw is rigid. Thread snakes have well-developed pelvic girdles, and some have vestigial hind limbs in the form of small spurs. They do not have left lungs, and females do not have left oviducts. The rudimentary eyes are small, and each one is covered by a scale.

All thread snakes live underground, where they feed on termites and their larvae. They use their tiny mouths to grasp the soft-bodied insects and squeeze them dry. Some species (perhaps all of them) produce pheromones that protect them from attack by soldier termites. Thread snakes appear to be egg-layers, although the reproductive method of several species has not been recorded. The family is found in practically all parts of the world where there are termites: North America, Central and South America, Africa, Arabia, and the Middle East.

GENUS: LEPTOTYPHLOPS
85 SPECIES

SIZE: Small and slender.
DISTRIBUTION: North America (California and Texas), Central and South America, Africa, Arabia, and the Middle East.
HABITAT: Subterranean.
FOOD: Termites.
REPRODUCTION: Egg-layers.

SPECIES:
Leptotyphlops affinis
Leptotyphlops albifrons
Leptotyphlops albipunctus
Leptotyphlops albiventer
Leptotyphlops algeriensis
Leptotyphlops anthracinus
Leptotyphlops asbolepis
Leptotyphlops australis
Leptotyphlops bicolor
Leptotyphlops bilineatus
Leptotyphlops blanfordi
Leptotyphlops borapeliotes
Leptotyphlops borrichianus
Leptotyphlops boueti
Leptotyphlops boulengeri
Leptotyphlops brasiliensis
Leptotyphlops bressoni
Leptotyphlops brevicaudus
Leptotyphlops brevissimus
Leptotyphlops burii
Leptotyphlops cairi
Leptotyphlops calypso
Leptotyphlops collaris

Leptotyphlops columbi
Leptotyphlops conjunctus,
    Cape Thread Snake
Leptotyphlops cupinensis
Leptotyphlops debilis
Leptotyphlops diaplocius
Leptotyphlops dimidiatus
Leptotyphlops dissimilis
Leptotyphlops distanti,
    Distant's Thread Snake
Leptotyphlops dugandi
Leptotyphlops dulcis,
    Texas Blind Snake
Leptotyphlops emini
Leptotyphlops filiformis
Leptotyphlops goudotii
Leptotyphlops gracilior,
    Slender Thread Snake
Leptotyphlops guayaquilensis
Leptotyphlops humilis,
    Western Blind Snake (US)
Leptotyphlops joshuai
Leptotyphlops koppesi
Leptotyphlops labialis,
    Damara Thread Snake
Leptotyphlops leptipilepta
Leptotyphlops longicaudus,
    Long-tailed Thread Snake
Leptotyphlops macrolepis
Leptotyphlops macrops
Leptotyphlops macrorhynchus,
    Beaked Thread Snake
Leptotyphlops macrurus
Leptotyphlops maximus
Leptotyphlops melanotermus
Leptotyphlops melanurus
Leptotyphlops munoai
Leptotyphlops narirostris
Leptotyphlops nasalis
Leptotyphlops natatrix
Leptotyphlops nicefori
Leptotyphlops nigricans,
    Black Thread Snake
Leptotyphlops nursii
Leptotyphlops occidentalis,
    Western Thread Snake (Africa)
Leptotyphlops pembae
Leptotyphlops perreti
Leptotyphlops peruvianus
Leptotyphlops phillipsi
Leptotyphlops pyrites
Leptotyphlops reticulatus
Leptotyphlops rostratus
Leptotyphlops rubrolineatus
Leptotyphlops rufidorsus
Leptotyphlops salgueiroi
Leptotyphlops scutifrons,
    Peter's Thread Snake
Leptotyphlops septemstriatus
Leptotyphlops signatus
Leptotyphlops striatulus
Leptotyphlops subcrotillus
Leptotyphlops sundevalli
Leptotyphlops teaguei
Leptotyphlops telloi,
    Tello's Thread Snake
Leptotyphlops tenellus
Leptotyphlops tesselatus
Leptotyphlops tricolor
Leptotyphlops undecimstriatus

Leptotyphlops unguirostris
Leptotyphlops vellardi
Leptotyphlops weyrauchi
Leptotyphlops wilsoni

GENUS: RHINOLEPTUS
1 SPECIES

SIZE: Small.
DISTRIBUTION: Central Africa (Senegal and Guinea).
HABITAT: Subterranean.
FOOD: Thought to be ants and termites.
REPRODUCTION: Thought to be an egg-layer.
NOTES: Poorly known.

SPECIES:
Rhinoleptus koniagui

ANOMALEPIDAE

4 GENERA CONTAINING 15 SPECIES

This is the most primitive snake family. Very little is known about its members, which are perhaps the least known of all vertebrates. All members are very small with smooth, shiny scales; slender, cylindrical bodies; and short tails. Most are brown or black, although some species have yellow or white heads and tails. Members of some genera have a pair of teeth on the lower jaw, while others have no teeth at all. The eyes are rudimentary.

Anomalepidae spend nearly all their time below ground and feed mostly on termites. Their method of reproduction is unknown, although it is assumed that they lay eggs. The family is restricted to tropical Central and South America.

GENUS: ANOMALEPIS
4 SPECIES

SIZE: Small and slender.
DISTRIBUTION: Central America and northern South America.
HABITAT: Subterranean, in forests.
FOOD: Termites.
REPRODUCTION: Thought to be egg-layers.
NOTES: Poorly known.

SPECIES:
Anomalepis aspinosus
Anomalepis colombius
Anomalepis flavapices
Anomalepis mexicanus

GENUS: HELMINTHOPHIS
3 SPECIES

SIZE: Small, to 1 ft.(30 cm)
DISTRIBUTION: Northern South America.
HABITAT: Subterranean.
FOOD: Termites.
REPRODUCTION: Thought to be egg-layers.
NOTES: Poorly known.

SPECIES:
Helminthophis flavoterminatus
Helminthophis frontalis
Helminthophis praeocularis

GENUS: LIOTYPHLOPS
7 SPECIES

SIZE: Small.
DISTRIBUTION: Central and northern South America.
HABITAT: Subterranean.
FOOD: Termites.
REPRODUCTION: Thought to be egg-layers.
NOTES: Poorly known.

SPECIES:
Liotyphlops albirostris
Liotyphlops anops
Liotyphlops argaleus
Liotyphlops beui
Liotyphlops schubarti
Liotyphlops ternetzii
Liotyphlops wilderi

GENUS: TYPHLOPHIS
1 SPECIES

SIZE: Small.
DISTRIBUTION: Central and northern South America.
HABITAT: Subterranean.
FOOD: Termites.
REPRODUCTION: Thought to be an egg-layer.
NOTES: Poorly known.

SPECIES:
Typhlophis squamosus

TYPHLOPIDAE
BLIND SNAKES

5 GENERA CONTAINING 218 SPECIES

Blind snakes are small with smooth, shiny scales, cylindrical bodies, and short tails, which often end in a small spine. Most are brown, black, or pinkish, but some species have faint stripes or blotches. They have teeth in the upper jaw only and rudimentary eyes.

Burrowing species that feed almost entirely on termites and ants, they are found in a variety of environments, but usually avoid very dry soils. Individuals may be found resting beneath partially buried logs or stones. They appear to be egg-layers, although the reproductive habits of the majority of species in this family are not known. Members are found in Central and South America, Africa, southern Asia, and Australasia, with one species in southeastern Europe.

GENUS: **ACUTOTYPHLOPS**
4 SPECIES

SIZE: Small.
DISTRIBUTION: Bougainville Island, New Guinea, and the Solomon Islands.
HABITAT: Subterranean.
FOOD: Unknown, but thought to be small invertebrates.
REPRODUCTION: Unknown, but thought to be egg-layers.
NOTES: Poorly known; the genus was first described in 1995.

SPECIES:
Acutotyphlops infralabialis
Acutotyphlops kunuaensis
Acutotyphlops solomonis
Acutotyphlops subocularis

GENUS: **CYCLOTYPHLOPS**
1 SPECIES

SIZE: Small, to just over $5\frac{1}{2}$ in (14 cm).
DISTRIBUTION: Southeastern Sulawesi and Indonesia.
HABITAT: Clearings in secondary forests.
FOOD: Unknown, but thought to be ants and termites.
REPRODUCTION: Unknown, but thought to be an egg-layer.
NOTES: The genus and species were first described in 1994; only two specimens are known.

SPECIES:
Cyclotyphlops deharvengi

GENUS: **RAMPHOTYPHLOPS**
52 SPECIES

SIZE: Small, to about 8 in (20 cm), occasionally larger.
DISTRIBUTION: India, Southeast Asia, New Guinea, Australia, and surrounding islands. *R. braminus* has been introduced to many parts of the tropical and subtropical world, including South Africa, Madagascar, Central America, and Florida.
HABITAT: Subterranean, including in plantations.
FOOD: Ants and termites.
REPRODUCTION: Egg-layers, where known. *R. braminus* is unique among snakes, being the world's only parthenogenic (all-female) species (see p. 31).

NOTES: Several species are newly described, and a number are known from only a single specimen.

SPECIES:
Ramphotyphlops acuticauda
Ramphotyphlops affinis
Ramphotyphlops albiceps
Ramphotyphlops angusticeps
Ramphotyphlops australis
Ramphotyphlops batillus
Ramphotyphlops bituberculatus
Ramphotyphlops braminus,
  Brahminy Blind Snake
Ramphotyphlops broomi
Ramphotyphlops centralis
Ramphotyphlops chamodracaena
Ramphotyphlops cumingii
Ramphotyphlops depressus
Ramphotyphlops diversus
Ramphotyphlops endoterus
Ramphotyphlops erycinus
Ramphotyphlops exocoeti
Ramphotyphlops flaviventer
Ramphotyphlops grypus
Ramphotyphlops guentheri
Ramphotyphlops hamatus
Ramphotyphlops howi
Ramphotyphlops kimberleyensis
Ramphotyphlops leptosoma
Ramphotyphlops leucoproctus
Ramphotyphlops ligatus
Ramphotyphlops lineatus
Ramphotyphlops lorenzi
Ramphotyphlops margaretae
Ramphotyphlops melanocephalus
Ramphotyphlops micromma
Ramphotyphlops minimus
Ramphotyphlops multilineatus
Ramphotyphlops nigrescens
Ramphotyphlops nigroterminatus
Ramphotyphlops olivaceus
Ramphotyphlops pilbarensis
Ramphotyphlops pinguis
Ramphotyphlops polygrammicus
Ramphotyphlops proximus
Ramphotyphlops silvia
Ramphotyphlops similis
Ramphotyphlops suluensis
Ramphotyphlops supranasalis
Ramphotyphlops tovelli
Ramphotyphlops troglodytes
Ramphotyphlops unguirostris
Ramphotyphlops waitii
Ramphotyphlops wiedii
Ramphotyphlops willeyi
Ramphotyphlops yampiensis
Ramphotyphlops yirrikalae

GENUS: **RHINOTYPHLOPS**
28 SPECIES

SIZE: Small, to about 1 ft (30 cm). One species, *R. schlegelii*, is the world's largest worm snake at nearly 3 ft 3 in (1 m).
DISTRIBUTION: Africa, Asia (two species), Middle East (one species).
HABITAT: Subterranean, usually found in dry soils.

FOOD: Ants and termites.
REPRODUCTION: Egg-layers.
NOTES: Sometimes classified as members of the genus *Typhlops*.

SPECIES:
Rhinotyphlops acutus
Rhinotyphlops anomalus
Rhinotyphlops ataeniatus
Rhinotyphlops boylei,
  Boyle's Blind Snake
Rhinotyphlops caecus
Rhinotyphlops crossii
Rhinotyphlops debilis
Rhinotyphlops erythraeus
Rhinotyphlops feae
Rhinotyphlops gracilis
Rhinotyphlops graueri
Rhinotyphlops kibarae
Rhinotyphlops lalandei,
  Delalande's Blind Snake
Rhinotyphlops leucocephalus
Rhinotyphlops lumbriciformis
Rhinotyphlops newtoni
Rhinotyphlops pallidus
Rhinotyphlops praeocularis
Rhinotyphlops rufescens
Rhinotyphlops schinzi,
  Beaked Blind Snake
Rhinotyphlops schlegelii,
  Schlegel's Blind Snake
Rhinotyphlops scortecci
Rhinotyphlops simoni
Rhinotyphlops somalicus
Rhinotyphlops stejnegeri
Rhinotyphlops sudanensis
Rhinotyphlops unitaeniatus
Rhinotyphlops wittei

GENUS: **TYPHLOPS**
133 SPECIES

SIZE: Small.
DISTRIBUTION: Central and South America, Africa, the Middle East, and Asia. One species, *T. vermicularis*, just enters southeastern Europe.
HABITAT: Subterranean.
FOOD: Ants and termites, where known.
REPRODUCTION: Egg-layers, where known.
NOTES: The sole Madagascan species, *T. grandidieri*, is sometimes placed in a separate genus, *Xenotyphlops*.

SPECIES:
Typhlops albanalis
Typhlops andamanensis
Typhlops angolensis
Typhlops arenarius
Typhlops ater
Typhlops beddomi
Typhlops blanfordii
Typhlops bibronii,
  Bibron's Blind Snake
Typhlops biminensis
Typhlops bisubocularis
Typhlops bothriorhynchus
Typhlops brongersmianus
Typhlops caecatus

Typhlops canlaonensis
Typhlops capensis
Typhlops capitulatus
Typhlops cariei
Typhlops castanotus
Typhlops catapontus
Typhlops caymanensis
Typhlops collaris
Typhlops comoroensis
Typhlops congestus
Typhlops conradi
Typhlops costaricensis
Typhlops cuneirostris
Typhlops decorosus
Typhlops decorsei
Typhlops depressiceps
Typhlops diardi
Typhlops disparilis
Typhlops domerguei
Typhlops dominicanus
Typhlops elegans
Typhlops epactius
Typhlops euproctus
Typhlops exiguus
Typhlops filiformis
Typhlops fletcheri
Typhlops floweri
Typhlops fornasinii,
  Fornasini's Blind Snake
Typhlops fredparkeri
Typhlops fuscus
Typhlops giadinhensis
Typhlops gierrai
Typhlops gonavensis
Typhlops grandidieri
Typhlops granti
Typhlops hectus
Typhlops hedraeus
Typhlops hypogius
Typhlops hypomethes
Typhlops hypsobothrius
Typhlops inconspicuus
Typhlops inornatus
Typhlops jamaicensis
Typhlops jerdoni
Typhlops khoratensis
Typhlops klemmeri
Typhlops koekkoeki
Typhlops koshunnesis
Typhlops kraali
Typhlops lankaensis
Typhlops lehneri
Typhlops leucomelas
Typhlops leucostictus
Typhlops limbrickii
Typhlops lineolatus
Typhlops longissimus
Typhlops loveridgei
Typhlops lumbricalis
Typhlops luzonensis
Typhlops mackinnoni
Typhlops madagascariensis
Typhlops malcolmi
Typhlops manilae
Typhlops manni
Typhlops marxi
Typhlops mcdowelli
Typhlops microcephalus
Typhlops microstomus
Typhlops minuisquamus

Typhlops mirus
Typhlops monastus
Typhlops monensis
Typhlops mucronatus
Typhlops muelleri
Typhlops mutilatus
Typhlops oatesi
Typhlops obtusus,
   Slender Blind Snake
Typhlops ocularis
Typhlops oligolepis
Typhlops pammeces
Typhlops paucisquamus
Typhlops platycephalus
Typhlops platyrhynchus
Typhlops porrectus
Typhlops punctatus
Typhlops pusillus
Typhlops reticulatus
Typhlops reuteri
Typhlops richardi
Typhlops rondoensis
Typhlops rostellatus
Typhlops ruber
Typhlops ruficaudus
Typhlops schmidti
Typhlops schmutzi
Typhlops schwartzi
Typhlops siamensis
Typhlops socotranus
Typhlops steinhausi
Typhlops sulcatus
Typhlops syntherus
Typhlops tasymicris
Typhlops tenebrarum
Typhlops tenuicollis
Typhlops tenuis
Typhlops tetrathyreus
Typhlops thurstoni
Typhlops tindalli
Typhlops titanops
Typhlops trangensis
Typhlops trinitatus
Typhlops uluguruensis
Typhlops unilineatus
Typhlops veddae
Typhlops vermicularis,
   European Worm Snake
Typhlops verticalis
Typhlops violaceus
Typhlops wilsoni
Typhlops yonenagae
Typhlops zenkeri

ANOMOCHILIDAE
DWARF PIPE SNAKES

1 GENUS CONTAINING 2 SPECIES

The two species belonging to the genus *Anomochilus* are very rare, very poorly known, and have only recently been placed in their own family. Superficially they are similar to the members of the Cylindropheidae family, with which they were formerly grouped. They are found in Malaysia, Sumatra, and Borneo.

GENUS: **ANOMOCHILUS**
2 SPECIES

SIZE: Small, not more than 1 ft 4 in (40 cm)
DISTRIBUTION: Malaysia, Sumatra, and Borneo.
HABITAT: Subterranean.
FOOD: Unknown.
REPRODUCTION: Unknown.

SPECIES:
   Anomochilus leonardi
   Anomochilus weberi

ANILIIDAE
SOUTH AMERICAN PIPE SNAKE

1 GENUS CONTAINING 1 SPECIES

The South American Pipe Snake is placed in a family on its own, although it was formerly included in Cylindropheidae.

GENUS: **ANILIUS**
1 SPECIES

SIZE: Medium, to a maximum of 3 ft 3 in (1 m), but usually smaller.
DISTRIBUTION: South America (Amazon basin).
HABITAT: Forests and swamps, where it burrows in mud.
FOOD: Snakes and other burrowing reptiles and amphibians.
REPRODUCTION: Live-bearer.
NOTES: A red and black false coral snake.

SPECIES:
   Anilius scytale

CYLINDROPHEIDAE
ASIAN PIPE SNAKES

1 GENUS CONTAINING 9 SPECIES

Asian pipe snakes are small and dark with boldly marked, black and white undersides. The tail is waved in the air if the snake is disturbed. All burrow. They are found in Asia, from Sri Lanka and India, down into the Malay Peninsula, Borneo, and parts of Indonesia.

GENUS: **CYLINDROPHIS**
9 SPECIES

SIZE: Small, to 2 ft 3½ in (70 cm) at most.
DISTRIBUTION: Sri Lanka, India, and Southeast Asia.
HABITAT: Forests, in underground tunnels.
FOOD: Eels, caecilians, and other snakes.
REPRODUCTION: Live-bearers.

SPECIES:
   Cylindrophis aruensis
   Cylindrophis boulengeri
   Cylindrophis engkariensis
   Cylindrophis isolepis
   Cylindrophis lineatus
   Cylindrophis maculatus
   Cylindrophis melanotus
   Cylindrophis opisthorhodus
   Cylindrophis ruffus

UROPELTIDAE
SHIELD-TAILED SNAKES

8 GENERA CONTAINING 46 SPECIES

All individuals are small and cylindrical. Some have a pelvic girdle, but others do not, which means that the family represents an evolutionary stage in snakes' transition from primitive to more advanced characteristics. The left lung is either absent or greatly reduced in size. The snakes spend most of their time beneath the surface, in leaf-litter, soil, or mud, and many species are poorly known. All are thought to eat burrowing invertebrates and other small snakes. The family is restricted to southern India and Sri Lanka.

GENUS: **BRACHYOPHIDIUM**
1 SPECIES

SIZE: Very small.
DISTRIBUTION: Southern India.
HABITAT: Unknown.
FOOD: Thought to be earthworms.
REPRODUCTION: Thought to be a live-bearer.

SPECIES:
   Brachyophidium rhodogaster

GENUS: **MELANOPHIDIUM**
3 SPECIES

SIZE: Medium.
DISTRIBUTION: Southern India.
HABITAT: Montane forests.
FOOD: Thought to be earthworms.
REPRODUCTION: Thought to be live-bearers.

SPECIES:
   Melanophidium bilineatum
   Melanophidium punctatum
   Melanophidium wynaudense

GENUS: **PLATYPLECTRURUS**
2 SPECIES

SIZE: Small.
DISTRIBUTION: Southern India and Sri Lanka, although P. madurensis is known from only one specimen in Sri Lanka.
HABITAT: Montane forests.
FOOD: Thought to be earthworms.
REPRODUCTION: Live-bearers, producing small litters.

SPECIES:
   Platyplectrurus madurensis
   Platyplectrurus trilineatus

GENUS: **PLECTRURUS**
4 SPECIES

SIZE: Small.
DISTRIBUTION: Southern India.
HABITAT: Unknown.
FOOD: Thought to be earthworms.
REPRODUCTION: Thought to be live-bearers.

SPECIES:
   Plectrurus aureus
   Plectrurus canaricus
   Plectrurus guentheri
   Plectrurus perroteti

GENUS: **PSEUDOTYPHLOPS**
1 SPECIES

SIZE: Small, to about 1 ft 8 in (50 cm) .
DISTRIBUTION: Sri Lanka.
HABITAT: Fields, where it lives in humus.
FOOD: Earthworms.
REPRODUCTION: Live-bearer.
NOTES: The specific name was given in error, because the species was thought to come from the Philippines.

SPECIES:
   Pseudotyphlops philippinus

GENUS: **RHINOPHIS**
11 SPECIES

SIZE: Small, to about 1 ft (30 cm) , except for R. oxyrhynchus, which grows to 1 ft 10½ in (57 cm) .
DISTRIBUTION: Southern India and Sri Lanka.
HABITAT: Forests and plantations, where they burrow in soil and leaf-litter. Also under rotting logs and in silted-up drains.
FOOD: Earthworms.
REPRODUCTION: Live-bearers, where known.
NOTES: Some species are rare, known from only a few specimens.

SPECIES:
   Rhinophis blythii
   Rhinophis dorsimaculatus
   Rhinophis drummondhayi
   Rhinophis fergusonianus
   Rhinophis oxyrhynchus
   Rhinophis philippinus
   Rhinophis porrectus
   Rhinophis punctatus
   Rhinophis sanguineus
   Rhinophis travancoricus
   Rhinophis trevelyana

GENUS: **TERETRURUS**
1 SPECIES

SIZE: Small.
DISTRIBUTION: Southern India.
HABITAT: Unknown.
FOOD: Thought to be earthworms.
REPRODUCTION: Thought to be a
live-bearer.
NOTES: Very rare, and poorly known.

SPECIES:
Teretrurus sanguineus

GENUS: **UROPELTIS**
23 SPECIES

SIZE: Small.
DISTRIBUTION: Southern India (20 species)
and Sri Lanka (3 species).
HABITAT: Varied, but all are burrowers.
FOOD: Thought to be earthworms.
REPRODUCTION: Live-bearers.
NOTES: Some species are rare; *U. ruhunae*,
for instance, is known from a single
specimen.

SPECIES:
Uropeltis articeps
Uropeltis beddomii
Uropeltis broughami
Uropeltis ceylanicus
Uropeltis dindigalensis
Uropeltis ellioti
Uropeltis grandis
Uropeltis liura
Uropeltis macrolepis
Uropeltis macrorhynchus
Uropeltis maculatus
Uropeltis melanogaster
Uropeltis myhendrae
Uropeltis nitidus
Uropeltis ocellatus
Uropeltis petersi
Uropeltis phillipsi
Uropeltis pulneyensis
Uropeltis rubrolineatus
Uropeltis rubromaculatus
Uropeltis ruhanae
Uropeltis smithi
Uropeltis woodmasoni

LOXOCEMIDAE
CENTRAL AMERICAN SUNBEAM
SNAKE

1 GENUS CONTAINING 1 SPECIES

A family of one species, from Central
America, formerly thought to be a New
World python.

GENUS: **LOXOCEMUS**
1 SPECIES

SIZE: Medium, growing to just over 3 ft 3
in (1 m), and stocky.
DISTRIBUTION: Central America.
HABITAT: Scrub and deciduous dry forests.
FOOD: Varied, including lizards, small
rodents, and the eggs of lizards (iguanas
in particular).
REPRODUCTION: Egg-layer.

SPECIES:
● *Loxocemus bicolor* (p. 36)

XENOPELTIDAE
ASIAN SUNBEAM SNAKES

1 GENUS CONTAINING 2 SPECIES

This family of two species from the Far
East bears a superficial resemblance to
Loxocemus. Both have a compressed,
spade-shaped head for burrowing, and
smooth, glossy, highly iridescent scales.

GENUS: **XENOPELTIS**
2 SPECIES

SIZE: Medium, to over 3 ft 3 in (1 m), and
cylindrical.
DISTRIBUTION: China and Southeast Asia.
HABITAT: Lightly wooded areas and open
ground, including plantations, gardens,
and parks.
FOOD: Reptiles and small mammals.
REPRODUCTION: Egg layers.
NOTES: *X. hainanensis* was described only
in 1972, and its natural history is poorly
known in comparison to that of the
other species.

SPECIES:
Xenopeltis hainanensis
● *Xenopeltis unicolor*,
Sunbeam Snake, Iridescent Earth
Snake (p. 37)

BOIDAE
BOAS

2 SUBFAMILIES CONTAINING 7 GENERA AND
36 SPECIES

This family, which previously included the
pythons, contains some of the world's
largest snakes, such as the Anaconda and
the Common Boa (*Boa constrictor*). They
are not all large, however, and the smallest
species, the North American Rubber Boa,
rarely grows to more than.1 ft 11½ in
(60 cm) in total length. Boas are
characterized by small scales on the head
and body. The body scales are usually
smooth, but can occasionally be rough, as
in the Rough-scaled Sand Boa, *Eryx
conicus*. All have muscular bodies that are
used to constrict prey. Some species have
heat pits bordering the mouth.

Boas have varied lifestyles, from
burrowing to semiaquatic to arboreal, and
are found in most tropical and
subtropical parts of the world. The
greatest species diversity occurs in the
West Indies, where there are many
species of *Epicrates*, several of them
restricted to one or two small islands.

All boas are live-bearers with one
notable exception - the Calabar Ground
Boa, *Charina reinhardtii*, which lays eggs.
Until recently, it was considered to be a
python and was placed in a separate
genus, *Calabaria*.

There are 36 species (although there is
some controversy about the classification
of the Green Anaconda) divided into two
subfamilies - Boinae and Erycinae. There
is a distinct division between the families,
both in appearance and lifestyle. The
Boinae are found in Central and South
America, New Guinea, South Pacific
islands, and the West Indies, while the
Erycinae are found in North America,
North, West, and East Africa, the Middle
East, and Central and southern Asia.

SUBFAMILY: BOINAE

5 GENERA CONTAINING 23 SPECIES

The members of the Boinae family can
grow to a large size and may have heat
pits between the scales bordering the
jaws. They are found in Central and
South America, the Caribbean region,
the South Pacific region, and Madagascar,
but are absent from Africa and Australia.

GENUS: **BOA**
BOAS
4 SPECIES

SIZE: Medium to very large. The Common
Boa grows to more than 9 ft 10 in (3 m)
in length.
DISTRIBUTION: Central and South
America (*B. constrictor*) and Madagascar.
The Common Boa has one of the
largest latitudinal geographic ranges
of any snake, from Mexico in the
north to Argentina in the south,
and it also occurs on a number of
Caribbean islands.
HABITAT: Varied, from dry desert scrub to
tropical rain forest.
FOOD: Birds and mammals.
REPRODUCTION: Live-bearers.
NOTES: Until recently, the Madagascan
species used to be placed in separate
genera, *Acrantophis* and *Sanzinia*.

SPECIES:
● *Boa constrictor*,
Common Boa (pp. 40–1)
● *Boa dumerili*,
Dumeril's Boa (pp. 48–9)
Boa madagascariensis,
Madagascan Ground Boa
Boa mandrita,
Madagascan Tree Boa

GENUS: **CANDOIA**
PACIFIC BOAS
3 SPECIES

SIZE: Medium to large and stocky.
DISTRIBUTION: New Guinea and
neighboring South Pacific islands.
HABITAT: Forests.
FOOD: Lizards, birds, and mammals.
REPRODUCTION: Live-bearers.
NOTES: Pacific boas are unusual among
boas in having keeled scales. One
species, *C. bibroni*, is long, slender, and
highly arboreal, while the other two are
stockier and live mostly on the ground.
C. aspera, the smallest species, lives in
leaf-litter and is often found
near streams. Its shape and markings
resemble those of vipers; it might be a
mimic of the highly venomous Death
Adder, *Acantophis*, from the same region.

SPECIES:
Candoia aspera,
Viper Boa
Candoia bibroni,
Pacific Tree Boa
Candoia carinata,
Pacific Ground Boa

GENUS: **CORALLUS**
TREE BOAS
4 SPECIES

SIZE: Large, to over 6 ft 6 in (2 m).
DISTRIBUTION: Central and South America.
HABITAT: Forests.
FOOD: Lizards, birds, and mammals.
REPRODUCTION: Live-bearers.
NOTES: *C. cropanii* is sometimes placed
in a separate genus, *Xenoboa*. It is the
world's rarest boa – only three known
specimens have been collected to date,
all from the vicinity of São Paulo, Brazil.

SPECIES:
Corallus annulatus,
Annulated Boa
● *Corallus caninus*,
Emerald Tree Boa (pp. 38–9)
Corallus cropanii,
Cropan's Boa
Corallus hortulanus,
Amazon Tree Boa
or Cook's Tree Boa

GENUS: EPICRATES
10 SPECIES

SIZE: Small to large. *E. angulifer*, for instance, grows to nearly 13 ft 1 in (4 m).

DISTRIBUTION: Central and South America (*E. cenchria*) and the West Indies (other species).

HABITAT: Typically rain forests, but also beaches, rocky places, and plantations.

FOOD: Lizards (small species), birds, and mammals.

REPRODUCTION: Live-bearers.

NOTES: *E. cenchria*, the only species found on the mainland of Central and South America, is divided into a number of distinct forms, or subspecies.

SPECIES:
Epicrates angulifer,
  Cuban Boa
● *Epicrates cenchria*,
  Rainbow Boa (pp. 42–3)
Epicrates chrysogaster,
  Turks Island Boa
Epicrates exsul,
  Abaco Boa
Epicrates fordi,
  Ford's Boa
Epicrates gracilis,
  Vine Boa
Epicrates inornatus,
  Puerto Rican Boa
Epicrates monensis,
  Virgin Islands Boa
Epicrates striatus,
  Haitian Boa
Epicrates subflavus,
  Jamaican Boa

GENUS: EUNECTES
ANACONDAS
2 SPECIES

SIZE: Very large; *E. murinus* is the largest snake in the world.

DISTRIBUTION: South America.

HABITAT: Swamps and flooded forests.

FOOD: Turtles, crocodilians, birds ,and mammals.

REPRODUCTION: Live-bearers.

NOTES: Two additional species, *E. barbouri* and *E. deschauenseei*, have been described from Marajo Island in the mouth of the Amazon, but their validity as separate species is dubious.

SPECIES:
● *Eunectes murinus*,
  Anaconda or Green Anaconda
  (pp. 44–5)
Eunectes notaeus,
  Yellow Anaconda

SUBFAMILY: ERYCINAE
2 GENERA CONTAINING 13 SPECIES

The Erycinae tend to be smaller than members of the Boinaie. They lack heat pits, have stocky, cylindrical bodies, and short tails. They are burrowing or semiburrowing snakes.

GENUS: CHARINA
3 SPECIES

SIZE: Small to medium, with stocky bodies and short tails.

DISTRIBUTION: North America (*C. bottae* and *C. trivirgata*) and West Africa (*C. reinhardtii*)

HABITAT: Pinewoods (*C. bottae*), deserts and coastal scrub (*C. trivirgata*), and tropical forests (*C. reinhardtii*). All species are semiburrowing.

FOOD: Small mammals.

REPRODUCTION: The American species are live-bearers; the African species are egg-layers.

NOTES: Until recently the genus *Charina* comprised a single species: the Rubber Boa, *C. bottae*. However, two other species have been added to the genus: the Rosy Boa, formerly *Lichanura trivirgata*, and the Calabar Ground Boa, formerly *Calabaria reinhardtii*.

SPECIES:
Charina bottae,
  Rubber Boa
● *Charina reinhardtii*,
  Calabar Ground Boa (pp.50–1)
● *Charina trivirgata*,
  Rosy Boa (pp. 46–7)

GENUS: ERYX
SAND BOAS
10 SPECIES

SIZE: Small to medium, with stout, cylindrical bodies.

DISTRIBUTION: North and East Africa, the Middle East, Central and southern Asia. One species, *E. jaculus*, is found just inside Europe, in the Balkan region.

HABITAT: Arid regions, beneath rocks or in burrows.

FOOD: Lizards, small mammals, and ground-nesting birds.

REPRODUCTION: Live-bearers.

NOTES: Three of the species from north-east Africa are poorly known.

SPECIES:
Eryx colubrinus,
  Egyptian Sand Boa or Kenyan Sand Boa
Eryx conicus,
  Rough-scaled Sand Boa
Eryx elegans

Eryx jaculus,
  Turkish Sand Boa or Javelin Sand Boa
Eryx jayakari,
  Arabian Sand Boa
Eryx johnii
Eryx miliaris
Eryx muelleri
Eryx somalicus
Eryx tataricus

PYTHONIDAE
PYTHONS

8 GENERA CONTAINING 26 SPECIES

The python family contains all the "other" giant snakes - those species that are not boas. However, there are also small to medium-sized members in the family, including a few that do not exceed 3 ft 3 in (1 m) in length. Pythons may have large or small scales on the top of their heads, and many species have heat pits along the margins of their jaws, although these are lacking in the two members of the genus *Aspidites*, the Papuan Python, *Apodora papuana*, and the Ringed Python, *Bothrochilus boa* (which is a python, despite its specific name).

Like the boas, pythons have exploited a number of habitats, although there are no highly adapted burrowing species. All the pythons lay eggs which they coil around and guard, or brood, for the duration of their development.

Pythons are found in Australia, Papua New Guinea, Indonesia, Timor, Africa, and southern and Southeast Asia. At present, there are 26 species grouped into 8 genera. This arrangement has been changed many times recently, so it is possible that there will be more changes in the future.

GENUS: ANTARESIA
SOUTHERN PYTHONS
4 SPECIES

SIZE: Small to medium, to about 4 ft 11 in (1.5 m). *A. perthensis*, with a maximum length of 1 ft 11^1/$_2$ in (60 cm), is the smallest python.

DISTRIBUTION: Australia.

HABITAT: Deserts and wooded areas. *A. perthensis* often lives in termite mounds.

FOOD: Lizards and small mammals.

REPRODUCTION: Egg-layers.

NOTES: All four species have heat pits.

SPECIES:
● *Antaresia childreni*,
  Children's Python (p. 60)
● *Antaresia maculosa*,
  Spotted Python (p. 61)

Antaresia perthensis,
  Anthill Python
Antaresia stimsoni,
  Stimson's Python

GENUS: APODORA
1 SPECIES

SIZE: Large, to over 9 ft 10 in (3 m), and heavily built.

DISTRIBUTION: New Guinea.

HABITAT: Lowland forests and grasslands.

FOOD: Mainly mammals up to the size of wallabies, and occasionally other snakes.

REPRODUCTION: Egg-layer.

NOTES: It has no heat pits. Previously placed in the genus *Liasis*.

SPECIES:
Apodora papuana,
  Papuan Olive Python

GENUS: ASPIDITES
2 SPECIES

SIZE: Moderately large, up to about 8 ft 2 in (2.5 m).

DISTRIBUTION: Australia.

HABITAT: Varied, from humid forests to arid deserts.

FOOD: Birds, small mammals, and other reptiles, including venomous snakes.

REPRODUCTION: Egg-layers.

NOTES: They have no heat pits.

SPECIES:
Aspidites melanocephalus, Black-headed Python
Aspidites ramsayi,
  Woma

GENUS: BOTHROCHILUS
1 SPECIES

SIZE: Moderately large, to about 4 ft 11 in (1.5 m), and slender.

DISTRIBUTION: Papua New Guinea

HABITAT: Forests and plantations, where it is secretive and semiburrowing.

FOOD: Lizards and small mammals.

REPRODUCTION: Egg-layer.

NOTES: It has no heat pits. Previously placed in the genus *Liasis*.

SPECIES:
Bothrochilus boa,
  Ringed Python

GENUS: LEIOPYTHON
1 SPECIES

SIZE: Large, to 8 ft 2 in (2.5 m).

DISTRIBUTION: New Guinea and surrounding islands, including Australian territory in the Torres Straits.

HABITAT: Rain forests.

FOOD: Lizards and small mammals.
REPRODUCTION: Egg-layer.
NOTES: It has heat pits. Formerly included in the genus *Liasis*.

SPECIES:
Leiopython albertisii,
 D'Alberti's Python

GENUS: **LIASIS**
3 SPECIES

SIZE: Medium to large.
DISTRIBUTION: Australia, New Guinea, and some Indonesian islands.
HABITAT: Open country, marshes, and forests.
FOOD: Fish, amphibians, lizards, snakes, birds, and mammals.
REPRODUCTION: Egg-layers.
NOTES: All three species have heat pits. *L. fuscus* is sometimes considered to be a variant of *L. mackloti*.

SPECIES:
Liasis fuscus,
 Australian Water Python
Liasis mackloti,
 Macklot's Python or Speckled Python
Liasis olivaceus,
 Olive Python

GENUS: **MORELIA**
7 SPECIES

SIZE: Medium to large; *M. amethistina* may grow to 16 ft 5 in (5 m) or more.
DISTRIBUTION: Australia, New Guinea, and neighboring islands.
HABITAT: Varied, including deserts, grasslands, and forests.
FOOD: Reptiles, birds, and mammals up to the size of wallabies.
REPRODUCTION: Egg-layers.
NOTES: They have prominent heat pits. *M. viridis*, formerly *Chondropython viridis*, is totally arboreal, closely paralleling the South American Emerald Tree Boa in appearance and habits.

SPECIES:
Morelia amethistina,
 Amethystine Python
Morelia boeleni,
 Boelen's Python
Morelia bredli,
 Central Australian Carpet Python or Desert Carpet Python
Morelia carinata,
 Rough-scaled Python
Morelia oenpelliensis,
 Oenpelli Python
● *Morelia spilota*,
 Carpet Python or Diamond Python (pp. 52–3)
● *Morelia viridis*,
 Green Tree Python (pp. 62–3)

GENUS: **PYTHON**
7 SPECIES

SIZE: Medium to huge. Often heavily built.
DISTRIBUTION: Africa, southern and Southeast Asia, and Australasia (Timor).
HABITAT: Varied, from rocky deserts (*P. anchietae*) to rain forests.
FOOD: Almost exclusively warm-blooded prey, mostly mammals. Some are known to have eaten small humans.
REPRODUCTION: Egg-layers.
NOTES: There are no burrowing, aquatic, or highly arboreal species.

SPECIES:
Python anchietae,
 Angolan Python
● *Python curtus*,
 Blood Python or Short-tailed Python (pp. 58–9)
● *Python molurus*,
 Indian Python, Burmese Python, or Asian Rock Python (pp. 54–5)
● *Python regius*,
 Royal Python or Ball Python (pp. 64–5)
● *Python reticulatus*,
 Reticulated Python (pp. 56–7)
Python sebae,
 African Rock Python
Python timoriensis,
 Timor Python

TROPIDOPHEIDAE
WOOD SNAKES

4 GENERA CONTAINING 21 SPECIES

Although members of this family used to be placed within the Boidae, they are now considered to form a separate family. They are small to medium-sized snakes and occur in a variety of colors and patterns. Some species are capable of limited physiological color changes, often becoming paler at night. Their eyes have vertically elliptical pupils. Unlike the boas and pythons, they have a well-developed tracheal lung. Males of all species have pelvic girdles and vestigial legs in the form of small spurs. Females of some species also have pelvic girdles and spurs, but the spurs are smaller than those of the males. Females of other species lack pelvic girdles altogether.

These are secretive snakes, living among leaf-litter and under rocks and logs. They are active at night and feed on a variety of prey, including invertebrates, amphibians, lizards, and small mammals, which they may constrict. Some species are partially arboreal. They give birth to live young after a long gestation period.

They are found in the Caribbean region, and in Central and South America.

GENUS: **EXILIBOA**
1 SPECIES

SIZE: Small.
DISTRIBUTION: Southern Mexico.
HABITAT: Montane cloud forests.
FOOD: Unknown.
REPRODUCTION: Thought to be a live-bearer.
NOTES: Very rare; known from only a handful of specimens.

SPECIES:
Exiliboa placata,
 Oaxaca Boa

GENUS: **TRACHYBOA**
EYELASH BOAS
2 SPECIES

SIZE: Small, to just over 1 ft (30 cm).
DISTRIBUTION: Central and northern South America.
HABITAT: Tropical forests.
FOOD: Thought to be lizards and small mammals.
REPRODUCTION: Live-bearers.
NOTES: Secretive and not well known. Characterized by clusters of scales over each eye.

SPECIES:
Trachyboa boulengeri
Trachyboa gularis

GENUS: **TROPIDOPHIS**
WOOD SNAKES
16 SPECIES

SIZE: Small to medium, with fairly stout bodies.
DISTRIBUTION: West Indies, especially Cuba (13 species), South America (3 species).
HABITAT: Damp places, such as forests, plantations, and parks.
FOOD: Invertebrates, amphibians, lizards, and small mammals.
REPRODUCTION: Live-bearers.

SPECIES:
Tropidophis battersbyi,
 Battersby's Wood Snake
Tropidophis canus,
 Bahamas Wood Snake
Tropidophis caymanensis,
 Cayman Islands Wood Snake
Tropidophis feicki,
 Feick's Wood Snake
Tropidophis fuscus,
 Brown Wood Snake
Tropidophis greenwayi,
 Turks and Caicos Wood Snake
● *Tropidophis haetianus*,
 Haitian Wood Snake (p. 66)
Tropidophis maculatus,
 Spotted Wood Snake
● *Tropidophis melanurus*,
 Cuban Wood Snake (p. 67)

Tropidophis nigriventris
Tropidophis pardalis,
 Leopard Wood Snake
Tropidophis paucisquamis
Tropidophis pilsbryi
Tropidophis semicinctus
Tropidophis taczanowskyi
Tropidophis wrighti,
 Wright's Wood Snake

GENUS: **UNGALIOPHIS**
BANANA BOAS
2 SPECIES

SIZE: Small to medium, to about 1 ft 8 in (50 cm), and slender.
DISTRIBUTION: Central America.
HABITAT: Forests. Partially arboreal.
FOOD: Frogs, lizards, and small mammals.
REPRODUCTION: Live-bearers.
NOTES: They are sometimes accidentally transported in bunches of bananas.

SPECIES:
Ungaliophis continentalis
Ungaliophis panamensis

BOLYERIIDAE
ROUND ISLAND BOAS

2 GENERA CONTAINING 2 SPECIES

This is a small family of only two species, one of which is thought to be extinct. They have no pelvic girdles, and it is this characterization that separates them from the true boas and tropidophids. The left lung is greatly reduced. They are small to medium-sized snakes that probably feed exclusively on lizards. One species lays eggs; reproduction in the other species has not been confirmed.

Confined to the tiny island of Round Island in the Indian Ocean, north of Mauritius, these snakes have suffered greatly from habitat devastation, due largely to the activities of two introduced mammals: goats and rabbits.

GENUS: **BOLYERIA**
1 SPECIES

SIZE: Small.
DISTRIBUTION: Round Island.
HABITAT: Soil-filled, rocky fissures.
FOOD: Thought to be lizards.
REPRODUCTION: Unknown, but thought to have laid eggs.
NOTES: Thought to be extinct; the last specimen was seen in 1975.

SPECIES:
Bolyeria multicarinata,
 Round Island Burrowing Boa

GENUS: CASAREA
1 SPECIES

SIZE: Medium, with a flattened head.
DISTRIBUTION: Round Island.
HABITAT: Rocky places.
FOOD: Thought to be lizards.
REPRODUCTION: Egg-layer.
NOTES: Very rare; its natural history is poorly known.

SPECIES:
Casarea dussumieri,
    Round Island Keel-scaled Boa

ACROCHORDIDAE
WART SNAKES OR FILE SNAKES

1 GENUS CONTAINING 3 SPECIES

Three strange aquatic species comprise this family, which includes some primitive and some advanced characteristics. They have small granular scales and loose skin that hangs in folds around their bodies; out of the water they are effectively helpless. Two out of the three species are dull gray in color, but *A. javanicus* has bold white bands, especially when young. They all catch small fish, eels, and crustaceans, using their rough, granular scales to grasp them between coils.

File snakes are found in Southeast Asia, northern Australia, and Papua New Guinea.

GENUS: ACROCHORDUS
3 SPECIES

SIZE: Medium to large, to 8 ft 2 in (2.5 m) in *A. arafurae*, and very thickset.
DISTRIBUTION: Southeast Asia, northern Australia, and Papua New Guinea.
HABITAT: Aquatic, living in marine and brackish water, and freshwater.
FOOD: Fish and crustaceans.
REPRODUCTION: Live-bearers, only giving birth every eight to ten years.

SPECIES:
Acrochordus arafurae,
    Arafura File Snake or Elephant Trunk Snake
Acrochordus granulatus,
    Little File Snake
Acrochordus javanicus,
    Javan File Snake

COLUBRIDAE
COLUBRIDS

305 GENERA CONTAINING 1,858 SPECIES

The Colubridae is a huge family, containing nearly 2,000 members. These species all share a number of fundamental characteristics: they lack a pelvic girdle, a functional left lung, and a coronoid bone (a small bone in the lower jaw that is present in some of the more primitive snakes). With few exceptions, their heads are covered in large, symmetrical, plate-like scales (like members of the cobra family, but unlike most boas, pythons, and vipers).

Despite these similarities, colubrids are enormously diverse. They range in size from tiny snakes less than 1 ft (30 cm) long to large species measuring up to 9 ft 10 in (3 m) or more. They may be elongated or chunky, and may be colored almost any hue. Colubrids may burrow, swim, or climb, and live in just about every habitat, from freshwater lakes and swamps to the most arid deserts. They eat a huge variety of prey, from small invertebrates up to moderately large mammals. Some species constrict their prey, while others merely grasp it and proceed to swallow. A relatively small number have venom-delivering fangs at the rear of their jaws with which they envenomate and subdue their prey. Most lay eggs, although a sizable proportion, notably those from cooler environments, give birth to live young.

Members of this family are found in nearly every corner of the world, except in the very coldest places and in central and southern Australia. They are most common in warmer regions, with their numbers falling off toward the higher latitudes.

The Colubridae, as currently understood, is not a natural grouping, but contains snakes from a number of evolutionary lines. A number of subfamilies are recognized; some are well defined, but in others, there is considerable debate over the assignment of species. However, until the family is rearranged into smaller units, there is no sensible alternative but to treat colubrids as a single large unit.

GENUS: ACHALINUS
11 SPECIES

SIZE: Small.
DISTRIBUTION: China and Southeast Asia.
HABITAT: Unknown.
FOOD: Thought to eat worms and slugs.
REPRODUCTION: Egg-layers.
NOTES: Poorly known, secretive snakes.

SPECIES:
Achalinus ater
Achalinus braconnieri
Achalinus formosanus
Achalinus hainanus
Achalinus jinggangensis
Achalinus loochoensis
Achalinus meiguensis
Achalinus niger
Achalinus rufescens
Achalinus spinalis
Achalinus werneri

GENUS: ADELOPHIS
2 SPECIES

SIZE: Small.
DISTRIBUTION: Mexico.
HABITAT: Damp places.
FOOD: Earthworms.
REPRODUCTION: Live-bearers.
NOTES: Poorly known.

SPECIES:
Adelophis copei
Adelophis foxi

GENUS: ADELPHICOS
5 SPECIES

SIZE: Small.
DISTRIBUTION: Central America (Guatemala and Chiapas, Mexico).
HABITAT: Pine, oak, and cloud forests, where they are semifossorial (adapted for digging).
FOOD: Earthworms.
REPRODUCTION: Egg-layers.

SPECIES:
Adelphicos daryi
Adelphicos latifasciatus
Adelphicos nigrilatus
Adelphicos quadrivirgatus
Adelphicos veraepacis

GENUS: AELUROGLENA
1 SPECIES

SIZE: Small
DISTRIBUTION: Ethiopia and northern Somalia.
HABITAT: Desert and semidesert.
FOOD: Unknown.
REPRODUCTION: Unknown.
NOTES: Described in 1898 and seldom collected since.

SPECIES:
Aeluroglena cucullata

GENUS: AFRONATRIX
1 SPECIES

SIZE: Medium.
DISTRIBUTION: Africa.
HABITAT: Varied, but always close to water.
FOOD: Frogs and possibly fish.
REPRODUCTION: Thought to be an egg-layer.
NOTES: Poorly known.

SPECIES:
Afronatrix anoscopus

GENUS: AHAETULLA
ASIAN VINE SNAKES OR LONG-NOSED TREE SNAKES
8 SPECIES

SIZE: Long, up to 6 ft 6 in (2 m) , and very slender.
DISTRIBUTION: Sri Lanka, India, China, and Southeast Asia.
HABITAT: Forests, plantations, and cultivated places; completely arboreal.
FOOD: Mainly lizards, but also small mammals and birds.
REPRODUCTION: Live-bearers.
NOTES: Green or brown, with elongated heads and pointed snouts. The eyes have horizontally elliptical pupils, which are useful for judging distance. Rear-fanged, but not particularly dangerous to humans. They were previously placed in the genus *Dryophis*.

SPECIES:
Ahaetulla dispar
Ahaetulla fasciolata
Ahaetulla fronticincta
Ahaetulla mycterizans
Ahaetulla nasuta
Ahaetulla perroteti
Ahaetulla prasina
Ahaetulla pulverulenta

GENUS: ALLUAUDINA
2 SPECIES

SIZE: Small, typically up to 1 ft 4 in (40 cm).
DISTRIBUTION: Madagascar.
HABITAT: Forests.
FOOD: Unknown.
REPRODUCTION: Thought to be egg-layers.
NOTES: Rare and poorly known. *A. mocquardi* is known from only two specimens, both taken in caves at the same locality.

SPECIES:
Alluaudina bellyi
Alluaudina mocquardi

GENUS: ALSOPHIS
13 SPECIES

SIZE: Moderately long, and slender.
DISTRIBUTION: West Indies, South America, and the Galapagos Islands.
HABITAT: Varied.
FOOD: Lizards.
REPRODUCTION: Thought to be egg-layers.

NOTES: Fast-moving snakes, which are active by day. Two species, *A. ater* and *A. sanctaecrucis*, may be extinct; others are on the verge of extinction.

SPECIES:
Alsophis anomalus
Alsophis antiguae
Alsophis antillensis
Alsophis ater
Alsophis biserialis
Alsophis cantherigerus
Alsophis melanichinus
Alsophis occidentalis
Alsophis portoricensis
Alsophis rijersmai
Alsophis rufiventris
Alsophis sanctaecrucis
Alsophis vudii

GENUS: AMASTRIDIUM
1 SPECIES

SIZE: Small, to a maximum of 2 ft 4½ in (72 cm).
DISTRIBUTION: Central America (Mexico to Panama).
HABITAT: Forests, where it is terrestrial.
FOOD: Thought to be frogs.
REPRODUCTION: Unknown.

SPECIES:
Amastridium veliferum

GENUS: AMBLYODIPSAS
9 SPECIES

SIZE: Small, with cylindrical bodies.
DISTRIBUTION: Africa south of the Sahara.
HABITAT: Dry, sandy soil, where it burrows.
FOOD: Other burrowing reptiles, amphibians, and small mammals.
REPRODUCTION: Mostly egg-layers, but *A. concolor* may be a live-bearer.
NOTES: They have a pair of grooved, venom-delivering fangs below the eyes.

SPECIES:
Amblyodipsas concolor
Amblyodipsas dimidiata
Amblyodipsas katangensis
Amblyodipsas microphthalma
Amblyodipsas polylepis
Amblyodipsas rodhaini
Amblyodipsas teitana
Amblyodipsas unicolor
Amblyodipsas ventrimaculata

GENUS: AMPHIESMA
43 SPECIES

SIZE: Small.
DISTRIBUTION: Southeast Asia, India, Sri Lanka, China, and Japan.
HABITAT: Swamps, marshes, lakes, and slow-moving rivers as well as damp forests. Some species are semiaquatic.
FOOD: Amphibians and fish.
REPRODUCTION: Egg-layers.

SPECIES:
Amphiesma atemporalis
Amphiesma beddomei
Amphiesma bitaeniata
Amphiesma boulengeri
Amphiesma celebica
Amphiesma concelarum
Amphiesma craspedogaster
Amphiesma deschauenseei
Amphiesma elongata
Amphiesma flavifrons
Amphiesma frenata
Amphiesma groundwateri
Amphiesma inas
Amphiesma ishigakiense
Amphiesma johannis
Amphiesma khasiensis
Amphiesma metusia
Amphiesma miyajimae
Amphiesma modesta
Amphiesma montana
Amphiesma monticola
Amphiesma nicobarensis
Amphiesma novaeguineae
Amphiesma octolineata
Amphiesma optata
Amphiesma parallela
Amphiesma pealii
Amphiesma petersii
Amphiesma platyceps
Amphiesma popei
Amphiesma pryeri
Amphiesma punctiventris
Amphiesma sanguinea
Amphiesma sarasinora
Amphiesma sarawacensis
Amphiesma sauteri
Amphiesma sieboldii
Amphiesma stolata
Amphiesma truncata
Amphiesma venningi
Amphiesma vibakari
Amphiesma viperina
Amphiesma xenura

GENUS: AMPHIESMOIDES
1 SPECIES

SIZE: Small.
DISTRIBUTION: China.
HABITAT: Semiaquatic.
FOOD: Unknown.
REPRODUCTION: Unknown.
NOTES: Rare and poorly known.

SPECIES:
Amphiesmoides ornaticeps

GENUS: AMPLORHINUS
1 SPECIES

SIZE: Small.
DISTRIBUTION: Southern Africa.
HABITAT: Damp places.
FOOD: Frogs and lizards.
REPRODUCTION: Live-bearer.
NOTES: Rear-fanged, though not dangerous to humans.

SPECIES:
Amplorhinus multimaculatus

GENUS: ANOPLOHYDRUS
1 SPECIES

SIZE: Small, 1 ft 5 in (43 cm).
DISTRIBUTION: Sumatra.
HABITAT: Wet forests. Thought to be semiaquatic.
FOOD: Unknown.
REPRODUCTION: Unknown.
NOTES: Known from only a single specimen described in 1909.
SPECIES:
Anoplohydrus aemulans

GENUS: ANTILLOPHIS
2 SPECIES

SIZE: Medium and slender.
DISTRIBUTION: Cuba, Haiti, and neighboring islands.
HABITAT: Lightly forested and open places.
FOOD: Lizards.
REPRODUCTION: Egg-layers.
NOTES: Diurnal.

SPECIES:
Antillophis andreai
Antillophis parvifrons

GENUS: APLOPELTURA
1 SPECIES

SIZE: Medium.
DISTRIBUTION: Southeast Asia.
HABITAT: Rain forests, in vegetation and on the ground.
FOOD: Snails.
REPRODUCTION: Thought to be an egg-layer.
NOTES: It is very elongated, with a square head and mottled brown and black markings. Closely parallels the *Dipsas* species from Central and South America.

SPECIES:
Aplopeltura boa

GENUS: APOSTOLEPIS
21 SPECIES

SIZE: Small.
DISTRIBUTION: South America.
HABITAT: Forests, where they spend most of their time underground.
FOOD: Invertebrates, small frogs, and lizards.
REPRODUCTION: Unknown.

SPECIES:
Apostolepis ambiniger
Apostolepis assimilis
Apostolepis barrioi
Apostolepis cearensis
Apostolepis coronata
Apostolepis dorbignyi
Apostolepis erythronata
Apostolepis flavotorquata
Apostolepis goiasensis
Apostolepis intermedia
Apostolepis longicaudata
Apostolepis niceforoi
Apostolepis nigroterminata
Apostolepis polylepis
Apostolepis pymi
Apostolepis quinquelineata
Apostolepis rondoni
Apostolepis tenuis
Apostolepis ventrimaculata
Apostolepis villaricae
Apostolepis vittata

GENUS: ARGYROGENA
1 SPECIES

SIZE: Medium and slender.
DISTRIBUTION: India.
HABITAT: Open countryside.
FOOD: Mainly lizards.
REPRODUCTION: Thought to be an egg-layer.
FOOD: Diurnal and fast-moving.

SPECIES:
Argyrogena fasciolata

GENUS: ARIZONA
1 SPECIES

SIZE: Moderately large.
DISTRIBUTION: North America.
HABITAT: Deserts and dry places.
FOOD: Lizards, other snakes, and small mammals.
REPRODUCTION: Egg-layer, producing 20 or more eggs.

SPECIES:
Arizona elegans,
Glossy Snake

GENUS: ARRHYTON
12 SPECIES

SIZE: Small.
DISTRIBUTION: West Indies and Cuba.
HABITAT: Varied.
FOOD: Amphibians and their eggs, and lizards.
REPRODUCTION: Thought to be egg-layers.
NOTES: Rear-fanged, though not dangerous to humans. Otherwise poorly known.

SPECIES:
Arrhyton ainictum
Arrhyton callilaemum

Arrhyton dolichura
Arrhyton exiguum
Arrhyton funereum
Arrhyton landoi
Arrhyton polylepis
Arrhyton procerum
Arrhyton supernum
Arrhyton taeniatum
Arrhyton tanyplectum
Arrhyton vittatum

GENUS: ASPIDURA
6 SPECIES

SIZE: Small.
DISTRIBUTION: Sri Lanka.
HABITAT: Forests, among leaf-litter.
FOOD: Mostly earthworms.
REPRODUCTION: Egg-layers.
NOTES: Nocturnal.

SPECIES:
Aspidura brachyorrhos
Aspidura copii
Aspidura deraniyagalae
Aspidura drummondhayi
Aspidura guentheri
Aspidura trachyprocta

GENUS: ATRACTUS
89 SPECIES

SIZE: Very small.
DISTRIBUTION: Central and South America.
HABITAT: Rain forests, among leaf-litter.
FOOD: Mainly invertebrates.
REPRODUCTION: Egg-layers.
NOTES: Most species are dark, and some have a brighter collar marking. Some species are known from only one or two specimens and have very localized distributions; others are only recently described.

SPECIES:
Atractus albuquerquei
Atractus alphonsehogei
Atractus andinus
Atractus arrangoi
Atractus badius
Atractus balzani
Atractus biseriatus
Atractus bocki
Atractus bocourti
Atractus boettgeri
Atractus boulengerii
Atractus canedii
Atractus carrioni
Atractus clarki
Atractus collaris
Atractus crassicaudatus
Atractus duidensis
Atractus dunni
Atractus ecuadorensis
Atractus elaps
Atractus emigdioi
Atractus emmeli
Atractus erythromelas

Atractus favae
Atractus flammigerus
Atractus fuliginosus
Atractus gaigeae
Atractus guentheri
Atractus indistinctus
Atractus insipidus
Atractus iridescens
Atractus lancinii
Atractus lasallei
Atractus latifrons
Atractus lehmanni
Atractus limitaneus
Atractus loveridgei
Atractus maculatus
Atractus major
Atractus manizalesensis
Atractus mariselae
Atractus melanogaster
Atractus melas
Atractus micheli
Atractus microrhynchus
Atractus modestus
Atractus multicinctus
Atractus nicefori
Atractus nigricaudus
Atractus nigriventris
Atractus obesus
Atractus obtusirostris
Atractus occidentalis
Atractus occipitoalbus
Atractus oculotemporalis
Atractus pamplonensis
Atractus pantostictus
Atractus paravertebralis
Atractus paucidens
Atractus pauciscutatus
Atractus peruvianus
Atractus poeppigi
Atractus potschi
Atractus punctiventris
Atractus resplendens
Atractus reticulatus
Atractus riveroi
Atractus roulei
Atractus sanctaemartae
Atractus sanguineus
Atractus schach
Atractus serranus
Atractus snethlageae
Atractus steyermarki
Atractus subbicinctum
Atractus taeniatus
Atractus torquatus
Atractus trihedrurus
Atractus trilineatus
Atractus trivittatus
Atractus univittatus
Atractus variegatus
Atractus ventrimaculatus
Atractus vertebralis
Atractus vertebrolineatus
Atractus vittatus
Atractus wagleri
Atractus werneri
Atractus zidoki

GENUS: ATRETIUM
2 SPECIES

SIZE: Small to medium.
DISTRIBUTION: India and Sri Lanka (*A. schistosum*) and China (*A. yunnanensis*).
HABITAT: Wet and damp places, where they are aquatic or semiaquatic.
FOOD: Fish and frogs.
REPRODUCTION: Thought to be egg-layers.
NOTES: The Chinese species is rare and hardly known.

SPECIES:
Atretium schistosum
Atretium yunnanensis

GENUS: BALANOPHIS
1 SPECIES

SIZE: Small
DISTRIBUTION: Sri Lanka.
HABITAT: Forests, where it lives among leaf-litter.
FOOD: Frogs.
REPRODUCTION: Egg-layer.

SPECIES:
Balanophis ceylonensis

GENUS: BITIA
1 SPECIES

SIZE: Small DISTRIBUTION: Myanmar, Thailand, and the Malay Peninsula.
HABITAT: Estuaries and river mouths.
FOOD: Fish.
REPRODUCTION: Live-bearer.
NOTES: The narrow head and compressed tail help the snake to swim.

SPECIES:
Bitia hydroides

GENUS: BLYTHIA
1 SPECIES

SIZE: Small.
DISTRIBUTION: Northern India, Myanmar, Tibet, and southern China.
HABITAT: Unknown, but thought to burrow.
FOOD: Unknown.
REPRODUCTION: Unknown.

SPECIES:
Blythia reticulata

GENUS: BOGERTOPHIS
RATSNAKES
2 SPECIES

SIZE: Medium to large.
DISTRIBUTION: North America (southern US and northern Mexico).

HABITAT: Rocky deserts, in gulleys, gorges, and relatively humid microhabitats.
FOOD: Mainly small mammals.
REPRODUCTION: Egg-layers, producing up to 20 eggs.
NOTES: Powerful, constricting species with large eyes and heavily keeled scales. Active mostly at night. Formerly placed in the genus *Elaphe*.

SPECIES:
Bogertophis rosaliae
● *Bogertophis subocularis*, Trans-Pecos Ratsnake (pp. 76–7)

GENUS: BOIGA
30 SPECIES

SIZE: Moderately large.
DISTRIBUTION: Africa, southern Asia, Southeast Asia, the Philippines, the Indonesian archipelago, and northern Australia.
HABITAT: Varied, including forests, lightly wooded places, and mangrove forests. All species are highly arboreal.
FOOD: Mainly arboreal lizards and mammals, including bats.
REPRODUCTION: Egg-layers.
NOTES: Rear-fanged, but unlikely to pose a serious threat to humans. One species, the Brown Tree Snake, *Boiga irregularis*, has been accidentally introduced to several islands, notably Guam, where it has become a menace through its depredations of native birdlife and domestic animals.

SPECIES:
Boiga andamanensis
Boiga angulata
Boiga barnesi
Boiga beddomei
Boiga blandingii
Boiga ceylonensis
● *Boiga cyanea*, Green-eyed Cat Snake (p. 109)
Boiga cynodon, Dog-toothed Cat Snake
● *Boiga dendrophila*, Mangrove Snake (p. 108)
Boiga dightoni
Boiga drapiezii, White-spotted Cat Snake
Boiga flavescens
Boiga forsteni
Boiga gokool
Boiga hexogonata
Boiga irregularis, Brown Tree Snake
Boiga jaspidea
Boiga kraepelini
Boiga multifasciata
Boiga multitemporalis
Boiga multomaculata
Boiga nigriceps
Boiga nuchalis
Boiga ocellata
Boiga ochracea

Boiga philippina
Boiga pulverulenta
Boiga quincunciata
Boiga saengsomi
Boiga trigonata

GENUS: BOTHROLYCUS
1 SPECIES

SIZE: Small
DISTRIBUTION: Central Africa.
HABITAT: Unknown.
FOOD: Unknown.
REPRODUCTION: Unknown.

SPECIES:
Bothrolycus ater

GENUS: BOTHROPHTHALMUS
1 SPECIES

SIZE: Small
DISTRIBUTION: Central and West Africa.
HABITAT: Moist montane forests.
FOOD: Unknown.
REPRODUCTION: Unknown.

SPECIES:
Bothrophthalmus lineatus

GENUS: BRACHYOPHIS
1 SPECIES

SIZE: Small.
DISTRIBUTION: Kenya and Somalia.
HABITAT: Unknown.
FOOD: Unknown.
REPRODUCTION: Unknown.
NOTES: Poorly known. Its relationships with other colubrids are unclear.

SPECIES:
Brachyophis revoili

GENUS: BRACHYORRHUS
1 SPECIES

SIZE: Small.
DISTRIBUTION: The Indonesian archipelago.
HABITAT: Unknown.
FOOD: Unknown.
REPRODUCTION: Unknown.

SPECIES:
Brachyorrhus albus

GENUS: BRYGOPHIS
1 SPECIES

SIZE: Large.
DISTRIBUTION: Madagascar.
HABITAT: Unknown.
FOOD: Essentially unknown.
REPRODUCTION: Unknown.

NOTES: Known from only a single specimen, which was reddish brown with white spots. It had previously eaten a large chameleon.

SPECIES:
Brygophis coulangesi

GENUS: BUHOMA
2 SPECIES

SIZE: Medium.
DISTRIBUTION: Madagascar.
HABITAT: Forests.
FOOD: Unknown.
REPRODUCTION: Unknown.
NOTES: Formerly placed in the genus *Geodipsas*.

SPECIES:
Buhoma boulengeri
Buhoma infralineatus

GENUS: CALAMARIA
REED SNAKES AND WORM SNAKES
56 SPECIES

SIZE: Small.
DISTRIBUTION: India, Myanmar, southern and southwestern China, Southeast Asia, and the Indonesian archipelago.
HABITAT: Forests and damp places, where they live underground in burrows.
FOOD: Earthworms and other soft-bodied invertebrates.
REPRODUCTION: Egg-layers.

SPECIES:
Calamaria abstrusa
Calamaria acutirostris
Calamaria albiventer
Calamaria alidae
Calamaria apraeocularis
Calamaria baluensis
Calamaria battersbyi
Calamaria bicolor
Calamaria bitorques
Calamaria boesemani
Calamaria borneensis
Calamaria brachyura
Calamaria brongersmai
Calamaria buchi
Calamaria ceramensis
Calamaria crassa
Calamaria curta
Calamaria doederleini
Calamaria eiselti
Calamaria everetti
Calamaria forcarti
Calamaria gervaisii
Calamaria grabowskyi
Calamaria gracillima
Calamaria griswoldi
Calamaria hilleniusi
Calamaria javanica
Calamaria joloensis
Calamaria lateralis
Calamaria lautensis

Calamaria leucogaster
Calamaria linnaei
Calamaria lowi
Calamaria lumbricoidea
Calamaria lumholtzi
Calamaria margaritophora
Calamaria mecheli
Calamaria melanota
Calamaria modesta
Calamaria muelleri
Calamaria nuchalis
Calamaria palavanensis
Calamaria pavimentata
Calamaria pendleburyi
Calamaria pfefferi
Calamaria prakkei
Calamaria rebentischi
Calamaria schlegeli
Calamaria schmidti
Calamaria septentrionalis
Calamaria suluensis
Calamaria sumatrana
Calamaria ulmeri
Calamaria vermiformis
Calamaria virgulata
Calamaria yunnanensis

GENUS: CALAMODONTOPHIS
1 SPECIES

SIZE: Small.
DISTRIBUTION: Southern Brazil.
HABITAT: Unknown.
FOOD: Unknown.
REPRODUCTION: Unknown.
NOTES: Rear-fanged, but otherwise poorly known.

SPECIES:
Calamodontophis paucidens

GENUS: CALAMORHABDIUM
2 SPECIES

SIZE: Very small.
DISTRIBUTION: The Celebes (Sulawesi and Bacan).
HABITAT: Unknown.
FOOD: Unknown.
REPRODUCTION: Unknown.
NOTES: A third, unnamed species is known from a single specimen. It was taken from the stomach of a snake belonging to the cobra family (*Maticora bivirgata*) on the Indonesian island of Sumatra in 1940.

SPECIES:
Calamorhabdium acuticeps
Calamorhabdium kuekenthali

GENUS: CANTORIA
2 SPECIES

SIZE: Small.
DISTRIBUTION: The coasts of India, the Malay peninsula, Indonesia and the Andaman Islands (*C. violacea*), and Prins Hendrick Island, New Guinea (*C. annulata*).
HABITAT: Coastal waters and estuaries. Semiaquatic.
FOOD: Mainly fish.
REPRODUCTION: Live-bearers.

SPECIES:
Cantoria annulata
Cantoria violacea

GENUS: CARPHOPHIS
WORM SNAKES
2 SPECIES

SIZE: Very small.
DISTRIBUTION: Eastern North America.
HABITAT: Damp places, where they are found under debris.
FOOD: Mainly earthworms and other soft-bodied invertebrates.
REPRODUCTION: Egg-layers.
NOTES: They are black or dark brown above, pink below. *C. vermis* is sometimes considered a subspecies of *C. amoenus*.

SPECIES:
Carphophis amoenus
Carphophis vermis,
  Worm Snake

GENUS: CEMOPHORA
1 SPECIES

SIZE: Small.
DISTRIBUTION: Southeastern North America.
HABITAT: Burrowing in the ground and hiding under bark.
FOOD: Smaller snakes and lizards.
REPRODUCTION: Egg-layer, producing up to six elongated eggs.
NOTES: Brightly colored red, black, and white.

SPECIES:
Cemophora coccinea,
  Scarlet Snake

GENUS: CERBERUS
2 SPECIES

SIZE: Medium.
DISTRIBUTION: Southeast Asia, the Indonesian archipelago, New Guinea, and tropical Australia.
HABITAT: Estuaries, mangrove swamps, and mud flats, where they are totally aquatic.
FOOD: Fish and marine crustaceans.

REPRODUCTION: Live-bearers.
NOTES: Rear-fanged, but not considered dangerous to humans.

SPECIES:
Cerberus microlepis
Cerberus rynchops,
Bockadam

GENUS: CERCASPIS
1 SPECIES

SIZE: Medium and slender.
DISTRIBUTION: Sri Lanka.
HABITAT: Moist places, where it is terrestrial.
FOOD: Lizards and snakes.
REPRODUCTION: Egg-layer.
NOTES: The bold black and white bands mimic those of the highly venomous krait, *Bungarus ceylonicus*, from the same region. Nocturnal.

SPECIES:
Cercaspis carinatus,
Sri Lankan Wolf Snake

GENUS: CERCOPHIS
1 SPECIES

SIZE: Medium.
DISTRIBUTION: Southeast Asia.
HABITAT: Forests, where it is highly arboreal.
FOOD: Mainly lizards.
REPRODUCTION: Egg-layer.

SPECIES:
Cercophis auratus

GENUS: CHAMAELYCUS
2 SPECIES

SIZE: Small.
DISTRIBUTION: West Africa.
HABITAT: Forests, where they live in burrows.
FOOD: Unknown.
REPRODUCTION: Unknown.

SPECIES:
Chamaelycus christyi
Chamaelycus fasciatus

GENUS: CHERSODROMUS
2 SPECIES

SIZE: Small.
DISTRIBUTION: Mexico.
HABITAT: Unknown.
FOOD: Unknown.
REPRODUCTION: Unknown.

SPECIES:
Chersodromus liebmanni
Chersodromus rubriventris

GENUS: CHILOMENISCUS
SAND SNAKES
4 SPECIES

SIZE: Small.
DISTRIBUTION: The Sonoran Desert of southwestern North America, and on islands in the Gulf of California (*C. punctatissimus* and *C. savagei*).
HABITAT: Dry, sandy places.
FOOD: Invertebrates, including scorpions.
REPRODUCTION: Egg-layers.
NOTES: The flattened heads and smooth, shiny scales are adaptations for "sand swimming."

SPECIES:
Chilomeniscus cinctus,
Banded Sand Snake
Chilomeniscus punctatissimus
Chilomeniscus savagei
Chilomeniscus stramineus

GENUS: CHIONACTIS
SHOVEL-NOSED SNAKES
2 SPECIES

SIZE: Small.
DISTRIBUTION: Southwestern North America.
HABITAT: Gravelly or sandy deserts, where they "swim" through the sand just below the surface.
FOOD: Invertebrates and insect larvae.
REPRODUCTION: Egg-layers, producing one to three small, elongated eggs.
NOTES: Brightly colored false coral snakes with flattened heads and smooth, shiny scales. A third species, *C. saxatilis*, appears to have been wrongly described.

SPECIES:
Chionactis occipitalis,
Shovel-nosed Snake
Chionactis palarostris,
Organ Pipe Shovel-nosed Snake

GENUS: CHIRONIUS
24 SPECIES

SIZE: Small to medium, and slender.
DISTRIBUTION: Central and northern South America.
HABITAT: In forests and lightly wooded areas, where they live on the ground and in low vegetation.
FOOD: Lizards, birds, and small rodents.
REPRODUCTION: Egg-layers.

SPECIES:
Chironius barrioi
Chironius bicarinatus
Chironius carinatus
Chironius cinnamomeus
Chironius cochranae
Chironius exoletus
Chironius flavolineatus
Chironius flavopictus
Chironius foveatus
Chironius fuscus
Chironius grandisquamis
Chironius holochlorus
Chironius laevicollis
Chironius laurenti
Chironius melas
Chironius monticola
Chironius multiventris
Chironius pyrrhopogon
Chironius quadricarinatus
Chironius schlueteri
Chironius scurrulus
Chironius spixii
Chironius vicinus
Chironius vincenti

GENUS: CHRYSOPELEA
FLYING SNAKES OR TREE SNAKES
5 SPECIES

SIZE: Moderately large snakes with slender bodies.
DISTRIBUTION: India, Sri Lanka, Myanmar, Malaysia, southern China, the Indonesian archipelago, and the Philippines.
HABITAT: Forests and plantations, where they are arboreal.
FOOD: Arboreal lizards, frogs, and mammals.
REPRODUCTION: Egg-layers.
NOTES: They can flatten their undersurfaces to create a highly wind-resistant shape, enabling them to glide from treetops. Rear-fanged, but not considered particularly dangerous to humans.

SPECIES:
Chrysopelea ornata
Chrysopelea paradisi,
Paradise Tree Snake
Chrysopelea pelias
Chrysopelea rhodopleuron
Chrysopelea taprobanica

GENUS: CLELIA
MUSSURANAS
9 SPECIES

SIZE: Large.
DISTRIBUTION: Central and South America.
HABITAT: Forests.
FOOD: Other snakes, including venomous ones, and mammals, which they constrict.
REPRODUCTION: Egg-layers.
NOTES: Active mainly at night.

SPECIES:
Clelia bicolor
Clelia clelia
Clelia equatoriana
Clelia errabunda
Clelia montana
Clelia occipitolutea
Clelia quimi
Clelia rustica
Clelia scytalina

GENUS: CLONOPHIS
1 SPECIES

SIZE: Small to about 1 ft 11½ in (60 cm).
DISTRIBUTION: North America.
HABITAT: Damp places, including swamps.
FOOD: Earthworms and slugs.
REPRODUCTION: Live-bearer.

SPECIES:
Clonophis kirtlandii,
Kirtland's Water Snake

GENUS: COLLORHABDIUM
1 SPECIES

SIZE: Small.
DISTRIBUTION: The Cameron Highlands, Malaysia.
HABITAT: Montane forest.
FOOD: Unknown.
REPRODUCTION: Unknown.
NOTES: A secretive snake that has been found only on a few occasions.

SPECIES:
Collorhabdium williamsoni

GENUS: COLUBER
WHIP-SNAKES AND RACERS
29 SPECIES

SIZE: Medium to large, mostly slender.
DISTRIBUTION: North America (*C. constrictor*), Europe, North Africa, West Africa, the Middle East, Central Asia, and Indochina.
HABITAT: Varied.
FOOD: Lizards and small mammals. They hunt mainly on the ground, but will sometimes climb into low vegetation in pursuit of prey.
REPRODUCTION: Egg-layers.
NOTES: They defend themselves vigorously by biting, although they are harmless to humans. Diurnal. The genus will probably be divided into several smaller ones at a later date (see *Eremiophis*, for instance).

SPECIES:
Coluber algirus
Coluber brevis
Coluber caspius,
Caspian Whip-snake
Coluber constrictor,
Racer
Coluber cypriensis
Coluber dorri
Coluber elegantissimus
Coluber florulentus
Coluber gemonensis,
Balkan Whip-snake
Coluber hippocrepis,
Horseshoe Snake
Coluber insulanus
Coluber jugularis
Coluber manseri

Coluber messanai
Coluber mormon
Coluber najadum
Coluber nummifer
Coluber rogersi
Coluber rubriceps
Coluber schmidti
Coluber sinai
Coluber smithi
Coluber socotrae
Coluber spinalis
Coluber thomasi
Coluber variabilis
Coluber ventromaculatus
Coluber venzmeri
Coluber viridiflavus,
   Dark Green Snake

GENUS: **COMPSOPHIS**
1 SPECIES

SIZE: Small.
DISTRIBUTION: Madagascar.
HABITAT: Unknown.
FOOD: Unknown.
REPRODUCTION: Unknown.
NOTES: Known from only a single juvenile specimen that was brown with a dark stripe along its back. Nothing is known about its natural history, and all attempts to find additional specimens have so far failed.

SPECIES:
Compsophis albiventris

GENUS: **CONIOPHANES**
13 SPECIES

SIZE: Small
DISTRIBUTION: North, Central, and South America (southern Texas to Peru).
HABITAT: Varied. They live on the ground.
FOOD: Invertebrates, frogs, and lizards.
REPRODUCTION: Egg-layers.
NOTES: Rear-fanged, although not normally considered dangerous to humans. The fragile tails, which are easily broken, have been found in the stomachs of coral snakes.

SPECIES:
Coniophanes alvarezi
Coniophanes andresensis
Coniophanes bipunctatus
Coniophanes dromiciformis
Coniophanes fissidens
Coniophanes flangivirgatus
Coniophanes imperialis
Coniophanes joanae
Coniophanes lateritius
Coniophanes meridanus
Coniophanes piceivittis
Coniophanes quinquevittatus
Coniophanes schmidti

GENUS: **CONOPHIS**
ROAD GUARDERS
5 SPECIES

SIZE: Moderately large, to about 3 ft 3 in (1 m) in length.
DISTRIBUTION: Central America.
HABITAT: Dry forests and clearings, including beaches.
FOOD: They chase and eat lizards and snakes. They also eat frogs, toads, and small mammals.
REPRODUCTION: Egg-layers.
NOTES: They have enlarged rear fangs and potent venom. The bites can be painful to humans and may cause localized swelling. They are active, diurnal species.

SPECIES:
Conophis biserialis
Conophis lineatus
Conophis nasus
Conophis pulcher
Conophis vittatus

GENUS: **CONTIA**
1 SPECIES

SIZE: Small, to about 1 ft 6 in (45 cm).
DISTRIBUTION: Western North America.
HABITAT: Open woodland and grassy places, usually near water.
FOOD: Slugs.
REPRODUCTION: Egg-layer.

SPECIES:
Contia tenuis,
   Sharp-tailed Snake

GENUS: **CORONELLA**
SMOOTH SNAKES
2 SPECIES

SIZE: Small.
DISTRIBUTION: Europe and North Africa (*C. girondica* only).
HABITAT: Varied; dry to damp places, from mountains to sea level.
FOOD: Mainly lizards, but also nestling rodents.
REPRODUCTION: *C. austriaca* is a live-bearer; the other species is an egg-layer.

SPECIES:
Coronella austriaca,
   Smooth Snake
Coronella girondica,
   Southern Smooth Snake

GENUS: **CRISANTOPHIS**
1 SPECIES

SIZE: Medium and slender.
DISTRIBUTION: Mexico.
HABITAT: Dry forests.

FOOD: Unknown.
REPRODUCTION: Thought to be an egg-layer.

SPECIES:
Crisantophis nevermanni

GENUS: **CROTAPHOPELTIS**
5 SPECIES

SIZE: Medium.
DISTRIBUTION: The southern half of Africa.
HABITAT: Damp, marshy places.
FOOD: Frogs and toads.
REPRODUCTION: Egg-layers.
NOTES: They have fangs toward the back of their mouths, but are not considered dangerous to humans.

SPECIES:
Crotaphopeltis acarina
Crotaphopeltis barotseensis,
   Barotse Water Snake
Crotaphopeltis degeni
Crotaphopeltis hotamboeia,
   Herald Snake or Red-lipped Snake
Crotaphopeltis tornieri

GENUS: **CRYOPHIS**
1 SPECIES

SIZE: Medium.
DISTRIBUTION: Mexico.
HABITAT: Unknown.
FOOD: Unknown.
REPRODUCTION: Unknown.
NOTES: Rare and poorly known.

SPECIES:
Cryophis hallbergi

GENUS: **CRYPTOLYCUS**
1 SPECIES

SIZE: Small.
DISTRIBUTION: Mozambique.
HABITAT: Unknown.
FOOD: Amphisbaenians (worm lizards).
REPRODUCTION: Egg-layer.

SPECIES:
Cryptolycus nanus,
   Dwarf Wolf Snake

GENUS: **CYCLOCORUS**
2 SPECIES

SIZE: Small.
DISTRIBUTION: Philippines.
HABITAT: Under rotting logs and vegetation.
FOOD: Thought to eat other snakes.
REPRODUCTION: Unknown.
NOTES: Rare and poorly known.

SPECIES:
Cyclocorus lineatus
Cyclocorus nuchalis

GENUS: **CYCLOPHIOPS**
3 SPECIES

SIZE: Medium and slender.
DISTRIBUTION: Indochina.
HABITAT: Unknown.
FOOD: Thought to feed mostly on invertebrates.
REPRODUCTION: Egg-layers.

SPECIES:
Cyclophiops doriae
Cyclophiops major
Cyclophiops multicinctus

GENUS: **DARLINGTONIA**
1 SPECIES

SIZE: Small.
DISTRIBUTION: Haiti.
HABITAT: Unknown.
FOOD: Small frogs.
REPRODUCTION: Unknown.

SPECIES:
Darlingtonia haetiana

GENUS: **DASYPELTIS**
EGG-EATING SNAKES
6 SPECIES

SIZE: Medium, to about 3 ft 3 in (1 m).
DISTRIBUTION: Central and southern Africa.
HABITAT: Varied, from arid semideserts to forests.
FOOD: Birds' eggs, which they engulf whole, then crush in their throats.
REPRODUCTION: Egg-layers.
NOTES: They often mimic the appearance and behavior of venomous adders from the same region. They have several adaptations in connection with their specialized diet.

SPECIES:
Dasypeltis atra
Dasypeltis fasciata
Dasypeltis inornata,
   Southern Brown Egg-eater
Dasypeltis medici,
   East African Egg-eater
Dasypeltis palmarum
● *Dasypeltis scabra*,
   Common Egg-eater or
   Rhombic Egg-eater (pp. 70–1)

GENUS: **DENDRELAPHIS**
19 SPECIES

SIZE: Medium to large, with slender bodies.
DISTRIBUTION: India, Sri Lanka, Myanmar, southern China, Indochina, Southeast Asia, the Indonesian archipelago, and northern Australia.

HABITAT: Forests, where they are highly arboreal, although they also enter water.
FOOD: Mainly lizards and amphibians, but also fish.
REPRODUCTION: Egg-layers.

SPECIES:
Dendrelaphis bifrenalis
Dendrelaphis calligastra,
　Northern Tree Snake
Dendrelaphis caudolineatus
Dendrelaphis cyanochloris
Dendrelaphis formosus
Dendrelaphis gastrostictus
Dendrelaphis gorei
Dendrelaphis grandoculis
Dendrelaphis humayuni
Dendrelaphis lorentzi
Dendrelaphis meeki
Dendrelaphis oliveri
Dendrelaphis papuensis
Dendrelaphis pictus
Dendrelaphis punctulata,
　Common Tree Snake
Dendrelaphis salomonis
Dendrelaphis striatus
Dendrelaphis subocularis
Dendrelaphis tristis

GENUS: DENDROLYCUS
1 SPECIES

SIZE: Unknown
DISTRIBUTION: Dem. Rep. of Congo
HABITAT: Forests.
FOOD: Unknown.
REPRODUCTION: Unknown.

SPECIES:
Dendrolycus elapsoides

GENUS: DENDROPHIDION
FOREST RACERS
8 SPECIES

SIZE: Small and very slender.
DISTRIBUTION: Central and South America (Mexico to northern Bolivia).
HABITAT: Humid lowland forests, where they are mainly terrestrial, but may also climb.
FOOD: Rodents, lizards, and frogs.
REPRODUCTION: Thought to be egg-layers.

SPECIES:
Dendrophidion bivittatus
Dendrophidion boshelli
Dendrophidion brunneus
Dendrophidion dendrophis
Dendrophidion nuchalis
Dendrophidion paucicarinatum
Dendrophidion percarinatum
Dendrophidion vinitor

GENUS: DIADOPHIS
1 SPECIES

SIZE: Highly variable; small to medium depending on the subspecies.
DISTRIBUTION: North America.
HABITAT: Varied: it occurs in dry and moist habitats, and is often found under rocks, logs, and garbage.
FOOD: Earthworms, slugs and other invertebrates, small amphibians, and small reptiles. Large forms sometimes eat nestling rodents.
REPRODUCTION: Egg-layer.

SPECIES:
Diadophis punctatus,
　Ringneck Snake

GENUS: DIAPHOROLEPIS
2 SPECIES

SIZE: Moderately large snakes.
DISTRIBUTION: Panama, Colombia, and Ecuador.
HABITAT: Unknown, but thought to be terrestrial.
FOOD: Unknown.
REPRODUCTION: Thought to be egg-layers.

SPECIES:
Diaphorolepis laevis
Diaphorolepis wagneri

GENUS: DINODON
8 SPECIES

SIZE: Small and stocky.
DISTRIBUTION: Myanmar, southern China, and northern Indochina.
HABITAT: Moist forests.
FOOD: Poorly known, but thought to be amphibians and fish.
REPRODUCTION: Egg-layers.

SPECIES:
Dinodon flavozonatum
Dinodon gammiei
Dinodon japonicus
Dinodon orientalis
Dinodon rosozonatum
Dinodon rufozonatum
Dinodon semicarinatum
Dinodon septentrionalis

GENUS: DIPSADOBOA
6 SPECIES

SIZE: Small and slender.
DISTRIBUTION: Africa.
HABITAT: Forests, where they are arboreal.
FOOD: Geckos and frogs.
REPRODUCTION: Egg-layers.
NOTES: Rear-fanged, though not dangerous to humans. Active at night.

SPECIES:
Dipsadoboa aulicus
Dipsadoboa duchesnii
Dipsadoboa elongata
Dipsadoboa shrevei
Dipsadoboa unicolor
Dipsadoboa werneri

GENUS: DIPSAS
THIRST SNAKES, SNAIL-EATERS, OR SNAIL-SUCKERS
33 SPECIES

SIZE: Long and slender.
DISTRIBUTION: Central and South America (Mexico to Brazil).
HABITAT: Rain forests, where they are mainly arboreal.
FOOD: They feed only on snails and slugs, for which they have special adaptations to their jaws, resulting in squarish heads.
REPRODUCTION: Egg-layers.
NOTES: The bodies are flattened from side to side as an adaptation to an arboreal lifestyle. Some species are brightly colored.

SPECIES:
Dipsas albifrons
Dipsas articulata
Dipsas bicolor
Dipsas boettgeri
Dipsas brevifacies
Dipsas catesbyi
Dipsas chaparensis
Dipsas copei
Dipsas ellipsifera
Dipsas gaigeae
Dipsas gracilis
Dipsas incerta
Dipsas indica
Dipsas infrenalis
Dipsas latifasciata
Dipsas latifrontalis
Dipsas longicaudata
Dipsas maxillaris
Dipsas neivai
Dipsas oreas
Dipsas pavonina
Dipsas perijanensis
Dipsas peruana
Dipsas poecilolepis
Dipsas polylepis
Dipsas pratti
Dipsas sanctijoannis
Dipsas schunkii
Dipsas temporalis
Dipsas tenuissima
Dipsas variegata
Dipsas vermiculata
Dipsas viguieri

GENUS: DIPSINA
1 SPECIES

SIZE: Small and slender.
DISTRIBUTION: Southern and south-western Africa.

HABITAT: Dry sandy areas with rocks.
FOOD: Lizards.
REPRODUCTION: Egg-layer.
NOTES: The head has a hooked snout and large eyes.

SPECIES:
Dipsina multimaculata,
　Dwarf Beaked Snake

GENUS: DISPHOLIDUS
1 SPECIES

SIZE: Large but slender.
DISTRIBUTION: Throughout Africa south of the Sahara.
HABITAT: Forests, where it is arboreal.
FOOD: Hunting by day, it specializes in chameleons, but also takes other lizards. It kills its prey by grasping and chewing, using its venom fangs.
REPRODUCTION: Egg-layer, producing clutches of up to 25 eggs.
NOTES: One of the few rear-fanged snakes that has caused human fatalities.

SPECIES:
● *Dispholidus typus,*
　Boomslang (pp. 110–11)

GENUS: DITAXODON
1 SPECIES

SIZE: Unknown.
DISTRIBUTION: Brazil.
HABITAT: Unknown.
FOOD: Unknown.
REPRODUCTION: Unknown.
NOTES: Extremely rare and poorly known.

SPECIES:
Ditaxodon taeniatus

GENUS: DITYPOPHIS
1 SPECIES

SIZE: Small.
DISTRIBUTION: The isolated island of Socotra, off the Arabian Peninsula.
HABITAT: The island is dry. Details of the snake's preferences are unknown.
FOOD: Unknown.
REPRODUCTION: Unknown.
NOTES: Rare and poorly known.

SPECIES:
Ditypophis vivax

GENUS: DREPANOIDES
1 SPECIES

SIZE: Small.
DISTRIBUTION: South America.
HABITAT: Forests, where it lives on the ground and in leaf-litter.
FOOD: Unknown.

REPRODUCTION: Unknown.

NOTES: Brightly colored, similar to a coral snake.

SPECIES:

Drepanoides anomalus

GENUS: **DROMICODRYAS**
2 SPECIES

SIZE: Small and slender.
DISTRIBUTION: Madagascar.
HABITAT: Forests.
FOOD: Thought to be lizards.
REPRODUCTION: Thought to be egg-layers.
NOTES: Active during the day.

SPECIES:

Dromicodryas bernieri
Dromicodryas quadrilineatus

GENUS: **DROMICUS**
8 SPECIES

SIZE: Small to medium, and slender.
DISTRIBUTION: The Galapagos Islands and the West Indies.
HABITAT: Varied.
FOOD: Varied, including lizards, amphibians, and small mammals.
REPRODUCTION: Egg-layers.
NOTES: Active, diurnal species. Sometimes placed in the genus *Liophis*.

SPECIES:

Dromicus angustilineatus
Dromicus calliaemus
Dromicus chamissonis
Dromicus exiguum
Dromicus funereum
Dromicus inca
Dromicus polylepis
Dromicus tachymenoides

GENUS: **DROMOPHIS**
2 SPECIES

SIZE: Moderately long, but slender.
DISTRIBUTION: Tropical Africa.
HABITAT: Forests and damp places.
FOOD: Frogs and small mammals.
REPRODUCTION: Unknown.

SPECIES:

Dromophis lineatus
Dromophis praeornatus

GENUS: **DRYADOPHIS** SEE MASTIGODRYAS

GENUS: **DRYMARCHON**
1 SPECIES

SIZE: Large, sometimes to 8 ft 2 in (2.5 m).
DISTRIBUTION: North, Central, and northern South America.

HABITAT: Varied; dry pine hammocks and palmetto scrub to tropical forests.
FOOD: Fish, frogs, other reptiles, birds, and mammals.
REPRODUCTION: Egg-layer.
NOTES: The species shows great variation in color throughout its range. Diurnal, and often basks in the sun.

SPECIES:

● *Drymarchon corais,*
 Indigo Snake or Cribo (pp. 98–9)

GENUS: **DRYMOBIUS**
TROPICAL RACERS
4 SPECIES

SIZE: Fairly long, and slender.
DISTRIBUTION: North America (southern Texas) through Central America and into South America.
HABITAT: Varied.
FOOD: Mainly amphibians.
REPRODUCTION: Egg-layers.
NOTES: Active in the day.

SPECIES:

Drymobius chloroticus
Drymobius margaritiferus
Drymobius melanotropis
Drymobius rhombifer

GENUS: **DRYMOLUBER**
2 SPECIES

SIZE: Long and slender.
DISTRIBUTION: South America
HABITAT: Varied.
FOOD: Mainly lizards.
REPRODUCTION: Egg-layers.

SPECIES:

Drymoluber brazili
Drymoluber dichrous

GENUS: **DRYOCALAMUS**
6 SPECIES

SIZE: Small.
DISTRIBUTION: Sri Lanka, India, Southeast Asia, and the Philippines.
HABITAT: Forests, where they are arboreal.
FOOD: Thought to be invertebrates, frogs, and lizards.
REPRODUCTION: Unknown.
NOTES: Poorly known. Nocturnal.

SPECIES:

Dryocalamus davisonii
Dryocalamus gracilis
Dryocalamus nympha
Dryocalamus philippinus
Dryocalamus subannulatus
Dryocalamus tristrigatus

GENUS: **DRYOPHIOPS**
2 SPECIES

SIZE: Small (*D. philippina*) to medium.
DISTRIBUTION: Southeast Asia and the Philippines.
HABITAT: Forests, where they are aboreal.
FOOD: Small lizards.
REPRODUCTION: *D. rubescens* is a live-bearer, but the reproductive method of the other species is unknown.

SPECIES:

Dryophiops philippina
Dryophiops rubescens

GENUS: **DUBERRIA**
SLUG-EATING SNAKES
2 SPECIES

SIZE: Small, to about 1 ft 4 in (40 cm).
DISTRIBUTION: Southern Africa.
HABITAT: Among grass and under logs, in damp situations.
FOOD: Slugs and snails.
REPRODUCTION: Live-bearers.
NOTES: Secretive.

SPECIES:

Duberria lutrix,
 Common Slug-eater
Duberria variegata,
 Variegated Slug-eater or
 Spotted Slug-eater

GENUS: **ECHINANTHERA**
12 SPECIES

SIZE: Small.
DISTRIBUTION: South America.
HABITAT: Unknown.
FOOD: Unknown.
REPRODUCTION: Unknown.
NOTES: Contains several species that formerly belonged to the genus *Rhadinea*.

SPECIES:

Echinanthera affinis
Echinanthera amoenus
Echinanthera bilineata
Echinanthera brevirostris
Echinanthera cephalomaculata
Echinanthera cephalostriata
Echinanthera cyanopleura
Echinanthera melanostigma
Echinanthera occipitalis
Echinanthera persimilis
Echinanthera poecilopogon
Echinanthera undulata

GENUS: **EIRENIS**
18 SPECIES

SIZE: Small.
DISTRIBUTION: From North Africa, throughout Turkey and the Middle East, and into northwestern India.

HABITAT: Among rocks and other debris.
FOOD: Invertebrates and small lizards.
REPRODUCTION: Egg-layers, where known.
NOTES: Secretive. Some species are very poorly known and others are only recently described.

SPECIES:

Eirenis africana
Eirenis aurolineatus
Eirenis barani
Eirenis collaris
Eirenis coronella
Eirenis coronelloides
Eirenis decemlineata
Eirenis eiselti
Eirenis frenatus
Eirenis hakkariensis
Eirenis iranica
Eirenis levantinus
Eirenis lineomaculata
Eirenis modestus
Eirenis persicus
Eirenis punctatolineatus
Eirenis rothii
Eirenis thospitis

GENUS: **ELACHISTODON**
1 SPECIES

SIZE: Small.
DISTRIBUTION: India.
HABITAT: Unknown.
FOOD: Birds' eggs, paralleling the African *Dasypeltis*.
REPRODUCTION: Thought to be an egg-layer.
NOTES: Very rare and poorly known.

SPECIES:

Elachistodon westermanni,
 Indian Egg-eating Snake

GENUS: **ELAPHE**
RAT SNAKES AND RACERS
33 SPECIES

SIZE: Small to large, from about 1 ft 6 in (45 cm) to more than 6 ft 6 in (2 m).
DISTRIBUTION: North and Central America (five species), Europe, and Asia.
HABITAT: Varied, including forests, swamps, rain forests, caves, mountains, and even deserts.
FOOD: Most eat small mammals and birds, although some also take amphibians and lizards, and, possibly, invertebrates.
REPRODUCTION: Egg-layers, except for the semiaquatic *E. rufodorsata*, from China, which seems out of place in this genus.
NOTES: The genus is in serious need of revision. Some species have already been removed, to *Bogertophis*, *Gonyosoma*, and *Senticolis*. An additional species, *E. enganensis*, from Indonesia, is sometimes recognized, although it is more commonly regarded as a subspecies of *E. subradiata*.

SPECIES:
- *Elaphe bairdi*,
  Baird's Rat Snake (pp. 74–5)
  Elaphe bimaculata,
  Twin-spotted Rat Snake
  Elaphe cantoris,
  Cantor's Rat Snake
  Elaphe carinata,
  Keeled Rat Snake
  Elaphe climacophora,
  Japanese Rat Snake
  Elaphe conspicillata,
  Japanese Forest Rat Snake
  Elaphe davidi,
  David's Rat Snake
  Elaphe dione,
  Dione's or Steppe Rat Snake
  Elaphe erythrura,
  Philippine Rat Snake
  Elaphe flavirufa,
  Mexican Night Snake or Central
  American Rat Snake
  Elaphe flavolineata,
  Yellow-striped Rat Snake
- *Elaphe guttata*,
  Corn Snake or Red Rat Snake
  (pp. 72–3)
  Elaphe helena,
  Indian Trinket Snake
  Elaphe hodgsoni,
  Hodgson's Rat Snake
  Elaphe hohenackeri,
  Transcaucasian Rat Snake
  Elaphe leonardi,
  Leonard's Rat Snake
  Elaphe longissima,
  Aesculapian Snake
- *Elaphe mandarina*,
  Mandarin Rat Snake (pp. 78–9)
  Elaphe moellendorffi,
  Moellendorff's Rat Snake
  Elaphe obsoleta,
  American Rat Snake
  Elaphe perlacea,
  Pearl-banded Rat Snake
  Elaphe persica,
  Persian Rat Snake
  Elaphe porphyracea,
  Red Mountain Rat Snake
  Elaphe quadrivirgata,
  Japanese Four-lined Snake
  Elaphe quatuorlineata,
  Four-lined Snake
  Elaphe radiata,
  Copperhead Rat Snake
  Elaphe rufodorsata,
  Red-backed Rat Snake
  Elaphe scalaris,
  Ladder Snake
  Elaphe schrenckii,
  Russian or Amur Rat Snake
- *Elaphe situla*,
  Leopard Snake (pp. 96–7)
  Elaphe subradiata,
  Indonesian Rat Snake
  Elaphe taeniura,
  Beauty Snake
  Elaphe vulpina,
  Fox Snake

GENUS: ELAPOIDIS
1 SPECIES

SIZE: Small.
DISTRIBUTION: Borneo, Sumatra, and Java.
HABITAT: Hills and mountains, in wet and damp places, where it burrows.
FOOD: Unknown.
REPRODUCTION: Egg-layer.

SPECIES:
Elapoides fusca

GENUS: ELAPOMOJUS
1 SPECIES

SIZE: Small.
DISTRIBUTION: Brazil.
HABITAT: Forests.
FOOD: Unknown.
REPRODUCTION: Unknown.
NOTES: Rare and poorly known.

SPECIES:
Elapomojus dimidiatus

GENUS: ELAPOMORPHUS
12 SPECIES

SIZE: Small.
DISTRIBUTION: South America.
HABITAT: Varied; a secretive, burrowing species.
FOOD: Thought to be earthworms and other invertebrates.
REPRODUCTION: Unknown.
NOTES: Poorly known.

SPECIES:
Elapomorphus bilineatus
Elapomorphus bollei
Elapomorphus dimidiatus
Elapomorphus lemniscatus
Elapomorphus lepidus
Elapomorphus mertensi
Elapomorphus nasutus
Elapomorphus punctatus
Elapomorphus quinquelineatus
Elapomorphus spegazzinii
Elapomorphus tricolor
Elapomorphus wuchereri

GENUS: ELAPOTINUS
1 SPECIES

SIZE: Small.
DISTRIBUTION: Tropical Africa.
HABITAT: Unknown.
FOOD: Unknown.
REPRODUCTION: Unknown.
NOTES: Rare and almost completely unknown. Its relationships with other snakes are still unclear.

SPECIES:
Elapotinus picteti

GENUS: EMMOCHLIOPHIS
1 SPECIES

SIZE: Small.
DISTRIBUTION: Ecuador.
HABITAT: Forested Andean slopes.
FOOD: Unknown.
REPRODUCTION: Unknown.
NOTES: The few details are known from only one specimen.

SPECIES:
Emmochliophis fugleri

GENUS: ENHYDRIS:
21 SPECIES

SIZE: Generally small, although *E. bocourti* grows to over 3 ft 3 in (1 m).
DISTRIBUTION: India, China, Southeast Asia, New Guinea, and northern Australia.
HABITAT: Totally aquatic, found in ponds, marshes, and hill streams.
FOOD: Fish, frogs, and their larvae (tadpoles).
REPRODUCTION: Live-bearers; the young are born in the water.
NOTES: The cylindrical bodies have smooth glossy scales, and the eyes point upward.

SPECIES:
Enhydris albomaculata
Enhydris alternans
Enhydris bennetti
Enhydris bocourti,
  Bocourt's Water Snake
Enhydris chinensis
Enhydris doriae
Enhydris dussumieri
Enhydris enhydris
Enhydris indica
Enhydris innominata
Enhydris jagorii
Enhydris longicauda
Enhydris maculosa
Enhydris matannensis
Enhydris pahangensis
Enhydris pakistanica
Enhydris plumbea
Enhydris polylepis,
  Macleay's Water Snake
Enhydris punctata
Enhydris sieboldi
Enhydris smithi

GENUS: ENULIUS
3 SPECIES

SIZE: Small and slender.
DISTRIBUTION: Central and northern South America.
HABITAT: Dry and moist forests, where they are burrowers.
FOOD: Unknown, but thought to be invertebrates.
REPRODUCTION: Unknown.
NOTES: Poorly known.

SPECIES:
Enulius flavitorques
Enulius oligostichus
Enulius sclateri

GENUS: EREMIOPHIS
6 SPECIES

SIZE: Large and slender.
DISTRIBUTION: India, Pakistan, and western China.
HABITAT: Dry, open places.
FOOD: Mainly lizards.
REPRODUCTION: Egg-layers.
NOTES: Previously placed in the genus *Coluber*. Swift, diurnal hunters.

SPECIES:
Eremiophis bholanathi
Eremiophis gracilis
Eremiophis karelini
Eremiophis ravergieri
Eremiophis rhodorhachis
Eremiophis ventromaculatus

GENUS: ERIDIPHAS
1 SPECIES

SIZE: Small to medium.
DISTRIBUTION: Baja California, Mexico.
HABITAT: Dry, rocky places.
FOOD: Mainly lizards.
REPRODUCTION: Egg-layer.

SPECIES:
Eridiphas slevini,
  Baja Night Snake

GENUS: ERPETON
1 SPECIES

SIZE: Medium.
DISTRIBUTION: Thailand and Indochina.
HABITAT: Totally aquatic.
FOOD: Fish. It rests among dense aquatic vegetation waiting to ambush its prey.
REPRODUCTION: Live-bearer. The young are born underwater.
NOTES: The body is almost rectangular in cross section, the head is flattened, and there are two strange, fleshy appendages projecting from the snout. The ventral scales are reduced to a thin, raised ridge.

SPECIES:
Erpeton tentaculatum,
  Tentacled Snake, Fishing Snake

GENUS: ERYTHROLAMPRUS
FALSE CORAL SNAKES
6 SPECIES

SIZE: Small.
DISTRIBUTION: Central and South America.
HABITAT: Forests, where they are terrestrial.
FOOD: Other reptiles.

REPRODUCTION: Egg-layers.
NOTES: Brightly banded, like a coral snake. Rear-fanged, though not dangerous to humans.

SPECIES:
Erythrolamprus aesculapii
Erythrolamprus bauperthuisii
Erythrolamprus bizona
Erythrolamprus guentheri
Erythrolamprus mimus
Erythrolamprus pseudocorallus

GENUS: **ETHERIDGEUM**
1 SPECIES

SIZE: Small.
DISTRIBUTION: Sumatra.
HABITAT: Unknown.
FOOD: Unknown.
REPRODUCTION: Unknown.
NOTES: Known from only a single specimen described in 1924.

SPECIES:
Etheridgeum pulchrum

GENUS: **FARANCIA**
2 SPECIES

SIZE: Large, occasionally to 6 ft 6 in (2 m).
DISTRIBUTION: North America (Florida and adjoining states).
HABITAT: Semiaquatic, in or near swamps, ditches, and lakes, often where there is plenty of cover.
FOOD: Frogs, tadpoles, eels, and the eel-like salamanders belonging to the genus *Amphiuma*.
REPRODUCTION: Egg-layers, depositing the eggs in an underground chamber.

SPECIES:
Farancia abacura,
    Mud Snake
Farancia erytrogramma,
    Rainbow Snake

GENUS: **FICIMIA**
HOOK-NOSED SNAKES
6 SPECIES

SIZE: Small.
DISTRIBUTION: North and Central America (southern Texas to northern Honduras).
HABITAT: Varied, from arid semideserts to forests.
FOOD: Mainly on spiders and centipedes.
REPRODUCTION: Egg-layers.
NOTES: Rear-fanged, though not dangerous to humans. Two species are each known from only a single specimen.

SPECIES:
Ficimia olivacea
Ficimia publia,
    Yucatan Hook-nosed Snake

Ficimia ramirezi
Ficimia ruspator
Ficimia streckeri,
    Mexican Hook-nosed Snake
Ficimia variegata

GENUS: **FIMBRIOS**
1 SPECIES

SIZE: Small.
DISTRIBUTION: Southeast Asia.
HABITAT: Thought to be forests, where they are terrestrial.
FOOD: Unknown.
REPRODUCTION: Unknown.
NOTES: Rare and poorly known. It has a patch of spiky scales on the lower jaw, the function of which is unknown. Nocturnal.

SPECIES:
Fimbrios klossi

GENUS: **FORDONIA**
1 SPECIES

SIZE: Small.
DISTRIBUTION: Around the coasts of Southeast Asia, the Philippines, New Guinea, and northern Australia.
HABITAT: Coastal mudflats and mangrove forests.
FOOD: Crabs, which it constricts, then eats piece by piece.
REPRODUCTION: Live-bearer.
NOTES: A highly specialized species.

SPECIES:
Fordonia leucobalia,
    White-bellied Mangrove Snake

GENUS: **GASTROPYXIS**
1 SPECIES

SIZE: Medium, but very slender.
DISTRIBUTION: Tropical Africa.
HABITAT: Forests.
FOOD: Frogs.
REPRODUCTION: Unknown.
NOTES: Sometimes included in the genus *Hapsidophrys*.

SPECIES:
Gastropyxis smaragdina

GENUS: **GEARGAS**
1 SPECIES

SIZE: Small.
DISTRIBUTION: Mexico.
HABITAT: Unknown, but thought to burrow.
FOOD: Unknown.
REPRODUCTION: Unknown.
NOTES: Rare and poorly known.

SPECIES:
Geargas redimitus

GENUS: **GEODIPSAS**
6 SPECIES

SIZE: Medium.
DISTRIBUTION: West Africa (*G. depressiceps*), East Africa (*G. procterae* and *G. vauerecegae*), and Madagascar.
HABITAT: Mainly terrestrial, although they have been found in low vegetation.
FOOD: Unknown.
REPRODUCTION: Unknown.
NOTES: Rare and poorly known snakes. Nocturnal.

SPECIES:
Geodipsas depressiceps
Geodipsas laphystia
Geodipsas procterae
Geodipsas vauerecegae
Geodipsas vinckei
Geodipsas zenyi

GENUS: **GEOPHIS**
EARTH SNAKES
41 SPECIES

SIZE: Small, slender snakes.
DISTRIBUTION: Central and northern South America (northern Mexico to Colombia).
HABITAT: Varied, on the ground.
FOOD: Earthworms and other soft-bodied invertebrates
REPRODUCTION: Egg-layers, where known.
NOTES: Active mainly at night. Although 41 species are listed, it is likely that many of these are mere variants and that the correct total of species is significantly less than this.

SPECIES:
Geophis alasukai
Geophis anocularis
Geophis betaniensis
Geophis bicolor
Geophis blanchardi
Geophis brachycephalus
Geophis cancellatus
Geophis carinosus
Geophis chalybeus
Geophis championi
Geophis downsi
Geophis dubius
Geophis duellmani
Geophis dugesii
Geophis dunni
Geophis fulvoguttatus
Geophis godmani
Geophis hoffmanni
Geophis immaculatus
Geophis incomptus
Geophis isthmicus
Geophis laticinctus
Geophis laticollaris
Geophis latifrontalis
Geophis maculiferus
Geophis mutitorques
Geophis nasalis
Geophis nigrocinctus
Geophis omiltemanus

Geophis petersii
Geophis pyburni
Geophis rhodogaster
Geophis rostralis
Geophis russatus
Geophis ruthveni
Geophis sallaei
Geophis semiannulatus
Geophis semidoliatus
Geophis sieboldi
Geophis tarascae
Geophis zeledoni

GENUS: **GERARDA**
1 SPECIES

SIZE: Small.
DISTRIBUTION: Around the coasts and estuaries of Sri Lanka, India, Myanmar, and Thailand.
HABITAT: Mangrove forests; highly aquatic.
FOOD: Unknown; thought to be fish.
REPRODUCTION: Live-bearer.

SPECIES:
Gerarda prevostiana

GENUS: **GOMESOPHIS**
1 SPECIES

SIZE: Small.
DISTRIBUTION: Brazil.
HABITAT: Unknown.
FOOD: Unknown.
REPRODUCTION: Unknown.

SPECIES:
Gomesophis brasiliensis

GENUS: **GONGYLOSOMA**
3 SPECIES

SIZE: Small.
DISTRIBUTION: Southeast Asia (Indonesia, the Malay Peninsula, and Thailand).
HABITAT: Hilly countryside, often close to water.
FOOD: Invertebrates, amphibians, and lizards.
REPRODUCTION: Thought to be egg-layers.
NOTES: Previously included in the genus *Liopeltis*.

SPECIES:
Gongylosoma baliodeirus
Gongylosoma longicauda
Gongylosoma scripta

GENUS: **GONIONOTOPHIS**
3 SPECIES

SIZE: Small.
DISTRIBUTION: West Africa.
HABITAT: Rain forests.
FOOD: Thought to be frogs.
REPRODUCTION: Unknown.

SPECIES:
Gonionotophis brussauxi
Gonionotophis grantii
Gonionotophis klingi

GENUS: **GONYOPHIS**
1 SPECIES

SIZE: Large.
DISTRIBUTION: The Malay Peninsula and Borneo.
HABITAT: Forested hills.
FOOD: Thought to be lizards and small mammals.
REPRODUCTION: Thought to be an egg-layer.
NOTES: Closely related to the similar *Chrysopelea* species.

SPECIES:
Gonyophis margaritatus

GENUS: **GONYOSOMA**
RAT SNAKES OR RACERS
4 SPECIES

SIZE: Large.
DISTRIBUTION: Southeast Asia.
HABITAT: Forests, where they are highly arboreal.
FOOD: Frogs, lizards, birds, and small mammals.
REPRODUCTION: Egg-layers.
NOTES: Mostly bright green in color. Previously included in the genus *Elaphe*.

SPECIES:
Gonyosoma frenata
Gonyosoma janseni,
  Celebes Black-tailed Rat Snake or Celebes Black-tailed Racer
● *Gonyosoma oxycephalum,*
  Red-tailed Racer or Red-tailed Rat Snake (pp. 106–7)
Gonyosoma prasina,
  Green Bush Rat Snake or Green Bush Racer

GENUS: **GRAYIA**
4 SPECIES

SIZE: Large.
DISTRIBUTION: West Africa.
HABITAT: Semiaquatic.
FOOD: Thought to be fish.
REPRODUCTION: Thought to be egg-layers.
NOTES: Poorly known.

SPECIES:
Grayia caesar
Grayia ornata
Grayia smythii
Grayia tholloni

GENUS: **GYALOPION**
HOOK-NOSED SNAKES
2 SPECIES

SIZE: Small.
DISTRIBUTION: Central and northern South America.
HABITAT: Dry places.
FOOD: Mainly spiders.
REPRODUCTION: Egg-layers.
NOTES: *G. quadrangularis* is bright red, and mimics the black and white coral snake. Both species are nocturnal. They are closely related to *Ficimia* species, also known as hook-nosed snakes.

SPECIES:
Gyalopion canum
Gyalopion quadrangularis

GENUS: **HAEMORRHOIS**
5 SPECIES

SIZE: Medium.
DISTRIBUTION: The northeastern corner of Africa (Somalia, northern Kenya).
HABITAT: Unknown.
FOOD: Unknown.
REPRODUCTION: Unknown.
NOTES: Rare and poorly known.

SPECIES:
Haemorrhois caudalineata
Haemorrhois citernii
Haemorrhois keniensis
Haemorrhois somalicus
Haemorrhois taylori

GENUS: **HAPLOCERCUS**
1 SPECIES

SIZE: Small.
DISTRIBUTION: Sri Lanka.
HABITAT: Forests, usually under rotting logs.
FOOD: Earthworms.
REPRODUCTION: Egg-layer.

SPECIES:
Haplocercus ceylonensis

GENUS: **HAPSIDOPHRYS**
1 SPECIES

SIZE: Medium, and slender.
DISTRIBUTION: Tropical Africa.
HABITAT: Forests, where it is highly arboreal.
FOOD: Frogs.
REPRODUCTION: Unknown.

SPECIES:
Hapsidophrys lineatus

GENUS: **HELICOPS**
15 SPECIES

SIZE: Small.
DISTRIBUTION: South America
HABITAT: Aquatic and semiaquatic.
FOOD: Thought to be fish.
REPRODUCTION: Live-bearers, although *H. angulatus* may sometimes lay eggs.

SPECIES:
Helicops angulatus
Helicops carinicaudus
Helicops danieli
Helicops gomesi
Helicops hagmanni
Helicops hogei
Helicops leopardinus
Helicops modestus
Helicops pastazae
Helicops petersi
Helicops pictiventris
Helicops polylepis
Helicops scalaris
Helicops trivittatus
Helicops yacu

GENUS: **HELOPHIS**
1 SPECIES

SIZE: Unknown.
DISTRIBUTION: Dem. Rep. of Congo.
HABITAT: Unknown.
FOOD: Unknown.
REPRODUCTION: Unknown.
NOTES: Rarely collected.

SPECIES:
Helophis schoutedeni

GENUS: **HEMIRHAGERRHIS**
BARK SNAKES
2 SPECIES

SIZE: Small.
DISTRIBUTION: Africa.
HABITAT: Wooded grasslands, where they are arboreal.
FOOD: Lizards.
REPRODUCTION: Egg-layers.
NOTES: Nocturnal, hiding beneath loose bark during the day.

SPECIES:
Hemirhagerrhis kelleri
Hemirhagerrhis nototaenia,
  Bark Snake or Mopane Snake

GENUS: **HETERODON**
HOGNOSE SNAKES
3 SPECIES

SIZE: Small to medium, nearly 3 ft 3 in (1 m), with stocky bodies.
DISTRIBUTION: North America.
HABITAT: Varied, but often dry places with sandy soil.

FOOD: Mainly toads, but also ground-nesting birds and small mammals.
REPRODUCTION: Egg-layers
NOTES: When alarmed they flatten their bodies, hiss, make mock strikes, and, as a last resort, may pretend to be dead.

SPECIES:
● *Heterodon nasicus,*
  Western Hognose Snake (pp. 94–5)
Heterodon platyrhinos,
  Eastern Hognose Snake
Heterodon simus,
  Southern Hognose Snake

GENUS: **HETEROLIODON**
1 SPECIES

SIZE: Small.
DISTRIBUTION: Madagascar.
HABITAT: Unknown.
FOOD: Unknown.
REPRODUCTION: Unknown.

SPECIES:
Heteroliodon occipitalis

GENUS: **HEURNIA**
1 SPECIES

SIZE: Small, less than 3 ft 3 in (1 m).
DISTRIBUTION: New Guinea.
HABITAT: Semiaquatic
FOOD: Fish.
REPRODUCTION: Live-bearer.
NOTES: Closely related to the *Enhydris* species.

SPECIES:
Heurnia ventromaculata

GENUS: **HOLOGERRHUM**
1 SPECIES

SIZE: Small.
DISTRIBUTION: The island of Luzon, Philippines.
HABITAT: Unknown.
FOOD: Unknown.
REPRODUCTION: Unknown.

SPECIES:
Hologerrhum philippinum

GENUS: **HOMALOPSIS**
1 SPECIES

SIZE: Medium.
DISTRIBUTION: India, Myanmar, Indo-china, and Southeast Asia.
HABITAT: Fresh and brackish water.
FOOD: Fish and frogs. Can become a pest in fisheries.
REPRODUCTION: Live-bearer.

SPECIES:
Homalopsis buccata,
    Puff-faced Water Snake

GENUS: HORMONOTUS
1 SPECIES

SIZE: Unknown.
DISTRIBUTION: West Africa.
HABITAT: Unknown.
FOOD: Unknown.
REPRODUCTION: Unknown.

SPECIES:
Hormonotus modestus

GENUS: HYDRABLABES
2 SPECIES

SIZE: Small.
DISTRIBUTION: Borneo.
HABITAT: Forests, where they burrow.
FOOD: Unknown.
REPRODUCTION: Unknown.
NOTES: Rare and poorly known.

SPECIES:
Hydrablabes periops
Hydrablabes praefrontalis

GENUS: HYDRAETHIOPS
2 SPECIES

SIZE: Small.
DISTRIBUTION: West and Central Africa.
HABITAT: Semiaquatic.
FOOD: Thought to be amphibians and fish.
REPRODUCTION: Unknown.
NOTES: Related to *Afronatrix*, but
    otherwise poorly known

SPECIES:
Hydraethiops laevis
Hydraethiops melanogaster

GENUS: HYDRODYNASTES
2 SPECIES

SIZE: Large, heavy-bodied.
DISTRIBUTION: South America.
HABITAT: Semiaquatic.
FOOD: Frogs and toads; also small mammals.
REPRODUCTION: Egg-layers.

SPECIES:
Hydrodynastes bicinctus
Hydrodynastes gigas,
    False Water Cobra

GENUS: HYDROMORPHUS
3 SPECIES

SIZE: Small.
DISTRIBUTION: Central America.
HABITAT: Unknown.

FOOD: Unknown.
REPRODUCTION: Thought to be egg-layers.
NOTES: Secretive and poorly known.

SPECIES:
Hydromorphus clarki
Hydromorphus concolor
Hydromorphus dunni

GENUS: HYDROPS
2 SPECIES

SIZE: Medium.
DISTRIBUTION: Northern South America,
    to the east of the Andes.
HABITAT: Highly aquatic.
FOOD: Amphibians and fish.
REPRODUCTION: Thought to be egg-layers.

SPECIES:
Hydrops martii
Hydrops triangularis

GENUS: HYPOPTOPHIS
1 SPECIES

SIZE: Small.
DISTRIBUTION: Central Africa.
HABITAT: Unknown.
FOOD: Unknown.
REPRODUCTION: Unknown.

SPECIES:
Hypoptophis wilsoni

GENUS: HYPSIGLENA
NIGHT SNAKES
2 SPECIES

SIZE: Small.
DISTRIBUTION: North and Central
    America.
HABITAT: Varied, but usually dry and rocky
    places.
FOOD: Lizards, which they hunt at night.
    Also small snakes and mammals.
REPRODUCTION: Egg-layers.

SPECIES:
Hypsiglena tanzeri
Hypsiglena torquata,
    Spotted Night Snake

GENUS: HYPSIRHYNCHUS
1 SPECIES

SIZE: Medium and heavy-bodied.
DISTRIBUTION: Haiti.
HABITAT: Unknown.
FOOD: Lizards, especially those of the
    genus *Anolis.*
REPRODUCTION: Unknown.

SPECIES:
Hypsirhynchus ferox

GENUS: IALTRIS
3 SPECIES

SIZE: Medium and slender.
DISTRIBUTION: Hispaniola (Haiti and the
    Dominican Republic).
HABITAT: Unknown.
FOOD: Unknown.
REPRODUCTION: Thought to be egg-layers.
NOTES: Rear-fanged, though not dangerous
    to humans.

SPECIES:
Ialtris agyrtes
Ialtris dorsalis
Ialtris parishi

GENUS: IGUANOGNATHUS
1 SPECIES

SIZE: Small.
DISTRIBUTION: Sumatra.
HABITAT: Unknown.
FOOD: Unknown.
REPRODUCTION: Unknown.
NOTES: A rare snake that has been
    collected only a few times.

SPECIES:
Iguanognathus werneri

GENUS: IMANTODES
BLUNT-HEADED VINE SNAKES
6 SPECIES

SIZE: To about 3 ft 3 in (1 m) in length,
    but exceedingly elongated.
DISTRIBUTION: Central and South America.
HABITAT: Totally arboreal, hiding in
    bromeliad plants during the day and
    hunting at night.
FOOD: Lizards and frogs that rest or sleep
    on the extreme tips of leaves and twigs.
REPRODUCTION: Egg-layers, producing
    small clutches of elongated eggs.
NOTES: Rear-fanged, though not dangerous
    to humans. The heads are wide, with
    blunt snouts and huge eyes. Some
    species have a row of greatly enlarged
    dorsal scales running along the center
    of the back.

SPECIES:
Imantodes cenchoa
Imantodes gemmistratus
Imantodes inornatus
Imantodes lentiferus
Imantodes phantasma
Imantodes tenuissimus

GENUS: INTERNATUS
2 SPECIES

SIZE: Small.
DISTRIBUTION: Southeast Asia (Indonesia,
    Malaysia, and Thailand).
HABITAT: Forests.

FOOD: Snails.
REPRODUCTION: Egg-layers.
NOTES: Previously included in the genus
    Pareas.

SPECIES:
Internatus laevis
Internatus malaccanus

GENUS: ITHYCYPHUS
5 SPECIES

SIZE: Fairly large, to about 4 ft 11 in
    (1.5 m).
DISTRIBUTION: Madagascar.
HABITAT: Forests, where they are highly
    arboreal.
FOOD: Frogs and lizards, including
    chameleons.
REPRODUCTION: Egg-layers.
NOTES: Rear-fanged, though not dangerous
    to humans.

SPECIES:
Ithycyphus blanci
Ithycyphus goudoti
Ithycyphus miniatus
Ithycyphus oursi
Ithycyphus perineti

GENUS: LAMPROPELTIS
KINGSNAKES
8 SPECIES

SIZE: Small to fairly large.
DISTRIBUTION: North, Central, and South
    America.
HABITAT: Deserts, mountains, and forests.
FOOD: Lizards, other snakes, birds, and
    mammals.
REPRODUCTION: Egg-layers.
NOTES: Several are brightly colored
    false coral snakes, with rings of red,
    black, and white. Species may be active
    during the day or night, depending on
    their habitat.

SPECIES:
- *Lampropeltis alterna,*
    Gray-banded Kingsnake (pp. 84)
    Lampropeltis calligaster,
    Prairie Kingsnake
- *Lampropeltis getula,*
    Common Kingsnake (pp. 82–3)
- *Lampropeltis mexicana,*
    Mexican Kingsnake (pp. 85)
- *Lampropeltis pyromelana,*
    Sonoran Mountain Kingsnake
    (pp.86–7)
    Lampropeltis ruthveni,
    Queretaro Kingsnake
- *Lampropeltis triangulum,*
    Milk Snake (pp. 88–9)
    Lampropeltis zonata,
    Californian Mountain Kingsnake

GENUS: **LAMPROPHIS**
HOUSE SNAKES
14 SPECIES

SIZE: Small to medium.
DISTRIBUTION: Africa and the Seychelles (*L. geometricus*).
HABITAT: Varied, from deserts to forests, and around human dwellings.
FOOD: Lizards and small mammals. They are powerful constrictors.
REPRODUCTION: Egg-layers.

SPECIES:
Lamprophis abyssinicus
Lamprophis aurora,
    Aurora House Snake
Lamprophis erlangeri
Lamprophis fiskii,
    Fisk's House Snake
● *Lamprophis fuliginosus*,
    Brown House Snake (pp.104–5)
Lamprophis fuscus,
    Yellow-bellied House Snake
Lamprophis geometricus,
    Seychelles House Snake
Lamprophis guttatus,
    Spotted House Snake
Lamprophis inornatus,
    Olive House Snake
Lamprophis lineatus
Lamprophis maculatus
Lamprophis olivaceus
Lamprophis swazicus,
    Swazi House Snake
Lamprophis virgatus

GENUS: **LANGAHA**
MADAGASCAN VINE SNAKES
3 SPECIES

SIZE: Long and extremely slender.
DISTRIBUTION: Madagascar.
HABITAT: Rain forests, where they are totally arboreal.
FOOD: Lizards, especially geckos.
REPRODUCTION: Egg-layers, producing small clutches of eggs.
NOTES: An appendage on the tip of the snouts is flattened like a leaf in females, but is more elongated and pointed in males. Females of two species also have enlarged scales jutting out above their eyes. Active mainly in the early morning.

SPECIES:
Langaha alluaudi
Langaha madagascariensis
Langaha pseudoalluaudi

GENUS: **LEIMADOPHIS**
3 SPECIES

SIZE: Small.
DISTRIBUTION: Central and South America.
HABITAT: Moist situations such as rain forests.

FOOD: Fish, frogs, including their tadpoles, and lizards.
REPRODUCTION: Egg-layers.
NOTES: Rear-fanged, though not dangerous to humans. Sometimes included in the genus *Liophis*.

SPECIES:
Leimadophis atahuallpae
Leimadophis pygmaeus
Leimadophis simonsii

GENUS: **LEIOHETERODON**
MADAGASCAN HOGNOSE SNAKES
3 SPECIES

SIZE: Large and robust.
DISTRIBUTION: Madagascar.
HABITAT: Dry and forested areas.
FOOD: Reptile eggs that they dig up using their upturned snouts.
REPRODUCTION: Egg-layers.

SPECIES:
Leioheterodon geayi
Leioheterodon madagascariensis
Leioheterodon modestus

GENUS: **LEPTODEIRA**
CAT-EYED SNAKES
9 SPECIES

SIZE: Mostly small, and slender.
DISTRIBUTION: North, Central, and South America (Texas to northern Argentina and Paraguay)
HABITAT: Varied. They occur mainly on the ground but also climb into low vegetation.
FOOD: Lizards, frogs, toads, and tadpoles. *L. septentrionalis* (and possibly others) specializes in eating the eggs of leaf-nesting tree frogs.
REPRODUCTION: Egg-layers.
NOTES: Rear-fanged, though not dangerous to humans.

SPECIES:
Leptodeira annulata
Leptodeira bakeri
Leptodeira frenata
Leptodeira maculata
Leptodeira nigrofasciata
Leptodeira punctata
Leptodeira rubricata
Leptodeira septentrionalis,
    Northern Cat-eyed Snake
Leptodeira splendida

GENUS: **LEPTODRYMUS**
1 SPECIES

SIZE: Fairly large.
DISTRIBUTION: Central America.
HABITAT: Montane rain forests.
FOOD: Unknown.
REPRODUCTION: Unknown.

NOTES: Rare; its natural history is unknown.

SPECIES:
Leptodrymus pulcherrimus

GENUS: **LEPTOPHIS**
PARROT SNAKES
10 SPECIES

SIZE: Long and slender.
DISTRIBUTION: Central and South America (northwestern Mexico to Argentina and Paraguay).
HABITAT: Varied, including uplands. Partially arboreal.
FOOD: Amphibians, lizards, snakes, small birds (and their eggs), and small mammals.
REPRODUCTION: Egg-layers.
NOTES: The upper surfaces are often bright green. Rear-fanged, though not dangerous to humans. When alarmed they open their mouths widely to display bright blue inner parts. Active during the day.

SPECIES:
Leptophis ahaetulla
Leptophis cupreus
Leptophis depressirostris
Leptophis diplotropis
Leptophis mexicanus
Leptophis modestus
Leptophis nebulosus
Leptophis riveti
Leptophis santamartensis
Leptophis stimsoni

GENUS: **LEPTUROPHIS**
1 SPECIES

SIZE: Large.
DISTRIBUTION: Indonesia, Malaysia (including Borneo), and Thailand.
HABITAT: Lowland rain forests, often close to streams and in dense vegetation.
FOOD: Frogs, lizards, and birds.
REPRODUCTION: Thought to be an egg-layer.

SPECIES:
Lepturophis albofuscus

GENUS: **LIMNOPHIS**
1 SPECIES

SIZE: Small, to about 1 ft 11½ in (60 cm).
DISTRIBUTION: Southern Africa.
HABITAT: Semiaquatic, in marshy places.
FOOD: Fish and amphibians.
REPRODUCTION: Egg-layer.

SPECIES:
Limnophis bicolor

GENUS: **LIOHETEROPHIS**
1 SPECIES

SIZE: Small.
DISTRIBUTION: Brazil.
HABITAT: Damp places.
FOOD: Frogs.
REPRODUCTION: Unknown.

SPECIES:
Lioheterophis iheringi

GENUS: **LIOPELTIS**
14 SPECIES

SIZE: Small and slender.
DISTRIBUTION: South and Southeast Asia.
HABITAT: Mostly terrestrial, living in tropical rain forests, cultivated fields, and plantations.
FOOD: Thought to feed on invertebrates, amphibians, and lizards.
REPRODUCTION: Egg-layers.
NOTES: There is some confusion over the validity of some of the species listed.

SPECIES:
Liopeltis calamaria
Liopeltis doriae
Liopeltis frenatus
Liopeltis hamptoni
Liopeltis herminae
Liopeltis kikuzatoi
Liopeltis major
Liopeltis multicinctus
Liopeltis nicobariensis
Liopeltis philipinus
Liopeltis rappi
Liopeltis semicarinatus
Liopeltis stoliczkae
Liopeltis tricolor

GENUS: **LIOPHIDIUM**
8 SPECIES

SIZE: Small.
DISTRIBUTION: Madagascar (seven species) and the Comoros (*L. mayottensis*).
HABITAT: Sandy places or on forest floors.
FOOD: Unknown.
REPRODUCTION: Unknown.
NOTES: Poorly known: there is only one recorded specimen of *L. apperti* and two of *L. therezieni*.

SPECIES:
Liophidium apperti
Liophidium chabaudi
Liophidium mayottensis
Liophidium rhodogaster
Liophidium therezieni
Liophidium torquatum
Liophidium trilineatum
Liophidium vaillanti

GENUS: LIOPHIS
59 SPECIES

SIZE: Small to fairly large.
DISTRIBUTION: Central and South America and the West Indies.
HABITAT: Varied.
FOOD: Mostly lizards, but also frogs and fish.
REPRODUCTION: Egg-layers.
NOTES: Rear-fanged, though not dangerous to humans. Active during the day. Some species (*L. coralliventris, L. flavifrenatus, L. lineatus,* and *L. paucidens*) are sometimes included in a separate genus, *Lygophis*.

SPECIES:
Liophis albiceps
Liophis albiventris
Liophis almadensis
Liophis amarali
Liophis amazonicus
Liophis andinus
Liophis anomalus
Liophis atraventer
Liophis bimaculatus
Liophis brazili
Liophis breviceps
Liophis canaima
Liophis carajascinsis
Liophis ceii
Liophis chrysostomus
Liophis cobella
Liophis coralliventris
Liophis cursor
Liophis dilepis
Liophis epinephalus
Liophis festae
Liophis flavifrenatus
Liophis fraseri
Liophis frenatus
Liophis guentheri
Liophis ingeri
Liophis jaegeri
Liophis joberti
Liophis juliae
Liophis leucogaster
Liophis lineatus
Liophis longiventris
Liophis maryellenae
Liophis melanauchen
Liophis melanostigma
Liophis melanotus
Liophis meridionalis
Liophis miliaris
Liophis mossoroensis
Liophis obtusus
Liophis oligolepis
Liophis ornatus
Liophis paucidens
Liophis perfuscus
Liophis poecilogyrus
Liophis problematicus
Liophis pseudocobella
Liophis purpurans
Liophis reginae
Liophis sagittifer
Liophis steinbachi
Liophis subocularis
Liophis taeniurus
Liophis triscalis
Liophis typhlus
Liophis vanzolinii
Liophis viridis
Liophis williamsi
Liophis zweifeli

GENUS: LIOPHOLIDOPHIS
10 SPECIES

SIZE: Long and slender.
DISTRIBUTION: Madagascar.
HABITAT: Varied, from swamps to forests and clearings.
FOOD: Mainly frogs.
REPRODUCTION: Egg-layers.
NOTES: Several species are only recently discovered.

SPECIES:
Liopholidophis dolicocercus
Liopholidophis epistibes
Liopholidophis grandidieri
Liopholidophis infrasignatus
Liopholidophis lateralis
Liopholidophis pinguis
Liopholidophis pseudolateralis
Liopholidophis rhadinaea
Liopholidophis sexlineatus
Liopholidophis stumpffi

GENUS: LYCODON
26 SPECIES

SIZE: Small to medium.
DISTRIBUTION: Asia.
HABITAT: Varied, including villages and farms. Terrestrial or slightly arboreal.
FOOD: Lizards and snakes, although other prey may be taken.
REPRODUCTION: Egg-layers, where known.
NOTES: The taxonomy of the genus is confused: the number of species listed here may be greatly exaggerated.

SPECIES:
Lycodon alcalai
Lycodon aulicus
Lycodon bibonius
Lycodon butleri
Lycodon capucinus
Lycodon chrysoprateros
Lycodon dumerili
Lycodon effraenis
Lycodon fasciatus
Lycodon flavomaculatus
Lycodon florensis
Lycodon jara
Lycodon kundui
Lycodon laoensis
Lycodon mackinnoni
Lycodon muelleri
Lycodon osmanhilli
Lycodon paucifasciatus
Lycodon ruhstrati
Lycodon solivagus
Lycodon stormi
Lycodon striatus
Lycodon subcinctus
Lycodon tessellatus
Lycodon tiwarii
Lycodon travancoricus

GENUS: LYCODONOMORPHUS
6 SPECIES

SIZE: Medium.
DISTRIBUTION: Africa.
HABITAT: Semiaquatic.
FOOD: Fish, frogs, and tadpoles.
REPRODUCTION: Egg-layers.

SPECIES:
Lycodonomorphus bicolor
Lycodonomorphus laevissimus
Lycodonomorphus leleupi
Lycodonomorphus rufulus
Lycodonomorphus subtaeniatus
Lycodonomorphus whytii

GENUS: LYCODRYAS
3 SPECIES

SIZE: Long and slender.
DISTRIBUTION: Indian Ocean region.
HABITAT: Unknown.
FOOD: Lizards and frogs.
REPRODUCTION: Thought to be egg-layers.
NOTES: Several Madagascan species that used to be in this genus have recently been moved to the genus *Stenophis*.

SPECIES:
Lycodryas maculatus
Lycodryas sanctijohannts
Lycodryas seychellensis

GENUS: LYCOGNATHOPHIS
1 SPECIES

SIZE: Medium.
DISTRIBUTION: Seychelles.
HABITAT: Apparently terrestrial.
FOOD: Unknown.
REPRODUCTION: Unknown.
NOTES: Very poorly known.

SPECIES:
Lycognathophis seychellensis

GENUS: LYCOPHIDION
WOLF SNAKES
15 SPECIES

SIZE: Small.
DISTRIBUTION: Africa.
HABITAT: Unknown.
FOOD: Lizards and snakes.
REPRODUCTION: Egg-layers.
NOTES: The name derives from the elongated front fangs.

SPECIES:
Lycophidion capense
Lycophidion depressirostre
Lycophidion hellmichi
Lycophidion irroratum
Lycophidion laterale
Lycophidion meleagre
Lycophidion namibianum
Lycophidion ornatum
Lycophidion polylepis
Lycophidion pygmaeum
Lycophidion semiannule
Lycophidion semicinctum
Lycophidion taylori
Lycophidion uzungwense
Lycophidion variegatum

GENUS: LYSTROPHIS
SOUTH AMERICAN HOGNOSE SNAKES
6 SPECIES

SIZE: Small to medium, but stocky.
DISTRIBUTION: South America.
HABITAT: Varied.
FOOD: Thought to be toads.
REPRODUCTION: Egg-layers.
NOTES: Some species are brightly colored and may mimic the venomous coral snakes from the same region. They have upturned snouts.

SPECIES:
Lystrophis dorbignyi
Lystrophis histricus
Lystrophis matogrossiensis
Lystrophis natteri
Lystrophis pulcher
Lystrophis semicinctus

GENUS: LYTORHYNCHUS
LEAF-NOSED SNAKES
7 SPECIES

SIZE: Small.
DISTRIBUTION: North Africa, the Middle East, and Central Asia.
HABITAT: Dry places, including sand dunes and gravel deserts.
FOOD: Geckos and other lizards.
REPRODUCTION: Egg-layers.
NOTES: The rostral scale is enlarged and has a similar shape to that of North American leaf-nosed snakes (*Phyllorhynchus*), which live in similar habitats and are thought to have a similar diet.

SPECIES:
Lytorhynchus diadema
Lytorhynchus gaddi
Lytorhynchus gasperetti
Lytorhynchus kennedyi
Lytorhynchus maynardi
Lytorhynchus paradoxus
Lytorhynchus ridgewayi

GENUS: **MACROCALAMUS**
MOUNTAIN REED SNAKES
3 SPECIES

SIZE: Small.
DISTRIBUTION: Malay Peninsula.
HABITAT: Montane forests.
FOOD: Thought to be worms and slugs.
REPRODUCTION: Egg-layers.

SPECIES:
Macrocalamus jasoni
Macrocalamus lateralis
Macrocalamus tweediei

GENUS: **MACROPISTHODON**
4 SPECIES

SIZE: Medium.
DISTRIBUTION: India, Sri Lanka, southern
China, and parts of Southeast Asia.
HABITAT: Fields and grasslands.
FOOD: Mainly frogs.
REPRODUCTION: Egg-layers.
NOTES: Rear-fanged, but innocuous. The
broad heads and markings mimic those
of the dangerously venomous pit vipers
belonging to the genus *Agkistrodon* from
the same region.

SPECIES:
Macropisthodon flaviceps
Macropisthodon plumbicolor
Macropisthodon rhodomelas
Macropisthodon rudis

GENUS: **MACROPOPHIS**
4 SPECIES

SIZE: Small to medium.
DISTRIBUTION: Philippines
HABITAT: Semiaquatic, often found along
mountain streams.
FOOD: Thought to be amphibians and fish.
REPRODUCTION: Unknown.
NOTES: Sometimes placed in the genus
Tropidonophis.

SPECIES:
Macropophis barbouri
Macropophis dendrophiops
Macropophis halmaherica
Macropophis hypomela

GENUS: **MACROPROTODON**
1 SPECIES

SIZE: Small.
DISTRIBUTION: Western Europe, North
Africa, and parts of the Middle East.
HABITAT: Dry and rocky places.
FOOD: Lizards, which it catches while they
are asleep.
REPRODUCTION: Egg-layer.
NOTES: Rear-fanged, though not dangerous
to humans. Completely nocturnal.

SPECIES:
Macroprotodon cucullatus,
Cowled Snake or False Smooth Snake

GENUS: **MADAGASCAROPHIS**
4 SPECIES

SIZE: Medium, with thickset bodies.
DISTRIBUTION: Madagascar.
HABITAT: Varied: on the ground and in
trees and bushes.
FOOD: Frogs, lizards, including
chameleons, other snakes, and birds.
REPRODUCTION: Egg-layers, producing
small clutches of eggs.
NOTES: Most active after rain.

SPECIES:
Madagascarophis citrinus
Madagascarophis colubrina
Madagascarophis meridionalis
Madagascarophis ocellatus

GENUS: **MALPOLON**
2 SPECIES

SIZE: Large, growing to 6 ft 6 in (2 m)
or more.
DISTRIBUTION: Southern Europe, North
Africa, and the Middle East.
HABITAT: Varied, but often dry, scrubby
hillsides and semiarid deserts.
FOOD: Lizards and other snakes, which
they hunt during the day.
REPRODUCTION: Egg-layers.
NOTES: Rear-fanged snakes that bite
readily. Although not life-threatening,
the bites can cause nausea, localized
pain, and swelling.

SPECIES:
Malpolon moilensis
Malpolon monspessulanus,
Montpellier Snake

GENUS: **MANOLEPIS**
1 SPECIES

SIZE: Small.
DISTRIBUTION: Mexico.
HABITAT: Unknown.
FOOD: Unknown.
REPRODUCTION: Unknown.

SPECIES:
Manolepis putnami

GENUS: **MASTICOPHIS**
COACHWHIPS
10 SPECIES

SIZE: Long and slender.
DISTRIBUTION: North, Central, and
northern South America.
HABITAT: Deserts, sparse forests,
and beaches.

FOOD: Lizards, snakes, and small
mammals
REPRODUCTION: Egg-layers.
NOTES: Active hunters during the day, using
speed to overwhelm their prey. They bite
readily but are not dangerous to humans.

SPECIES:
Masticophis anthonyi
Masticophis aurigulus,
Cape Whip-snake
Masticophis bilineatus,
Sonoran Whip-snake
Masticophis flagellum,
Coachwhip
Masticophis lateralis,
Striped Racer
Masticophis mentovarius
Masticophis pulchriceps
Masticophis schotti,
Schott's Whipsnake
Masticophis stigodryas
Masticophis taeniatus,
Striped Whipsnake

GENUS: **MASTIGODRYAS**
12 SPECIES

SIZE: Medium with slender bodies.
DISTRIBUTION: Central and South America
(Mexico to Argentina).
HABITAT: Varied, but usually open country.
FOOD: Amphibians, lizards, snakes, birds,
and small mammals.
REPRODUCTION: Egg-layers.
NOTES: Active by day. Up to four species
are sometimes placed in a separate
genus, *Dryadophis.*

SPECIES:
Mastigodryas amarali
Mastigodryas bifossatus
Mastigodryas boddaerti
Mastigodryas bruesi
Mastigodryas cliftoni
Mastigodryas danieli
Mastigodryas dorsalis
Mastigodryas heathii
Mastigodryas melanolomus
Mastigodryas pleei
Mastigodryas pulchriceps
Mastigodryas sanguiventris

GENUS: **MEHELYA**
FILE SNAKES
10 SPECIES

SIZE: Medium to large.
DISTRIBUTION: Africa south of the Sahara.
HABITAT: Varied; grasslands, forests, and
rocky, mountainous places.
FOOD: Mostly lizards and snakes.
REPRODUCTION: Egg-layers, producing
small clutches of eggs.
NOTES: The slender bodies are triangular
when viewed in cross section, and have
knobbly scales.

SPECIES:
Mehelya capensis,
Cape File Snake
Mehelya crossi
Mehelya egbensis
Mehelya guirali
Mehelya laurenti
Mehelya nyassae,
Black File Snake
Mehelya poensis
Mehelya riggenbachi
Mehelya stenophthalmus
Mehelya vernayi,
Angolan File Snake

GENUS: **MEIZODON**
2 SPECIES

SIZE: Small.
DISTRIBUTION: Tropical Africa.
HABITAT: Unknown.
FOOD: Lizards and frogs.
REPRODUCTION: Egg-layers.
NOTES: Two other species are sometimes
recognized, but are more commonly
assigned as races of *M. semiornatus.*

SPECIES:
Meizodon coronatus
Meizodon semiornatus

GENUS: **MICROPISTHODON**
1 SPECIES

SIZE: Medium and slender.
DISTRIBUTION: Madagascar.
HABITAT: Unknown, but thought to
be arboreal.
FOOD: Thought to eat lizards and frogs.
REPRODUCTION: Egg-layer.
NOTES: Known from only a few
specimens. Thought to be diurnal.

SPECIES:
Micropisthodon ochraceus

GENUS: **MIMOPHIS**
1 SPECIES

SIZE: Small and slender.
DISTRIBUTION: Madagascar.
HABITAT: On the ground in forests and
more open habitats.
FOOD: Thought to be lizards.
REPRODUCTION: Unknown, but thought
to be an egg-layer.

SPECIES:
Mimophis mahfalensis

GENUS: **MONTASPIS**
1 SPECIES

SIZE: Small.
DISTRIBUTION: South Africa, in the Natal
Drakensberg Mountains.

HABITAT: Wetlands above the tree line at nearly 9,850 ft (3,000 m) altitude.
FOOD: Frogs.
REPRODUCTION: Unknown.
NOTES: Only recently described from a small number of specimens.

SPECIES:
  Montaspis gilvomaculata

GENUS: **MYERSOPHIS**
1 SPECIES

SIZE: Moderately large.
DISTRIBUTION: Banaue in the Philippines.
HABITAT: Unknown.
FOOD: Unknown.
REPRODUCTION: Unknown.
NOTES: Rare and known from only a few specimens.

SPECIES:
  Myersophis alpestris

GENUS: **MYRON**
1 SPECIES

SIZE: Small.
DISTRIBUTION: New Guinea and extreme northern Australia.
HABITAT: Mudflats and mangrove forests.
FOOD: Crabs and small fish.
REPRODUCTION: Live-bearer.

SPECIES:
  Myron richardsonii,
    Richardson's Gray Mangrove Snake

GENUS: **NATRICITERES**
MARSH SNAKES
3 SPECIES

SIZE: Small and slender.
DISTRIBUTION: Tropical Africa.
HABITAT: Swamps and marshes.
FOOD: Frogs.
REPRODUCTION: Egg-layers.
NOTES: They can discard the tail if it is grasped by a predator.

SPECIES:
  Natriciteres fuliginoides
  Natriciteres olivacea
  Natriciteres variegata

GENUS: **NATRIX**
EURASIAN WATER SNAKES
4 SPECIES

SIZE: Medium to large.
DISTRIBUTION: Europe, Western Asia, and North Africa.
HABITAT: Water and damp places.
FOOD: Mainly amphibians and fish, but the Grass Snake also takes small mammals and birds.

REPRODUCTION: Egg-layers, the eggs of the Grass Snake often being deposited in communal sites.
NOTES: The habits of the newly described *N. megalocephala* are poorly known.

SPECIES:
  Natrix maura,
    Viperine Snake
  Natrix megalocephala,
    Big-headed Grass Snake
● *Natrix natrix,*
    Grass Snake (p. 68–9)
  Natrix tessellata,
    Dice Snake or Tessellated Snake

GENUS: **NERODIA**
AMERICAN WATER SNAKES
7 SPECIES

SIZE: Medium to large, and stocky.
DISTRIBUTION: Southeastern North America and Baja California, Mexico.
HABITAT: Aquatic and semiaquatic, in swamps, lakes, and coastal marshes.
FOOD: Mostly amphibians and fish.
REPRODUCTION: Live bearers. The young can number nearly 100 in some species.
NOTES: Some species are divided into several subspecies, some of which are sometimes regarded as full species.

SPECIES:
  Nerodia clarkii
    Salt Marsh Snake
  Nerodia cyclopion,
    Mississippi Green Water Snake
  Nerodia erythrogaster,
    Plain-bellied Water Snake
● *Nerodia fasciata,*
    Banded Water Snake or Southern Water Snake (pp. 90–1)
  Nerodia floridana
    Florida Green Water Snake
  Nerodia harteri,
    Brazo Water Snake
  Nerodia rhombifer,
    Diamondback Water Snake
  Nerodia sipedon,
    Northern Water Snake
  Nerodia taxispilota,
    Brown Water Snake

GENUS: **NINIA**
COFFEE SNAKES
11 SPECIES

SIZE: Small.
DISTRIBUTION: Central and South America.
HABITAT: Leaf-litter.
FOOD: Invertebrates, small lizards, and frogs.
REPRODUCTION: Egg-layers.
NOTES: Only six species are recognized by some authorities.

SPECIES:
  Ninia atrata

  Ninia celata
  Ninia cerroensis
  Ninia diademata
  Ninia espinali
  Ninia hudsoni
  Ninia maculata
  Ninia oxynota
  Ninia pavimentata
  Ninia psephota
  Ninia sebae

GENUS: **NOTHOPSIS**
1 SPECIES

SIZE: Small.
DISTRIBUTION: Central America.
HABITAT: Humid forests, where it is possibly aquatic or semiaquatic.
FOOD: Unknown.
REPRODUCTION: Unknown.

SPECIES:
  Nothopsis rugosus

GENUS: **OLIGODON**
KUKRI SNAKES
71 SPECIES

SIZE: Small to medium, with chunky bodies.
DISTRIBUTION: Asia (the Middle East, through Central Asia and India, Myanmar, southern China, and into the Malay Peninsula).
HABITAT: Varied.
FOOD: Varied, including amphibians, small mammals, and, especially, the eggs of reptiles.
REPRODUCTION: All the known species are egg-layers.
NOTES: The snouts are slightly upturned. Long, curved fangs at the back of the mouths (similar to the kukri knives used by the Gurkha soldiers from the same part of the world) are used for slashing the shells of reptiles and for defense, although they are harmless to humans. The species may be nocturnal or diurnal.

SPECIES:
  Oligodon affinis
  Oligodon albocinctus
  Oligodon ancorus
  Oligodon annulifer
  Oligodon arnensis
  Oligodon barroni
  Oligodon bellus
  Oligodon bitorquatus
  Oligodon brevicauda
  Oligodon calamarius
  Oligodon catenatus
  Oligodon chinensis
  Oligodon cinereus
  Oligodon cruentatus
  Oligodon cyclurus
  Oligodon dorsalis
  Oligodon dorsolateralis
  Oligodon durheimi
  Oligodon eberhardti

  Oligodon erythrogaster
  Oligodon erythrorhachis
  Oligodon everetti
  Oligodon forbesi
  Oligodon formosanus
  Oligodon hamptoni
  Oligodon inornatus
  Oligodon jacobi
  Oligodon joynsoni
  Oligodon juglandifer
  Oligodon kunmigeosis
  Oligodon lacroixi
  Oligodon lungshenensis
  Oligodon macrurus
  Oligodon maculatus
  Oligodon mcdougalli
  Oligodon melaneus
  Oligodon melanozonatus
  Oligodon meyerinkii
  Oligodon modestum
  Oligodon mouhoti
  Oligodon multizonatus
  Oligodon nikhili
  Oligodon ningshaanensis
  Oligodon notospilus
  Oligodon ocellatus
  Oligodon octolineatus
  Oligodon ornatus
  Oligodon perkinsi
  Oligodon petronellae
  Oligodon planiceps
  Oligodon praefrontalis
  Oligodon propinquus
  Oligodon pulcherrimus
  Oligodon purpuraescens
  Oligodon quadrilineatus
  Oligodon rhombifer
  Oligodon signatus
  Oligodon splendidus
  Oligodon subcarinatus
  Oligodon sublineatus
  Oligodon taeniatus
  Oligodon taeniolatus
  Oligodon theobaldi
  Oligodon torquatus
  Oligodon travancoricus
  Oligodon trilineatus
  Oligodon unicolor
  Oligodon venustus
  Oligodon vertebralis
  Oligodon waandersi
  Oligodon woodmasoni

GENUS: **OPHEODRYS**
GREEN SNAKES
2 SPECIES

SIZE: Small and very slender.
DISTRIBUTION: North America.
HABITAT: Grasses and other low vegetation, where they are terrestrial.
FOOD: Invertebrates, including spiders and caterpillars.
REPRODUCTION: Both species are egg-layers, but the eggs of *O. vernalis* hatch after a very short period of incubation and the species may even be live-bearers in parts of its range.
NOTES: Diurnal. *O. vernalis* is sometimes

placed in a separate genus, *Liochlorophis*. Two additional species from Mexico are sometimes recognized.

SPECIES:
- *Opheodrys aestivus*, Rough Green Snake (pp. 80–81)
  Opheodrys vernalis, Smooth Green Snake

GENUS: **OPISTHOPLUS**
1 SPECIES

SIZE: Unknown.
DISTRIBUTION: Brazil
HABITAT: Unknown.
FOOD: Unknown.
REPRODUCTION: Unknown.
NOTES: A rare and obscure snake about which almost nothing appears to be known.

SPECIES:
  Opisthoplus degener

GENUS: **OPISTHOTROPIS**
14 SPECIES

SIZE: Small to medium.
DISTRIBUTION: Southern China, Indochina, and the Philippines.
HABITAT: Aquatic or semiaquatic.
FOOD: Fish, amphibians, freshwater shrimps, and earthworms.
REPRODUCTION: Thought to be egg-layers.
NOTES: Very rare and poorly known.

SPECIES:
  Opisthotropis alcalai
  Opisthotropis andersonii
  Opisthotropis balteatus
  Opisthotropis guangxiensis
  Opisthotropis jacobi
  Opisthotropis kikuzatoi
  Opisthotropis kuatunensis
  Opisthotropis lateralis
  Opisthotropis latouchii
  Opisthotropis maxwelli
  Opisthotropis praemaxillaris
  Opisthotropis rugosus
  Opisthotropis spenceri
  Opisthotropis typica

GENUS: **OREOCALAMUS**
1 SPECIES

SIZE: Small.
DISTRIBUTION: Borneo, and a small area in the Malay Peninsula at 3,300–6,000 ft (1,000–1,800 m).
HABITAT: Unknown.
FOOD: Unknown.
REPRODUCTION: Unknown.
NOTES: A rare snake that has only been collected on a few occasions and about which almost nothing is known.

SPECIES:
  Oreocalamus hanitschi

GENUS: **OXYBELIS**
VINE SNAKES
5 SPECIES

SIZE: Long and slender.
DISTRIBUTION: North, Central, and South America (Texas to Bolivia and Peru).
HABITAT: Forests, where they are arboreal.
FOOD: Mainly lizards.
REPRODUCTION: Egg-layers.
NOTES: They have rear fangs and bite readily, though they are not considered dangerous to humans.

SPECIES:
  Oxybelis aeneus, Brown Vine Snake
  Oxybelis argenteus
  Oxybelis brevirostris
  Oxybelis fulgidus
  Oxybelis wilsoni

GENUS: **OXYRHABDIUM**
2 SPECIES

SIZE: Moderately large.
DISTRIBUTION: Philippines.
HABITAT: Burrowing species, often found in rotting wood or leaf-litter.
FOOD: Unknown.
REPRODUCTION: Unknown.
NOTES: Although common, almost nothing is known of their natural history.

SPECIES:
  Oxyrhabdium leporinum
  Oxyrhabdium modestum

GENUS: **OXYRHOPUS**
13 SPECIES

SIZE: Medium, with fairly slender bodies.
DISTRIBUTION: Central and South America (Mexico to Peru).
HABITAT: Lowland forests, where they are terrestrial.
FOOD: Amphibians, lizards, snakes, and small mammals.
REPRODUCTION: Egg-layers.
NOTES: Boldly banded in red and black, or red, black, and white, and thought to mimic the venomous coral snakes from the region. Mainly nocturnal.

SPECIES:
  Oxyrhopus clathratus
  Oxyrhopus doliatus
  Oxyrhopus fitzingeri
  Oxyrhopus formosus
  Oxyrhopus guibei
  Oxyrhopus leucomelas
  Oxyrhopus marcapatae
  Oxyrhopus melanogenys
  Oxyrhopus occipitalis
  Oxyrhopus petola
  Oxyrhopus rhombifer
  Oxyrhopus trigeminus
  Oxyrhopus venezuelanus

GENUS: **PARAHELICOPS**
2 SPECIES

SIZE: Small.
DISTRIBUTION: Southeast Asia (Thailand and Vietnam).
HABITAT: Unknown.
FOOD: Unknown.
REPRODUCTION: Unknown.
NOTES: Very rare and poorly known.

SPECIES:
  Parahelicops annamensis
  Parahelicops boonsongi

GENUS: **PARARHABDOPHIS**
1 SPECIES

SIZE: Medium.
DISTRIBUTION: Southeast Asia.
HABITAT: Unknown.
FOOD: Unknown.
REPRODUCTION: Unknown.

SPECIES:
  Pararhabdophis chapaensis

GENUS: **PARARHADINAEA**
2 SPECIES

SIZE: Small.
DISTRIBUTION: Madagascar.
HABITAT: Thought to be burrowers in leaf-litter.
FOOD: Unknown.
REPRODUCTION: Unknown.
NOTES: Very few specimens are known.

SPECIES:
  Pararhadinea albignaci
  Pararhadinea melanogaster

GENUS: **PAREAS**
ASIAN SLUG-EATERS
18 SPECIES

SIZE: Small.
DISTRIBUTION: Southern China and Southeast Asia, including the island of Borneo.
HABITAT: Humid forests and plantations.
FOOD: Slugs and snails; the skulls and jaws are modified for extracting them from their shells.
REPRODUCTION: Egg-layers.

SPECIES:
  Pareas boulengeri
  Pareas carinatus
  Pareas chinensis
  Pareas formosensis
  Pareas hamptoni
  Pareas iwasakii
  Pareas kuangtungensis
  Pareas laevis
  Pareas macularius
  Pareas malaccanus
  Pareas margaritophorus

  Pareas monticola
  Pareas nuchalis
  Pareas stanleyi
  Pareas tamdaoensis
  Pareas tropidonotus
  Pareas vertebralis
  Pareas yunnanensis

GENUS: **PHILODRYAS**
25 SPECIES

SIZE: Moderately long, but slender.
DISTRIBUTION: South America.
HABITAT: Forests, where they are arboreal.
FOOD: Frogs, lizards, snakes, birds, and bats.
REPRODUCTION: Egg-layers.
NOTES: Active by day. *P. lividum* was previously placed in the genus *Platyinion*.

SPECIES:
  Philodryas aestivus
  Philodryas arnoldi
  Philodryas baroni
  Philodryas bolivianus
  Philodryas borelli
  Philodryas burmeisteri
  Philodryas carbonelli
  Philodryas chamissonis
  Philodryas elegans
  Philodryas inca
  Philodryas laticeps
  Philodryas latirostris
  Philodryas lividum
  Philodryas mattogrossensis
  Philodryas nattereri
  Philodryas olfersii
  Philodryas oligolepis
  Philodryas patagoniensis
  Philodryas psammophideus
  Philodryas pseudoserra
  Philodryas serra
  Philodryas simonsii
  Philodryas tachymenoides
  Philodryas varius
  Philodryas viridissimus

GENUS: **PHILOTHAMNUS**
GREEN SNAKES, BUSH SNAKES
17 SPECIES

SIZE: Small and slender.
DISTRIBUTION: The southern half of Africa.
HABITAT: Varied, but always well-vegetated.
FOOD: Mainly frogs.
REPRODUCTION: Egg-layers.

SPECIES:
  Philothamnus angolensis, Western Bush Snake
  Philothamnus battersbyi
  Philothamnus bequaerti
  Philothamnus carinatus
  Philothamnus dorsalis
  Philothamnus girardi
  Philothamnus heterodermus

Philothamnus heterolepidotus
Philothamnus hoplogaster,
    Green Bush Snake
Philothamnus hughesi
Philothamnus irregularis
Philothamnus macrops
Philothamnus natalensis,
    Natal Green Snake
Philothamnus nitidus
Philothamnus ornatus,
    Ornate Bush Snake
Philothamnus punctatus
Philothamnus semivariegatus,
    Spotted Bush Snake

GENUS: PHIMOPHIS
5 SPECIES

SIZE: Small.
DISTRIBUTION: Central and South America.
HABITAT: Burrowers.
FOOD: Thought to be mainly invertebrates.
REPRODUCTION: Egg-layers.
NOTES: They have modified, upturned snouts, the purpose of which is unclear.

SPECIES:
Phimophis guerini
Phimophis guianensis
Phimophis iglesiasi
Phimophis lineaticollis
Phimophis vittatus

GENUS: PHYLLORHYNCHUS
LEAF-NOSED SNAKES
2 SPECIES

SIZE: Small.
DISTRIBUTION: Western North America (Sonoran Desert).
HABITAT: Dry places.
FOOD: Small lizards, especially geckos, and their eggs.
REPRODUCTION: Egg-layers.
NOTES: The common name is derived from the modified scale found at the tip of the snout.

SPECIES:
Phyllorhynchus browni,
    Saddled Leaf-nosed Snake
Phyllorhynchus decurtatus,
    Spotted Leaf-nosed Snake

GENUS: PITUOPHIS
GOPHER, PINE, AND BULL SNAKES
5 SPECIES

SIZE: Medium to large, with stout, muscular bodies.
DISTRIBUTION: North and Central America.
HABITAT: Varied, from deserts to pinewoods and cultivated fields.
FOOD: Small mammals, up to the size of squirrels and rabbits.
REPRODUCTION: Egg-layers.

NOTES: They hiss loudly if threatened and some forms bite viciously. The Louisiana Pine Snake, *P. ruthveni*, is one of the rarest snakes in North America.

SPECIES:
Pituophis catenifer,
    Gopher Snake, Bull Snake
Pituophis deppei,
    Mexican Gopher Snake
Pituophis lineaticollis,
    Central American Gopher Snake
● *Pituophis melanoleucus*,
    Pine Snake (pp. 92–3)
Pituophis ruthveni,
    Louisiana Pine Snake

GENUS: PLAGIOPHOLIS
5 SPECIES

SIZE: Small.
DISTRIBUTION: China, Myanmar, and Thailand.
HABITAT: Terrestrial; otherwise unknown.
FOOD: Unknown.
REPRODUCTION: Unknown.

SPECIES:
Plagiopholis blakewayi
Plagiopholis delacouri
Plagiopholis nuchalis
Plagiopholis styani
Plagiopholis unipostocularis

GENUS: PLIOCERCUS
6 SPECIES

SIZE: Medium.
DISTRIBUTION: Central and South America (Amazon basin).
HABITAT: Lowland rain forests.
FOOD: Mainly frogs.
REPRODUCTION: Egg-layers.

SPECIES:
Pliocercus andrewsi
Pliocercus annellatus
Pliocercus arubricus
Pliocercus dimidiatus
Pliocercus elapoides
Pliocercus euryzonus

GENUS: POECILOPHOLIS
1 SPECIES

SIZE: Small.
DISTRIBUTION: West Africa (Cameroon).
HABITAT: Unknown.
FOOD: Unknown.
REPRODUCTION: Unknown.
NOTES: Very rare and poorly known.

SPECIES:
Poecilopholis cameronensis

GENUS: PROSYMNA
SHOVEL-SNOUTED SNAKES
15 SPECIES

SIZE: Small and slender.
DISTRIBUTION: Southern half of Africa.
HABITAT: Varied; usually dry places, where they burrow in loose, sandy soil.
FOOD: Reptile eggs.
REPRODUCTION: Egg-layers, producing small numbers of elongated eggs.
NOTES: Active at night.

SPECIES:
Prosymna ambigua,
    East African Shovelsnout
Prosymna angolensis,
    Angolan Shovelsnout
Prosymna bivittata,
    Two-striped Shovelsnout
Prosymna frontalis,
    Southwestern Shovelsnout
Prosymna greigerti
Prosymna janii,
    Mozambique Shovelsnout
Prosymna meleagris
Prosymna ornatissima
Prosymna pitmani
Prosymna ruspolii
Prosymna semifasciata
Prosymna somalica
Prosymna sundevalli,
    Sundevall's Shovelsnout
Prosymna varius
Prosymna visseri,
    Visser's Shovelsnout

GENUS: PSAMMODYNASTES
MOCK VIPERS
2 SPECIES

SIZE: Small.
DISTRIBUTION: Southeast Asia, including the Indonesian archipelago and the Philippine Islands.
HABITAT: Forests.
FOOD: Lizards and frogs.
REPRODUCTION: Live-bearers.
NOTES: They have deep, angular heads; large eyes; and vertical pupils; very much like vipers. Nocturnal.

SPECIES:
Psammodynastes pictus
Psammodynastes pulverulentus

GENUS: PSAMMOPHIS
SAND SNAKES
23 SPECIES

SIZE: Small to moderately large, with slender bodies.
DISTRIBUTION: Africa and the Middle East; one species (*P. condanarus*) is found in Myanmar and Thailand and another (*P. lineolatus*) in western China.
HABITAT: Varied but usually open grasslands, deserts, and cultivated places.

FOOD: Mainly lizards, which they pursue with great speed.
REPRODUCTION: Egg-layers.
NOTES: Rear-fanged; bites from some of the larger species can result in localized pain and swelling in humans.

SPECIES:
Psammophis aegyptius
Psammophis angolensis,
    Dwarf Sand Snake
Psammophis ansorgii
Psammophis biseriatus
Psammophis brevirostris
Psammophis condanarus
Psammophis crucifer,
    Cross-marked Sand Snake
Psammophis elegans
Psammophis jallae,
    Jalla's Sand Snake
Psammophis leightoni,
    Cape Sand Snake
Psammophis leithii
Psammophis lineolatus
Psammophis longifrons
Psammophis notostictus,
    Karoo Sand Snake
Psammophis phillipsi,
    Olive Sand Snake
Psammophis pulcher
Psammophis punctulatus
Psammophis rukwae
Psammophis schokari
Psammophis sibilans,
    Hissing Sand Snake
Psammophis subtaeniatus,
    Stripe-bellied Sand Snake
Psammophis tanganicus
Psammophis trigrammus,
    Western Sand Snake

GENUS: PSAMMOPHYLAX
SKAAPSTEKERS
3 SPECIES

SIZE: Small to medium.
DISTRIBUTION: Southern Africa.
HABITAT: Grasslands and scrub.
FOOD: Frogs, lizards, and small mammals.
REPRODUCTION: Various: *P. tritaeniatus* and *P. rhombeatus* are egg-layers, but some populations of *P. variabilis* lay eggs, while others are live-bearers.
NOTES: Rear-fanged. They produce small amounts of very potent venom, but are not considered dangerous to humans (nor to sheep, despite their name, which means "sheep killer" in Afrikaans).

SPECIES:
Psammophylax rhombeatus,
    Spotted Skaapsteker or Rhombic Skaapsteker
Psammophylax tritaeniatus,
    Striped Skaapsteker
Psammophylax variabilis,
    Gray-bellied Grass Snake

GENUS: **PSEUDABLABES**
1 SPECIES

SIZE: Small.
DISTRIBUTION: South America
HABITAT: Unknown.
FOOD: Unknown.
REPRODUCTION: Unknown.

SPECIES:
Pseudablabes agassizii

GENUS: **PSEUDASPIS**
1 SPECIES

SIZE: Large, to over 6 ft 6 in (2 m).
DISTRIBUTION: Southern Africa.
HABITAT: Open country: grassland, scrub, deserts, and hillsides.
FOOD: Small mammals.
REPRODUCTION: Live-bearer. Young can number up to 100 in exceptional cases.

SPECIES:
Pseudaspis cana,
Mole Snake

GENUS: **PSEUDOBOA**
4 SPECIES

SIZE: Medium.
DISTRIBUTION: Central and South America.
HABITAT: Rain forests, where they live mostly on the ground.
FOOD: Lizards, snakes, and small mammals.
REPRODUCTION: Egg-layers, sometimes laying their eggs in ant nests.
NOTES: Rear-fanged, though not dangerous to humans. Active at night.

SPECIES:
Pseudoboa coronata
Pseudoboa haasi
Pseudoboa neuwiedii
Pseudoboa nigra

GENUS: **PSEUDOBOODON**
3 SPECIES

SIZE: Small to medium.
DISTRIBUTION: The highlands of Ethiopia.
HABITAT: Unknown.
FOOD: Unknown.
REPRODUCTION: Unknown.
NOTES: Apparently closely related to the house snakes, *Lamprophis*, but rare and poorly known.

SPECIES:
Pseudoboodon boehmi
Pseudoboodon gascae
Pseudoboodon lemniscatus

GENUS: **PSEUDOERYX**
1 SPECIES

SIZE: Fairly large.
DISTRIBUTION: Brazil and Paraguay.
HABITAT: Aquatic.
FOOD: Thought to eat fish and amphibians.
REPRODUCTION: Unknown.
NOTES: Its natural history is practically unknown.

SPECIES:
Pseudoeryx plicatilis

GENUS: **PSEUDOFICIMIA**
1 SPECIES

SIZE: Small.
DISTRIBUTION: Mexico.
HABITAT: Unknown.
FOOD: Unknown.
REPRODUCTION: Unknown.
NOTES: A rare snake about which almost nothing is known. Presumed to be similar in habits to the hook-nosed snakes, *Ficimia* species, which it resembles.

SPECIES:
Pseudoficimia frontalis.

GENUS: **PSEUDOLEPTODEIRA**
2 SPECIES

SIZE: Small.
DISTRIBUTION: Mexico
HABITAT: Terrestrial, otherwise unknown.
FOOD: Thought to be lizards and frogs.
REPRODUCTION: Egg-layers.

SPECIES:
Pseudoleptodeira latifasciata
Pseudoleptodeira uribei

GENUS: **PSEUDORABDION**
11 SPECIES

SIZE: Small.
DISTRIBUTION: Southeast Asia.
HABITAT: Forests, in leaf-litter and other debris.
FOOD: Thought to be earthworms and other soft-bodied invertebrates.
REPRODUCTION: Thought to be egg-layers.

SPECIES:
Pseudorabdion albonuchalis
Pseudorabdion ater
Pseudorabdion collaris
Pseudorabdion eiselti
Pseudorabdion longiceps
Pseudorabdion mcnamarae
Pseudorabdion montanum
Pseudorabdion oxycephalum
Pseudorabdion sarasinorum
Pseudorabdion saravacensis
Pseudorabdion taylor

GENUS: **PSEUDOTOMODON**
1 SPECIES

SIZE: Medium.
DISTRIBUTION: Western Argentina.
HABITAT: Unknown.
FOOD: Unknown.
REPRODUCTION: Live-bearer.
NOTES: Very rare and poorly known.

SPECIES:
Pseudotomodon trigonatus

GENUS: **PSEUDOXENODON**
11 SPECIES

SIZE: Small to medium.
DISTRIBUTION: China and Southeast Asia.
HABITAT: Terrestrial.
FOOD: Lizards and frogs.
REPRODUCTION: Thought to be egg-layers.

SPECIES:
Pseudoxenodon bambusicola
Pseudoxenodon baramensis
Pseudoxenodon dorsalis
Pseudoxenodon fukienensis
Pseudoxenodon inornatus
Pseudoxenodon jacobsonii
Pseudoxenodon karlschmidti
Pseudoxenodon macrops
Pseudoxenodon popei
Pseudoxenodon stejnegeri
Pseudoxenodon striaticaudatus

GENUS: **PSEUDOXYRHOPUS**
10 SPECIES

SIZE: Small.
DISTRIBUTION: Madagascar
HABITAT: Unknown; thought to be a burrowing species, often turning up beneath rotting logs and other debris.
FOOD: Some species may feed on frogs.
REPRODUCTION: Unknown.

SPECIES:
Pseudoxyrhopus ambreensis
Pseudoxyrhopus ankafinaensis
Pseudoxyrhopus heterurus
Pseudoxyrhopus imerinae
Pseudoxyrhopus kely
Pseudoxyrhopus microps
Pseudoxyrhopus punctatus
Pseudoxyrhopus quinquelineatus
Pseudoxyrhopus sokosoko
Pseudoxyrhopus tritaeniatus

GENUS: **PSEUSTES**
3 SPECIES

SIZE: Long and slender.
DISTRIBUTION: Central and South America, including Trinidad.
HABITAT: Forests, where they are terrestrial, although they occasionally climb into low vegetation while hunting.

FOOD: Birds, lizards, and amphibians.
REPRODUCTION: Egg-layers.

SPECIES:
Pseustes poecilonotus
Pseustes sexcarinatus
Pseustes sulphureus

GENUS: **PSOMOPHIS**
3 SPECIES

SIZE: Small.
DISTRIBUTION: Central and South America.
HABITAT: Forests, especially in leaf-litter and decaying logs.
FOOD: Earthworms.
REPRODUCTION: Egg-layers.
NOTES: Described in 1994; formerly placed in the genus *Rhadinea*.

SPECIES:
Psomophis genimaculatus
Psomophis jobertsi
Psomophis obtusus

GENUS: **PTYAS**
ASIAN RAT SNAKES
5 SPECIES

SIZE: Large to very large, and powerful.
DISTRIBUTION: Asia.
HABITAT: Varied, often found around villages and towns.
FOOD: Rodents, amphibians, lizards, snakes, and birds.
REPRODUCTION: Egg-layers.
NOTES: Active during the day. They are killed in massive numbers for the skin trade and are disappearing from many of the places where they were formerly abundant. Four former species (*P. carinatus, P. dhumnades, P. fuscus,* and *P. nigromarginatus*) are now placed in the genus *Zaocys*.

SPECIES:
Ptyas dipsas
Ptyas korros
Ptyas luzonensis
Ptyas mucosus
Ptyas tornieri

GENUS: **PTYCHOPHIS**
1 SPECIES

SIZE: Small.
DISTRIBUTION: Brazil.
HABITAT: Damp places, where it is semi-aquatic.
FOOD: Frogs and fish.
REPRODUCTION: Live-bearer.
NOTES: Rear-fanged and potentially harmful to humans.

SPECIES:
Ptychophis flavovirgatus

GENUS: PYTHONODIPSAS
1 SPECIES

SIZE: Small, to about 1 ft 11½ in (60 m).
DISTRIBUTION: Namibia and Angola.
HABITAT: Rocky deserts.
FOOD: Small lizards and rodents.
REPRODUCTION: Unknown.
NOTES: It is unusual among colubrids because the head is covered with many small, fragmented scales. The nostrils point upward. It has large rear fangs, but is not considered dangerous to humans. It shelters by day in sand and is often found at the base of the equally unusual *Welwischia* plants.

SPECIES:
Pythonodipsas carinata,
Western Keeled Snake

GENUS: RABDION
1 SPECIES

SIZE: Small.
DISTRIBUTION: Sulawesi.
HABITAT: Unknown.
FOOD: Unknown.
REPRODUCTION: Unknown.
NOTES: Rare and poorly known.

SPECIES:
Rabdion forsteni

GENUS: REGINA
CRAYFISH SNAKES
4 SPECIES

SIZE: Small to medium.
DISTRIBUTION: North America.
HABITAT: Invariably found near water.
FOOD: Crustaceans and the aquatic larvae of insects. *R. septemvittata* has one of the most specialized diets of any snake: it only eats newly molted crayfish.
REPRODUCTION: Live-bearers.
NOTES: Closely related to the *Nerodia* species, to which they bear a resemblance.

SPECIES:
Regina alleni,
Striped Swamp Snake
Regina grahami,
Graham's Water Snake
Regina rigida,
Glossy Water Snake
Regina septemvittata,
Queen Snake

GENUS: RHABDOPHIS
17 SPECIES

SIZE: Medium, usually less than 3 ft 3 in (1 m).
DISTRIBUTION: Central and Southeast Asia, India, China, and Japan.
HABITAT: Ponds, swamps, flooded areas, and slow-moving rivers.
FOOD: Fish and frogs.
REPRODUCTION: Egg-layers.
NOTES: Rear-fanged and dangerous; at least one species, *R. tigrinus*, has caused human fatalities.

SPECIES:
Rhabdophis angeli
Rhabdophis auriculata
Rhabdophis callichroma
Rhabdophis ceylonensis
Rhabdophis chrysargoides
Rhabdophis chrysargus
Rhabdophis conspicillatus
Rhabdophis himalayanus
Rhabdophis leonardi
Rhabdophis lineata
Rhabdophis murudensis
Rhabdophis nigrocinctus
Rhabdophis nuchalis
Rhabdophis spilogaster
Rhabdophis subminiatus
Rhabdophis swinhonis
Rhabdophis tigrinus

GENUS: RHABDOPS
2 SPECIES

SIZE: Small.
DISTRIBUTION: India, northern Myanmar, and China.
HABITAT: Unknown.
FOOD: Thought to be invertebrates.
REPRODUCTION: Unknown.

SPECIES:
Rhabdops bicolor
Rhabdops olivaceus

GENUS: RHACHIDELUS
1 SPECIES

SIZE: Fairly large, over 3 ft 3 in (1 m) long, and stocky.
DISTRIBUTION: Brazil and Argentina.
HABITAT: Forests, where it is terrestrial.
FOOD: Mainly birds.
REPRODUCTION: Egg-layer.
NOTES: Active by day.

SPECIES:
Rhachidelus brazili

GENUS: RHADINAEA
43 SPECIES

SIZE: Small.
DISTRIBUTION: North, Central, and South America, from North Carolina (*R. flavilata*) to Argentina.
HABITAT: Varied but often damp, wooded places, under logs and forest debris.
FOOD: Earthworms and other invertebrates, frogs, frogs' eggs, and small reptiles.

REPRODUCTION: Egg-layer, producing small clutches of eggs.
NOTES: Secretive. There is some doubt over the validity of certain species.

SPECIES:
Rhadinaea altamontana
Rhadinaea anochoreta
Rhadinaea beui
Rhadinaea bogertorum
Rhadinaea calligaster
Rhadinaea cuneata
Rhadinaea decipiens
Rhadinaea decorata
Rhadinaea dumerilli
Rhadinaea flavilata
Rhadinaea forbesi
Rhadinaea fulviceps
Rhadinaea fulvivittis
Rhadinaea gaigeae
Rhadinaea godmani
Rhadinaea guentheri
Rhadinaea hannsteini
Rhadinaea hempsteadae
Rhadinaea hesperia
Rhadinaea kanalchutchan
Rhadinaea kinkelini
Rhadinaea lachrymans
Rhadinaea lateristriga
Rhadinaea laureata
Rhadinaea macdougalli
Rhadinaea marcellae
Rhadinaea montana
Rhadinaea montecristi
Rhadinaea multilineata
Rhadinaea myersi
Rhadinaea omiltemana
Rhadinaea pachyura
Rhadinaea pilonaorum
Rhadinaea pinicola
Rhadinaea posadasi
Rhadinaea pulveriventris
Rhadinaea quinquelineata
Rhadinaea sargenti
Rhadinaea schistosa
Rhadinaea serperaster
Rhadinaea stadelmani
Rhadinaea taeniata
Rhadinaea vermiculaticeps

GENUS: RHADINOPHANES
1 SPECIES

SIZE: Small.
DISTRIBUTION: South America.
HABITAT: Unknown.
FOOD: Unknown.
REPRODUCTION: Unknown.
NOTES: Rare and poorly known.

SPECIES:
Rhadinophanes monticola

GENUS: RHAMNOPHIS
2 SPECIES

SIZE: Small.
DISTRIBUTION: West and Central Africa.
HABITAT: Tropical forests.
FOOD: Unknown.
REPRODUCTION: Unknown.
NOTES: Very rare and poorly known.

SPECIES:
Rhamnophis aethiopissa
Rhamnophis batesii

GENUS: RHAMPHIOPHIS
BEAKED SNAKES
4 SPECIES

SIZE: Medium to large, and stocky.
DISTRIBUTION: Africa.
HABITAT: Dry, scrubby countryside.
FOOD: Reptiles, birds, and small mammals.
REPRODUCTION: Egg-layers.

SPECIES:
Rhamphiophis acutus
Rhamphiophis marudiensis
Rhamphiophis oxyrhynchus
Rhamphiophis rubropunctatus

GENUS: RHINOBOTHRYUM
2 SPECIES

SIZE: Large and slender, with blunt heads.
DISTRIBUTION: Central and South America.
HABITAT: Forests, where they are arboreal.
FOOD: Unknown.
REPRODUCTION: Unknown.
NOTES: Brightly banded, like the coral snake, *Micrurus alleni*, which lives in the same region. Nocturnal.

SPECIES:
Rhinobothryum bovallii
Rhinobothryum lentiginosum

GENUS: RHINOCALAMUS
1 SPECIES

SIZE: Small.
DISTRIBUTION: Southeast Asia.
HABITAT: Varied; a burrower.
FOOD: Earthworms and other soft-bodied invertebrates.
REPRODUCTION: Egg-layer.

SPECIES:
Rhinocalamus dimidiatus

GENUS: RHINOCHEILUS
1 SPECIES

SIZE: Medium, to nearly 3 ft 3 in (1 m).
DISTRIBUTION: North America and northern Mexico.
HABITAT: Dry places, where it is terrestrial.

FOOD: Mostly lizards, but also snakes, small mammals, and birds.
REPRODUCTION: Egg-layer.
NOTES: Largely nocturnal. A second form, *R. lecontei antoni*, may be a separate species.

SPECIES:
Rhinocheilus lecontei,
Long-nosed Snake

GENUS: RHYNCHOCALAMUS
8 SPECIES

SIZE: Small and slender.
DISTRIBUTION: Middle East.
HABITAT: Dry places.
FOOD: Invertebrates and small reptiles.
REPRODUCTION: Thought to be egg-layers.
NOTES: There is confusion over the number of species in this genus; some of those listed may not be valid.

SPECIES:
Rhynchocalamus arabicus
Rhynchocalamus dorsolateralis
Rhynchocalamus eberhardti
Rhynchocalamus melanocephalus
Rhynchocalamus phaenochalinus
Rhynchocalamus propinquis
Rhynchocalamus satunini
Rhynchocalamus violaceus

GENUS: RHYNCHOPHIS
1 SPECIES

SIZE: Medium.
DISTRIBUTION: China and North Vietnam.
HABITAT: Forests, where it is arboreal.
FOOD: Unknown.
REPRODUCTION: Unknown.
NOTES: The body is slender and bright green, and the narrow head has an unusual upturned fleshy "horn" on the tip of the snout.

SPECIES:
Rhynchophis boulengeri

GENUS: SALVADORA
PATCH-NOSED SNAKES
7 SPECIES

SIZE: Up to about 3 ft 3 in (1 m) in length, with slender bodies.
DISTRIBUTION: North and Central America.
HABITAT: Dry sandy and rocky places.
FOOD: Mainly lizards and snakes.
REPRODUCTION: Egg-layers
NOTES: Fast-moving, diurnal hunters.

SPECIES:
Salvadora bairdi
Salvadora deserticola,
Big Bend Patch-nosed Snake
Salvadora grahamiae,
Mountain Patch-nosed Snake

Salvadora hexalepis,
Western Patch-Nosed Snake
Salvadora intermedia
Salvadora lemniscata
Salvadora mexicana

GENUS: SAPHENOPHIS
5 SPECIES

SIZE: Small.
DISTRIBUTION: South America (Colombia, Ecuador, and Peru).
HABITAT: Humid forests.
FOOD: Unknown.
REPRODUCTION: Unknown.
NOTES: Rare and poorly known. Some species have been included in *Lygophis* in the past.

SPECIES:
Saphenophis antioquiensis
Saphenophis atahuallpae
Saphenophis boursieri
Saphenophis sneiderni
Saphenophis tristriatus

GENUS: SCAPHIODONTOPHIS
4 SPECIES

SIZE: Small.
DISTRIBUTION: Central and South America.
HABITAT: Forests.
FOOD: Thought to be lizards and snakes.
REPRODUCTION: Egg-layers.

SPECIES:
Scaphiodontophis annulatus
Scaphiodontophis carpicinctus
Scaphiodontophis dugandi
Scaphiodontophis venustissimus

GENUS: SCAPHIOPHIS
2 SPECIES

SIZE: Up to 3 ft 3 in (1 m).
DISTRIBUTION: Central and West Africa.
HABITAT: Unknown.
FOOD: Unknown.
REPRODUCTION: Egg-layer.

SPECIES:
Scaphiophis albopunctatus
Scaphiophis raffreyi

GENUS: SCOLECOPHIS
1 SPECIES

SIZE: Small and slender.
DISTRIBUTION: Central America.
HABITAT: Forests.
FOOD: Centipedes.
REPRODUCTION: Egg-layer.
NOTES: A brightly marked false coral snake.

SPECIES:
Scolecophis atrocinctus

GENUS: SEMINATRIX
1 SPECIES

SIZE: Small.
DISTRIBUTION: Southeastern US.
HABITAT: Still waters, especially where there is a covering of floating plants.
FOOD: Fish, frogs, tadpoles, salamanders, and leeches.
REPRODUCTION: Live-bearer.

SPECIES:
Seminatrix pygaea,
Black Swamp Snake

GENUS: SENTICOLIS
1 SPECIES

SIZE: Long, to 6 ft 6 in (2 m), but quite slender.
DISTRIBUTION: North and Central America.
HABITAT: Forests, where it is semi-arboreal.
FOOD: Lizards, birds, and small mammals.
REPRODUCTION: Egg-layer.
NOTES: Formerly placed in the genus *Elaphe*.

SPECIES:
Senticolis triaspis,
Neotropical Rat Snake

GENUS: SIBON
SOUTH AMERICAN SLUG-EATERS
15 SPECIES

SIZE: Small: often quite long, but very slender and with rounded heads.
DISTRIBUTION: Central and South America.
HABITAT: Forests, where they are highly arboreal.
FOOD: Slugs and snails, for which they have specially modified jaws.
REPRODUCTION: Egg-layers.

SPECIES:
Sibon annulata
Sibon annuliferus
Sibon anthracops
Sibon argus
Sibon carri
Sibon dimidiata
Sibon dunni
Sibon fasciata
Sibon fischeri
Sibon longifrenis
Sibon nebulata
Sibon philippii
Sibon sanniola
Sibon sartorii
Sibon zweifeli

GENUS: SIBYNOMORPHUS
10 SPECIES

SIZE: Small.
DISTRIBUTION: South America.
HABITAT: Forests and clearings.
FOOD: Slugs and snails.
REPRODUCTION: Thought to be egg-layers.

SPECIES:
Sibynomorphus inaequifasciatus
Sibynomorphus lavillai
Sibynomorphus mikanii
Sibynomorphus neuwiedi
Sibynomorphus oneilli
Sibynomorphus turgidus
Sibynomorphus vagrans
Sibynomorphus vagus
Sibynomorphus ventrimaculatus
Sibynomorphus williamsi

GENUS: SIBYNOPHIS
10 SPECIES

SIZE: Small and slender.
DISTRIBUTION: India, Sri Lanka, southern China, and Southeast Asia.
HABITAT: Forests.
FOOD: Unknown.
REPRODUCTION: Egg-layers.
NOTES: Secretive and poorly known.

SPECIES:
Sibynophis bistrigatus
Sibynophis bivittatus
Sibynophis chinensis
Sibynophis collaris
Sibynophis geminatus
Sibynophis grahami
Sibynophis melanocephalus
Sibynophis sagittarius
Sibynophis subpunctatus
Sibynophis triangularis

GENUS: SIMOPHIS
2 SPECIES

SIZE: Small and slender.
DISTRIBUTION: Brazil.
HABITAT: Fields and clearings.
FOOD: Unknown.
REPRODUCTION: Unknown.

SPECIES:
Simophis rhinostoma
Simophis rhodei

GENUS: SINONATRIX
5 SPECIES

SIZE: Fairly large, to about 3 ft 3 in (1 m.)
DISTRIBUTION: China and Vietnam.
HABITAT: Swamps, marshes, and pools.
FOOD: Fish and amphibians.
REPRODUCTION: Live-bearers, where known.

SPECIES:
Sinonatrix aquaefasciata
Sinonatrix annularis
Sinonatrix bellula
Sinonatrix dunni
Sinonatrix percarinata

GENUS: **SIPHLOPHIS**
5 SPECIES

SIZE: Small to medium.
DISTRIBUTION: Central and South America.
HABITAT: Forests, where they are arboreal.
FOOD: Frogs and lizards.
REPRODUCTION: Egg-layers.
NOTES: Rear-fanged and capable of causing localized pain and swellings in humans. Active at night.

SPECIES:
Siphlophis cervinus
Siphlophis leucocephalus
Siphlophis longicaudatus
Siphlophis pulcher
Siphlophis worontzowi

GENUS: **SONORA**
GROUND SNAKES
4 SPECIES

SIZE: Small.
DISTRIBUTION: North America and Mexico.
HABITAT: Dry places.
FOOD: Insects, spiders, and scorpions.
REPRODUCTION: Egg-layers.
NOTES: The markings are extremely variable and various color forms have sometimes been regarded as separate species.

SPECIES:
Sonora aemula
Sonora episcopa
Sonora michoacanensis
Sonora semiannulata

GENUS: **SORDELLINA**
1 SPECIES

SIZE: Small.
DISTRIBUTION: Brazil.
HABITAT: Damp places, near water.
FOOD: Frogs and tadpoles.
REPRODUCTION: Egg-layer.

SPECIES:
Sordellina punctata

GENUS: **SPALEROSOPHIS**
6 SPECIES

SIZE: Fairly large, to more than 3 ft 3 in (1 m).
DISTRIBUTION: North Africa and the Middle East.
HABITAT: Deserts and scrub.

FOOD: Rodents, birds, and probably lizards.
REPRODUCTION: Egg-layers.

SPECIES:
Spalerosophis arenarius
Spalerosophis atriceps
Spalerosophis diadema
Spalerosophis dolichospilus
Spalerosophis josephscorteccii
Spalerosophis microlepis

GENUS: **SPILOTES**
1 SPECIES

SIZE: Large, to over 6 ft 6 in (2 m).
DISTRIBUTION: Central and South America, from Mexico to Argentina.
HABITAT: Varied, but often dry forests, where they are highly arboreal. Often associated with human dwellings.
FOOD: Amphibians, reptiles, birds, birds' eggs, bats, and other mammals.
REPRODUCTION: Egg-layer.
NOTES: The narrow body is brightly marked in black and yellow and has a prominent ridge along the back. A well-known and common species that defends itself vigorously by biting, although it is harmless to humans.

SPECIES:
Spilotes pullatus,
Tiger Snake, Chicken Snake, Thunder Snake

GENUS: **STEGONOTUS**
10 SPECIES

SIZE: Medium to large.
DISTRIBUTION: Southeast Asia, including the Philippines and New Guinea, and northern Australia.
HABITAT: Varied.
FOOD: Fish, frogs, and tadpoles.
REPRODUCTION: Egg-layers.

SPECIES:
Stegonotus batjanensis
Stegonotus borneensis
Stegonotus cucullatus,
Slaty-gray Snake
Stegonotus diehli
Stegonotus dumerilii
Stegonotus guentheri
Stegonotus heterurus
Stegonotus modestus
Stegonotus muelleri
Stegonotus parvus

GENUS: **STENOPHIS**
15 SPECIES

SIZE: Long and slender.
DISTRIBUTION: Madagascar.
HABITAT: Forests, where they are highly arboreal.

FOOD: Unknown, but thought to be arboreal lizards.
REPRODUCTION: Live-bearers, where known.
NOTES: Several species are newly described and some are known from only a handful of specimens.

SPECIES:
Stenophis arctifasciatus
Stenophis betsileanus
Stenophis capuroni
Stenophis carleti
Stenophis citrinus
Stenophis gaimardi
Stenophis granuliceps
Stenophis guentheri
Stenophis iarakaensis
Stenophis inopinae
Stenophis inornatus
Stenophis jaosoloa
Stenophis pseudogranuliceps
Stenophis tulearensis
Stenophis variabilis

GENUS: **STENORRHINA**
2 SPECIES

SIZE: Medium, with stout bodies.
DISTRIBUTION: Central and northern South America, from Mexico to Ecuador.
HABITAT: Lowland forests and grasslands.
FOOD: Invertebrates, especially spiders and scorpions.
REPRODUCTION: Egg-layers.

SPECIES:
Stenorrhina degenhardtii
Stenorrhina freminvillei

GENUS: **STILOSOMA**
1 SPECIES

SIZE: Small, very slender.
DISTRIBUTION: Central Florida.
HABITAT: Dry, sandy pinewoods, where it is a burrower.
FOOD: Small snakes and lizards.
REPRODUCTION: Egg-layer.

SPECIES:
Stilosoma extenuatum,
Short-tailed Snake

GENUS: **STOLICZKAIA**
2 SPECIES

SIZE: Small.
DISTRIBUTION: India (*S. khasiensis*) and Borneo.
HABITAT: Montane species.
FOOD: Unknown.
REPRODUCTION: Unknown.
NOTES: Rare snakes whose natural history and relationships are poorly known.

SPECIES:
Stoliczkaia borneensis
Stoliczkaia khasiensis

GENUS: **STORERIA**
4 SPECIES

SIZE: Small.
DISTRIBUTION: North and Central America, from Canada to Honduras.
HABITAT: Damp places, including gardens, parks, fields, and hillsides.
FOOD: Invertebrates such as slugs, snails, and insects.
REPRODUCTION: Live-bearers.

SPECIES:
Storeria dekayi,
Brown Snake
Storeria hidalgoensis
Storeria occipitomaculata,
Red-bellied Snake
Storeria storerioides

GENUS: **SYMPHIMUS**
2 SPECIES

SIZE: Small, to about 1 ft 8 in (50 cm), and slender.
DISTRIBUTION: Mexico.
HABITAT: Dry and moist forests.
FOOD: Insects, especially grasshoppers and crickets.
REPRODUCTION: Thought to be egg-layers.
NOTES: Partially arboreal.

SPECIES:
Symphimus leucostomus
Symphimus mayae

GENUS: **SYMPHOLIS**
1 SPECIES

SIZE: Small.
DISTRIBUTION: Mexico.
HABITAT: Dry forests and scrub, where it lives in burrows.
FOOD: Thought to be lizards.
REPRODUCTION: Unknown.
NOTES: Very little is known about this secretive species.

SPECIES:
Sympholis lippiens

GENUS: **SYNOPHIS**
3 SPECIES

SIZE: Small to medium.
DISTRIBUTION: Colombia and Ecuador.
HABITAT: Damp places.
FOOD: Thought to be lizards.
REPRODUCTION: Egg-layers.

SPECIES:

Synophis bicolor
Synophis lasallei
Synophis miops

GENUS: TACHYMENIS
7 SPECIES

SIZE: Small.
DISTRIBUTION: Northwestern South America.
HABITAT: Dry situations.
FOOD: Thought to be lizards.
REPRODUCTION: Live-bearers.

SPECIES:

Tachymenis affinis
Tachymenis attenuata
Tachymenis chilensis
Tachymenis elongata
Tachymenis peruviana
Tachymenis surinamensis
Tachymenis tarmensis

GENUS: TAENIOPHALLUS
5 SPECIES

SIZE: Small.
DISTRIBUTION: South America.
HABITAT: Unknown.
FOOD: Unknown.
REPRODUCTION: Unknown.
NOTES: Poorly known; some species are only recently described.

SPECIES:

Taeniophallus affinis
Taeniophallus bilineatus
Taeniophallus brevirostris
Taeniophallus occipitalis
Taeniophallus persimilis

GENUS: TANTALOPHIS
1 SPECIES

SIZE: Small.
DISTRIBUTION: South-central Mexico.
HABITAT: Pine and cloud forests at high altitudes.
FOOD: Unknown.
REPRODUCTION: Unknown.
NOTES: Rare and poorly known.

SPECIES:

Tantalophis discolor

GENUS: TANTILLA
BLACK-HEADED AND CROWNED SNAKES
60 SPECIES

SIZE: Very small and slender.
DISTRIBUTION: North, Central, and South America, from central US to Argentina.
HABITAT: Varied, from deserts to forests.
FOOD: Insects and their larvae.

REPRODUCTION: Egg-layers, producing from one to three eggs.
NOTES: The many species are all very similar, usually brown with a black "cap" on the top of the heads. Several have small geographic ranges. Secretive snakes, which are active mainly at night and hide under stones, logs, and debris by day.

SPECIES:

Tantilla albiceps
Tantilla alticola
Tantilla andinista
Tantilla armillata
Tantilla atriceps,
    Mexican Black-headed Snake
Tantilla bairdi
Tantilla bocourti
Tantilla brevicauda
Tantilla brevis
Tantilla briggsi
Tantilla calamarina
Tantilla canula
Tantilla capistrata
Tantilla cascadae
Tantilla coronadoi
Tantilla coronata,
    Southeastern Crowned Snake
Tantilla cucullata
Tantilla cuesta
Tantilla cuniculator
Tantilla deppei
Tantilla deviatrix
Tantilla equatoriana
Tantilla excubitor
Tantilla flavilineata
Tantilla fraseri
Tantilla gracilis,
    Flat-headed Snake
Tantilla hobartsmithi,
    Southwestern Black-headed Snake
Tantilla insulamontana
Tantilla jani
Tantilla lempira
Tantilla longifrontalis
Tantilla melanocephala
Tantilla mexicana
Tantilla miniata
Tantilla miyatai
Tantilla moesta
Tantilla morgani
Tantilla nigra
Tantilla nigriceps,
    Plains Black-headed Snake
Tantilla oaxacae
Tantilla oolitica,
    Rim Rock Crowned Snake
Tantilla petersi
Tantilla planiceps,
    Californian Black-headed Snake
Tantilla relicta,
    Florida Crowned Snake
Tantilla reticulata
Tantilla rubra
Tantilla schistosa
Tantilla semicincta
Tantilla shawi
Tantilla slavensi
Tantilla striata

Tantilla supracincta
Tantilla taeniata
Tantilla tayrae
Tantilla tecta
Tantilla trilineata
Tantilla vermiformis
Tantilla virgata
Tantilla wilcoxi,
    Chihuahuan Black-headed Snake
Tantilla yaquia,
    Yaqui Black-headed Snake

GENUS: TANTILLITA
3 SPECIES

SIZE: Very small.
DISTRIBUTION: Central America.
HABITAT: Lowland forests.
FOOD: Invertebrates.
REPRODUCTION: Egg-layers.
NOTES: Closely related to the *Tantilla* species, which they resemble.

SPECIES:

Tantillita brevissima
Tantillita canula
Tantillita lintoni

GENUS: TELESCOPUS
TIGER SNAKES, CAT SNAKES
16 SPECIES

SIZE: Medium, but slender.
DISTRIBUTION: Africa, the Balkan region of Europe (*T. fallax*), and the Near East.
HABITAT: Varied, but usually in dry, rocky places.
FOOD: Lizards and small rodents.
REPRODUCTION: Egg-layers.
NOTES: Rear-fanged, though not dangerous to humans. Thoroughly nocturnal.

SPECIES:

Telescopus beetzi,
    Namib Tiger Snake
Telescopus dhara
Telescopus fallax,
    European Cat Snake
Telescopus gabesiensis
Telescopus gezirae
Telescopus guentheri
Telescopus guidimakensis
Telescopus hoogstraali
Telescopus iberus
Telescopus nigriceps
Telescopus obtusus
Telescopus pulcher
Telescopus rhinopoma
Telescopus semiannulatus,
    Eastern Tiger Snake
Telescopus tessellatus
Telescopus variegatus

GENUS: TETRALEPIS
1 SPECIES

SIZE: Small.
DISTRIBUTION: Java.
HABITAT: Cool, montane forests.
FOOD: Unknown.
REPRODUCTION: Unknown.
NOTES: Rare and poorly known.

SPECIES:

Tetralepis fruhstorferi

GENUS: THAMNODYNASTES
6 SPECIES

SIZE: Small to medium-sized, and stocky.
DISTRIBUTION: South America.
HABITAT: Forests, where they are terrestrial or arboreal.
FOOD: Thought to be lizards.
REPRODUCTION: Live-bearers.
NOTES: Rear-fanged; the bites can cause local pain and swelling in humans. Active mainly at night.

SPECIES:

Thamnodynastes chaquensis
Thamnodynastes chimanta
Thamnodynastes pallidus
Thamnodynastes rutilus
Thamnodynastes strigatus
Thamnodynastes strigilis

GENUS: THAMNOPHIS
GARTER SNAKES AND RIBBON SNAKES
28 SPECIES

SIZE: Small to fairly large, to over 3 ft 3 in (1 m) in some cases, with slender bodies.
DISTRIBUTION: North and Central America.
HABITAT: Usually damp places, often near water.
FOOD: Earthworms, fish, amphibians and their tadpoles, and, sometimes, small mammals.
REPRODUCTION: Live-bearers, with litters of up to 100 young in some species.
NOTES: Active by day.

SPECIES:

Thamnophis angustirostris
Thamnophis atratus
Thamnophis brachystoma,
    Short-headed Garter Snake
Thamnophis butleri,
    Butler's Garter Snake
Thamnophis chrysocephalus
Thamnophis couchii,
    Western Aquatic Garter Snake
Thamnophis cyrtopsis,
    Black-necked Garter Snake
Thamnophis elegans,
    Terrestrial Garter Snake
Thamnophis eques,
    Mexican Garter Snake
Thamnophis exsul

Thamnophis fulvus
Thamnophis gigas
Thamnophis godmani
Thamnophis hammondii,
   Two-striped Garter Snake
● *Thamnophis marcianus*,
   Checkered Garter Snake
   (pp. 100–1)
Thamnophis melanogaster
Thamnophis mendax
Thamnophis ordinoides,
   Northwestern Garter Snake
Thamnophis proximus,
   Western Ribbon Snake
Thamnophis radix,
   Plains Garter Snake
Thamnophis rufipunctatus,
   Narrow-headed Garter Snake
Thamnophis sauritus,
   Eastern Ribbon Snake
Thamnophis scalaris
Thamnophis scaliger
● *Thamnophis sirtalis*,
   Eastern Garter Snake (pp. 102–3)
Thamnophis sumichrasti
Thamnophis valida,
   Baja Garter Snake
Thamnophis vicinus

GENUS: **THELOTORNIS**
TWIG SNAKES
2 SPECIES

SIZE: Long, to nearly 6 ft 6 in (2 m), and extremely slender and twiglike.
DISTRIBUTION: Africa south of the Sahara.
HABITAT: Rain forests and shrubby grasslands, where they are totally arboreal.
FOOD: Lizards and birds.
REPRODUCTION: Egg-layers.
NOTES: The heads are elongated and pointed, and the large eyes have keyhole-shaped pupils. Active by day.

SPECIES:
Thelotornis capensis,
   Twig Snake or Bird Snake
Thelotornis kirtlandii,
   Kirtland's Twig Snake

GENUS: **THERMOPHIS**
1 SPECIES

SIZE: Fairly small.
DISTRIBUTION: Tibet.
HABITAT: Mountains at about 14,750 ft (4,500 m).
FOOD: Unknown.
REPRODUCTION: Unknown.

SPECIES:
Thermophis baileyi

GENUS: **THRASOPS**
TREE SNAKES
4 SPECIES

SIZE: Large.
DISTRIBUTION: Tropical Africa.
HABITAT: Forests, where they are arboreal.
FOOD: Frogs, lizards, and small mammals.
REPRODUCTION: Egg-layers.

SPECIES:
Thrasops aethiopissa
Thrasops flavifularis
Thrasops jacksonii,
   Jackson's Tree Snake
Thrasops occidentalis

GENUS: **TOLUCA**
4 SPECIES

SIZE: Small.
DISTRIBUTION: Central Mexico.
HABITAT: Montane woods and forests.
FOOD: Unknown.
REPRODUCTION: Unknown.

SPECIES:
Toluca amphistricha
Toluca conica
Toluca lineata
Toluca megalodon

GENUS: **TOMODON**
2 SPECIES

SIZE: Small.
DISTRIBUTION: Brazil and Argentina.
HABITAT: Forests.
FOOD: Unknown.
REPRODUCTION: Unknown.

SPECIES:
Tomodon dorsatus
Tomodon ocellatus

GENUS: **TOXICODRYAS**
2 SPECIES

SIZE: Unknown.
DISTRIBUTION: West and Central Africa.
HABITAT: Unknown.
FOOD: Unknown.
REPRODUCTION: Unknown.
NOTES: Extremely rare and poorly known.

SPECIES:
Toxicodryas blandingii
Toxicodryas pulverulenta

GENUS: **TRACHISCHIUM**
5 SPECIES

SIZE: Small.
DISTRIBUTION: Northern India and Myanmar.
HABITAT: Forests. Thought to be terrestrial.

FOOD: Unknown.
REPRODUCTION: Unknown.
NOTES: Thought to be nocturnal.

SPECIES:
Trachischium fuscum
Trachischium guentheri
Trachischium laeve
Trachischium monticola
Trachischium tenuiceps

GENUS: **TRETANORHINUS**
CENTRAL AMERICAN SWAMP SNAKES
4 SPECIES

SIZE: Small.
DISTRIBUTION: Central America to northern South America, and the West Indies.
HABITAT: Shallow, heavily weeded bodies of water. *T. nigroluteus* has been found swimming in the ocean.
FOOD: Fish, frogs, and tadpoles.
REPRODUCTION: Egg-layers.
NOTES: Nocturnal.

SPECIES:
Tretanorhinus mocquardi
Iretanorhinus nigroluteus
Tretanorhinus taeniatus
Tretanorhinus variabilis

GENUS: **TRIMETOPON**
6 SPECIES

SIZE: Small.
DISTRIBUTION: Central America.
HABITAT: Rain forests.
FOOD: Unknown.
REPRODUCTION: Unknown.

SPECIES:
Trimetopon barbouri
Trimetopon gracile
Trimetopon pliolepis
Trimetopon simile
Trimetopon slevini
Trimetopon viquezi

GENUS: **TRIMORPHODON**
LYRE SNAKES
2 SPECIES

SIZE: Medium, up to about 3 ft 3 in (1 m), with slender bodies.
DISTRIBUTION: North and Central America.
HABITAT: Dry, scrubby places, frequently among rocks.
FOOD: Mainly lizards, although snakes and small mammals, including bats, are sometimes taken.
REPRODUCTION: Egg-layers.
NOTES: Rear-fanged, though not dangerous to humans. Several subspecies of *T. biscutatus* are sometimes regarded as distinct species.

SPECIES:
Trimorphodon biscutatus
Trimorphodon tau

GENUS: **TRIPANURGOS**
1 SPECIES

SIZE: Medium, with very slender bodies, flattened from side to side.
DISTRIBUTION: Central and South America, including the island of Trinidad.
HABITAT: Forests, where it is largely arboreal.
FOOD: Mainly frogs.
REPRODUCTION: Egg-layer.

SPECIES:
Tripanurgos compressus

GENUS: **TROPIDOCLONION**
1 SPECIES

SIZE: Small.
DISTRIBUTION: North America.
HABITAT: Varied, in grasslands, gardens, parks, and fields.
FOOD: Earthworms.
REPRODUCTION: Live-bearer.

SPECIES:
Tropidoclonion lineatum,
   Lined Snake

GENUS: **TROPIDODRYAS**
2 SPECIES

SIZE: Medium, to about 3 ft 3 in (1 m).
DISTRIBUTION: Southern Brazil.
HABITAT: Forests, where they are thought to be arboreal.
FOOD: Frogs, lizards, birds, and small mammals.
REPRODUCTION: Unknown.

SPECIES:
Tropidodryas pseudoserra
Tropidodryas serra

GENUS: **TROPIDONOPHIS**
AUSTRALASIAN KEELBACKS
12 SPECIES

SIZE: Medium, to about 3 ft 11 in (1.2 m).
DISTRIBUTION: New Guinea and Borneo. One species (*T. mairii*) also occurs in northern Australia.
HABITAT: Semiaquatic, such as swamps, marshes, pools, and ditches.
FOOD: Mainly fish and frogs, but occasionally small lizards.
REPRODUCTION: Egg-layers.
NOTES: A complex genus. Certain species are sometimes known under the older name of *Macropophis*, which is here reserved for four species from the Philippine Islands. *T. flavifrons* and

T. muruensis, from Borneo, are sometimes placed in *Natrix*. Other species have been included in various other genera in the past.

SPECIES:
Tropidonophis aenigmaticus
Tropidonophis elongatus
Tropidonophis flavifrons
Tropidonophis mairii,
Keelback, Freshwater Snake
Tropidonophis montanus
Tropidonophis multiscutellatus
Tropidonophis muruensis
Tropidonophis novaeguinea
Tropidonophis parkeri
Tropidonophis picturata
Tropidonophis statisticus
Tropidonophis truncata

GENUS: **UMBRIVAGA**
3 SPECIES

SIZE: Small.
DISTRIBUTION: Northern South America.
HABITAT: Terrestrial.
FOOD: Unknown.
REPRODUCTION: Unknown.
NOTES: Poorly known.

SPECIES:
Umbrivaga mertensi
Umbrivaga pyburni
Umbrivaga pygmaea

GENUS: **UROMACER**
4 SPECIES

SIZE: Medium to large, and slender.
DISTRIBUTION: Hispaniola and surrounding islands.
HABITAT: Forests.
FOOD: Lizards, especially *Anolis* species.
REPRODUCTION: Thought to be egg-layers.

SPECIES:
Uromacer catesbyi
Uromacer frenatus
Uromacer oxyrhynchus
Uromacer wetmorei

GENUS: **UROMACERINA**
1 SPECIES

SIZE: Medium and slender.
DISTRIBUTION: Brazil.
HABITAT: Forests, where they are thought to be arboreal.
FOOD: Arboreal lizards.
REPRODUCTION: Thought to be an egg-layer.
NOTES: Poorly known.

SPECIES:
Uromacerina ricardinii

GENUS: **VIRGINIA**
EARTH SNAKES
3 SPECIES

SIZE: Small, to about 1 ft (30 cm) or less.
DISTRIBUTION: Southeastern North America.
HABITAT: Under rocks and debris, usually in damp places.
FOOD: Earthworms.
REPRODUCTION: Live-bearers.
NOTES: Secretive. *V. pulchra* may be a subspecies of *V. valeriae*.

SPECIES:
Virginia pulchra,
Mountain Earth Snake
Virginia striatula,
Rough Earth Snake
Virginia valeriae,
Smooth Earth Snake

GENUS: **WAGLEROPHIS**
1 SPECIES

SIZE: Medium and stocky.
DISTRIBUTION: South America.
HABITAT: Damp places in forests.
FOOD: Amphibians, especially toads.
REPRODUCTION: Egg-layer.
NOTES: Long rear-fangs, with which it punctures the bodies of toads. The effect of its venom on humans is not known.

SPECIES:
Waglerophis merremi

GENUS: **WALLOPHIS**
1 SPECIES

SIZE: Small.
DISTRIBUTION: India.
HABITAT: Unknown.
FOOD: Unknown.
REPRODUCTION: Egg-layer.
NOTES: Previously included in *Coronella*. A second species, *W. bella*, is referred to *Oligodon*, as *O. bellus*.

SPECIES:
Wallophis brachyura

GENUS: **XENELAPHIS**
2 SPECIES

SIZE: Large, to 6 ft 6 in (2 m) or more.
DISTRIBUTION: Thailand, the Malay Peninsula, Borneo, and Java.
HABITAT: Semiaquatic, in swamps.
FOOD: Mainly frogs.
REPRODUCTION: Egg-layers.
NOTES: Poorly known.

SPECIES:
Xenelaphis ellipsifer
Xenelaphis hexagonotus,
Malaysian Brown Snake

GENUS: **XENOCHROPHIS**
ASIAN KEELBACKS
9 SPECIES

SIZE: Medium, to over 3 ft 3 in (1 m) in some species.
DISTRIBUTION: From Afghanistan, through to Southeast Asia and the Indonesian archipelago. One species, *X. piscator*, is found throughout the genus' range; the others have more limited distributions.
HABITAT: Damp places, usually near open water.
FOOD: Fish and amphibians.
REPRODUCTION: Egg-layers.
NOTES: Rear-fanged; capable of giving a painful, but not serious, bite.

SPECIES:
Xenochrophis asperrimus
Xenochrophis cerasogaster
Xenochrophis flavipunctatus
Xenochrophis maculatus,
Spotted Keelback
Xenochrophis piscator,
Asian Keelback
Xenochrophis punctulatus
Xenochrophis sanctijohannis
Xenochrophis trianguligerus,
Red-sided Keelback
Xenochrophis vittatus,
Striped Keelback

GENUS: **XENODERMUS**
1 SPECIES

SIZE: Small, to about 2 ft 3½ in (70 cm).
DISTRIBUTION: The Malay Peninsula, Java, Sumatra, and Borneo.
HABITAT: Damp forests, marshes, paddies, and irrigation ditches. Semiaquatic and semiburrowing.
FOOD: Frogs.
REPRODUCTION: Egg-layer.
NOTES: An unusual, sluggish species that shows no obvious affinities to other colubrid snakes.

SPECIES:
Xenodermus javanicus

GENUS: **XENODON**
FALSE VIPERS
7 SPECIES

SIZE: Medium to large, with stout bodies.
DISTRIBUTION: Central and South America (Mexico to Argentina).
HABITAT: Rain forests, especially alongside watercourses.
FOOD: Toads.
REPRODUCTION: Egg-layers.
NOTES: Bad tempered and rear-fanged. Their bites are painful, though not thought to be especially dangerous.

SPECIES:
Xenodon bertholdi
Xenodon guentheri
Xenodon neuwiedii
Xenodon rabdocephalus
Xenodon severus
Xenodon suspectus
Xenodon werneri

GENUS: **XENOPHIDION**
2 SPECIES

SIZE: Small.
DISTRIBUTION: Sabah, Borneo (*X. acanthognathus*) and Selangar, Malaysia (*X. schaeferi*).
HABITAT: Primary rain forest.
FOOD: Worms, insects, and their larvae.
REPRODUCTION: Thought to be egg-layers.
NOTES: Only described in 1995 and, therefore, poorly known as yet.

SPECIES:
Xenophidion acanthognathus
Xenophidion schaeferi

GENUS: **XENOPHOLIS**
3 SPECIES

SIZE: Small and slender.
DISTRIBUTION: South America, in the Amazon basin.
HABITAT: Damp forests.
FOOD: Mainly frogs.
REPRODUCTION: Unknown, but likely to be egg-layers.

SPECIES:
Xenopholis reticulatus
Xenopholis scalaris
Xenopholis undulatus

GENUS: **XYLOPHIS**
2 SPECIES

SIZE: Small.
DISTRIBUTION: Southern India.
HABITAT: Thought to be semiburrowing.
FOOD: Unknown.
REPRODUCTION: Unknown.
NOTES: Secretive snakes about which little is known.

SPECIES:
Xylophis perroteti
Xylophis stenorhynchus

GENUS: **ZAOCYS**
4 SPECIES

SIZE: Large.
DISTRIBUTION: Northern India, Myanmar, China, and Southeast Asia.
HABITAT: Forests, fields, and around villages.
FOOD: Birds and small mammals.

REPRODUCTION: Egg-layers.

NOTES: Sometimes placed in the genus *Ptyas*.

SPECIES:

Zaocys carinatus
Zaocys dhumnades
Zaocys fuscus
Zaocys nigromarginatus

ATRACTASPIDIDAE
BURROWING ASPS

8 GENERA CONTAINING 62 SPECIES

Members of the enigmatic Atractaspididae family are generally small to medium-sized, slender, cylindrical snakes with smooth, shiny scales. Most are dull in color. They have an extraordinarily varied arrangement of the teeth and fangs, which has led to confusion over classification. Some members have hinged fangs and powerful venoms, but others are of no danger to humans.

Burrowing asps live underground, in tunnels. They feed mostly on other reptiles, especially amphisbaenians, although members of the genus *Aparallactus* eat centipedes. All the species for which reproductive mode is known are egg-layers, with one possible exception (*Amblyodipsas concolor*).

Atractaspidids are found almost exclusively in Africa, with one species in the Middle East. Members of the family have at various times been placed in the Colubridae, Viperidae, and Elapidae families. They have a variety of common names, several of them misleading. The African harlequin snakes, genus *Homoroselaps*, are sometimes placed in this family, but are currently assigned to the Elapidae.

GENUS: **AMBLYODIPSAS**
PURPLE-GLOSSED SNAKES
9 SPECIES

SIZE: Small.

DISTRIBUTION: Africa south of the Sahara.

HABITAT: Varied; burrowing in loose soil.

FOOD: Burrowing reptiles, amphibians, and small mammals.

REPRODUCTION: All egg-layers except *A. concolor*, which may be a live-bearer under certain circumstances.

NOTES: Venomous, with a pair of grooved, venom-delivering fangs below the eyes, but not dangerous to humans.

SPECIES:

Amblyodipsas concolor,
Natal Purple-glossed Snake
Amblyodipsas dimidiata
Amblyodipsas katangensis

Amblyodipsas microphthalma,
Eastern Purple-glossed Snake
Amblyodipsas polylepis
Amblyodipsas rodhaini
Amblyodipsas teitana
Amblyodipsas unicolor
Amblyodipsas ventrimaculata,
Kalahari Purple-glossed Snake

GENUS: **APARALLACTUS**
CENTIPEDE-EATERS
11 SPECIES

SIZE: Small, to about 1 ft 11½ in (60 cm).

DISTRIBUTION: Africa south of the Sahara.

HABITAT: Burrowers in sandy soil, rotting logs, abandoned termite nests, and other debris.

FOOD: Centipedes.

REPRODUCTION: Egg-layers, producing small clutches.

NOTES: Venomous, but of no danger to humans.

SPECIES:

Aparallactus capensis,
Cape Centipede-eater
Aparallactus guentheri,
Black Centipede-eater
Aparallactus jacksonii
Aparallactus lineatus
Aparallactus lunulatus,
Reticulated Centipede-eater
Aparallactus modestus
Aparallactus moeruensis
Aparallactus niger
Aparallactus nigriceps,
Mozambique Centipede-eater
Aparallactus turneri
Aparallactus werneri

GENUS: **ATRACTASPIS**
STILETTO SNAKES, BURROWING ASPS
16 SPECIES

SIZE: Small to medium.

DISTRIBUTION: Africa and the Middle East (*A. engaddensis*).

HABITAT: Varied, burrowing in loose or sandy soil.

FOOD: Small vertebrates: lizards, especially skinks, snakes, and nestling rodents.

REPRODUCTION: Egg-layers.

NOTES: They have large, partially hinged fangs and powerful venoms. They can bite without opening their mouths, by moving their fangs sideways and using them to stab their prey. This makes them very difficult to handle safely, and there have been human fatalities. All the species look similar and the number of species may be greater than those listed. Some authorities recognize 18 or more species.

SPECIES:

Atractaspis aterrima,
Slender Stiletto Snake
Atractaspis battersbyi,
Battersby's Stiletto Snake
Atractaspis bibronii,
Bibron's Stiletto Snake
Atractaspis boulengeri,
Central African Stiletto Snake
Atractaspis coalescens,
Black Stiletto Snake
Atractaspis congica,
Congo Stiletto Snake
Atractaspis corpulenta,
Fat Stiletto Snake
Atractaspis dahomeyensis,
Dahomey Stiletto Snake
Atractaspis duerdeni,
Duerden's Stiletto Snake
Atractaspis engaddensis,
Ein Geddi Stiletto Snake
Atractaspis engdahli,
Engdahl's Stiletto Snake
Atractaspis irregularis,
Variable Stiletto Snake
Atractaspis leucomelas,
Ogaden Stiletto Snake
Atractaspis microlepidota,
Small-scaled Stiletto Snake
Atractaspis reticulata,
Reticulated Stiletto Snake
Atractaspis scorteccii,
Somali Stiletto Snake

GENUS: **CHILORHINOPHIS**
BLACK AND YELLOW BURROWING SNAKES
3 SPECIES

SIZE: Small.

DISTRIBUTION: Central Africa.

HABITAT: Forests, where they live in burrows.

FOOD: Thought to feed on amphisbaenians (worm lizards) and other burrowing reptiles.

REPRODUCTION: Unknown.

NOTES: They have venom fangs near the front of their upper jaw.

SPECIES:

Chilorhinophis butleri,
Butler's Black and Yellow Burrowing Snake
Chilorhinophis carpenteri,
Carpenter's Black and Yellow Burrowing Snake
Chilorhinophis gerardi,
Gerard's Black and Yellow Burrowing Snake

GENUS: **MACRELAPS**
1 SPECIES

SIZE: Medium.

DISTRIBUTION: South Africa.

HABITAT: Coastal bush, where it burrows in leaf-litter.

FOOD: Reptiles, amphibians, and small mammals.

REPRODUCTION: Egg-layer.

NOTES: It has a potentially dangerous bite.

SPECIES:

Macrelaps microlepidotus,
Natal Black Snake

GENUS: **MICRELAPS**
4 SPECIES

SIZE: Small.

DISTRIBUTION: Central Africa.

HABITAT: Burrowing species, but otherwise unknown.

FOOD: Thought to feed on other burrowing reptiles and their eggs.

REPRODUCTION: Thought to be egg-layers.

SPECIES:

Micrelaps bicoloratus
Micrelaps boettgeri
Micrelaps muelleri
Micrelaps vaillanti

GENUS: **POLEMON**
13 SPECIES

SIZE: Small.

DISTRIBUTION: West and Central Africa.

HABITAT: Burrowers.

FOOD: Unknown.

REPRODUCTION: Unknown.

NOTES: Rare and secretive snakes, whose natural history – including their relationships with other snakes – is poorly known. Various species have been placed in the genera *Cyanodontophis*, *Elapocalamus*, and *Miodon* in the past.

SPECIES:

Polemon acanthias
Polemon barthii
Polemon bocourti
Polemon christyi
Polemon collaris
Polemon fulvicollis
Polemon gabonensis
Polemon gracilis
Polemon griseiceps
Polemon leopoldi
Polemon neuwiedi
Polemon notatus
Polemon robutus

GENUS: **XENOCALAMUS**
QUILL-SNOUTED SNAKES
5 SPECIES

SIZE: Small, to about 2 ft 7½ in (80 cm), and very slender.

DISTRIBUTION: Central and southern Africa.

HABITAT: Burrowers in sandy soil.

FOOD: Amphisbaenians (worm lizards).

REPRODUCTION: Egg-layers.

NOTES: Technically venomous, but not known to bite and of no danger to humans.

SPECIES:
Xenocalamus bicolor,
Bicolored Quill-snouted Snake
Xenocalamus mechowii,
Elongated Quill-snouted Snake
Xenocalamus michellii,
Mitchell's Quill-snouted Snake
Xenocalamus sabiensis,
Sabi Quill-snouted Snake
Xenocalamus transvaalensis,
Transvaal Quill-snouted Snake

ELAPIDAE

COBRAS, KRAITS, MAMBAS, CORAL SNAKES, AND SEA SNAKES

60 GENERA CONTAINING 291 SPECIES

Superficially, the members of the cobra family resemble many of the colubrids, to which they are undoubtedly closely related. They differ mostly in their dentition: cobras and their relatives have a pair of hollow, fixed, front fangs through which they deliver their venom.

Here the land cobras are dealt with first, followed by the marine species.

TERRESTRIAL COBRAS

43 GENERA CONTAINING 229 SPECIES

Apart from the typical hooded cobras, which are familiar if only through movies and cartoons of snake-charmers, this family contains a number of brightly colored snakes, often known as coral snakes in America, Africa, and Australia, where they occur, as well as several nondescript, dark-colored members, mostly from Australia. Their taxonomic relationships with the marine cobras (sea snakes) are still the subject of much speculation.

The mambas, kraits, taipans, brown snakes, Australian copperheads, and tiger snakes are further examples of highly venomous species within the family. The sea snakes and sea kraits (which are sometimes placed in separate families) are also dangerously venomous, although they rarely find themselves in conflict with humans. A number of genera of small, generally inoffensive and secretive snakes makes up the rest of the family.

Cobras are found in much of the world, but are more common in the southern hemisphere. Australia has a particularly rich selection of species, making up for its lack of vipers and near lack of colubrids.

GENUS: **ACANTHOPHIS**
DEATH ADDERS
3 SPECIES

SIZE: Medium, but very heavy-bodied.
DISTRIBUTION: Australasia (Australia and New Guinea).
HABITAT: Various.
FOOD: Lizards, birds, and small mammals.
REPRODUCTION: Live-bearers.
NOTES: Very dangerous species that are the ecological counterparts of vipers, which are not found in the same region. There may be additional species in New Guinea, as yet undescribed.

SPECIES:
Acanthophis antarcticus,
Common Death Adder
● *Acanthophis praelongus,*
Northern Death Adder (pp. 118–19)
Acanthophis pyrrhus,
Desert Death Adder

GENUS: **ASPIDELAPS**
2 SPECIES

SIZE: Small, to about 2 ft 7½ in (80 cm).
DISTRIBUTION: Southern Africa.
HABITAT: Dry places, usually those with sandy soil.
FOOD: Amphibians, lizards, snakes, and small mammals.
REPRODUCTION: Egg-layers.
NOTES: Deaths from bites are very rare.

SPECIES:
Aspidelaps lubricus,
(African) Coral Snake
Aspidelaps scutatus,
Shield-nosed Snake

GENUS: **ASPIDOMORPHUS**
NEW GUINEA CROWNED SNAKES
3 SPECIES

SIZE: Small, to about 1 ft 4 in (40 cm).
DISTRIBUTION: New Guinea and the Moluccas.
HABITAT: Forests; in decaying wood and vegetation, and other debris.
FOOD: Unknown.
REPRODUCTION: Unknown, but thought to be egg-layers.
NOTES: Rare, secretive snakes whose natural history, and the effects of their venom, are poorly known.

SPECIES:
Aspidomorphus lineaticollis
Aspidomorphus muelleri
Aspidomorphus schlegeli

GENUS: **AUSTRELAPS**
AUSTRALIAN COPPERHEADS
3 SPECIES

SIZE: Large, to about 5 ft 6 in (1.7 m).
DISTRIBUTION: Southeastern Australia, including Tasmania.
HABITAT: Damp places.
FOOD: Amphibians and reptiles.
REPRODUCTION: Live-bearers.
NOTES: Very dangerous, though not usually aggressive. Sometimes the three species are regarded as forms of a single species.

SPECIES:
Austrelaps labialis,
Kangaroo Island Copperhead
Austrelaps ramsayi,
Northern Copperhead
Austrelaps superbus,
Southern Copperhead

GENUS: **BOULENGERINA**
WATER COBRAS
2 SPECIES

SIZE: Moderately large, and thickset.
DISTRIBUTION: Central Africa.
HABITAT: Aquatic.
FOOD: Fish.
REPRODUCTION: Egg-layers.
NOTES: Potentially dangerous to humans, but usually inoffensive.

SPECIES:
Boulengerina annulata,
Banded Water Cobra
Boulengerina christyi,
Congo Water Cobra

GENUS: **BUNGARUS**
KRAITS
12 SPECIES

SIZE: Medium to large; slender, with cylindrical, compressed, or triangular bodies.
DISTRIBUTION: Asia (India and Sri Lanka to southern China and Southeast Asia).
HABITAT: Varied, often around human dwellings. Terrestrial.
FOOD: Other snakes.
REPRODUCTION: Egg-layers.
NOTES: Highly venomous and potentially lethal to humans. Nocturnal.

SPECIES:
Bungarus andamanensis,
Andaman Krait
Bungarus bungaroides
Bungarus caeruleus,
Indian Krait
Bungarus candidus
Bungarus ceylonicus,
Sri Lankan Krait
Bungarus fasciatus
Bungarus flaviceps
Bungarus lividus

Bungarus magnimaculatus
Bungarus multicinctus
Bungarus niger,
Black Krait
Bungarus sindanus

GENUS: **CACOPHIS**
CROWNED SNAKES
3 SPECIES

SIZE: Small, to about 2 ft 5½ in (75 cm).
DISTRIBUTION: Eastern Australia.
HABITAT: Various, under leaves or debris.
FOOD: Unknown.
REPRODUCTION: Egg-layers.
NOTES: Secretive and poorly known. The venom is thought to be too mild to be dangerous to humans.

SPECIES:
Cacophis harriettae,
White-crowned Snake
Cacophis krefftii,
Dwarf-crowned Snake
Cacophis squamulosus,
Golden-crowned Snake

GENUS: **CALLIOPHIS**
11 SPECIES

SIZE: Small and slender.
DISTRIBUTION: Southern and Southeast Asia.
HABITAT: Forests.
FOOD: Other reptiles, especially burrowing species.
REPRODUCTION: Thought to be egg-layers.
NOTES: Secretive; its relationships are poorly understood. The venom is not thought to be dangerous to humans.

SPECIES:
Calliophis beddomei
Calliophis bibroni
Calliophis calligaster
Calliophis gracilis
Calliophis japonicus
Calliophis kelloggi
Calliophis macclellandi
Calliophis maculiceps
Calliophis melanurus
Calliophis nigrescens
Calliophis sauteri

GENUS: **DEMANSIA**
AUSTRALIAN WHIP-SNAKES
8 SPECIES

SIZE: Small to medium, and slender.
DISTRIBUTION: Australia and southern New Guinea.
HABITAT: Varied, from deserts to rain forests.
FOOD: Frogs, lizards, and reptile eggs.
REPRODUCTION: Egg-layers.
NOTES: Considered too small to be of any great danger to humans. Diurnal and

fast-moving. Two forms (*D. calodera* and *D. rufescens*) are sometimes regarded as subspecies of *D. olivaceae*.

SPECIES:
Demansia atra,
  Black Whip-snake
Demansia calodera
Demansia olivacea
Demansia papuensis
Demansia psammophis,
  Yellow-faced Whip-snake
Demansia rufescens
Demansia simplex
Demansia torquata,
  Collared Whip-snake

GENUS: **DENDROASPIS**
MAMBAS
4 SPECIES

SIZE: Medium to large, sometimes reaching 13 ft 1 in (4 m), with slender bodies.
DISTRIBUTION: Tropical and southern Africa.
HABITAT: Forests and lightly wooded grassland. Three species, which are green, are arboreal; the fourth (the Black Mamba) lives on the ground.
FOOD: Birds and small mammals.
REPRODUCTION: Egg-layers.
NOTES: Extremely dangerous to humans, though not usually aggressive. Active during the day.

SPECIES:
Dendroaspis angusticeps,
  Eastern Green Mamba
Dendroaspis jamesoni,
  Jameson's Mamba
Dendroaspis polylepis,
  Black Mamba
● *Dendroaspis viridis*,
  West African Green Mamba
  (pp. 120–1)

GENUS: **DENISONIA**
2 SPECIES

SIZE: Small, to 1 ft 11¹/₂ in (60 cm), and stocky.
DISTRIBUTION: Eastern Australia.
HABITAT: Lightly wooded places.
FOOD: Mainly frogs.
REPRODUCTION: *D. maculata* is a live-bearer, *D. devisi* is unknown.
NOTES: Dangerous to humans, though probably not lethal. Secretive and nocturnal.

SPECIES:
Denisonia devisi,
  De Vis' Banded Snake
Denisonia maculata,
  Ornamental Snake

GENUS: **DRYSDALIA**
4 SPECIES

SIZE: Small and slender.
DISTRIBUTION: Southern Australia.
HABITAT: Unknown.
FOOD: Lizards, including skinks.
REPRODUCTION: Live-bearers, where known.
NOTES: Not considered dangerous to humans. Secretive and nocturnal.

SPECIES:
Drysdalia coronata,
  Crowned Snake
Drysdalia coronoides,
  White-lipped Snake
Drysdalia mastersii,
  Masters' Snake
Drysdalia rhodogaster

GENUS: **ECHIOPSIS**
2 SPECIES

SIZE: Small.
DISTRIBUTION: Southern Australia.
HABITAT: Dry places.
FOOD: Frogs, lizards, birds, and small mammals.
REPRODUCTION: *E. curta* is a live-bearer, *E. atriceps* is unknown.
NOTES: Not considered dangerous to humans. *E. atriceps* is rare and hardly known. Nocturnal.

SPECIES:
Echiopsis atriceps
Echiopsis curta,
  Bardick

GENUS: **ELAPOGNATHUS**
1 SPECIES

SIZE: Small, to 1 ft 4 in (40 cm).
DISTRIBUTION: Southwestern Australia.
HABITAT: Edges of swamps.
FOOD: Unknown.
REPRODUCTION: Thought to be a live-bearer.
NOTES: Not considered dangerous to humans.

SPECIES:
Elapognathus minor,
  Little Brown Snake

GENUS: **ELAPSOIDEA**
AFRICAN GARTER SNAKES
8 SPECIES

SIZE: Small to medium, but to over 3 ft 3 in (1 m) in one form.
DISTRIBUTION: Africa south of the Sahara.
HABITAT: Varied, from arid places to woodland.
FOOD: Mainly other reptiles, but also amphibians and small mammals.

REPRODUCTION: Egg-layers.
NOTES: Not considered dangerous to humans. Juveniles are often brightly colored "coral" snakes. *E. chelazzii*, from Somalia, is known from only two specimens, and *E. broadleyi* was only described in 1997.

SPECIES:
Elapsoidea broadleyi,
  Broadley's Garter Snake
Elapsoidea chelazzii,
  Southern Somali Garter Snake
Elapsoidea guentheri,
  Gunther's Garter Snake
Elapsoidea laticincta,
  Central African Garter Snake
Elapsoidea loveridgei,
  East African Garter Snake
Elapsoidea nigra,
  Usumbara Garter Snake
Elapsoidea semiannulata,
  Half-banded Garter Snake
Elapsoidea sundevallii,
  Sundevall's Garter Snake

GENUS: **FURINA**
5 SPECIES

SIZE: Small, exceptionally to 3 ft 3 in (1 m) (*F. tristis*).
DISTRIBUTION: Australia and New Guinea (*F. tristis*).
HABITAT: Varied, from deserts to gardens.
FOOD: Thought to be small lizards.
REPRODUCTION: Egg-layers where known.
NOTES: Not considered dangerous to humans.

SPECIES:
Furina barnardi,
  Yellow-naped Snake
Furina diadema,
  Red-naped Snake
Furina dunmalli,
  Dunmall's Snake
Furina ornata,
  Orange-naped Snake
Furina tristis,
  Brown-headed Snake

GENUS: **HEMACHATUS**
1 SPECIES

SIZE: Medium, to 4 ft 11 in (1.5 m).
DISTRIBUTION: Southern Africa.
HABITAT: Grassland.
FOOD: Mainly toads.
REPRODUCTION: Live-bearer.
NOTES: A very dangerous spitter, potentially causing blindness, but rarely lethal.

SPECIES:
Hemachatus haemachatus,
  Rinkhals, Spitting Cobra

GENUS: **HEMIASPIS**
2 SPECIES

SIZE: Small, to 1 ft 11¹/₂ in (60 cm).
DISTRIBUTION: Eastern Australia.
HABITAT: Wet and dry forests.
FOOD: Frogs and lizards, especially skinks.
REPRODUCTION: Live-bearers.
NOTES: Not considered dangerous to humans. Active at night and by day.

SPECIES:
Hemiaspis damelii,
  Gray Snake
Hemiaspis signata,
  Black-bellied Swamp Snake

GENUS: **HOMOROSELAPS**
HARLEQUIN SNAKES
2 SPECIES

SIZE: Small, to 1 ft 9¹/₂ in (55 cm).
DISTRIBUTION: Southern Africa.
HABITAT: Often found in termite mounds.
FOOD: Legless skinks, thread snakes, blind snakes, and other small snakes.
REPRODUCTION: Egg-layers.
NOTES: Brightly colored. Not considered dangerous to humans because of their small size. Formerly classified as burrowing asps (Atractaspididae). *H. dorsalis* is rare and its natural history is hardly known.

SPECIES:
Homoroselaps dorsalis,
  Striped Harlequin Snake
Homoroselaps lacteus,
  Spotted Harlequin Snake

GENUS: **HOPLOCEPHALUS**
3 SPECIES

SIZE: Small to medium, the largest up to 2 ft 11¹/₂ in (90 cm).
DISTRIBUTION: Eastern Australia.
HABITAT: Varied, often in forests. *H. bungaroides* is restricted to rocky outcrops, where it lives underneath flaking slabs.
FOOD: Frogs, lizards, birds, and mammals.
REPRODUCTION: Live-bearers.
NOTES: Aggressive, with painful, though fairly innocuous, bites.

SPECIES:
Hoplocephalus bitorquatus,
  Pale-headed Snake
Hoplocephalus bungaroides,
  Broad-headed Snake
Hoplocephalus stephensii,
  Stephens' Banded Snake

GENUS: **LOVERIDGELAPS**
1 SPECIES

SIZE: Medium, to about 2 ft 7½ in (80 cm).
DISTRIBUTION: Solomon Islands.
HABITAT: Forests, often near streams.
FOOD: Frogs, lizards, and worm snakes.
REPRODUCTION: Unknown.
NOTES: Rare and poorly known. Boldly banded in black and white. Its bite is potentially dangerous to humans.

SPECIES:
Loveridgelaps elapoides,
    Solomon's Small-eyed Snake or
    Shark of the Jungle

GENUS: **MATICORA**
2 SPECIES

SIZE: Small (*M. intestinalis*) to large, and slender.
DISTRIBUTION: Southeast Asia.
HABITAT: Forests and fields, where they are semiburrowing.
FOOD: Snakes.
REPRODUCTION: Egg-layers.
NOTES: Brightly colored. Generally inoffensive, but, with huge venom glands extending for one third the length of the body, they are potentially dangerous.

SPECIES:
Maticora bivirgata,
    Blue Coral Snake
Maticora intestinalis

GENUS: **MICROPECHIS**
1 SPECIES

SIZE: Large, to 6 ft 6 in (2 m), and stocky.
DISTRIBUTION: New Guinea and some of its satellite islands.
HABITAT: Rain forests, swamps, and plantations.
FOOD: Frogs, lizards, snakes, and small mammals.
REPRODUCTION: Unknown.
NOTES: Highly dangerous, with several recorded fatalities.

SPECIES:
Micropechis ikaheka,
    New Guinea Small-eyed Snake

GENUS: **MICRUROIDES**
1 SPECIES

SIZE: Small, to about 1 ft 8 in (50 cm), and slender.
DISTRIBUTION: North America (Arizona and northwestern Mexico).
HABITAT: Arid deserts and scrub.
FOOD: Lizards and snakes.
REPRODUCTION: Egg-layer.
NOTES: Brightly banded in red, black, and white. Dangerous.

SPECIES:
Micruroides euryxanthus,
    Sonoran Coral Snake

GENUS: **MICRURUS**
CORAL SNAKES
61 SPECIES

SIZE: Small to moderately large, with some species reaching 4 ft 11 in (1.5 m).
DISTRIBUTION: North, Central, and South America.
HABITAT: Varied, from dry deserts to humid rain forests. Invariably terrestrial.
FOOD: Other reptiles, especially burrowing forms such as amphisbaenians.
REPRODUCTION: Egg-layers.
NOTES: The slender bodies are brightly colored with red, black, and white or yellow bands. Some tropical species also have blue bands. Despite having small mouths and short fangs, all coral snakes are potentially dangerous, and there have been many human fatalities. Usually nocturnal. The list of species includes a number that are sometimes regarded as subspecies.

SPECIES:
Micrurus alleni,
    Allen's Coral Snake
Micrurus ancoralis,
    Regal Coral Snake
Micrurus annellatus
Micrurus averyi,
    Black-headed Coral Snake
Micrurus bernadi,
    Blotched Coral Snake
Micrurus bocourti,
    Ecuadorian Coral Snake
Micrurus bogerti,
    Bogert's Coral Snake
Micrurus browni,
    Brown's Coral Snake
Micrurus catamayensis
Micrurus clarki,
    Clark's Coral Snake
Micrurus collaris
Micrurus corallinus,
    Painted Coral Snake
Micrurus decoratus,
    Brazilian Coral Snake
Micrurus frontalis diana
Micrurus diastema,
    Variable Coral Snake
Micrurus dissoleucus,
    Pygmy Coral Snake
Micrurus distans,
    West Mexican Coral Snake
Micrurus dumerilii,
    Dumeril's Coral Snake
Micrurus elegans,
    Elegant Coral Snake
Micrurus ephippifer,
    Oaxacan Coral Snake
Micrurus filiformis,
    Slender Coral Snake
Micrurus frontalis,
    Southern Coral Snake

Micrurus frontifasciatus,
    Bolivian Coral Snake
Micrurus fulvius,
    Eastern Coral Snake
Micrurus hemprichii,
    Hemprich's Coral Snake
Micrurus hippocrepis,
    Mayan Coral Snake
Micrurus ibiboboca,
    Caatinga Coral Snake
Micrurus isozonus,
    Venezuelan Coral Snake
Micrurus langsdorffi,
    Langsdorff's Coral Snake
Micrurus laticollaris
Micrurus latifasciatus,
    Broad-ringed Coral Snake
Micrurus lemniscatus,
    South American Coral Snake
Micrurus limbatus,
    Tuxtlan Coral Snake
Micrurus margaritiferus,
    Speckled Coral Snake
Micrurus medemi
Micrurus mertensi,
    Merten's Coral Snake
Micrurus mipartitus,
    Red-tailed Coral Snake
Micrurus multifasciatus,
    Many-banded Coral Snake
Micrurus multiscutatus,
    Cauca Coral Snake
Micrurus narduccii,
    Andean Black-backed Coral Snake
Micrurus nebularis
Micrurus nigrocinctus,
    Central American Coral Snake
Micrurus paraensis
Micrurus peruvianus,
    Peruvian Coral Snake
Micrurus petersi,
    Peters' Coral Snake
Micrurus proximans
Micrurus psyches,
    Carib Coral Snake
Micrurus putumayensis
Micrurus pyrrhocryptus
Micrurus remotus
Micrurus ruatanus,
    Roatán Coral Snake
Micrurus sangilensis,
    Santander Coral Snake
Micrurus scutiventris
Micrurus spixii,
    Amazonian Coral Snake
Micrurus spurelli,
    Colombian Coral Snake
Micrurus steindachneri,
    Steindachner's Coral Snake
Micrurus stewarti,
    Panamanian Coral Snake
Micrurus stuarti,
    Stuart's Coral Snake
Micrurus surinamensis,
    Aquatic Coral Snake
Micrurus fulvius tenere
Micrurus tschudii,
    Desert Coral Snake

GENUS: **NAJA**
COBRAS
17 SPECIES

SIZE: Medium to large, reaching over 6 ft 6 in (2 m) in some cases, and fairly stout.
DISTRIBUTION: Africa and southern Southeast Asia.
HABITAT: Varied, from deserts to forests, and including fields, plantations, and human dwellings.
FOOD: Highly adaptable, eating fish, amphibians, lizards, snakes, birds, and mammals.
REPRODUCTION: Egg-layers.
NOTES: All cobras are dangerous and capable of giving a lethal bite. Several species in Africa and in Asia also spit venom. Hoods are spread only when the snakes are alarmed. Active by day and night depending on species. The Asian species were formerly regarded as different forms of one widespread species.

SPECIES:
• Naja atra
    Chinese Cobra (pp. 114)
Naja haje,
    Egyptian Cobra
• Naja kaouthia
    Monacled Cobra (pp. 115)
Naja katiensis,
    West African Brown Spitting Cobra
Naja melanoleuca,
    Forest Cobra
Naja mossambica,
    Mozambique Spitting Cobra
Naja naja,
    Asiatic Cobra
Naja nigricollis,
    Black-necked Spitting Cobra
Naja nivea,
    Cape Cobra
Naja oxiana
• Naja pallida,
    Red Spitting Cobra (pp. 112–13)
Naja philippinensis
Naja sagittifera
Naja samarensis
Naja siamensis
Naja sputatrix
Naja sumatrana

GENUS: **NOTECHIS**
TIGER SNAKES
2 SPECIES

SIZE: Moderately large, to 4 ft 11 in (1.5 m) , and stocky.
DISTRIBUTION: Southern Australia, including Tasmania.
HABITAT: Varied, from marshes to dry, rocky places.
FOOD: Mainly frogs and small mammals, but the population of *N. ater* living on small islands depends almost entirely on the seasonally abundant mutton bird chicks.
REPRODUCTION: Live-bearers.

NOTES: Highly venomous, responsible for a large proportion of human deaths from snakebite in Australia.

SPECIES:
Notechis ater,
Black Tiger Snake
Notechis scutatus,
Eastern Snake or Mainland Tiger Snake

GENUS: **OGMODON**
1 SPECIES

SIZE: Small.
DISTRIBUTION: Vitu Levi, one of the Fijian Islands.
HABITAT: Mountain valleys, where it is burrowing and secretive.
FOOD: Thought to be earthworms and other soft-bodied invertebrates.
REPRODUCTION: Unknown.
NOTES: A rare species whose natural history is poorly known. Not likely to be dangerous to humans.

SPECIES:
Ogmodon vitianus

GENUS: **OPHIOPHAGUS**
1 SPECIES

SIZE: Very large, to over 16 ft 5 in (5 m), and, therefore, the world's longest venomous snake.
DISTRIBUTION: India, Southeast Asia, and the Philippines.
HABITAT: Humid woods and forests; occasionally in fields and near human dwellings.
FOOD: Other snakes.
REPRODUCTION: Egg-layer. The female stays near the eggs throughout their incubation.
NOTES: Highly venomous, but not normally aggressive.

SPECIES:
Ophiophagus hannah,
King Cobra

GENUS: **OXYURANUS**
TAIPANS
2 SPECIES

SIZE: Large, to 8 ft 2 in (2.5 m) and, therefore, the largest venomous snake in Australia.
DISTRIBUTION: Australia and New Guinea.
HABITAT: Varied, mainly in lightly wooded places and grasslands, including gardens.
FOOD: Small mammals, especially rats.
REPRODUCTION: Egg-layers.
NOTES: Rare. Extremely dangerous, with powerful venom and an erratic temperament.

SPECIES:
Oxyuranus microlepidotus,
Fierce Snake or Inland Taipan
Oxyuranus scutellatus,
Taipan

GENUS: **PARANAJA**
1 SPECIES

SIZE: Small, to about 2 ft 7½ in (80 cm), and stout.
DISTRIBUTION: West Africa.
HABITAT: Forests and forest edges.
FOOD: Unknown.
REPRODUCTION: Egg-layer.
NOTES: Rare and poorly known. Not considered to be especially dangerous to humans.

SPECIES:
Paranaja multifasciata,
Burrowing Cobra

GENUS: **PARAPISTOCALAMUS**
1 SPECIES

SIZE: Small, to about 1 ft 8 in (50 cm), and slender.
DISTRIBUTION: Bougainville Island, New Guinea.
HABITAT: Forests.
FOOD: Unknown.
REPRODUCTION: Unknown.
NOTES: Rare and poorly known. Not likely to be dangerous to humans because of its small size.

SPECIES:
Parapistocalamus hedigeri,
Bougainville Coral Snake

GENUS: **PSEUDECHIS**
BROWN SNAKES
6 SPECIES

SIZE: Large, up to 6 ft 6 in (2 m).
DISTRIBUTION: Australia and New Guinea.
HABITAT: Varied, from tropical forests to deserts.
FOOD: Frogs, lizards, snakes, and small mammals.
REPRODUCTION: Egg-layers.
NOTES: Dangerously venomous.

SPECIES:
Pseudechis australis,
Mulga Snake or King Brown Snake
Pseudechis butleri
● *Pseudechis colletti,*
Collett's Snake (pp. 116–17)
Pseudechis guttatus,
Spotted Black Snake
Pseudechis papuanus,
Papuan Black Snake
Pseudechis porphyriacus,
Red-bellied Black Snake

GENUS: **PSEUDOHAJE**
TREE COBRAS
2 SPECIES

SIZE: Large, up to 8 ft 2 in (2.5 m).
DISTRIBUTION: Central and West Africa.
HABITAT: Forests, where it is highly arboreal.
FOOD: Amphibians and possibly small mammals.
REPRODUCTION: Egg-layers.
NOTES: Both species are poorly known and no bites have been recorded. Thought to be dangerous to humans.

SPECIES:
Pseudohaje goldii,
Gold's Tree Cobra
Pseudohaje nigra,
Black Tree Cobra

GENUS: **PSEUDONAJA**
7 SPECIES

SIZE: Moderately large, up to 4 ft 11 in (1.5 m).
DISTRIBUTION: Australia and New Guinea.
HABITAT: Mainly open places, including dunes and grasslands, but sometimes in lightly wooded places.
FOOD: Frogs, small lizards, and mammals.
REPRODUCTION: Egg-layers.
NOTES: Very dangerous to humans, with highly potent venom.

SPECIES:
Pseudonaja affinis,
Dugite
Pseudonaja guttata
Pseudonaja inframacula,
Peninsula Brown Snake
Pseudonaja ingrami,
Ingram's Brown Snake
Pseudonaja modesta,
Ringed Brown Snake
Pseudonaja nuchalis,
Western Brown Snake
Pseudonaja textilis,
Eastern Brown Snake

GENUS: **RHINOPLOCEPHALUS**
6 SPECIES

SIZE: Small, to about 1 ft 8 in (50 cm).
DISTRIBUTION: Australia and New Guinea.
HABITAT: Forests, woodlands, grassy places, and among rocks.
FOOD: Thought to be small lizards.
REPRODUCTION: Live-bearers, where known.
NOTES: Secretive and nocturnal, rarely encountered. Unlikely to be dangerous to humans.

SPECIES:
Rhinoplocephalus bicolor
Rhinoplocephalus boschmai,
Carpentaria Whip Snake
Rhinoplocephalus incredibilis
Rhinoplocephalus nigrescens,
Eastern Small-eyed Snake
Rhinoplocephalus nigrostriatus,
Black-striped Snake
Rhinoplocephalus pallidiceps,
Northern Small-eyed Snake

GENUS: **SALOMONELAPS**
1 SPECIES

SIZE: Medium, to just over 3 ft 3 in (1 m).
DISTRIBUTION: Solomon Islands and Bougainville Island in New Guinea.
HABITAT: Forests.
FOOD: Mainly lizards, especially skinks, but also frogs and snakes.
REPRODUCTION: Egg-layer.
NOTES: Poorly known. Bites may be dangerous to humans.

SPECIES:
Salomonelaps par,
Solomons Coral Snake

GENUS: **SIMOSELAPS**
AUSTRALIAN CORAL SNAKES
12 SPECIES

SIZE: Small, up to about 1 ft 11½ in (60 cm) long.
DISTRIBUTION: Australia.
HABITAT: Mostly dry, sandy places, where they live beneath the surface.
FOOD: Lizards, especially burrowing skinks.
REPRODUCTION: Egg-layers.
NOTES: Most species are boldly banded. Not considered dangerous to humans.

SPECIES:
Simoselaps anomalus
Simoselaps approximans
Simoselaps australis,
Coral Snake
Simoselaps bertholdi,
Desert Banded Snake
Simoselaps bimaculatus,
Western Black-naped Snake
Simoselaps calonotus,
Western Black-striped Snake
Simoselaps fasciolatus,
Narrow-banded Snake
Simoselaps incinctus
Simoselaps littoralis
Simoselaps minimus
Simoselaps semifasciatus,
Half-girdled snake
Simoselaps warro

GENUS: **SUTA**
9 SPECIES

SIZE: Small, mostly up to 1 ft 4 in (40 cm), but *S. ordensis* grows to 2 ft 5½ in (75 cm).
DISTRIBUTION: Australia and southern New Guinea.

HABITAT: Dry places, including heaths and woodlands.

FOOD: Lizards, especially skinks, and frogs.

REPRODUCTION: Live-bearers, where known.

NOTES: Not likely to be dangerous to humans because of their small size, but the bites of certain species are painful.

SPECIES:
Suta fasciata,
   Rosen's Snake
Suta flagellum,
   Little Whip Snake
Suta gouldii,
   Black-headed Snake
Suta monachus,
   Hooded Snake
Suta nigriceps
Suta ordensis
Suta punctata,
   Little Spotted Snake
Suta spectabilis
Suta suta,
   Curl Snake

GENUS: **TOXICOCALAMUS**
NEW GUINEA FOREST SNAKES
9 SPECIES

SIZE: Small to medium, from about 1 ft 8 in (50 cm) to nearly 3 ft 3 in (1 m).

DISTRIBUTION: New Guinea

HABITAT: Lowland and montane rain forest, grasslands, and gardens. Secretive and burrowing species, living under leaf-litter and other forest debris.

FOOD: Earthworms and other soft-bodied invertebrates and their larvae; perhaps also frogs.

REPRODUCTION: Egg-layers, where known.

NOTES: Very poorly known, but thought to be harmless to humans.

SPECIES:
Toxicocalamus buergersi
Toxicocalamus grandis
Toxicocalamus holopelturus
Toxicocalamus longissimus
Toxicocalamus loriae
Toxicocalamus misimae
Toxicocalamus preussi
Toxicocalamus spilolepidotus
Toxicocalamus stanleyanus

GENUS: **TROPIDECHIS**
1 SPECIES

SIZE: Medium, occasionally to about 3 ft 3 in (1 m).

DISTRIBUTION: Eastern Australia.

HABITAT: Forests.

FOOD: Frogs, reptiles, birds, and small mammals.

REPRODUCTION: Live-bearer.

NOTES: Aggressive and dangerous to humans.

SPECIES:
Tropidechis carinatus,
   Rough-scaled Snake

GENUS: **VERMICELLA**
BANDY-BANDIES
4 SPECIES

SIZE: Small, to 1 ft 11½ in (60 cm), and slender.

DISTRIBUTION: Australia.

HABITAT: Varied; burrowers.

FOOD: Blind snakes.

REPRODUCTION: Egg-layers.

NOTES: Boldly banded black and white. Too small to be considered dangerous to humans. *V. intermedia* and *V. vermiformis* are not always considered distinct species.

SPECIES:
Vermicella annulata,
   Bandy-bandy
Vermicella intermedia
Vermicella multifasciata,
   Northern Bandy-bandy
Vermicella vermiformis

GENUS: **WALTERINNESIA**
1 SPECIES

SIZE: Medium, to just over 3 ft 3 in (1 m), and thickset.

DISTRIBUTION: North Africa (Sinai) and the Middle East.

HABITAT: Deserts.

FOOD: Lizards, especially dabb lizards (*Uromastyx*), and possibly small mammals.

REPRODUCTION: Egg-layer.

NOTES: Dangerous; although it rarely bites, fatalities are known.

SPECIES:
Walterinnesia aegyptia,
   Desert Black Snake

MARINE SPECIES

17 GENERA CONTAINING 62 SPECIES

Some authorities consider that the marine species of the Elapidae should be placed in a separate family, the Hydropheidae. Others consider that this family should also include the Australian terrestrial elapids and that it should be subdivided to separate the sea snakes from the sea kraits. Here they are treated as part of the cobra family, while accepting that there are several important differences between the terrestrial elapids and the marine ones, and that there are also differences between the sea kraits, *Laticauda,* and the other sea snakes.

Although sea snakes and sea kraits are extremely venomous, they are generally inoffensive, and there are relatively few cases of human deaths from their bites. Most of them feed on fish, including eels, but some are specialists, feeding only on fish eggs. The sea kraits, *Laticauda* species, are the least perfectly adapted to a marine lifestyle and come ashore to lay eggs (with the possible exception of *L. crockeri*), but all the other species live completely aquatic lives and are thought to give birth to live young.

Marine species of the Elapidae are found in the Indian and Pacific Oceans and are most abundant around the coasts of northern Australia. Most species are associated with coral reefs, but the pelagic sea snake, *Pelamis platurus,* is an ocean-going wanderer, with large schools drifting right across the Pacific as far as the shores of Central America. There have been fears that this species would eventually find its way through the Panama Canal to populate the so far sea-snake-free Caribbean region.

GENUS: **ACALYPTOPHIS**
1 SPECIES

SIZE: Medium to large.

DISTRIBUTION: Coasts of northern Australia.

HABITAT: Reefs.

FOOD: Fish.

REPRODUCTION: Live-bearer, producing up to ten young.

SPECIES:
Acalyptophis peronii

GENUS: **AIPYSURUS**
7 SPECIES

SIZE: Medium to large; mostly under 3 ft 3 in (1 m), but *A. laevis* can grow to 6 ft 6 in (2 m).

DISTRIBUTION: Coasts of northern Australia, New Guinea, and New Caledonia.

HABITAT: Mostly found near reefs, although some frequent deeper water.

FOOD: Thought to be fish.

REPRODUCTION: Live-bearers, producing small litters of young.

NOTES: Some species are rarely seen and poorly known.

SPECIES:
Aipysurus apraefrontalis
Aipysurus duboisii
Aipysurus eydouxii
Aipysurus foliosquama
Aipysurus fuscus
Aipysurus laevis,
   Olive Sea Snake
Aipysurus tenuis

GENUS: **ASTROTIA**
1 SPECIES

SIZE: Large, to 6 ft 6 in (2 m), and very heavy-bodied.

DISTRIBUTION: Coasts of northern Australia, New Guinea, and Southeast Asia.

HABITAT: Coastal waters.

FOOD: Thought to be fish.

REPRODUCTION: Live-bearer.

SPECIES:
Astrotia stokesii

GENUS: **DISTEIRA**
4 SPECIES

SIZE: Moderately large, with some species to 4 ft 11 in (1.5 m).

DISTRIBUTION: Widespread, from the Persian Gulf to northern Australia.

HABITAT: Deep waters.

FOOD: Thought to be fish.

REPRODUCTION: Live-bearers.

NOTES: Poorly known. Usually collected accidentally in trawl nets.

SPECIES:
Disteira kingii
Disteira major
Disteira nigrocinctus
Disteira walli

GENUS: **EMYDOCEPHALUS**
TURTLE-HEADED SEA SNAKES
2 SPECIES

SIZE: Small, to less than 3 ft 3 in (1 m).

DISTRIBUTION: South China Sea and northern Australia.

HABITAT: Reefs, often in shallow water.

FOOD: Fish eggs.

REPRODUCTION: Live-bearers.

NOTES: They have no teeth or associated venom apparatus.

SPECIES:
Emydocephalus annulatus
Emydocephalus ijimae

GENUS: **ENHYDRINA**
2 SPECIES

SIZE: Medium, to 3 ft 11 in (1.2 m).

DISTRIBUTION: Coasts of northern Australia and southern New Guinea.

HABITAT: Shallow water in harbors, bays, and estuaries, and far up freshwater rivers.

FOOD: Fish.

REPRODUCTION: Live-bearers.

NOTES: Highly venomous, like other sea snakes, but unusual in being aggressive when disturbed. *E. zweifeli* was only described in 1985, from a single specimen taken in New Guinea. Its natural history is presumed to be similar to that of *E. schistosa.*

SPECIES:
Enhydrina schistosa
Enhydrina zweifeli

GENUS: EPHALOPHIS
1 SPECIES

SIZE: Small, to 1 ft 8 in (50 cm).
DISTRIBUTION: Coasts of Western Australia, around Broome.
HABITAT: Mangroves and estuarine mudflats.
FOOD: Unknown; probably fish.
REPRODUCTION: Live-bearer.

SPECIES:
Ephalophis greyi

GENUS: HYDRELAPS
1 SPECIES

SIZE: Small, to 1 ft 8 in (50 cm).
DISTRIBUTION: Coasts of northern Australia and southern Papua New Guinea.
HABITAT: Mudflats, especially near mangroves
FOOD: Probably fish.
REPRODUCTION: Live-bearer.

SPECIES:
Hydrelaps darwiniensis

GENUS: HYDROPHIS
30 SPECIES

SIZE: Small to large; from about 1 ft 8 in (50 cm) to more than 4 ft 11 in (1.5 m)
DISTRIBUTION: Widespread, from the Persian Gulf to the northern coasts of Australia and north to the Philippines.
HABITAT: Mainly shallow coastal waters, although some have occasionally been trawled from deeper waters. *H. semperi* is unique among sea snakes because it lives only in the freshwater Lake Taal on Luzon Island, Philippines.
FOOD: Fish, especially eels.
REPRODUCTION: Live-bearers.
NOTES: This large genus is likely to be divided into several smaller ones in the near future.

SPECIES:
Hydrophis atriceps
Hydrophis belcheri
Hydrophis bituberculatus
Hydrophis brooki
Hydrophis caerulescens
Hydrophis cantoris
Hydrophis coggeri
Hydrophis cyanocinctus
Hydrophis czeblukovi
Hydrophis elegans
Hydrophis fasciatus
Hydrophis gracilis
Hydrophis inornatus

Hydrophis klossi
Hydrophis lamberti
Hydrophis lapemoides
Hydrophis mamillaris
Hydrophis mcdowelli
Hydrophis melanocephalus
Hydrophis melanosoma
Hydrophis nigrocinctus
Hydrophis obscurus
Hydrophis ornatus
Hydrophis pacificus
Hydrophis parviceps
Hydrophis semperi
Hydrophis spiralis
Hydrophis stricticollis
Hydrophis torquatus
Hydrophis vorisi

GENUS: KERILIA
1 SPECIES

SIZE: Medium.
DISTRIBUTION: Southeast Asia.
HABITAT: Coastal waters.
FOOD: Probably fish.
REPRODUCTION: Live-bearer.
NOTES: Poorly known.

SPECIES:
Kerilia jerdonii

GENUS: KOLPOPHIS
1 SPECIES

SIZE: Unknown.
DISTRIBUTION: South China Sea from Thailand to Indonesia.
HABITAT: Coastal waters.
FOOD: Probably fish.
REPRODUCTION: Thought to be a live-bearer.
NOTES: Only recently discovered and still poorly known.

SPECIES:
Kolpophis annandalei

GENUS: LAPEMIS
2 SPECIES

SIZE: Medium, to about 3 ft 3 in (1 m).
DISTRIBUTION: Persian Gulf to northern Australian coasts.
HABITAT: Shallow coastal waters, reefs, and estuaries.
FOOD: Thought to be fish.
REPRODUCTION: Live-bearers.

SPECIES:
Lapemis curtus
Lapemis hardwickii

GENUS: LATICAUDA
SEA KRAITS
5 SPECIES

SIZE: Medium to large, to about 4 ft 11 in (1.5 m).
DISTRIBUTION: Southeast Asian and northern Australian coasts.
HABITAT: Rocky shores, mudflats, and reefs. *L. crockeri* is confined to the landlocked Lake Te-Nggano in the Solomon Islands.
FOOD: Fish, especially eels.
REPRODUCTION: Egg-layers, but there is some evidence that *L. crockeri* gives birth to live young.
NOTES: Partially terrestrial, the sea kraits come ashore to drink and to lay their eggs in sea caves. Considered to be part of a separate subfamily, or even family, from other sea snakes.

SPECIES:
Laticauda colubrina
Laticauda crockeri
Laticauda laticauda
Laticauda schistorhynchus
Laticauda semifasciata

GENUS: PARAHYDROPHIS
1 SPECIES

SIZE: Small, to about 1 ft 8 in (50 cm).
DISTRIBUTION: Coasts of northern Australia.
HABITAT: Coastal and estuarine mangroves and mudflats.
FOOD: Small fish
REPRODUCTION: Live-bearer.

SPECIES:
Parahydrophis mertoni

GENUS: PELAMIS
1 SPECIES

SIZE: Small, to less than 3 ft 3 in (1 m).
DISTRIBUTION: Widespread, from the east coast of Africa, across the Indian Ocean and the Pacific to the west coast of Central America. Occurs further south than other species.
HABITAT: Open water.
FOOD: Surface-dwelling fish.
REPRODUCTION: Live-bearer.
NOTES: Pelagic, drifting with the tides, often in huge numbers.

SPECIES:
Pelamis platurus,
  Yellow-bellied Sea Snake

GENUS: PRAESCUTATA
1 SPECIES

SIZE: Medium.
DISTRIBUTION: Persian Gulf to Indonesia.
HABITAT: Coastal waters.

FOOD: Probably fish.
REPRODUCTION: Live-bearer.
NOTES: Sometimes known as *Thalassophina viperina*.

SPECIES:
Praescutata viperina

GENUS: THALASSOPHIS
1 SPECIES

SIZE: Medium.
DISTRIBUTION: Coasts of Thailand and Indonesia.
HABITAT: Coastal waters.
FOOD: Fish.
REPRODUCTION: Live-bearer.

SPECIES:
Thalassophis anomalus

VIPERIDAE
VIPERS

4 SUBFAMILIES CONTAINING 30 GENERA AND 228 SPECIES

Most vipers are short and stout, with wide, triangular heads, and most have keeled scales, although there are exceptions in each case. The family is considered to be the most advanced of all snakes, with many features that are not found in any other families. These include the long, folding fangs with which they envenomate their prey and, in the group known as pit vipers, a pair of heat pits in their face that are more sensitive than those of the pythons, and which must, therefore, have evolved independently.

Vipers are found throughout much of the world, but are absent from Australasia and Madagascar. They have several adaptations that enable them to live in cold places, and the family includes the snakes that are found farthest north (*Vipera berus*) and farthest south (*Bothrops ammodytoides*) as well as the snake (*Gloydius himalayanus*) that is found at the highest altitude, at 16,000 ft (4,900 m) in the Himalayas.

There are four subfamilies, which are all well defined.

SUBFAMILY: AZEMIOPINAE

1 GENUS CONTAINING 1 SPECIES

A single species, *Azemiops feae*, considered to be the most primitive viper, is placed in this subfamily. It is banded orange on dark gray or black and has a yellow or buff head with large, platelike scales but no heat pits. Its natural history

183

is virtually unknown, but its venom is believed to be mild. It is one of the rarest vipers, found in temperate montane regions of northern Myanmar and southern China.

GENUS: AZEMIOPS
1 SPECIES

SIZE: Medium, to just under 3 ft 3 in (1 m), and slender.
DISTRIBUTION: China.
HABITAT: Cool, montane habitats up to 6,500 ft (2,000 m)
FOOD: Small mammals.
REPRODUCTION: Unknown.
NOTES: Very rare, with only a few known specimens.

SPECIES:
Azemiops feae,
Fea's Viper

SUBFAMILY: CAUSINAE

NIGHT ADDERS

1 GENUS CONTAINING 6 SPECIES

Slender, small vipers, all from the southern half of Africa, which have large platelike scales on top of their heads and, therefore, look more like colubrids than most other vipers. They are mostly dull brown in color, with saddles and blotches, although Causus resimus, the Green Night Adder, is brightly colored, as its name suggests. They all have specialized diets, feeding almost exclusively on toads. All the species are terrestrial.

GENUS: CAUSUS
NIGHT ADDERS
6 SPECIES

SIZE: Small,1 ft 11½–2 ft 3½ in (60–70 cm), and slender.
DISTRIBUTION: Africa south of the Sahara.
HABITAT: Varied, including grasslands, forests, and swamps. Often associated with damp places.
FOOD: Amphibians, especially toads.
REPRODUCTION: Egg-layers.
NOTES: They inject large amounts of venom, but their bites are unlikely to lead to serious consequences.

SPECIES:
Causus bilineatus,
Two-striped Night Adder
Causus defilippii,
Snouted Night Adder
Causus lichtensteinii,
Forest Night Adder
Causus maculatus,
West African Night Adder

Causus resimus,
Green Night Adder
Causus rhombeatus,
Rhombic Night Adder

SUBFAMILY: VIPERINAE

OLD WORLD VIPERS WITHOUT PITS

10 GENERA CONTAINING 67 SPECIES

The vipers in this subfamily are mostly small to medium-sized, heavily built snakes, with wide heads covered in small, fragmented scales. They typically have a dorsal pattern of blotches, often joined and sometimes forming a continuous zigzag. Many species, especially those belonging to the genus Bitis, appear to have colorful, even garish, patterns when seen out of habitat These markings disrupt the outline of the snakes to provide them with exceptional camouflage when they are resting on the appropriate substrates.

They are mostly terrestrial, with the exception of members of the African genus Atheris, which are known as bush vipers, although several of the European vipers also climb into low vegetation and bushes in search of nestling birds. Most species give birth to live young, but some lay eggs, and the reproduction of others is unknown.

This subfamily is restricted to Europe, Africa, and Asia.

GENUS: ADENORHINOS
1 SPECIES

SIZE: Small, to about 1 ft 4 in.(40 cm)
DISTRIBUTION: Western Tanzania, Africa.
HABITAT: Undergrowth on mountain slopes.
FOOD: Unknown.
REPRODUCTION: Unknown.
NOTES: Rare, with a small geographic range.

SPECIES:
Adenorhinos barbouri,
Uzungwe Viper or Barbour's Viper

GENUS: ATHERIS
BUSH VIPERS
10 SPECIES

SIZE: Small to medium, to about 2 ft 5½ in (75 cm), and relatively slender.
DISTRIBUTION: West, Central, and East Africa.
HABITAT: Forests and swamps. All except two species are arboreal.
FOOD: Frogs, lizards, and small mammals.
REPRODUCTION: Live-bearers.

NOTES: Dangerous to humans, although only A. squamiger has caused fatalities. A. laeviceps is sometimes regarded as a form of A. squamiger. Several species have extremely small geographic ranges and are known from only a few specimens.

SPECIES:
Atheris ceratophorus,
Usambara Bush Viper
Atheris chlorechis,
Western Bush Viper
Atheris desaixi,
Mount Kenya Bush Viper
Atheris hindii,
Kenya Montane Viper
Atheris hispidus,
Rough-scaled Bush Viper or Hairy Bush Viper
Atheris katangensis,
Shaba Bush Viper
Atheris laeviceps
Atheris nitschei,
Great Lakes Bush Viper
Atheris squamiger,
Green Bush Viper
Atheris superciliaris,
Lowland Viper or Swamp Viper

GENUS: BITIS
AFRICAN ADDERS
14 SPECIES

SIZE: Small to large: from a maximum of 10½ in (27 cm) in B. schneideri, to over 6 ft 6 in (2 m) in B. gabonica. Invariably stout with wide heads.
DISTRIBUTION: Africa.
HABITAT: Varied, from rain forests and grasslands to the most arid deserts.
FOOD: Lizards and small mammals.
REPRODUCTION: Live-bearers.
NOTES: Species that live on dunes, for example B. peringueyi, move by sidewinding. The larger species, notably the common Puff Adder, are among the most dangerous snakes in Africa. Small species give relatively harmless bites. Several species (B. heraldica, B. parviocula, and B. worthingtoni, for example) have rarely been collected and their natural history is relatively unknown. B. rubida was described only in 1997.

SPECIES:
● Bitis arietans,
Puff Adder (pp. 122–3)
Bitis atropos,
Berg Adder
Bitis caudalis,
Horned Adder
Bitis cornuta,
Many-horned Adder
● Bitis gabonica,
Gaboon Adder or Viper (pp. 128–9)
Bitis heraldica,
Angolan Adder

Bitis inornata,
Plain Mountain Adder
Bitis nasicornis,
Rhinoceros Viper
Bitis parviocula,
Ethiopian Mountain Adder
Bitis peringueyi,
Peringuey's Adder
Bitis rubida
Bitis schneideri,
Dwarf Adder
Bitis worthingtoni,
Kenyan Horned Viper
Bitis xeropaga,
Desert Mountain Adder

GENUS: CERASTES
NORTH AFRICAN DESERT VIPERS
3 SPECIES

SIZE: Short, to about 1 ft 11½ (60 cm), but very stout.
DISTRIBUTION: North Africa and the Middle East.
HABITAT: Sandy and rocky deserts.
FOOD: Small lizards and mammals.
REPRODUCTION: Egg-layers.
NOTES: Very heavily keeled scales. Capable of painful, though rarely fatal, bites. They may move by sidewinding.

SPECIES:
● Cerastes cerastes,
Desert Horned Viper (pp. 130–1)
Cerastes gasperettii,
Arabian Horned Viper
Cerastes vipera,
Sahara Horned Viper

GENUS: DABOIA
1 SPECIES

SIZE: Large, to well over 3 ft 3 in (1 m), and very heavily built.
DISTRIBUTION: India, Sri Lanka, Myanmar, Thailand, Bangladesh, Cambodia, southern China, Taiwan, Java, Komodo, and Flores.
HABITAT: Varied; found in most habitats except dense forests.
FOOD: Mammals.
REPRODUCTION: Live-bearer.
NOTES: Sometimes retained in the genus Vipera.

SPECIES:
Daboia russellii,
Russell's Viper

GENUS: ECHIS
CARPET OR SAW-SCALED VIPERS
8 SPECIES

SIZE: Small, all under 3 ft 3 in (1 m).
DISTRIBUTION: West and North Africa, through the Middle East and into India and Sri Lanka.

HABITAT: Dry grasslands and lightly wooded places.

FOOD: Varied, including spiders, scorpions, lizards, snakes, birds, and small mammals.

REPRODUCTION: Egg-layers.

NOTES: Responsible for the majority of fatal snakebites where they occur, partly because they are numerous and well camouflaged and therefore easily stepped on. They make a characteristic coil when disturbed, rubbing their scales together to produce a rasping·sound. The identification of the various species is difficult and their taxonomy is not completely fixed at present. A ninth species, *Echis varius*, from northeastern North Africa, is sometimes recognized.

SPECIES:
- *Echis carinatus*,
  Eastern Carpet Viper or Saw-scaled Viper (pp. 134–5)
- *Echis coloratus*,
  Burton's Viper or Painted Carpet Viper
- *Echis hughesi*,
  Hughes' Carpet Viper
- *Echis jogeri*,
  Joger's Carpet Viper
- *Echis leucogaster*,
  White-bellied Carpet Viper
- *Echis megalocephalus*
- *Echis ocellatus*,
  West African Carpet Viper
- *Echis pyramidum*,
  Northeast African Carpet Viper

GENUS: ERISTICOPHIS
1 SPECIES

SIZE: Small.

DISTRIBUTION: Afghanistan and northern Pakistan.

HABITAT: Sand deserts.

FOOD: Lizards and small mammals.

REPRODUCTION: Unknown.

NOTES: Rarely collected and poorly known.

SPECIES:
Eristicophis macmahoni,
  MacMahon's Viper

GENUS: MACROVIPERA
4 SPECIES

SIZE: Large, 3 ft 3 in–6 ft 6 in (1–2 m).

DISTRIBUTION: North Africa, southeastern Europe, and western Asia.

HABITAT: Deserts, rocky hillsides, and scrub.

FOOD: Small birds and mammals.

REPRODUCTION: Egg-layers.

NOTES: Dangerous, with serious, though rarely fatal, bites. Previously placed in the genus *Vipera*. The species *M. schweizeri* is endangered.

SPECIES:
Macrovipera deserti,
  Desert Viper
Macrovipera lebetina,
  Levant Viper
Macrovipera mauritanica,
  Moorish Viper
Macrovipera schweizeri,
  Milos Viper

GENUS: PSEUDOCERASTES
2 SPECIES

SIZE: Medium, occasionally up to 3 ft 3 in (1 m).

DISTRIBUTION: Middle East.

HABITAT: Sandy and rocky deserts.

FOOD: Lizards and small mammals.

REPRODUCTION: Thought to be live-bearers.

NOTES: They move by sidewinding. There are several subspecies, some of which, for instance *Pseudocerastes persicus fieldi*, are sometimes regarded as full species.

SPECIES:
Pseudocerastes persicus,
  Iranian Horned Viper

GENUS: VIPERA
23 SPECIES

SIZE: Small to moderately large.

DISTRIBUTION: Europe, western Asia, the Middle East, and North Africa.

HABITAT: Extremely varied, from mountainsides, meadows, and lightly wooded areas to rocky deserts, scree slopes, and high valleys.

FOOD: Insects, lizards, birds, and small mammals.

REPRODUCTION: Live-bearers.

NOTES: Many new species have been recently described, especially from Turkey and neighboring territories.

SPECIES:
Vipera albizona
- *Vipera ammodytes*,
  Long-nosed Viper or Sand Viper (pp. 124–5)
Vipera aspis,
  Asp or Aspic Viper
Vipera barani
- *Vipera berus*,
  Adder or Northern Viper (pp. 126–7)
Vipera bornmuelleri,
  Bornmuller's Viper
Vipera darevskii,
  Darevski's Viper
Vipera dinniki
Vipera eriwanensis
Vipera kaznakovi
Vipera latasti,
  Snub-nosed Viper
Vipera latifii,
  Latifi's Viper
Vipera lotievi
Vipera monticola
Vipera nikolskii
Vipera palaestinae
Vipera pontica,
  Pontic Viper
Vipera raddei
Vipera renardi
Vipera seoanei,
  Spanish Viper
Vipera ursinii,
  Orsini's Viper or Méadow Viper
Vipera wagneri,
  Wagner's Viper
Vipera xanthina

SUBFAMILY: CROTALINAE

PIT VIPERS

18 GENERA CONTAINING 154 SPECIES

Superficially, many pit vipers resemble the vipers in the Viperinae subfamily, but they all possess heat-sensitive organs in the form of a pair of deep and conspicuous facial pits between their eyes and nostrils.

Pit vipers may be terrestrial or arboreal, dull or bright in color, and live-bearers or egg-layers - they have explored a number of evolutionary options. These vipers are best equipped to hunt warm-blooded animals, which make up the majority of their food.

Pit vipers are found in the New World (North, Central, and South America) and the Old, in Africa and Asia.

GENUS: AGKISTRODON
10 SPECIES

SIZE: Medium, up to about 3 ft 3 in (1 m), and stocky.

DISTRIBUTION: North America (three species) and Asia.

HABITAT: Varied, from swamps to high, rocky mountain slopes.

FOOD: Mainly small birds and mammals, but a variety of other prey is taken by some species, including fish, frogs, and carrion by *A. piscivorus*.

REPRODUCTION: Live-bearers.

NOTES: The bites are dangerous to humans, though they rarely prove to be fatal.

SPECIES:
Agkistrodon bilineatus,
  Cantil.
Agkistrodon blomhoff
- *Agkistrodon contortrix*,
  Copperhead (pp. 138–9)
Agkistrodon intermedius
Agkistrodon monticola
Agkistrodon piscivorus,
  Cottonmouth
Agkistrodon saxatilis
Agkistrodon shedaoensis
Agkistrodon strauchi
Agkistrodon ussuriensis

GENUS: ATROPOIDES
3 SPECIES

SIZE: Small to medium, to just over 3 ft 3 in (1 m), but extremely stout.

DISTRIBUTION: Central America.

HABITAT: Rain and cloud forests.

FOOD: Amphibians, reptiles, and small mammals.

REPRODUCTION: Live-bearers.

NOTES: Venomous, but bites are unlikely to prove fatal. Previously placed in the genus *Porthidium*.

SPECIES:
Atropoides nummifer,
  Jumping Pit Viper
Atropoides olmec,
  Olmec Pit Viper
Atropoides picadoi,
  Picado's Pit Viper

GENUS: BOTHRIECHIS
PALM PIT VIPERS
7 SPECIES

SIZE: Medium; sometimes over 3 ft 3 in (1 m), but usually less.

DISTRIBUTION: Central America. *B. schlegelii* extends into South America as far as Ecuador.

HABITAT: Forests, where they are arboreal.

FOOD: Amphibians, reptiles, small birds, and mammals.

REPRODUCTION: Live-bearers.

NOTES: Bites are painful and have resulted in fatalities.

SPECIES:
Bothriechis aurifer,
  Yellow-blotched Palm Pit Viper
Bothriechis bicolor,
  Guatemalan Palm Pit Viper
Bothriechis lateralis,
  Side-striped Palm Pit Viper
Bothriechis marchi,
  March's Palm Pit Viper
Bothriechis nigroviridis,
  Black-speckled Palm Pit Viper
Bothriechis rowleyi,
  Rowley's Palm Pit Viper
Bothriechis schlegelii,
  Eyelash Viper

GENUS: BOTHRIOPSIS
7 SPECIES

SIZE: Medium to large, with some exceeding 4 ft 11 in (1.5 m).

DISTRIBUTION: Northern South America.

HABITAT: Forests.

FOOD: Amphibians, lizards, birds, and small mammals.

REPRODUCTION: Live-bearers.

NOTES: Sometimes included in the genus *Bothrops*.

SPECIES:
Bothriopsis albocarinata
Bothriopsis bilineata
Bothriopsis medusa
Bothriopsis oligolepis
Bothriopsis peruviana
Bothriopsis punctata
Bothriopsis taeniata

GENUS: **BOTHROPS**
LANCE-HEADED PIT VIPERS OR
FER-DE-LANCES
32 SPECIES

SIZE: Small to large, with some species reaching 8 ft 2 in (2.5 m) in length.
DISTRIBUTION: Central and South America (Mexico to Argentina).
HABITAT: Highly varied: rain forests, forest clearings, hillsides, grasslands, plantations, and fields, and even the Atacama Desert (*B. pictus*). Forest species are often encountered alongside streams and rivers.
FOOD: Amphibians, lizards, birds, and mammals.
REPRODUCTION: Live-bearers.
NOTES: Certain species are very dangerous due to their association with human habitation, excellent camouflage, and potent venom. *B. asper*, *B. atrox*, and *B. jararaca* are responsible for most of the snakebite fatalities recorded in Central and South America. Two additional species, *B. colombiensis* and *B. isabelae*, are usually considered to be forms of *B. atrox*.

SPECIES:
Bothrops alternatus,
    Urutu
Bothrops ammodytoides,
    Patagonian Lancehead
Bothrops andianus,
    Andean Lancehead
Bothrops asper,
    Terciopelo or Velvet Snake
Bothrops atrox,
    Common Lancehead
Bothrops barnetti,
    Barnett's Lancehead
Bothrops brazili,
    Brazil's Lancehead
Bothrops caribbaeus,
    Saint Lucia Lancehead
Bothrops colombianus,
    Colombian Lancehead
Bothrops cotiara,
    Cotiara
Bothrops erythromelas,
    Caatinga Lancehead
Bothrops fonsecai,
    Fonseca's Lancehead
Bothrops iglesiasi,
    Sertão Lancehead

Bothrops insularis,
    Golden Lancehead
Bothrops itapetiningae,
    São Paulo Lancehead
● *Bothrops jararaca*,
    Jararaca (pp. 136–7)
Bothrops jararacussu,
    Jararacussu
Bothrops jonathani
Bothrops lanceolatus,
    Martinique Lancehead
Bothrops leucurus,
    White-tailed Lancehead
Bothrops lojanus,
    Lojan Lancehead
Bothrops marajoensis,
    Marajó Lancehead
Bothrops microphthalmus,
    Small-eyed Lancehead
Bothrops moojeni,
    Brazilian Lancehead
Bothrops neuwiedi,
    Neuwied's Lancehead
Bothrops pictus,
    Desert Lancehead
Bothrops pirajai,
    Piraja's Lancehead
Bothrops pradoi,
    Prado's Lancehead
Bothrops pulcher,
    Dusky Lancehead
Bothrops sanctaecrucis,
    Bolivian Lancehead
Bothrops venezuelensis,
    Venezuelan Lancehead
Bothrops xanthogrammus,
    Cope's Lancehead

GENUS: **CALLOSELASMA**
1 SPECIES

SIZE: Large.
DISTRIBUTION: Southeast Asia (Malay Peninsula and some Indonesian islands).
HABITAT: Forests.
FOOD: Lizards, snakes, small birds, and mammals.
REPRODUCTION: Egg-layer. There is evidence that females coil around and guard their eggs.
NOTES: Bad-tempered and strongly inclined to bite, although bites are rarely serious.

SPECIES:
Calloselasma rhodostoma,
    Malaysian Pit Viper

GENUS: **CERROPHIDION**
3 SPECIES

SIZE: Small, 1 ft 8 in-2 ft 5½in (50-75 cm) in length.
DISTRIBUTION: Central America.
HABITAT: Montane forests of pine-oak, and cloud forests up to about 9,850 ft. (3,000 m). Terrestrial.
FOOD: Lizards and small mammals.
REPRODUCTION: Live-bearers.

NOTES: Sometimes included in the genus *Porthidium*.

SPECIES:
Cerrophidion barbouri
Cerrophidion godmani
Cerrophidion tzotzilorum

GENUS: **CROTALUS**
RATTLESNAKES
29 SPECIES

SIZE: Small to large, from 1 ft 8 in (50 cm) to over 6 ft 6 in (2 m) in exceptional circumstances.
DISTRIBUTION: North, Central, and South America.
HABITAT: Extremely varied: including temperate and tropical forests, grasslands, rocky and sandy deserts, and mountainsides.
FOOD: Lizards, birds, and small mammals.
REPRODUCTION: Live-bearers.
NOTES: The list of species includes several (*C. ruber*, *C. unicolor*, and *C. vegrandis*) that may be subspecies or geographical variations of other species.

SPECIES:
Crotalus adamanteus,
    Eastern Diamondback Rattlesnake
Crotalus aquilus,
    Queretaran Dusky Rattlesnake
● *Crotalus atrox*,
    Western Diamondback Rattlesnake (pp.140–1)
Crotalus basiliscus,
    Mexican West Coast Rattlesnake
Crotalus catalinensis,
    Santa Catalina Rattlesnake or Rattleless Rattlesnake
● *Crotalus cerastes*,
    Sidewinder (pp. 144)
● *Crotalus durissus*,
    Tropical Rattlesnake (pp. 142–3)
Crotalus enyo,
    Baja Rattlesnake
Crotalus exsul,
    Cedros Rattlesnake
Crotalus horridus,
    Timber Rattlesnake or Canebrake Rattlesnake
Crotalus intermedius,
    Mexican Small-headed Rattlesnake
Crotalus lannomi,
    Autlan Rattlesnake
Crotalus lepidus,
    Rock Rattlesnake
Crotalus mitchelli,
    Speckled Rattlesnake
Crotalus molossus,
    Black-headed Rattlesnake
Crotalus polystictus,
    Mexican Lance-headed Rattlesnake
Crotalus pricei,
    Twin-spotted Rattlesnake
Crotalus pusillus,
    Tancitaran Rattlesnake
Crotalus ruber,

Red Diamond Rattlesnake
Crotalus scutulatus,
    Mojave Rattlesnake
Crotalus stejnegeri,
    Long-tailed Rattlesnake
Crotalus tigris,
    Tiger Rattlesnake
Crotalus tortugensis,
    Tortuga Island Rattlesnake
Crotalus transversus,
    Cross-banded Mountain Rattlesnake
Crotalus triseriatus,
    Mexican Dusky Rattlesnake
Crotalus unicolor,
    Aruba Island Rattlesnake
Crotalus vegrandis,
    Uracoan Rattlesnake
Crotalus viridis,
    Pacific Rattlesnake
Crotalus willardi,
    Ridge-nosed Rattlesnake

GENUS: **DEINAGKISTRODON**
1 SPECIES

SIZE: Large.
DISTRIBUTION: Southeastern China and Taiwan.
HABITAT: Wooded mountains and hills.
FOOD: Amphibians, lizards, snakes, and mammals.
REPRODUCTION: Egg-layer.
NOTES: Common and highly dangerous, with a bite that often proves fatal. The common name refers to the supposed distance that a victim travels before succumbing.

SPECIES:
Deinagkistrodon acutus,
    Hundred-pace Snake

GENUS: **GLOYDIUS**
3 SPECIES

SIZE: Small, to 2 ft 5½ in (75 cm) at most.
DISTRIBUTION: Central Asia.
HABITAT: Mountain slopes, often at high altitude (to nearly 16,400 ft [5,000 m] in *G. himalayanus*).
FOOD: Lizards, snakes, and small mammals.
REPRODUCTION: Live-bearers.
NOTES: Previously included in the genus *Agkistrodon*.

SPECIES:
Gloydius halys,
    Siberian Pit Viper
Gloydius himalayanus,
    Himalayan Pit Viper
Gloydius tsushimaensis

GENUS: HYPNALE
HUMP-NOSED VIPERS
3 SPECIES

SIZE: Small; among the smallest pit vipers at 1 ft–1 ft 9½ in (30–55 cm), depending on species.
DISTRIBUTION: Southwestern India (Western Ghats) and Sri Lanka.
HABITAT: Forests, including rain forests, hillsides, plantations, and fields, often near human habitation.
FOOD: Frogs, lizards, snakes (including their eggs), and small mammals.
REPRODUCTION: Live-bearers.
NOTES: Venomous, although not aggressive.

SPECIES:
Hypnale hypnale,
   Hump-nosed Viper
Hypnale nepa,
   Sri Lankan Hump-nosed Viper
Hypnale walli,
   Wall's Hump-nosed Viper

GENUS: LACHESIS
1 SPECIES

SIZE: Very large, occasionally to over 9ft 10 in (3 m) and longer.
DISTRIBUTION: Central and South America.
HABITAT: Wet tropical forests and recently cleared land.
FOOD: Mammals.
REPRODUCTION: Egg-layer.
NOTES: The largest viper, with a fearsome reputation. Highly dangerous, though quite rare and secretive. The subspecies *Lachesis muta stenophrys* is sometimes elevated to a full species.

SPECIES:
Lachesis muta,
   Bushmaster

GENUS: OPHRYACUS
1 SPECIES

SIZE: Small, to about 2 ft 3½ in (70 cm).
DISTRIBUTION: Central Mexico.
HABITAT: Pine-oak and cloud forests.
FOOD: Unknown, but probably lizards and small mammals.
REPRODUCTION: Live-bearer.
NOTES: The effects of the venom are not known, although the bites are unlikely to be life-threatening.

SPECIES:
Ophryacus undulatus,
   Mexican Horned Viper

GENUS: OVOPHIS
4 SPECIES

SIZE: Small to medium.
DISTRIBUTION: Southeast Asia and the Far East (Borneo, Vietnam, the Ryukyu Islands, and Japan).
HABITAT: Forests.
FOOD: Lizards and small mammals.
REPRODUCTION: Egg-layers.
NOTES: Sometimes included in the genus *Trimeresurus*.

SPECIES:
Ovophis chaseni
Ovophis monticola,
   Mountain Pit Viper
Ovophis okinavensis
Ovophis tonkinensis

GENUS: PORTHIDIUM
HOGNOSE VIPERS
9 SPECIES

SIZE: Small, rarely more than 2 ft 3½ in (70 cm)
DISTRIBUTION: Central and South America.
HABITAT: Humid and dry tropical forests, where they are terrestrial.
FOOD: Frogs, lizards, and small mammals.
REPRODUCTION: Live-bearers.
NOTES: Venomous, though not usually considered to be very dangerous, except in the case of *P. nasutum*, which has caused human fatalities. Several snakes have been removed from this genus and placed in *Atropoides* and *Cerrophidion*.

SPECIES:
Porthidium dunni,
   Dunn's Hognose Viper
Porthidium hespere,
   Western Hognose Viper
Porthidium hyoprora,
   Amazonian Hognose Viper
Porthidium lansbergii,
   Lansberg's Hognose Viper
Porthidium melanurum,
   Black-tailed Viper
Porthidium nasutum,
   Rain forest Hognose Viper
Porthidium ophryomegas,
   Slender Hognose Viper
Porthidium volcanicum
Porthidium yucatanicum,
   Yucatán Hognose Viper

GENUS: SISTRURUS
PYGMY RATTLESNAKES
3 SPECIES

SIZE: Small to medium, from 1 ft 8 in (50 cm) to nearly 3 ft 3 in (1 m) occasionally.
DISTRIBUTION: Northeastern North America to southern Mexico.
HABITAT: Swamps and marshes, grasslands, pine woods, meadows, and forest clearings.
FOOD: Lizards and small mammals.
REPRODUCTION: Live-bearers.
NOTES: Capable of giving painful bites, but ones that are unlikely to have serious long-term effects on humans.

SPECIES:
Sistrurus catenatus,
   Massassauga
Sistrurus miliarius,
   Pygmy Rattlesnake
Sistrurus ravus,
   Mexican Pygmy Rattlesnake

GENUS: TRIMERESURUS
BAMBOO VIPERS AND ASIAN PIT VIPERS
36 SPECIES

SIZE: Small to medium.
DISTRIBUTION: Asia, from Sri Lanka and India through southern China and into Southeast Asia, the Indonesian archipelago, the Philippines, and Japan.
HABITAT: Varied: typically forests and thickets, but not all species are arboreal.
FOOD: Frogs, lizards, and small mammals.
REPRODUCTION: Mostly live-bearers, though some species are egg-layers.
NOTES: The genus is poorly studied. Many new species have been described recently, others have been removed to the genus *Ovophis*. There are likely to be more changes in the near future.

SPECIES:
- *Trimeresurus albolabris*,
   White-lipped Tree Viper
   (pp. 132–3)
Trimeresurus borneensis,
   Bornean Pit Viper
Trimeresurus brongersmai
Trimeresurus cantori
Trimeresurus cornutus
Trimeresurus elegans
Trimeresurus erythrurus
Trimeresurus fasciatus
Trimeresurus flavomaculatus
Trimeresurus flavoviridis
Trimeresurus gracilis
Trimeresurus gramineus
Trimeresurus hageni
Trimeresurus huttoni
Trimeresurus jerdonii
Trimeresurus kanburiensis
Trimeresurus kaulbacki
Trimeresurus labialis

Trimeresurus macrolepis
Trimeresurus macrops
Trimeresurus malabaricus
Trimeresurus mangshanensis
Trimeresurus medoensis
Trimeresurus mucrosquamatus
Trimeresurus popeiorum,
   Pope's Pit Viper
Trimeresurus puniceus,
   Leaf-nosed Pit Viper
Trimeresurus purpureomaculatus,
   Shore Pit Viper
Trimeresurus schultzei
Trimeresurus stejnegeri
Trimeresurus strigatus
Trimeresurus sumatranus,
   Sumatran Pit Viper
Trimeresurus tibetanus
Trimeresurus tokarensis
Trimeresurus trigonocephalus
Trimeresurus venustus
Trimeresurus xiangchengensis

GENUS: TROPIDOLAEMUS
1 SPECIES

SIZE: Medium, to about 3 ft 3 in (1 m).
DISTRIBUTION: Southeast Asia.
HABITAT: Forests and mangroves, where they are highly arboreal.
FOOD: Lizards, small birds, and mammals.
REPRODUCTION: Live-bearer.
NOTES: Formerly included in the genus *Trimeresurus*.

SPECIES:
Tropidolaemus wagleri,
   Wagler's Pit Viper

GLOSSARY

The terms below are defined as they apply to snakes and may have alternative or slightly different meanings in other contexts. Words in italics within an entry have their own entry in the glossary.

ADVANCED The term used to refer to characteristics that evolved relatively recently, and the *species*, *families*, etc., that display these characteristics. For example, hinged fangs are advanced characteristics and, therefore, vipers, which have hinged fangs, are members of an advanced family. The opposite of *primitive*.

AMPHISBAENIAN A member of a group of reptiles that is closely allied to snakes and lizards. They live below ground and (apart from three species) have no legs.

ARBOREAL Tree-dwelling.

BALLING A defensive response in which the snake rolls into a ball and hides its head inside its coils. (See p. 28.)

CAECILIAN A group of legless, wormlike amphibians that live in damp soil or water and are found in tropical countries.

CLOUD FOREST Tropical forest that is frequently cloaked in mist, usually located on hills or the flanks of mountains. This is the popular term for tropical montane forest.

COLUBRID A snake that belongs to the *family* Colubridae.

DESCRIBED SPECIES Any species for which a scientific description, including a scientific or Latin name, has been published in a reputable journal. Each new species must be recorded in this way.

DIURNAL Active during the day.

DORSAL Relating to the back. Dorsal scales, for instance, are the tilelike scales that cover the back and flanks of a snake's body.

ECTOTHERMIC Relying on outside sources, usually the sun, for body heat.

ELAPID Belonging to the *family* Elapidae, whose members include the cobras, coral snakes, mambas, sea snakes, and taipans.

FALSE CORAL SNAKE A term sometimes applied to certain brightly colored, harmless snakes that seem to mimic the appearance of venomous coral snakes, which are members of the cobra family. (See p. 26.)

FAMILY A scientific category containing *genera* considered to be closely related. Some snake families contain only one genus, but most have more than one. In zoology, family names always end in the suffix -idae.

FORM A group of organisms differing from others within the same *species* in, for example, pattern or coloring. Each variation is known as a separate form, e.g., striped form. See also *polymorphism*.

GENERALIST A *species* that operates over a wide ecological niche. For example, a species that feeds on a variety of prey and lives in different habitats. The opposite of *specialist*.

GENUS (plural **GENERA**) A scientific category consisting of one or more closely related *species*. All members of the same genus have the same generic name, e.g., *Lampropeltis* (a genus of kingsnakes).

HEAT PITS Facial pits, found in some boas and pythons and in all pit vipers, that detect small differences in temperature, such as those radiating from warm-blooded animals. (See p. 21.)

HOOD The area immediately behind the head of certain cobras. The snake can spread the hood by moving its ribs. The main purpose of the hood is to intimidate potential predators.

INTERSTITIAL SKIN The area of tissue between the scales. Interstitial skin is common to snakes and other reptiles. Also known as interscalar skin. (See p. 14.)

JACOBSON'S ORGAN An organ of smell situated in the roof of a snake's mouth. The tongue transfers scent particles to the Jacobson's organ, which connects to the brain via nerves. (See p. 20.)

KEELED SCALES Those scales with one or (rarely) two longitudinal ridges running down the center. (See p. 15.)

LIVE-BEARING See *viviparous*.

MONTANE FOREST A type of rain forest, usually at least 3,200 ft (1,000 m) above sea level. Characterized by high rainfall and/or frequent mists, and by an abundance of plants, such as mosses, that are epiphytic (growing on other plants). Often cool in comparison with other habitats at the same latitude, this type of forest is frequently inhabited by *specialist* snake species.

NOCTURNAL Active during the night.

OPISTHOGLYPHOUS Rear-fanged. Applied to snakes with enlarged fangs, often grooved, toward the rear of the mouth. (See p. 19.)

OVIPAROUS Egg laying.

OVOVIVIPAROUS Retaining fertilized eggs inside the body until just before or immediately after they hatch.

PARTHENOGENESIS The process whereby an unfertilized egg develops into an embryo. Parthenogenetic *species* can reproduce without mating and can thus consist only of females. Only one snake species, the flowerpot snake, *Ramphotyphlops braminus*, is parthenogenetic.

PELAGIC Inhabiting the middle and upper layers of the oceans.

POLYMORPHISM The occurrence of two or more distinct *forms* within a single population of the same *species*. (See p. 27.)

PRIMITIVE The term used to refer to characteristics that reflect an early ancestral evolutionary line and the *species*, *families*, etc. that are similar to that line. For example, thread snakes share many characteristics with some of the earliest known snakes and are therefore members of a primitive family. The opposite of *advanced*.

PROTEROGLYPHOUS Front-fanged. Applied to snakes that have enlarged, *venom*-delivering fangs in their upper jaw, including elapids, vipers, and some burrowing asps (Atractaspididae). (See p. 19.)

RELIC (or **RELICT**) A surviving population of a *species* or *family* that once had a large distribution, but now has only a fragmented or localized one.

ROSTRAL SCALES The scales at the very tip of a snake's snout. (See p. 15.)

SECONDARY FOREST Forest that has recolonized a cleared area.

SIDEWINDING A method of locomotion, practiced by some snakes living among sand dunes, in which the body moves forward at an angle of about 45 degrees. (See p. 17.)

SPECIALIST A *species* that operates over a narrow ecological niche. For example, a species that feeds on one or two other species or lives in a restricted habitat. The opposite of *generalist*.

SPECIES (plural and singular) A basic category of classification comprising a group of related organisms differing from others in the same *genus*. The most important classification in biology. A species' name consists of two Latin words: the generic name, followed by the specific name. *Crotalus*

atrox, for example, is a species of rattlesnake. Traditionally, species are reproductively isolated; they can interbreed with each other, but not with individuals of other species. This is not always so, however, and hybrids occasionally occur.

STRIDULATION The production of a sound by the rubbing together of two surfaces, such as the specialized, rough flank scales of several *species* of snake.

SUBCAUDAL SCALES The scales underneath a snake's tail. (See p. 15.)

SUBOCULAR SCALES Those scales immediately below the eye. Found only in some snake *species*. (See p. 15.)

SUBSPECIES A scientific category below the level of *species*. Used to denote differences in size, color, pattern, etc., between populations within a *species* that are found over a wide geographical area or on islands.

SUBSTRATE The ground or surface on which a *species* rests or lives.

TAXONOMY The science and practice of classification, in which organisms are arranged and named according to their relationships with one another.

TERRESTRIAL Living mostly on the ground.

TUBERCLES Small raised swellings or pimples. (See p. 21.)

UNDERSTORY Vegetated habitat below the forest canopy, usually consisting of shrubs, bushes, and grasses.

VENOM Modified saliva, the main purpose of which is to incapacitate prey. (See p. 24.)

VENTRAL SCALES Those scales on a snake's underside. (See p. 15.)

VERTEBRATES Animals with backbones (mammals, birds, reptiles, amphibians, and fish). All other animals are invertebrates.

VESTIGIAL LIMBS Undeveloped limbs that have diminished in size due to natural selection and are no longer functional.

VIVIPAROUS Giving birth to live young. The majority of snakes are not truly viviparous in the same way as mammals, since the embryos do not receive nourishment from their mothers. Instead, the eggs remain in the female's oviducts during development and hatch just before or after birth. Strictly speaking, such snakes are *ovoviviparous*.

INDEX

A

Acanthophis:
  praelongus, 118
  pyrrhus, 119
Acrochordidae family, 152
  classification, 34, 145
Acrochordus species, 30
adaptation to habitats, 9
Adder, 25, 126–27
African Carpet Viper, 134
African Mole Snake, 31
African Rock Python, 23, 31, 54
African Spitting Cobra, 28
Agkistrodon:
  contortix, 139
  piscivorus, 22
Ahaetulla, 20
Alethinophidia superfamily, 34, 145
Alsophis antigua, 33
Amazon Tree Boa, 21, 27, 39
amelanistic forms, 73
American Rat snake, 15
Amethystine Python, 12
Amphisbaenia suborder, 34
amphisbaenians, 8
anacondas, 44–45
anatomy, 16–17
Aniliidae family, 148
  classification, 34, 145
Anomalepidae family, 146
  classification, 34, 145
anomalepids, 13, 20
Anomochilidae family, 148
  classification, 34, 145
Anomochilus, 34
Antaresia:
  childreni, 60
  maculosa, 61
Antiguan Racer, 33
Aplopeltura boa, 81
aquatic/marine snakes, 11
  body shape, 13
  live-bearing, 31
  locomotion, 17
  right lung, 16
  types of prey, 22
  See also sea snakes
arboreal snakes:
  body shape, 13
  evolutionary convergence, 9
  live-bearing, 31
Argentine Rainbow Boa, 43
arid regions, adapting to, 10
Arizona Mountain Kingsnake, 86
articulation of skull bones, 18
Asian Pipe Snake, 28
Asian Slug-eating Snake, 81
Asian Tentacled Snake, 15
Atractaspididae family, 25, 177–78
  classification, 34, 145
audible warnings, 29
Australian Inland Taipan, 24

B

Baird, Spencer Fullerton, 74
Baird's Rat snake, 15, 74–75
Ball Python, 28
balling, 28
Banded Krait, 108
Banded Water Snake, 90–91
basking, 10, 11
binocular vision, 20, 111
Bitis:
  arietans, 123
  gabonica, 129
Black Adder, 127
Black Mamba, 24, 120
Black Pine Snake, 92
black snakes, 116
Black Tiger Snake, 117
blind snakes, 8, 31, 146–48
  classification, 145
Blood Python, 58–59
Boa:
  constrictor, 40
  dumerili, 48
boa constrictor, 40
boas, 38–51, 149–50
  classification, 34
  dispersal of, 9
  fossils, 8
  heat pits, 21
  hunting methods, 22, 23
  scales, 14, 15
  size of, 12
body shape, 13
body temperature/heat:
  regulating, 10, 11
body triads, 86
Bogertophis subocularis, 76
Boidae family, 38–51, 149–50
  classification, 34, 145
Boiga:
  cyanea, 109
  dendrophila, 108
Bolyeriidae family, 32, 151–52
  classification, 34, 145
bones of skull, 18, 19
Boomslang, 25, 29, 110–11
Bothrops:
  asper, 137
  jararaca, 136
Brahminy Blind Snake, 31
Brazilian Rainbow Boa, 42
breathing. *See* respiratory system
Brown House Snake, 104–5
  desert form, 105
Bull Snake, 93
bulls-eye markings, 78, 79
Burmese Python, 12, 54–55
  albino form, 54
burrowing, 8, 10, 11
burrowing asps, 19, 24, 177–78
  classification, 34
  side strike, 25

burrowing snakes:
  body shape, 13
  dorsal scales, 14
  seeing, 20
  tail, 15

C

Caenophidia subdivision, 34, 145
Calabar Ground Boa, 28, 50–51
California Kingsnake, 27, 83
California Mountain Kingsnake, 87
camouflage, 26
  Copperhead, 138
  cribo, 98
  Desert Horned Viper, 131
  Dumeril's Ground Boa, 49
  Gaboon Viper, 26, 129
  Reticulated Python, 57
  Rough Green Snake, 80
Candoia aspera, 27
captive breeding programs, 33
  Dumeril's Ground Boa, 48
Carpet Python, 52–53
carpet vipers, 25, 29, 134–35
Casarea dussumieri, 32
cascabel, 142
cat snakes, 109
cat-eyed snakes, 13, 109
Central American Centipede Snake, 81
Central Australian Carpet Python, 53
Central Baja Rosy Boa, 46
Cerastes cerastes, 131
Chappel Island Tiger Snake, 117
Charina:
  bottae, 12
  reinhardtii, 51
  trivirgata, 47
  trivirgata myriolepis, 47
  trivirgata roseofusca, 46
  trivirgata saslowi, 46
  trivirgata trivirgata, 46
Checkered Garter Snake, 100
Children, J.G., 60
Children's Python, 60
chin, 18
chin groove, 48
Chinese Cobra, 114
Chionactis occipitalis, 81
circulatory system, 16
classification, 34, 145
climbing snakes:
  body shape, 13
Coastal Rosy Boa, 46
cobras, 112–19, 178–83
  fangs, 18, 19
  large head scales, 15
  venom, 19, 24, 25

warning coloration, 26
coiling:
  brooding eggs, 60
  minimizing water loss, 11
cold conditions, adapting to, 10, 11
Collett's Snake, 116–17
coloration, 15
  defensive, 27
  warning, 26, 27
color change:
  Emerald Tree Boa, 15
  Haitian Wood Snake, 66
color scheme for venomous snakes, 26
Colubridae family, 68–111, 152–77
  classification, 34, 145
colubrids, 23, 68–111, 152–77
  fangs, 19
  large head scales, 15
  pupil shape, 20
  skull, 18
  venom, 19, 24, 25
Common Boa, 12, 20, 40–41
  swallowing prey, 23
Common Egg-eater, 70–71
Common Garter Snake, 31, 102
Common Kingsnake, 22, 82–83
compound bone, 18, 19
concealment, 27
concertina movement, 17
conditions, extreme living, 10
conservation, 32–33
constrictors, 23
continental land masses, 8, 9
Copperhead, 138–39
copulatory organs, *see* hemipenes
Coral Snake, 89
coral snakes, 26, 27, 89
Corallus:
  caninus, 39
  enhydris, 27
  hortulanus, 21
Corn Snake, 72–73
Cottonmouth, 22, 90
courtship, 30
cribo, 98
Crocodylia order, 34
Crotalus:
  atrox, 140
  cerastes, 144
  durissus, 142
  durissus vegrandis, 143
  ruber, 21
  scutulatus, 25
  willardi, 30
cuatro natrices (four nostrils), 21
Cuban Wood Snake, 67
Cylindropheidae family, 148

classification, 34, 145
Cylindrophis, 34
  ruffus, 28

D

Dasypeltis scabra, 71
day hunters. *See* diurnal (day) hunters
Death Adder, 9
death adders, 118–19
death, feigning, 28
defense:
  active, 24, 28–29
  passive, 26–27
  protection from scales, 14
defensive displays, 29
defensive posture:
  Calabar Ground Boa, 51
  carpet vipers, 134
  Common Egg-eater, 70
  Grass Snake, 69
  Red-tailed Rat snake, 107
  Royal Python, 64
  See also mimicry/mimics
deforestation, 32
  Madagascar, 49
dehydration, resisting, 11
Dendroaspis, 120
  polylepis, 24, 120
  viridis, 120
dentary bone, 18, 19
desert, adapting to the, 10
Desert Carpet Python, 53
Desert Death Adder, 119
Desert Horned Viper, 27, 29, 130–31
Desert Rosy Boa, 47
desert species, 10, 11, 27
desert vipers, 29
diamondbacks, 140–41
digestive system, 16, 17
dimorphic sexes:
  Nose-horned Viper, 124
Dispholidus typus, 111
diurnal (day) hunters, 23
  pupil shape, 20
dorsal scales, 14, 15
Drymarchon corais, 98
Dumeril's Ground Boa, 15, 48
Duvernoy's glands, 25
dwarf pipe snakes, 34, 148

E

earliest known snake, 8
Eastern Carpet Viper, 134–35
Eastern Diamondback, 140
Eastern Garter Snake, 102
Eastern Hognose Snake, 95
Echis, 135
  carinatus, 135

ecological niches, filling, 9
ectotherms, 10, 11
education, conservation, 33
egg chamber, 31
egg-eating snakes, 23, 70
egg incubation:
    Grass Snake, 69
    pythons, 60
egg-laying snakes, 31
egg-tooth, 31, 58
eggs, 31
    clutch size, 31
    development of, 30
eggs, eating, 23, 70
Elaphe, 107
    bairdi, 75
    guttata, 72
    mandarina, 79
    porphyracea, 107
    situla, 97
Elapidae family, 26, 112–21,
    178–83
    classification 34, 145
elapids:
    land, 25
    marine, 24
    venom, 24, 25
Emerald Tree Boa, 9, 15,
    38–39
endangered habitat. *See*
    habitat destruction
endangered snakes:
    Burmese Python, 55
    Common Boa, 40
    Dumeril's Ground Boa, 49
    San Francisco Garter Snake,
    102
    See also skin trade
energy, saving, 11
environment, adaptation to, 9,
    10–11
Epicrates:
    cenchria, 43
    cenchria alvarezi, 43
    cenchria crassus, 43
Erpeton tentaculatum, 15
Eunectes:
    murinus, 45
    notaeus, 45
evolution, 8–9
    dispersal, 8, 9
    origins, 8
    radiation, 9
evolutionary convergence, 9
excretory system, 17
extinctions, 32
eyes, 20
    and hunting, 23
    binocular vision, 20, 111
    swiveling, 58
eyespots, 43, 114, 115

F

false coral snakes, 26, 27
families (classification), 34
family tree (classification), 34
fangs, 19
    curved, 29

fixed front, 18
grooved, 19
hinged front, 18, 19, 24,
    126
hollow 18, 19
rear, 19, 25
replacement of, 19
sheathed, 140
specialized front, 25
Fawcett, Sir Percy, 12
feeding, 22–23
Fer-de-lance, 31, 137
fertilization, 30
file snakes, 15, 30, 152
flexible jaws. *See* jaws
fossil record of snakes, 8
front-fanged snakes, 19, 25

G

Gaboon Viper, 13, 26, 128–29
garter snakes, 20, 30, 100–3
    identifying, 103
    surviving the cold, 11
giant pythons, 12
giving birth, 31, 125
Glass Lizard, 8
golden pythons, 54
Gondwanaland, 9
Gonyosoma, 107
    oxycephala, 106
gopher snakes, 93
granular dorsal scales, 15
Grass Snake, 28, 68–69
    eating live prey, 22
Green Anaconda, 12, 44–45
Green Cat-eyed Snake, 13,
    109
Green Tree Python, 9, 62–63
Green Tree Viper, 109
Green Water Snake, 31
Gray-banded Kingsnake,
    84
ground-dwellers:
    body shape, 13

H

habitat destruction, 32
    Florida, 91
    Honduras, 40
    Madagascar, 49
    San Francisco area, 102
Haitian Wood Snake, 66
hatching, 31, 58
head scales, 14, 15
    modified, 14
heads, hiding, 28
hearing, 21
heart, 16
heat pits, 17, 21
heat, sensing, 21
Hemachatus haemachatus, 28
hemipenes, 17, 30
hemotoxic venom, 25
Heterodon nasicus, 94
hibernation, 10, 11, 30
    Adder, 127

California Mountain King-
    snake, 87
hiding places, 66
hissing, 11, 28, 29
hognose snakes, 22, 28,
    94–95
hood (cobra), 112, 114, 115
horizontal pupil, 20
horned adders, 15
horns, 130
human deaths by snakebites,
    24, 25
hunters, and pupil shape, 20
hunting methods, 22–23
    Carpet Python, 53
    Copperhead, 138

I

ice crystals, 11
Indian Python, 31
Indigo Snake, 98–99
internal systems, 16–17
interscalar skin, 14
interstitial skin, 14
intimidation, 28, 29
invertebrate eaters, 81
iridescence, 15, 37, 42
Iridescent Earth Snake, 37

J

Jacobson's organ, 17, 20
Jararaca, 136–37
jawbones, *see* jaws
jaws, 18, 19
    evolution of flexible, 18
Jersey Wildlife Preservation
    Trust, 33
Jersey Zoo, 33
Jungle Carpet Python, 53

K

keeled dorsal scales, 15
killing prey, *see* prey
King Cobra, 13
    digesting prey, 25
    threating posture, 29
    toxicity of venom, 24
kingsnakes, 22, 82–87
kraits, 13

L

labial scales, 14
Lampropeltis, 27
    alterna, 84
    getula, 82
    getula californiae, 83
    mexicana, 85
    mexicana mexicana, 85
    mexicana thayeri, 85
    pyromelana, 87
    triangulum, 89
    zonata, 87

Lamprophis:
    fuliginosus, 104
    fuliginosus mentalis, 105
lanceheads, 136–37
land drift, 8
land elapids, 25
Langaha madagascariensis, 14
Lapparentophis defrennei, 8
large head scales, 15
largest snakes, 12–13
    Common Boa, 12
    Green Anaconda, 12, 44
    pythons, 12
Lataste's Viper, 125
lateral undulation, 17
Laurasia, 9
legislation, conservation, 33
legless lizards, 8
Leopard Snake, 27, 96–97
Leptodeira septentrionalis, 22
Leptotyphlopidae family, 146
    classification, 34, 145
leptotyphlopids, 13, 20
Leptotyphlops bilineatus, 13
linear progression, 17
lingual fossa, 48
litter size, 31
live-bearing snakes, 31
lizards, 8
    as prey, 25
locomotion, 14, 17
longest snake:
    Reticulated Python, 12, 56
Long-nosed Tree Snake, 20
lower jawbone, 18, 19
Loxocemidae family, 36, 149
    classification, 34, 145
Loxocemus bicolor, 36
lungs, 16

M

Macrovipera schweizeri, 33
Madagascan Vine Snake, 14
male-to-male combat, 30, 126
mambas, 18, 120–21
Mandarin Rat snake, 78–79
Mangrove Snake, 108
marine elapids, 24
marine snakes, early, 8
Martinique Thread Snake, 13
mating, 30
mating ball, 30, 90
maxilla, 18, 19
mental groove, 48
Mexican Baird's Rat snake, 74,
    75
Mexican Burrowing Snake, 36
Mexican Kingsnake, 85
Mexican Rosy Boa, 46
Milk Snake, 27, 88–89
Milos Viper, 33
mimicry/mimics, 27, 70, 89
Moccasin, 138
moisture, balancing, 11
Mojave Rattlesnake, 25
Monocled Cobra, 115
Morelia:
    amethistina, 12

bredli, 53
spilota, 52
viridis, 63
mountain kingsnakes, 27
movement, 17
muscles, 17
myotoxic venom, 25

N

Naja:
    atra, 114
    kaouthia, 115
    pallida, 113
Natriciteres species, 28
Natrix natrix, 68
natural selection, 7, 12
nature reserves, 33
Nerodia:
    cyclopion, 31
    fasciata, 91
nervous system, 17
neurotoxic venom, 25
nocturnal (night) hunters, 23
    pupil shape, 20
Northern Death Adder,
    118–19
Northern Pine Snake, 92
Northern Viper, 126
Nose-horned Viper, 124
nostrils, 20
Notechis, 117
Nuevo Leon Kingsnake, 85

O

Opheodrys aestivus, 81
Ophiophagus hannah, 13
opistoglyphous snakes, 19
orders (classification), 34
organs, 16
ovaries, 17
Oxyuranus:
    microlepidotus, 24
    scutellatus, 13

P

Pacific Boa, 15
paired subcaudal scales, 15
pairs (sets) of species, 9
palatine bones, 18, 19
Pangaea, 8
Paraguayan Rainbow Boa,
    43
parthenogenetic (female-only)
    species, 31
pet trade, 32, 48
pets, domestic, 42, 72
pigments, 14, 15
Pine Snake, 92–93
pipe snakes, 8, 34, 148
pit vipers, 132–33, 138
    heat pits, 21
    island species, 133
Pituophis, 93
    melanoleucus, 93

Plains Garter Snake, 100, 103
playing dead, 28
Pliocercus elapoides, 28
polymorphism, 27
pre-anal scales, 14
predators of snakes, 26
prey:
    and constriction, 23, 61
    and use of venom, 25, 111
    detecting, 21
    digesting, 25
    eating, 18, 22
    lizards as, 25
    snakes as, 25, 26, 82
    striking at, 25
    subduing, 24
    swallowing, 41
    types of, 22
primitive living snakes, 8
    size, 13
    skulls, 18
proteroglyphous snakes, 19
Psammophis species, 28
Pseudaspis cana, 31
Pseudechis, 116
    colletti, 117
pterygoid bones, 18, 19
Pueblan Milk Snake, 88, 89
Puff Adder, 31, 122–23
    desert forms, 123
pupil shapes, 20
Python:
    curtus, 59
    molurus, 12, 31, 55
    regius, 65
    reticulatus, 56
    sebae, 12, 31
Pythonidae family, 52–65,
    150–51
    classification, 34, 145
pythons, 52–65, 150–51
    body shape, 13
    classification, 34
    clutch size, 31
    heat pits, 21
    hunting methods, 22, 23
    jaws, 18
    size, 12
    smooth scales, 15

Q
quadrate bone, 21

R
racers, 13, 20, 106–7
Rainbow Boa, 15, 42–43
rain forest destruction, 32
rasp, warning, 29
rat snakes, 72–79, 96–97, 107
    body shape, 13
    constrictors, 23
    hatching, 31
rattle, 15, 29, 141
rattlesnake roundups, 32, 140
rattlesnakes, 15, 29, 140–44
    as prey species, 82

breeding habits, 143
rear-fanged snakes, 19, 25
Red Diamond Rattlesnake, 21,
    140
Red Mountain Racer, 107
Red Rat snake, 72
Red-sided Garter Snake, 30
Red Spitting Cobra, 112–13
Red-tailed Rat snake, 106–7
reproduction, 30–31
reproductive system, 17
Reptila class, 34
reptiles, burrowing, 8
research, conservation, 33
respiratory system, 16
Reticulated Python, 12, 29,
    56–57
    clutch size, 31
reticulations, 52, 55
Rhinoceros Viper, 6
rhinoceros vipers, 15
Rhynchocephalia order, 34
ribs, 16
Ridge-nosed Rattlesnake, 30
Ringhals, 28
rostral scale, 14, 94
Rosy Boa, 15, 46–47
Rough Green Snake, 20,
    80–81
Round Island, 32, 33
Round Island Boa, 32, 151–52
round pupil, 20
Royal Python, 28, 64–65
Rubber Boa, 12

S
salt, correcting balance of, 11
San Diego Gopher Snake, 93
San Francisco Garter Snake,
    102–3
San Luis Potosí Kingsnake, 85
sand snakes, 13
Sauria suborder, 34
Saw-scaled Viper, 134
saw-scaled vipers, 25
scales, 14–15, 94, 118
    characteristics, 15
    coloration, 15
    functions of, 14
    specialized, 11, 15
    types of, 14, 15
Scaphiodontophis venustissimus,
    28
scents, analyzing, 20
Scolecophidia superfamily, 34,
    145
Scolecophis atrocinctus, 81
sea snakes, 11, 25, 31
    classification, 34
    types of prey, 22
secretions, foul-smelling, 28
seeing, 20
selective breeding, 72
sense organs, 20–21
Serpentes suborder, 34
shape. *See* body shape
shield-tailed snakes, 15,
    148–49

Short-tailed Python, 58
Shovel-nosed Snake, 81
side strike, 25
Sidewinder, 144
sidewinding, 17, 130, 144
Simoliophis, 8
Sinaloan Milk Snake, 88
single-sex snake, 31
single subcaudal scales, 15
size, 12–13
skeleton, 16, 17
skin, 14
shedding (sloughing), 13
skin trade, 32
    Burmese Python, 55
    Royal Python, 65
skull, 16, 18–19
    evolution of, 18
    flexibility of, 19
sloughing skin, 13
small head scales, 15
small snakes, 13
smelling, 20
smooth dorsal scales, 15
Smooth Green Snake, 80
snail- and slug-eating snakes,
    23
snake charmers, 115
snakes as prey, 25, 26, 82
snout, modified, 14
Snow Corn Snake, 73
snow corns, 73
Sonoran Mountain King-
    snake, 86–87
species, 8, 145
sperm, 17, 30
spine, 16
spitting, 29
spitting cobras, 28, 29
Spotted Python, 61
Squamata order, 8, 34
stapes, 21
stridulation, 11
subcaudal scales, 15
subfamilies, 145
subocular scales, 14
suborders (classification), 34
Sumatran Pit Viper, 133
Sunbeam Snake, 37, 149
sunbeam snakes, 37, 149
superfamilies (classification),
    34, 145
supraocular scales, 118

T
tail:
    loss, 28
    specialized scales, 15, 29
    to lure prey, 22
    vertebrae, 28
tail imitating head:
    Calabar Ground Boa, 28, 50
Taipan, 13, 24
teeth, 18–19, 24
    replacement of, 19
temperature, regulating body,
    10, 11
Terciopelo, 137

testes, 17
Testudines order, 34
Thamnophis:
    marcianus, 100
    sirtalis parietalis, 30
    sirtalis tetrataenia, 103
Thelotornis, 20
thermoreceptors, 21
thread snakes, 8, 18, 146
threatening posture, 29
tiger snakes, 117
tongue, 20
    and salt balance, 11
    blue, 107
    slot, 48
tracheal lung, 16
Trans-Pecos Rat snake, 76–77
    blonde form, 76
tree asp, *See Dendroaspis*
tree snakes, 20
triads, 86
Trimeresurus albolabris, 133
Tropical Rattlesnake, 142–43
Tropidophiidae family, 66–67,
    151
    classification, 34, 145
Tropidophis:
    haetianus, 66
    melanurus, 67
tubercles (pits), 21
twig snakes, 20, 25, 29
Typhlopidae family, 146–48
    classification, 34, 145
typhlopids, 13, 20

U
upper jawbone, 18, 19
uric acid, 11
Uropeltidae family, 148–49
    classification, 34, 145

V
venom, 24, 25
    injecting, 25
    producing, 24
    spraying, 29
    toxicity, 24, 25
venom duct, 19
venom gland, 19
venomous snakes, 24–25
    warning coloration, 26, 27
ventral scales, 14, 15
vertebrae, 16
vertical pupil, 20
vestigial:
    limbs, 17
    pelvic girdle, 17
vibrations, hearing, 21
Viper Boa, 27
Vipera, 125
    ammodytes, 124
    berus, 127
    latasti, 125
Viperidae family, 122–44,
    183–87
    classification, 34, 145

vipers, 122–31, 134–37,
    183–87
    body shape, 13
    dispersal of, 9
    fangs, 19, 24
    hunting methods, 22
    live-bearing, 31
    pupil shape, 20
    scales, 14, 15
    skull, 19
    venom, 19, 24, 25
    See also pit vipers

W
warm climates, living in, 10
warning:
    coloration, 26, 27
    signals, 29
    sounds, 15
wart snakes, 11, 15, 152
water snakes, 20, 90–91
West African Green Mamba,
    120–21
Western Diamondback
    Rattlesnake, 29, 140–41
Western Hognose Snake,
    94–95
whip-snakes, 13, 20
White-lipped Tree Viper,
    132–33
    identification of, 34
wood snakes, 28, 66–67, 151

X
Xenopeltidae family, 37, 149
    classification, 34, 145
Xenopeltis, 37
    unicolor, 37

Y
yarar, 136
yararaca, 136
Yellow Anaconda, 45

ACKNOWLEDGMENTS

Author's acknowledgments

Over the years I have benefited enormously from the expertise and good company of a number of fellow herpetologists while on snake-hunting trips to several parts of the world. Although they are too numerous to mention individually, I hope they all realize, nevertheless, that their contributions have been important to me.

More specifically, I would also like to thank the following people, listed alphabetically, who provided many of the snakes that I photographed for this project:

John and Linda Bird (for many specimens), the staff of Birdquest, Gretchen Davison, Richard Haigh, David Kershaw, Paul Rowley, Frank Schofield, and Cliff Stone.

In addition to loaning specimens, all these people also helped restrain and pose the snakes. In this respect, I am especially indebted to Paul Rowley of the Liverpool School of Tropical Medicine, who helped me photograph a number of highly dangerous species, and to Gretchen Davison, who has always been a willing helper when it comes to controlling uncooperative snakes in the studio, and who has also helped find and photograph snakes in the field.

Finally, thanks to Hugh Schermuly, Sally McEachern, and the other designers and editors of Schermuly Design, and to Stephanie Jackson, Adèle Hayward, and the rest of the editorial team at Dorling Kindersley, not only for all their hard work but also for helping make this book a pleasure to write.

Dorling Kindersley would like to thank the following:

Editors: Jane Simmonds for start-up project management; Tracey Beresford, Josephine Bryan, Claire Calman, and Nicola Munro for editorial assistance

Designers: Kate Poole for start-up project management; Tassy King as Senior Art Editor in the final stages of production

Administrative assistant: Chris Gordon

Schermuly Design Co. would like to thank the following:

Trevor Smith of Animal World for supplying and handling snakes for photography. Laura Wickenden for going lens to face with some very lively snakes. Mark O'Shea of West Midland Safari and Leisure Park for allowing us to photograph his cobras. Dr. Jennifer Daltry of Fauna and Flora International and Richard Gibson of the Jersey Wildlife Preservation Trust for sending transparencies and information on the Antiguan racer project. Lynn Bresler for proofreading and indexing. Didier Chatelus and Jenny Buzzard for DTP assistance.

DK Publishing, Inc. would like to thank John L. Behler of the Wildlife Conservation Society for his consulting work on this book.

Picture credits

Ardea London Ltd: 23 tc, Adrian Warren 120 br, Francois Gohier 30 bl, McDougal 23 tc
BBC Natural History Unit: 98 cl, Andrew Cooper 11 bl, Artur Tabor 25 bc, Jeff Foott 17 br, 140 cl, John Cancalosi 82 b, 117 bc, Jurgen Freund 11 br, Lynn M. Stone 95 tr, Martin Holmes 117 br, Steven David Miller 90 b
Biofotos: Slim Sreedharan 25 tc
Bruce Coleman Ltd: 25 l, Dr. Frieder Sauer 126 bl, Erwin and Peggy Bauer 72 cl
Chris Mattison: 4 br, 5 br, 6 r, 9 cl, cr, br, 10 br, bc, br, 12 tr, 13 tr, 14 bl, bc, tr, cr, 15 tl, tcl, tcr, tr, cl, ccl, ccr, cr, 17 tc, 18 cl, 20 tl, cl, bl, 19 cr, 29 bl, 31 tc, c, 33 tc, tr, 34 tr, 35 br, 36 cl, b, cr, 37 c, br, 38 tl, 39 c, br, 40 bl, 43 tl, tr, cr, 44 br, 46 cr, 47 tr, 49 br, 52 c, 53 br, 57 tr, 58 bl, 59 tc, 60 cr, b, 61 cr, b, 63 br, 66 t, tr, 67 bl, r, 70 tr, cr, 74 bl, 75 c, tr, 78 c, bl, 80 tl, c, br, 81 tr, cr, br, 82 cl, 83 c, 84 t, 85 cl, br, 86 c, 88 bc, 91 br, 93 br, 94 cl, r, 95 bc, 96 c, bl, 97 tr, 100 bl, r, 101 tr, 102 tl, r, 103 bc, br, 104 bl, c, 105 bl, 106 c, 107 tr, 110 tl, br, 111 tr, 116, 118 c, bl, 120 c, 121 tr, 122 c, 124, 125 tr, 127 br, 128 cl, r, 129 tr, 130 cl, 132 c, 133 r, 134 bl, 135 tl, c, 136 b, 137 tl, 142 r, 143 tr, 144 tr, b
Fauna and Flora International: 33 bl, bc, br
George McCarthy: 30 cb, 69 tr, 126 tr
Gerald Cubitt: 32 b
Jane Burton: 22 tr
Joe McDonald: endpapers, 130 bl, 131 cr, 140 tr
John Canceloni: 87 cr
John Visser: 70 cl, 70 bl
MPL Fogden: 137 br
Laura Wickenden: 5 tr, 10 tr, 12 c, 13 c, 14 br, 28 bl, 35 l, c, 40 c, 44 l, c, 46 tr, cl, 47 c, 48 bl, c, 50 c, br, 49 bl, 54 bl, cr, 55 tr, 56 c, 58 c, 62 c, 63 cr, 64 cl, bc, 65 c, 68 c, 71 c, 76 bl, tr, 77 c, 90 c, 92 c, bl, 99 c, 108 bl, 112 c, bl, 114 c, bl, 115 c, bl, 126 c
Michael & Patricia Fogden: 11 cb, 19 cb, 27 bl, 28 tr, 40 tr, 52 tr, 57 br, 89 tr, 119 br, 133 tc
FLPA: Chris Mattison 39 tl, M. Ranjiit 25 br
N.H.P.A.: Anthony Bannister 111 bl, Daniel Heuclin 125 bl, 143 br, Daniel Heuclin 113 tc, Daniel Heuclin 28 bl, 31 tr, 49 tl, E. Hanumantha Rao 29 tc, G.I. Bernard 24 tr, Ken Griffiths 118 tr, Martin Wendler 35 tr, 45 tr, Stephen Dalton 127 bc
Oxford Scientific Films: B.P. Kent 138 bl, M. Fogden 19 tr, Steve Tisner 26 bl, Z. Leszczynski 22 tc
Papilio Photographic: 29 t
Planet Earth Pictures: Brian Kenney 93 c, 123 bl, 138 br, Carol Farneti 32 tr, 63 br, Mary Clay 103 tr
Premaphotos Wildlife: K.G. Preston-Matham 27 c
Warren Photographic: Kim Taylor 24 b

Maps by Masumi Higo

Illustrations by Evi Antoniou

Back jacket photographs
Chris Mattison l, Bruce Coleman: Erwin and Peggy Bauer cr, Joe McDonald r